My Road From Yesterday
An Autobiography

CLIFFORD M. DRURY
Photograph at age 75 in 1973.

My Road From Yesterday
An Autobiography

by
Clifford Merrill Drury

With a Foreword by
THOMAS F. ANDREWS

THE ARTHUR H. CLARK COMPANY
GLENDALE, CALIFORNIA
1984

To My Grandchildren
Janet and Nancy Drury
and
Marcus Drury

Contents

Illustrations

Foreword

BY THOMAS F. ANDREWS

Fifty years ago this June a young minister with an earned doctorate from Edinburgh accepted an invitation to teach an adult Bible class at a Presbyterian campmeeting for the Nez Perce Indians. That summer's brief activity in the foothills of the Bitterroot Mountains convinced Clifford Drury, the former missionary to China and pastor of the First Presbyterian Church of Moscow, Idaho, that he had arrived in the West on the edge of a generation that was passing. That summer he proposed to write the history of the Oregon Mission and thereby save a story that otherwise might be lost to future generations.

What happened at Talmaks in 1934 is ably recounted in the pages that follow. It is sufficient to note here that the meetings and conversations that took place that summer launched a labor of love for one special man that persisted for half a century, produced some two dozen books and numerous articles, was recognized with awards and honors, and culminates this summer with the publication of an autobiography — the final act symbolizing both a love of labor and a labor of love.

Clifford Drury was especially fond of biographies and narrative histories. It is fitting therefore that his own story should be the concluding volume of the many works that have come from his pen. He had the good fortune to publish most of his books with Caxton Printers of Caldwell, Idaho, and Arthur H. Clark Company of Glendale, California, two of the outstanding publishers of Western Americana. It is also appropriate then that the Arthur H. Clark Company, publishers of his last twelve books, would bring his final work into print.

Under different circumstances one might be tempted to say that "number thirteen" proved unlucky for Clifford Drury, for he desired very much to hold the finished product of his labors in his hands, autograph copies for his many friends and admirers, and wait for the first reviews to come in. On the other hand, Clifford never thought of himself in those terms. (He once defined "luck" to me as "the meeting place between opportunity and preparation.") He believed that God had provided the opportunities in his life by placing him in the right place at the right time, over and over again. His task was to be prepared, and he lived his life to the full with that singleness of purpose — to serve his Lord as a productive Christian scholar.

Clifford Drury was fond of mentioning that, with few exceptions, all who had helped him gather material for the diaries he edited and

the biographies he authored had passed away. He often quoted from
Job 1:19 — "They all are dead; and I only am escaped to tell thee."
On April 18, 1984, in Pasadena, Clifford Merrill Drury, missionary,
pastor, chaplain, teacher and historian passed away. Because his life
was characterized by such an energetic love of labor, he was ready
to "go home" — as he termed it — when he had finished the task that
had been his primary scholarly concern for five decades: the history
of the Oregon Mission of the American Board. He will be missed by
all who knew him, yet he lives on, and in the pages that follow you
can share in the exciting adventure that was his. Clifford would be
pleased to have you along as his companion.

May, 1984
Westmont College
Santa Barbara, California

Introduction

Many have asked me: "How were you able to find source materials for each of your published twenty-five books? And then how were you able to get them published?" Although I have lectured frequently before service clubs, college assemblies, historical societies, and church groups, and although some of these lectures have been published, the time has come when I feel that I should write out a detailed account of my adventures in Americana which have covered nearly fifty years going back to 1934. Possibly some of my experiences and techniques will be a guide to younger historians who are just beginning their writing careers.

Through most of my life, I have kept a diary. I have also kept copies of hundreds of letters I have written and filed away memorabilia of various kinds which tell the story of some important events in my life. The time has come for me to clear out my files. It is better for me to write out the story of my life, condensing the wealth of source materials that I have, than to have someone dispose of these records after I am gone by throwing them into the trash can. Moreover, the Presbyterian Historical Society of Philadelphia has urged me to write my autobiography and then pass on to them the most important papers I have used. The others can be discarded.

I want this to be more than the story of my life. I want this to be a commentary on my generation. Having lived into the mid-eighties, and having lived abroad for over five years, I feel that I have important information as to how earlier generations have lived. Hence, I have taken pains to give prices, dates, and accounts of personal experiences through my many years which reach back to the beginning of this century.

This, then, is my autobiography. It is a story of my generation. It is "my road from yesterday."

IN APPRECIATION

I wish to express my appreciation to the following who have read all or part of the manuscript for this book and have made important corrections. Their encouragement made this book possible.

Mrs. Elam Anderson, McMinnville, Oregon
Mrs. J. Hudson Ballard, Corvallis, Oregon
Mr. and Mrs. James Black
Dr. Larry Byers and Mrs. Ted Lloyd, Sedro-Wooley, Washington
Mrs. Fred A. Clark, San Clemente, California
Mrs. Robert Evans, Early, Iowa
Mrs. Elton Gildow, Lacey, Washington
Mr. Jay Howe, Jr., Harrisonburg, Virginia
Mrs. Hillis Lory, Sun City, Arizona
Mr. Kenneth Platt, Moscow, Idaho
Dr. & Mrs. Stuart Seaton, Johnson City, Tennessee
Mrs. W. W. Taylor, West Vancouver, B.C.
Mr. & Mrs. A. W. Welch, Walla Walla, Washington
Mr. William S. White, Glendora, California
Rev. Robert Williams, Walnut Valley, California

CHAPTER ONE

My Ancestry

The Drury name can be traced back to a knight who entered England with William the Conqueror in 1066. This knight came from Rouvray, a town near Rouen in Normandy, France. Hence he was De Rouvray or Drury. The name was spelled phonetically for several centuries, hence the variations — Drewry, Drourie, and Drury.

The first Drury, or his immediate descendants, settled at Hawstead near Bury St. Edmunds, in Suffolk County, England, which remained the ancestral home of a Drury family for about 600 years. The British Museum in London has a copy of a book by John Cullen, *The History and Antiquities of Hawstead*, which contains the genealogy of the Drury family from 1066 to 1600. While a student at the University of Edinburgh, 1927-28, I was able to secure a copy of the reprinted edition of 1813. This copy is now in Drury College, Springfield, Missouri.

Another source for the history of the Drurys is Arthur Campling's *The History of Drury in the counties of Suffolk and Norfolk from the Conquest*, London, after 1913. This author, quoting from an older source with its antique spelling, included the following:

This right worshipful and most plentiful family of Drury descended from a gentleman of that name . . . who came from Normandy with King William, the Conqueror in 1066.

The offspring and issue of this Norman gentleman have multiplied greatlie increased, and prosperouslie continued untill this time, 1662, being divided and spread by sondrie branches into several branches, and settled house of good estimation in sondrie counties of this realme.

This family hath continued many years in good reputation; replenished with Knights and Squires, and greatlie honoured with soldiers of notable fame and memory."

Standing at Hawstead is a stone church called All Saints, centuries old, which contains several Drury memorials. Among the unique memorials is the tomb of Sir Roger Drury, flanked on either side by the tombs of his two wives. Over each tomb is a life-size bas-relief brass effigy. On Sir Roger's left was the effigy of his first wife with her eyes closed indicating that she was dead. On his other side was the effigy of his second wife with her eyes wide open, thus indicating that she was still living when her husband died.

In a shallow recess in the wall on the right side of the chancel, when viewed from the nave, is a statue of a girl of about fifteen years, a little less than life size. This memorializes Elizabeth Drury, the daughter of Sir Robert Drury. She was engaged to the Prince of Wales at the time of her death. She was depicted as half reclining, leaning on her right elbow. John Donne, who became dean of St. Paul's Cathedral in London, in 1621 wrote a poem on the occasion of the first anniversary of the death of Elizabeth Drury, and also, again, on the second anniversary. In this second poem are the following lines:

> Her pure and eloquent blood
> Spoke in her cheeks, and so distinctly wrought
> That one might almost say, her body thought.

In those days, the eldest son inherited both the title and the landed property. Younger sons were then obliged to seek their fortunes elsewhere. A number, including my ancestors, settled in Lincolnshire, to the north and west of Suffolk.

THE LINCOLNSHIRE DRURYS

My grandfather, Thomas Drury, migrated to Iowa in 1851 coming from a small village, Ashby-cum-Fenby, located about eight miles from the seaport town of Grimsby in Lincoln County, England. The unusual name arose out of the fact that two small settlements had been united. The word "cum" is a Latin word for "with." Sometime in the spring of 1919, I addressed a letter to the rector of the Anglican church at Ashby-cum-Fenby asking if the churchs records carried any reference to Thomas Drury.

The rector kindly replied giving the following information: "Thomas Drury married Elizabeth Jane Reynolds on October 2, 1826." The records showed that while Elizabeth Jane was able to sign her name, Thomas, being unable to write, signed with an "X" mark. The records also stated that Thomas came from Great Carlton and that he was a laborer in the employ of the Reynolds family.

Thomas and Elizabeth became the parents of three sons — William, baptized August 27, 1827; John, February 9, 1833; and Thomas, my grandfather, March 8, 1835. According to the church records, Thomas, the father, was buried on August 10, 1835, when my grandfather, Thomas George, was an infant only five months old.

When my wife and I were on our three-month tour of the British Isles in the late spring of 1966, we stopped over at Grimsby. The rector of the Anglican Church there kindly took us out to Ashby-cum-Fenby to show us the old stone church, called St. Peters, where my grandfather was baptized. One evidence of the age of this stone church was the grave of a crusader located in the vestibule.

The furniture of the church — the baptismal font, the pulpit, the pews — appeared to be very old. There were two memorials of special interest to me. The first was the elaborate tomb of Sir Christopher Wray and his wife Frances, a daughter of Sir William Drury of Hawstead.

The second memorial which attracted my attention was dedicated to the memory of Susanne Drury, the sister of Lady Wray, and, of course, a daughter of Sir William Drury. According to the account of her death found in Arthur Compling's *The History of the Family Drury:* "She . . . went a hunting whilst on a visit to Lady Wray . . . Being no horsewoman, they fastened her to her saddle with straps that she might not be dismounted. The animal became restive and ran away; galloping furiously across the country. Her head dashed against the branches of a tree, and the injuries were fatal. She was buried in the Ashby Church ,yard by where a splendid monument was erected to her memory." Susanne was only twenty-two years old when she died in 1606.

The presence of these memorials to members of the Drury family from Hawstead quickened my desire to trace out the lineage, generation by generation, which would link the Hawstead Drurys with my great-grandfather, Thomas Drury. There was a gap of about 200 years which needed to be filled. I was aware of this gap long before we visited Ashby-cum-Fenby and had sought the aid of an Anglican clergyman in the Diocesan Registry Office of the Anglican Cathedral in Lincoln. I was hopeful that some will would be found which would indicate some particular parish where my ancestors had lived. The clergyman examined eighty wills without finding any information of value to me.

My wife and I went to Lincoln, after our visit to Ashby-cum-Fenby, where we spent two days, May 25 and 26, 1966. This gave me time to visit the Registry Office and examine a number of Drury wills.

After reading a number of the Drury wills, I concluded that it would be futile to attempt to fill out my genealogical chart from such sources. Evidently many of my ancestors did not have enough property to justify making a will, as was the case of my great-grandfather. Thus the gap of about 200 years, from 1600 to 1794, in my genealogical chart remains blank. Even though I cannot name my ancestors generation by generation during these years, yet, because I bear the family name of DRURY, I know that I am a descendant of that knight from Rouvray in Normandy who entered England with William the Conqueror in 1066.

THREE DRURYS MIGRATE TO IOWA

The widow of Thomas Drury, Elizabeth Jane, was remarried to

George Sizer. They had two sons, George and Robert. Elizabeth Jane died on March 25, 1843.

In 1851, Mr. & Mrs. John Barker migrated to the United States with their two nephews, George and Robert Sizer, and the three Drury young men. William was then 24; John, 18; and Thomas, 16. They all settled in Clinton County, Iowa. William died during the following year without having been married. He lies buried in the Newberry Cemetery, Green Island, Iowa.

John Drury married Hannah Gibson and many of their descendants still live in Clinton County. John Drury died on August 1, 1874, and Hannah then married a man by the name of Addy. Hannah lived to be 93 years old, dying in 1933.

Very little documentation is available which tells of Thomas Drury's life for the eleven years he lived in Clinton County before he was killed in an accident in a sorghum mill on October 28, 1862. I have a copy of a deed issued to him on March 14, 1857, when he bought 80 acres of land in Clinton County for $7.00 an acre. Thomas applied for his naturalization papers on May 14, 1857, and received his final papers on March 12, 1860. He was then called upon to "absolutely and entirely renounce and adjure all allegiance and fidelity to every foreign Prince, Power, Potentate, State, and Sovereign, whatever and particularly to the Queen of Great Britain & Ireland." The reference here is to Queen Victoria.

Among those who migrated to Clinton County were members of the Davis family from Ontario, Canada. Among them was Sarah Elizabeth who was born at Hamilton, Ontario, on November 29, 1830. She and Thomas Drury were married on May 6, 1857. On November 10th of that year, Thomas bought 40 more acres of land for $400.00, or at a cost of $10.00 an acre. The land was located about two miles north of Bryant, Deep Creek Township, Clinton County. According to the record of this transaction, Thomas was able to pay $100.00 down and made arrangements to pay the balance in installments with 10% interest.

Thomas and Sarah were the parents of three children — Sarah Annette, born April 4, 1850; John Thomas, January 17, 1861; and William, my father, October 2, 1862. I remember my Grandmother Drury very well for I was in my ninth year when she died on April 29, 1906. I marvel to think that I knew the widows of two of the Drurys who were born at Ashby-cum-Fenby back in 1833 and in 1835.

Sarah Drury had, for a long time, wanted a carriage with a fringe on its top and Thomas had promised to buy one as soon as the mortgage on his last purchase of land had been paid. The day came when the final payment was made and then came the tragic accident.

Thomas stopped at a sorghum mill just at the time when a piece of metal from a spinning flywheel flew through the air and struck him in the head, killing him instantly The accident occurred on October 28, 1862, when Thomas was only 27½ years old. Sarah was left with three small children, the youngest of whom was my father, then only twenty-six days old.

Thus for the second time, a Thomas Drury was taken, leaving an infant son. Grandmother Drury was left with 120 acres of good Iowa farm land. Undoubtedly relatives came to her assistance.

CHAPTER TWO

The Drury Family in Sac County

Life was hard for my Grandmother who, with limited resources, had to raise her three little children. I remember my father telling me that often their meals consisted of corn bread and molasses. My father was not able to get any education beyond that at the common grade school in their vicinity. On September 3, 1876, when only seventeen years old, my father's sister, Annette, was married to David P. Bates and the couple moved to Hammond, Louisiana.

Living in the vicinity of the Drury family in Clinton County was the family of James Wilson consisting of the parents, five sons, and two daughters. They had come from Glasgow, Scotland, in 1853. The younger of the two girls, Sarah, and Will fell in love and evidently became engaged when Will was only eighteen.

According to a family tradition, sometime in the summer of 1880, a land salesman from Sioux City visited Clinton County extolling the excellence of the virgin soil of Sac County in northwest Iowa. My father, then in his eighteenth year, was fascinated with the glowing picture of the western paradise as painted by the salesman. So likewise was his friend, Robert Wilson, brother of Sarah, and about three years older than my father. The two decided to migrate to Sac County and each get a farm and invest their future in a new pioneer community.

On January 2, 1969, I wrote to an old friend and one who was our neighbor when we lived on the Boyer River farm asking him for his recollections regarding my father's journey across Iowa to Odebolt. He was John Schramm whose father's farm adjoined the Drury farm. In his reply, John stated that my father and Rob Wilson shipped their goods consisting of their horses, farm machinery, and personal belongings by train across the state to what was then the rail terminal at Vail, Iowa, a few miles east of Dennison, and about twenty miles to the southeast of Odebolt, their destination.

The two young men selected farms in Clinton Township. This township was named after Clinton County because so many from that county had settled in that area. No doubt this was the main reason why Rob and Will decided to settle there. The two selected farms located about eight miles to the northeast of Odebolt, which was their main shopping center. Most of the land between their farms and Odebolt lay uncultivated. Roads had not been laid out so it was customary to drive across the unbroken prairie when going to town.

In that part of Iowa, land was laid out like a checkerboard with thirty-six square miles in each township. Usually each square mile would be divided into four farms of 160 acres each. A school would be placed in the center of each segment of four square miles, thus there were nine schools in a township and no pupil would have to walk more than two miles to go to school, less if he cut across the fields.

Land records in Sac County show that my father bought 160 acres in Section 5 of Clinton Township for $15.00 an acre in December 1880. My father was then a little more than eighteen years old. He was able to make a down payment of $200.00 and promised to pay the balance within ten years with 10% interest. I remember that my father told me that he earned some money by breaking the virgin prairie for a neighbor with a walking plow for $2.00 an acre. This was difficult work and I doubt is he could have broken more than two acres a day. Robert Wilson bought a farm about a mile away from that owned by my father.

The farm that my father bought was supposed to have had "improvements," but when my father first saw what he had purchased, he discovered that these "improvements" needed improving. The barn was nothing more than a shed covered with straw for a make-shift roof. The well needed cleaning and relining. The house had a door that did not fit; steps that were broken; a chimney that did not draw; and a floor that needed repairs. All this was most disheartening, but the excellence of the soil more than compensated for the sad condition of the buildings. Being young and enthusiastic, my father tackled his problems with zest.

Both my father and his friend, Rob Wilson, "batched" for two years, often sharing one another's cooking. Shortly after the two had settled on their respective farms, they attended a public meeting of the local school board, which was District No. 1 of Clinton Township. Although neither of them were then married, both were elected to an office. Rob was elected treasurer and my father was made secretary. This was the beginning of my father's interest in public affairs, an interest which he pursued throughout the remainder of his life. He was elected to the House of Representatives of the Iowa Legislature in 1906 and reelected in 1908. He once told me that he could have gone further in the political field if he had had a better education.

In December 1882, my father returned to Clinton County where he and Sarah Wilson were married on the 28th. Both were then a few weeks beyond their twentieth birthdays. Will and Sarah became the parents of four children. Their names and birthdays are: Maud

Leone, April 21, 1884; Millard Wilson, April 21, 1887; Blanche Ann-ette, March 21, 1892; and Clara Mae, June 26, 1894.

In 1892 John Drury joined his brother Will and bought a farm across the road from where Will lived. To this place John brought his mother who kept house for him as John had never married. Sometime in 1893 Grandmother Drury entertained her first cousin, Mae Charity Dell, from Niagara Falls, Ontario, Canada. Mae, who became my mother, was then teaching school at Audubon, a town about forty-five miles southeast of where Will and John lived. Mae was born on November 2, 1864, near Hamilton, Ontario. She was able to take a course in a teacher's college at Hamilton and when she was twenty-nine or younger had accepted a call to be a teacher in Audubon. She had relatives there who, no doubt, had secured the position for her.

While visiting her cousin, my Grandmother, Mae became acquaint-ed with Will and Sarah Drury. A strong friendship developed between Mae and Sarah. When Sarah gave birth to her fourth child, a daugh-ter, on June 26, 1894, she was named Clara Mae, her second name being Mae after my mother. Years later when my mother gave birth to a daughter, she was named Sarah Miriam in memory of my father's first wife.

Shortly after moving to Clinton Township, John Drury decided that it would be more profitable to raise and fatten cattle than just to farm. So he bought 220 acres on the Boyer River for which he paid $35.00 an acre, largely on credit. This farm was ideally situated for the fattening of cattle as it had two large pastures. One on its west side through which a creek flowed and the other on the eastern side through which the Boyer River flowed. Perhaps when this latter stream entered the Missouri a little to the north of Omaha, it was large enough to be called a river, but when it flowed through the Drury farm, it would more properly have been called a creek. With these two streams, John did not need to worry about watering his livestock.

The two-story farm house was built in 1878 and is now torn down. The house had three bedrooms upstairs and two downstairs. It had no inside plumbing. A covered porch ran the length of the south side. Downstairs rooms also included a kitchen, pantry, and dining room. The house also had a basement which was sometimes used as a refuge when threatened with a cyclone.

The man who first erected the farm buildings loved trees for he planted an orchard of nearly two acres with a variety of summer and fall apples with some plum and cherry trees elsewhere. A windbreak of poplars lined the north side of the farmyard, with a thick grove of box elder trees and some cottonwoods along the west and south sides. The lane of about 500 feet long, which led from the road to the house, was lined with soft maple trees which, when I was a boy, were interlaced high overhead. Long before I ever heard of a street in London named Drury Lane, after one of the Hawstead Drurys, this was the only Drury Lane I knew.

John Drury died on November 1, 1893, and was the first of the Drurys to be buried in the family plot in the Odebolt cemetery. In the late spring of 1895, Sarah returned to her parental home in Clinton County for a visit, taking with her her baby Clara then about one year old. On June 5, 1895, Sarah died in the home of her parents and was buried in the Vernon Prairie Cemetery (Newberry Cemetery) where Thomas Drury lay buried. Following the death of Sarah, Grandmother Drury stepped into the Will Drury home and took care of the four children.

My father took over the Boyer River farm which John had purchased and assumed the debt of an unknown amount. Sometime during the spring of 1895, Will sold his first farm for $45.00 an acre, which is reported to have been the highest price ever paid for land in Sac County, and moved his family to the former John Drury farm. My father made many improvements. A new horse barn was erected in 1899 and a new cattle barn in 1903. Other buildings were also erected including several corn cribs, a cement block silo in 1914, and a garage, and icehouse. He bought an unneeded fuel shed from some school district and hauled it to the farm and converted it into a wash house in which he installed a one-cylinder gas engine to run the washing machine. He fenced the two pastures with hog-proof woven wire so that his herd of hogs, sometimes numbering up to 300, could be turned loose in them. I remember inserting rings into the snouts of the pigs to prevent them from rooting up the meadow.

Sometime in 1893, possibly before the death of his brother John, my father bought 160 acres of unimproved farm land in Boyer Valley Township for $25.00 an acre. Most of this land was in pasture through which the Boyer River ran, making it also an ideal place to pasture cattle. This farm was two miles from our home place. Thus with the farm that his brother once owned, my father became the owner of 380 acres of fine Iowa land.

Following the death of Sarah, his first wife, my father began a correspondence with Mae Dell, who was then living in Buffalo, New York. He evidently proposed through the mail and she accepted. Will then went to Buffalo and the two were married on January 26, 1897. They became the parents of the following six children, all of whom were born on the Boyer River farm: Clifford Merrill, November 7, 1897; Grover Eldridge, August 18, 1899; William Edward, March 5,

1901; Sarah Miriam, April 2, 1904; and the twins, Howard John and Homer Thomas, June 12, 1908. My mother died as the result of complications, following the birth of the twins, on June 30, 1908, and lies buried in the Drury plot in the Odebolt cemetery.

I should explain that I have gone by both of my first names. My father preferred calling me Clifford while my mother called me Merrill. I used my second name through High School and College but when I enlisted in World War I, the Army insisted on using my first name and since then I have been known as Clifford M. Drury.

Following the death of my mother, my father was left a widower with small children for the second time. Complicating the situation was the fact that one of the twins, Homer, had seizures during the first week of his life. This was later diagnosed as epilepsy. My father made arrangements with relatives of his first wife, Alex and Lou Wilson, to care for the twins. This they did for several years. Maud, my eldest sister, was married to Ferry Smith on April 30, 1902. All of the other seven children were at home following my mother's death. We also had a hired man who received $30.00 a month, plus room, board, and washing, and a hired girl, who was paid about $15.00 a month. Both were treated as members of the family. Thus, with my father, the table had to be set for ten three times a day.

Millard, my older brother, who became twenty-one in 1908, remained at home helping with the farm work until December 14, 1910, when he was married to Angie Evans of Early. He then started farming for himself. We three younger boys had chores to do as early as we were able. We were the first up in winter mornings and built the fires in the kitchen and dining room. I remember that I was milking cows when I was ten years old. As a boy, my father had to work hard and he expected the same of us.

I have before me as I write a clipping from the Early *News* from sometime in November 1958. Under the caption, "50 YEARS AGO," is the following item: "Hon. Will Drury of Clinton Township informs us that his three little sons, Clifford, Grover and Will husked over 1,000 bushels of corn for him this fall." In November 1908, I would have been eleven years old; Grover nine; and Willie (herafter known as Billy), seven.

Following the marriage of my father to my mother in January 1897, Grandmother Drury divided her time between staying with her daughter at Hammond, Louisiana, for six months, including the winter months, and staying with us for the other six months. I remember her as an energetic little woman who helped out with the house work. She even made our soap in a large black kettle which was suspended over a fire in the farmyard.

One fall, when I was seven or eight years old, my father took me with him when he took his mother to Wall Lake, about ten miles distant from our home, where she would catch a train for Chicago. There she would change to another train which would take her to Hammond, Louisiana. When the train arrived, my father told me to carry her suitcase to her reserved seat in the pullman car. I did so and as I was hurrying out my grandmother called me back to give me a farewell kiss. That was a mistake for in those few minutes, the conductor slammed the door shut and the train started for Chicago. I was frantic and besought the conductor to stop the train and let me get off. He calmed me down by saying that the train had to stop at the "Y" located about one mile east of the station and that I could get off there and walk back. This I did, and I still remember that long walk through the blackness of the night back to the station where my father was waiting for me. I wished then that my grandmother had not been so sentimental.

Grandmother Drury died at her daughter's home in Louisiana on April 29, 1906. Her body was sent back for burial in the Drury plot in the Odebolt cemetery. She had been a widow for forty-four years.

Shortly before my mother's death, my father secured the services of a young woman, Laura Gathman, to be our hired girl. After my mother died, Laura stayed on in the home for several weeks and then left. For a time another hired girl was secured. During these months, my two older sisters, Blanche, age 16, and Clara, 14, kept house. Clara entered high school in the fall of 1914 in Early and boarded through five days of the week. This gave added responsibility to Blanche. As the months passed, my father increasingly felt the need for a surrogate mother for the younger children. He proposed marriage to Laura Gathman and was accepted. The two were married in an Episcopal manse at Clinton, Iowa, on September 29, 1909. To this union were born two children, Joyce Jean on August 25, 1911, and Dean Allison on December 16, 1915. Joyce was the last of the Drurys to be born on the farm. Dean was born in the new house my father erected in Early in 1915.

The role of a stepmother is a difficult one, but especially so in our case for Laura had worked as a hired girl in our home and we then had called her Laura. Our father wanted us to call her mama, but this I could not do for I remembered my real mother. For years I avoided calling her by name in her presence. When I wrote to her during World War I and from China, I addressed her as Laura. Years passed before I realized how much she had done to keep the family together, especially the younger children, and how deserving she was of filial respect. Then I began to call her mother. Looking back, I feel that it might have been well if my father had had us

call her Aunt Laura rather than mama. Laura died on January 24,
1977, having passed her 97th birthday the preceding December 5th.
She, too, lies buried in the Odebolt cemetery.

Shortly after I began keeping company with the young lady who
became my wife in 1922, she asked me for the names of my brothers
and sisters in their chronological order. I then became aware that
the names formed a jingle rhyme. I told her that their names were:

> Maud, Millard, Blanche, Clara,
> Clifford, Grover, Will, Sarah,
> Howard, Homer, Joyce, Dean.
> Just one more would make thirteen.

LIFE ON AN IOWA FARM IN PRE-ELECTRICITY DAYS

I and those of my generation have lived through an age of transition. The introduction of electricity and the gasoline engine introduced a drastically new manner of living.

In my youth, the Iowa farmer was largely self-sustaining. On the
Drury farm we were always milking four or five cows which gave us
milk, cream, butter, and cottage (or Dutch) cheese. We had a flock
of chickens which ran free through the farmyard. During the spring
and summer months, our flock of hens would give us up to sixty
eggs a day. Eggs not needed for the table would be taken to the
Carlton Merchandise store in Early and sold for about 12¢ a dozen.

We raised our own vegetables, some of which we stored in the
basement of the house for winter use. We usually raised more po-
tatoes than were needed and sold the excess crop. We also stored
such winter apples from our orchard as Russets and Baldwins, but
since many of these were wormy, they did not last long. With the
exception of spraying our potato vines with a solution of paris green
(a mixture of copper acetate and arsenic), we used no insecticides,
and herbicides were then unknown. The modern use of these chemical compounds to control insects and weeds has had a devastating
effect on the bird life of the area.

My father usually devoted one acre to sweet corn and what we did
not eat in season, we dried by cutting the kernels from the cobs and
drying them as we did sliced apples. Since we had no pressure cooker,
the women of the household were unable to can peas and beans, but
they did can bushels of tomatoes in one or two-quart Ball fruit jars.
When in season, my father would buy boxes of peaches, pears, and
berries for canning. For several years, a good strawberry patch provided berries for eating and canning.

The farm even provided fuel for our cook stove as corn cobs and
wood from the grove of trees which surrounded the farm yard. My

father had to buy soft coal and anthracite for the heating stoves in the house. A bee hive provided us with honey and we harvested ice from the Boyer River in wintertime which we stored in an icehouse. This gave us ice until August. During winter months, we usually butchered one or two hogs. Arrangements were made with a neighbor for the smoking of hams and slabs of bacon as we had no smokehouse.

Farm life was very demanding. Cows had to be milked twice a day; the eggs had to be collected; and the animals fed. If my brothers and I went on a day's outing as to Lake View to swim or fish, we had to be back by 5:00 p.m. in order to do the chores. The idea of the whole family taking a month's vacation and traveling to some national park was unthinkable. The nearest to such an experience came in 1907 when the Redpath Chautauqua came to Sac City for a week and my father made arrangements for two tents to be reserved for us. We took turns going. It was there that I saw my first moving picture and my first Shakespeare play. And it was there that I heard William Jennings Bryan, the eloquent politician orator, and was bold enough to go up and shake his hand.

I wrote a more detailed account of my boyhood experiences on an Iowa farm which appeared in the winter issue, 1974, of the *Annals of Iowa*.

I began my public school education in September 1902, a few weeks before I reached my 5th birthday. The one-room schoolhouse was located about a quarter-mile from our home on an acre of land on the banks of the Boyer River. I recall how my first teacher, Miss Elizabeth Merchant, would take me up on her lap when teaching me my lessons. The number of pupils varied from five to about fifteen during the winter months when the older boys would return to school after harvesting the corn crops. Of course, all classes were held in that one room.

There was no well on the school grounds, so each day two of the older boys would be sent to the Manly home nearby to get a pail of drinking water. This we carried by putting a stick under the bail or handle. The pail full of water would then be placed on a bench near the door and a dipper would be hung on a nail nearby. If a pupil took more water in the dipper than he could drink, the part left over would simply be poured back into the pail. Finger signals were given to indicate certain requests. One finger on a raised arm meant — "Could I get a drink of water?" The raising of two fingers indicated a need to go to the out-of-doors privy. A simple nod from the teacher would give consent.

Since all classes were held in that one room, those who were not reciting could listen to those who were. Thus during the year, 1908-09, I followed all of the eighth grade classes and when the examinations for this grade arrived from the office of the County Superintendent of Schools, I took them and passed. I was then only eleven years old. So it was that I entered Early High School in the fall of 1909 when I was only eleven. My father let both Clara and me board in Early during the school year.

The high school department of the Early school occupied two rooms on the upper floor of a two-story building. During the time I was a student there, the total enrollment in high school numbered about thirty. In addition to the principal, there was one other teacher. The work for the 11th and 12 grades was combined and given on alternate years. No electives were offered. Only such basic subjects as English, history, mathematics, physiology, and Latin were scheduled.

At the beginning of my second year, when I was twelve years old, my father felt that I was then old enough to drive a horse back and forth to school. Clara then in her third year of high school rode with me. We had to be on the road before eight o'clock in order to be in school by nine o'clock. Classes were dismissed at 3:30 p.m., then came another hour of driving. I had to help with the milking and other chores both before leaving for school and after returning. This made it very difficult to do any homework. I recall the difficulty I experienced in finding time to read Scott's *Ivanhoe*. Also the one good reading light, fueled by kerosene, was on the dining room table and was shared by others in the family. There was little or no privacy for individual study.

Clara passed her 17th birthday in June 1911 and that year began teaching a country school. By that time my brother Grover was ready for high school so he joined me in driving the six miles to Early each day. Our father bought a blind horse which used to be a trotter in horse races for us to drive. The horse depended on us keeping a tight rein and when we let her go, she plunged ahead in absolute faith that we would guide her. I remember how in the coldest winter months we had to drive facing a north wind. Often the temperature dropped below zero. Sometimes we would heat bricks in the stove and then wrap them in newspapers and place them in the buggy under our lap robes in order to keep our feet warm.

When my father moved into Clinton Township in 1880, he bought two buffalo skins from some wandering Indians for 50¢ each. These were sent to a furrier to be lined and made into lap robes. I remember how Grover and I preferred using these buffalo robes over other kinds of blankets when we drove into the frigid north winds.

The only extra-curricular activities sponsored by the high school in my generation were a band, an annual oratorical contest, and a literary society which met every other Friday afternoon through the school year. Scheduled for one of these programs, I believe sometime in the spring of 1912, was a debate on the subject — "Resolved that the automobile will replace the horse on the average American farm." Elmer Evans, who later married my sister Clara, and I had the affirmative. Even though we brought forth every argument we could think of in favor of the automobile, we lost the debate. The passing of time has proved that the automobile has indeed replaced the horse on Iowa's farms, but such a possibility back in 1912 was unthinkable for the three judges who listened to our arguments.

I have kept a diary most of my life. Among my personal records is a small notebook which some live stock commission merchant in Chicago had given to my father. It provided space for short daily entries. The first entry in this, my first diary, was for Tuesday, March 1, 1910. I then wrote: "Today thought I would like to write a diary. Went to school today." The diary contains very little of interest beyond references to routine activities. On May 7, 1910, I noted that my father was adding a pantry and a bathroom to our house. The addition of the bathroom was for us a tremendous improvement. After these improvements were made, our father brought the twins home from the Wilsons who had kept them ever since my mother had died.

Among the records that I have saved through the years is my high school report card for my senior year, 1912-13. This shows that I received an "A" in each subject in both semesters.

The class of 1913 was graduated on May 30, 1913. The exercises were held in the town's "Opera House," which was nothing more than the hall over a drug store. There were six in my class, four boys and two girls, of whom only Ruth Hartsell and myself are still living. I was the youngest in the class, being only fifteen. I was still wearing knickerbocker pants with long black stockings which were held in place by elastic bands above my knees. Shortly before my graduation, my father bought me my first pair of long trousers but I was too embarrassed to wear them, so wore the knickerbockers. I was also then wearing button shoes which required a button hook to get them buttoned when I put them on.

I was the first member of the Will Drury family to be graduated from high school and in recognition of the occasion, my father gave me an open face gold watch. If my memory serves me correctly, he paid about $40.00 for it. Wrist watches were not then being worn. I was extremely proud of that watch and when wearing overalls, I carried the watch in the special pocket on the bib just over my heart.

I had a frightening experience shortly after my graduation from high school. I was plowing one day with a one-row cultivator. The row was nearly one-half mile long. I looked at my watch when I began one row and then when I came to the end, I looked again but the watch was gone. It had fallen out of my pocket! I tied the horses to a fence and then got down on my hands and knees and started back over the plowed row, pushing back the dirt, searching for the prized watch. About half way down the row, I found it! Thereafter I made certain that the watch was securely fastened in my pocket where it was placed.

Pleasant Hill Methodist Church

The amazing improvements in the country roads, made necessary by the coming of the automobile during the first years of the twentieth century, spelled the doom of two age-old institutions for the farmers — the country school and the country church. The highly important role that the country churches played in the social and religious life of the scattered farm communities should not be forgotten. The church that I attended in my youth was called the Pleasant Hill Methodist Episcopal Church. It was located about two miles east of where the Drury family lived. Actually there was no hill there, but only a gentle rise in the prairie. The church began about 1875 when some of the farm families met in homes on Sunday to sing familiar hymns and to worship.

Beginning about 1877, a Methodist minister from Wall Lake, about nine miles distant, would drive out on Sunday afternoons with his horse and buggy and conduct a service for these people. Finally, on June 20, 1889, this little group voted to build a church. An acre of land, which cost $50.00, was selected near schoolhouse No. 3, of Clinton Township and the cornerstone of the new church was laid on October 24, 1889. The total cash cost of the building, which measured 28 x 40 feet, was a little over $2,000.00. Some labor was donated. There were three Gothic style windows on each side of the sanctuary. The room was large enough to seat comfortably about seventy-five people. When crowded to capacity, another twenty-five could be seated. The church was supported by about fifteen families who lived within a radius of four miles of the church.

A Sunday school was held Sunday afternoons beginning at 2:00 o'clock. Those present would be divided into five or six classes. Of course there was a hubbub as the classes could not be separated from one another by more than one or two empty pews. My mother, who was deeply religious, taught a class of older boys and young men and was greatly beloved by them.

One Sunday, my sister Clara, then about fourteen years old, was

called upon to repeat the ten commandments. She got along famously
with the first nine but when she came to the 10th commandment,
she ran into a problem. Being deeply religious, her sensitive spirit
rebelled at saying what was to her a very bad word in that particular
commandment. She started repeating the commandment: "Thou
shalt not covet thy neighbor's house, thou shalt not covet thy neighbor's wife, nor his man servant, nor his maid servant, nor his ox,
nor his . . ." Then came a long pause. Her whole being rebelled at
the thought of saying what was to her a vulgar word, even if it were
in the Bible. She started again and again came to that objectionable
word. There followed a long pause, and finally she blurted out:
"Thou shalt not covet thy neighbor's ox, nor his donkey." Clara knew
her synonymns. The decorum of the assembly was shattered by a
spontaneous outburst of laughter, all to my sister's deep embarrass-
ment.

The preaching service was supposed to begin at 3:00 p.m., but the
minister was not always able to arrive by that time, so we would
have to wait. My mother was very faithful in her church attendance.
My father was not. I remember how both he and my mother were
obliged to stay in Des Moines for several months during the time
he served in the state legislature and that when the sessions were
over, both were very glad to be back home. At our first meal together,
my father said that he wanted to show his gratitude to God by saying the blessing at each meal. He did so thereafter. From this
experience and from others, I knew he was a religious man even
if he did not attend church regularly.

The church had a reed organ. Many of the songs sung at the worship
service laid heavy emphasis on the joys and rewards which awaited
the faithful in the next world. Such gospel songs were self-centered.
I recall the opening stanza of one of these songs was as follows:

> Will there be any stars, any stars, in my crown
> When at evening my sun goeth down?
> When I wake with the blest, in the mansions of rest,
> Will there be any stars in my crown?

Surely those hard-working men and women, who knew nothing of
the modern labor saving devices and comforts of today, needed the
assurances of a blessed hereafter when they would receive the well
earned rewards for their labors which they had not received in this
world.

Since my father did not follow the custom of handing out weekly
allowances of spending money to his children, I had to fall back on
my own ingenuity to make some extra money for incidental or per-

sonal expenses. I noticed that some of the weekly newspapers published in the nearby towns printed news of local country communities. I made contacts with the editors of the Sac *Sun*, the Odebolt *Chronicle*, and the Lake View *News* to be their reporter for the Pleasant Hill area. The Sac *Sun* paid me for the news which I sent in at .05¢ an inch after it was in type. The other two papers gave me an additional .06¢. I found that the best way to gather news items was right after church when the men and women would loiter a few minutes before departing for their homes. Then I would learn if a baby had been born or if anyone was sick or if anyone had taken a trip. After getting home from church I would use my father's Remington typewriter, and would use two carbon papers to make three copies — one for each paper. The editors did not object to the same news appearing in the other papers. Thus I was able to make at least $1.00 a week. Here was the beginning of my literary career. I was a paid newspaper reporter.

I sponsored another project which brought in about $10.00 a month in prizes. This was a Larkin Club made up of ten housewives, each of whom had promised to order $1.00 worth of Larkin products each month. The Larkin Company had its headquarters in Buffalo, New York. It carried a varied line of staple household items as soap, some canned goods, and incidentals. Each month one of the ladies got a $10.00 prize. I also got this amount in prizes and thus earned a camera, a tent, two hammocks, and a number of other items. I kept this project going for several years.

The Pleasant Hill church became a victim of the automobile and the coming of good roads, as did the country schools. The last service was held in the church in April 1948 and the church was demolished in September 1948. Today there is no sign that a church ever stood on the site. The grove of trees which once surrounded the lot is gone as are the sheds where we used to tie our horses. The one acre lot is now a part of a cornfield and only a few of the older people who pass that way ever remember that the Pleasant Hill Methodist Church once stood there.

CHAPTER THREE

Buena Vista College, 1914-1915

For the year and a half following my graduation from high school, I worked on my father's farm doing a full man's work even though I was only fifteen or sixteen years old. Sometime in February 1914, my father decided to visit his sister, Nettie, at Hammond, Louisiana. He took with him Laura, my stepmother, and their 2½ year old daughter, Joyce, and my brother and sister, Billy and Sarah. I was left in full charge of the farm. With me was my brother Grover, who was still driving back and forth to high school, and the twins, then approaching their sixth birthday. They were attending the country school near our home. Also, we had a hired girl, Kate Gathman, sister of my stepmother, who was doing the house work.

My father knew before he left for Louisiana that our hired man, Charlie Miller, who had worked for us several years, would be leaving in March to start farming for himself. The Miller family lived in the Wilcox farm house located about a quarter of a mile east of our home. My father gave me instructions as to how to find another hired man by getting in touch with some employment agency in Odebolt.

As soon as the Miller family vacated the house, I made inquiry and learned that there was in Odebolt a middle aged man who had recently been married and who was looking for a job on a farm. l drove over to Odebolt in a lumber wagon, for if he proved acceptable I would have to transport some of their belongings to the Wilcox house. After interviewing the man, whose name was Jack Lynch, I hired him and we put their belongings into the wagon and left for home.

Jack was about fifty years old and his bride, about twenty. She commented on the thirty years difference in their ages, but justified it by saying, "I would rather be an old man's darling than a young man's slave." Several years later she discovered that she and Jack were not legally married as the wedding ceremony which Jack arranged was a fake. She then left him.

During the five or six weeks my father was away, farm work consisted largely of taking care of the live stock, hauling manure to the fields, and mending fences. I soon discovered that I would have to be with Jack most of the time in order to get him to work.

My father was treasurer of the school board of Clinton township. In his absence I had the responsibility of writing the monthly pay checks for the teachers of the nine schools in the district.

Available reading material was scarce. My brothers and I subscribed for the *American Boy*. We three were friendly with a neigh-

bor's boy, Willie Millington, of about my age. He was the only child
in that family and his parents were very generous in buying books
for him to read. Among the books the parents selected were the
historical novels by the English author, G.A. Henty. I traveled with
him through the centuries and all over the world.

Reading these Henty books gave me my first real appreciation of
the drama and romance of history. Without being aware of what was
happening, the course of my life was being directed into the historical
field.

Although my father highly commended me for the way I had managed affairs on the farm during his absence, yet I knew that I was
not cut out to be a farmer. I loved reading too much. I took a correspondence course in grammar, shorthand, and some other subjects
in the early months of 1914, but I did not profit from these courses.

I constantly dreamed of going to college. At that time I had no
particular profession in mind. I thought some of being a lawyer or a
doctor, but never a minister. The Methodist ministers who drove out
each Sunday afternoon from Wall Lake to conduct services in the
Pleasant Hill Church had little opportunity to get acquainted with
the young people. After the service was over, they got into their
buggies and returned to their homes.

Since Buena Vista College at Storm Lake, Iowa, was located about
fifteen miles north of Early, it was the nearest college to my home
and, therefore, the place where I felt I should go.

In those days Buena Vista offered a special course during the winter
months for young men who were unable to take the college course,
and also a commercial course especially for young men who wanted
to learn shorthand and typewriting. During the 1915-16 year, twenty-
five young men were in the "short course" and fifteen men and women
in the commercial class. When I learned of these special courses, I
begged my father to let me enroll after I had finished picking corn.
This he consented to do and I was overjoyed.

My 17th birthday came on November 7 of that year, 1915. That
evening my father told Grover to take our Overland car and drive
to Early on some errand. I wanted to go also but he told me to stay
at home. While I was taking a bath, Grover returned with a carload
of young people. Other cars drove into our yard until some thirty-five
were present.

I have before me, as I write this page, a clipping from the Early
News which gives a report of my birthday party. The item states that
"It was a complete surprise which his sister, Mrs. Elmer Evans, had
planned." I marvel now to think how thirty-five guests would have
been able to gather in that small house in addition to the members

of the Drury family. Several years ago, when I had an opportunity to visit the old farm again, I measured the kitchen and found that it was only 9 x 12 feet and that the living room, or parlor as we used to call it, was 15 x 17. The dining room was about as large as the parlor. I wonder now how my father was able to get enough chairs for everyone to be seated. Perhaps some of the guests had to sit on the floor even when partaking of refreshments. This occasion was a very happy one for me.

I started another diary on that November 7th which I kept with fair regularity until Easter Sunday, April 4, 1915. Several of the first entries in this diary reveal my consuming eagerness to go to college. On November 12th, I wrote: "I can hardly wait to go to school. I am so tired of picking corn." According to my diary, I completed the corn picking on the 17th but the special courses for short term students did not begin at the college until the Monday after Thanksgiving.

My father took me to a clothing store in Odebolt and bought me about $50.00 worth of new clothes, including a suit which cost $24.00. I wrote in my diary that night: "First time in my life that I had had a high priced suit and two good suits at the same time." Later my father bought me an overcoat, shoes, a sweater, and a steamer trunk, but I forgot to ask for some shirts and new mittens.

I was then wearing on Sundays some hand-me-down shirts from my brother Millard which were at least one size too large. In those days we had to wear detachable collars which called for a collar button in front and one in the middle of the neck band in the back. With the neck band of Millard's old shirts one size larger than the collars, this meant a tuck in the shirt which was always uncomfortable. For mittens, I had been wearing two pairs of cotton corn husking mittens which I felt were not appropriate for college.

On Monday, November 23rd, I wrote in my diary: "One week from today I leave for college. Hurrah!" The entry closed with this cryptic note: "When there is a will, there is a way." That sentence quickened an old memory. I then desperately wanted some new shirts and a new pair of mittens of which I would not be ashamed. Since my father had been so generous in buying such an expensive outfit for me, I did not have the courage to go to him and ask for something more. I racked my brain to find some way to get the few dollars needed to get the extra items. And then I thought of the solution. I would take five or six roosters with me on my next trip to Odebolt and sell them. Nobody knew how many chickens we had. Moreover, I had all the work connected with raising the chickens, so I felt that I had a proprietary right to them.

I faced one serious obstacle in this money-raising scheme and that was my younger brother Grover. For several good reasons, he had become my vigilant critic, always quick to report any dereliction of duty on my part to our father. I recall three instances which, together, gave him ample reasons for suspicion. The first occurred while swimming in the Boyer River. We often would try to see who could hold his breath the longest while under water. I thought of a scheme to beat them. Holding our noses, we would each duck under the water at the same time. I would then quickly come up for a fresh whiff of air and then go down again. Under such circumstances, I always won until Grover grew suspicious at my continuous record-breaking feat and one day resurfaced just when I did. That incident alerted Grover to watch me.

Another of my tricks involved our favorite magazine, the *American Boy*. We three were avid readers of its continued stories and each wanted first chance to read the magazine when it arrived in the mail. Our mailman, who came out from Early driving a horse and buggy, usually arrived at our mailbox located at the foot of the lane at noontime. And I was usually there waiting for him. In order to avoid the controversy as to who should read the magazine first, I decided that a better way was for me to hide it when it came and then read it at my leisure. Afterwards I would put the magazine with the mail and then say to either Grover or Billy: "The *American Boy* came today. I'll let you read it first." This continued for several weeks and then Grover got suspicious of such magnanimity on my part and, after some investigations, discovered what I had been doing. I found it very difficult to fool Grover for long.

The third instance involved corn picking. Grover, although he was twenty-one months younger than I, was a better worker on the farm than I was. We could each go out to the corn field at the same time in the morning with individual wagons and he would always bring in a larger load of corn than I. One day we each went to the same field but in different locations. After picking for a short time, I found that my row led through a pumpkin patch. Those big yellow pumpkins gave me an idea. I filled the lower part of the wagon box with them and thus was able to bring in a much larger load than Grover had. That noon when I drove into the farmyard, I pulled up alongside his load. The difference was striking. Never before had I picked so much corn. Grover was astonished. He was mystified.

My scheme would have gone undetected had it not been that my father called me away to take care of some errand and asked Grover to unload my wagon. Perhaps my father had suspected what I had done. Grover soon found the pumpkins and with some glee made a pile of them by the wagon. These were later thrown to the hogs.

Remembering such experiences, I knew that Grover would raise a fuss if he discovered me taking a crate full of chickens to Odebolt to sell without having permission. I had to devise some way of getting the chickens crated and hidden until I left for town without him knowing about it. At that time we had divided our chores. I took care of the horses while he and Billy did the milking. I decided that the only safe course to follow was to get up earlier than Grover; do my work and then when Grover was busy milking, I would get the chickens and carry the crate to the end of the lane and hide it under the bridge. Then on my way to Odebolt, I could stop and pick it up.

I remember that I was harnessing my team of horses when Grover entered the barn. He was carrying a milk pail on one arm and a lantern on the other. He paused as he entered the barn and looked at me in astonishment.

"Why did you get up so early?" he asked. He felt that there must be some reason for my unusual behavior, and, indeed, there was but I was not in the mood to tell him.

"You take care of your chores," I answered, "and I'll take care of mine."

As soon as I knew that he and Billy were doing the milking, I hurried to the chicken house which was located back of the buildings on the north side of the farmyard. It was secluded and I was sure that they could not hear me. It was still dark so the chickens were still on their roosts. I had carried the crate to the place the night before. I entered quietly and picked out the ones I wanted and then with a double swipe, one hand around a chicken's neck and the other around its feet, I grabbed what I wanted. This I repeated at least five times. In order to prevent the roosters from crowing, I covered the crate with a blanket to keep the birds in the dark and quiet.

The next job was to get the crate down to the bridge. I dared not go the shortest way down the lane or through the barnyard lest I would be seen by someone in the house. So, I had to take a circuitous route around the buildings, through the cattle yard, down to the bridge. The box with the chickens and the blanket must have weighed at least fifty pounds and grew very heavy before I was able to hide it under the bridge. I was barely able to complete this task before it was time for breakfast. So far all had gone well and I was pleased with my accomplishments.

After breakfast, I deliberately loitered until our hired man had left with the other load of barley and my brothers were on their way to school. Then I started. I stopped at the bridge and with great difficulty lifted the crate with the birds to the top of the high wagon box. It taxed my strength to the limit. I have forgotten just how much I got in the sale of the chickens, but it was enough to buy the desired shirts and the mittens. This is why I wrote in my diary that evening: "When there is a will, there is a way."

COLLEGE LIFE, 1914-1915

Since the college held its registration for its winter courses on Monday, November 30, my father took me to Storm Lake on the previous day. The great day in my life had come. I wrote in my diary: "Outwardly, I may appear to be calm, but inwardly my soul leaps with joy."

My father arranged for me to board at Mrs. Mary Foote's, who set an excellent table for $4.00 a week. She already had two other boarders. I got a room in a private home located on the southwest corner of the campus, where the student union building is now located, for $2.50 a week. This I shared with another student.

I luxuriated in my new environment. How wonderful to get up in a warm room when it was below zero outside and not have to go out to the barn and milk the cows and do the chores. At times I had a guilty feeling. I felt sorry for my brothers, Grover and Billy, when I remembered that they had extra work to do because I was in college. But then I rationalized my situation by reasoning that some day they, too, would have the chance to go to college.

Buena Vista College was still in its infancy when I enrolled, being only twenty-three years old. It was founded in 1891 by the Presbyteries of Sioux City and Fort Dodge. During the first decades of the 20th century, Iowa was sprinkled with church-related colleges, many of which do not now exist.

When the Presbyterians were looking for a site for their new college, several towns, including Fort Dodge, vied with one another for the selection. Storm Lake, then boasting a population of about 1,600, was chosen partly because the town had no saloons and partly because a real estate company offered to donate eight acres for a campus and to erect a $25,000.00 building. Work on the building began in the fall of 1891 and was open for classes a year later. Actually some classes for the academic year, 1890-91, were held in the town's opera house.

Old Main, as the main building was called, was a four-story brick building including a basement, shallow enough so that half-sized windows could be placed. The basement contained the furnace, the men's toilets, class rooms, and a bookstore built into a corner of the hall. Upon entering the main front door, one was faced with a wide flight of stairs leading to the second or main floor. This was flanked on either side by stairways leading to the basement.

The second floor contained the administration offices, the library, the women's toilets, and several classrooms. The library then had about 8,000 volumes, if I remember correctly, including many books from the libraries of former ministers who were either retired or deceased. The third floor contained the chapel, the chemical and biological laboratories, and three small classrooms. The top floor had two large rooms, one on either side of the hallway, which were used by the two literary societies — the Franklin and the Star — for their semi-monthly meetings and also as classrooms when needed.

As I recall, all of the floors of Old Main were bare boards; no carpets or linoleum. I remember how noisy it was in the reading room of the library. Once the editor of the *Rudder,* our college annual, divided the student body into two groups — those who quietly closed the main door when entering or leaving the library, and those who did not. I was among the latter. It was so easy to let the big door slam shut with a bang.

The college owned three other buildings in addition to Old Main. These stood across the street to the east of the block-square campus. One was the President's residence; another was a house used by the music and domestic science departments; and the third was the girl's dormitory, large enough to accommodate thirty-four girls. This latter building was burned on June 21, 1915. Forty years were to pass before another women's dormitory was erected. In the meantime, all students from out of town had to find rooms in private homes.

The total enrollment at Buena Vista in 1914-15 was 105. Of this number, forty-seven were taking the four-year course leading to a B.A. degree; fourteen were in the academy which was the preparatory department for college; and the others were in the commercial department or taking the winter short courses. The academy was needed then because some students came from communities where there was no high school.

On Monday, November 30, I enrolled in two classes in the commercial department — shorthand and typewriting. I was also able to enter two freshman classes, English and Sociology. In order to be graduated in four years, a student had to earn on the average of fifteen units in each of the two semesters which made up an academic year. Since I enrolled late in the fall of 1914, and since my work in the commercial department was not accepted as equal to college courses, I later had to attend two summer schools in order to qualify for graduation in 1918.

I did not keep up the shorthand but my mastery of the touch system of typing proved to be of invaluable aid to me throughout my writing career. At the end of the second semester at Buena Vista, a contest was held in typing with $3.00 as first prize. Of course we did not have electric typewriters then but the old fashioned machines. I wrote in my diary for June 10: "Wrote 471 words with only 5 errors, average 44.6 words per minute for ten minutes." I have a recollection that once I wrote 103 words a minute for three minutes using old material.

No report on my college experiences would be complete without paying tribute to my teachers. They were excellent, deeply devoted to their work. Later I learned that they were serving on minimum salaries which were often in arrears. I owe much to them. One in particular played an important role in my life for some sixty-two years — Miss Mabelle Conquist who became Mrs. Elleroy Smith.

On December 4, 1914, only a few days after I had enrolled at the college, I noted in my diary: "I met Miss Conquist this evening." She was the "Professor of Oratory" at the college. She was only twenty-five years old when she joined the faculty in the fall of 1914, about eight years older than I. A bond of friendship quickly developed between us and I often went to her with my problems. She was as an older sister to me. I was present at her wedding in the spring of 1917 when she and the Rev. Elleroy Smith were married. They left that day for their mission field in Ningpo, China. They met my bride and myself at the dock in Shanghai, China, in March 1922 when we arrived to serve the American Protestant residents of that great city. We were in their home in Ningpo and they were in our home in Shanghai. After they retired, I visited in Omaha, Nebraska, and then after Roy died, I helped Mabelle get located in the Presbyterian retirement home for ex-missionaries at Westminster Gardens in Duarte, California, about twelve miles east of where my wife and I live. She passed away at that home on November 24, 1976. She was a precious and dear friend through many years, and our friendship began at Buena Vista on that December evening back in 1914.

Other lifelong friendships were started in those opening months of my college career. In the freshman class were two young men from Sioux City, both of whom were candidates for the Presbyterian ministry. They were Edmund Marousek, of Bohemian ancestry, and Harvey Hood. As I write now, in April 1980, Harvey Hood is one of my neighbors here at Monte Vista Grove Homes. With the exception of some relatives, I wrote more often to Ed Marousek through more than sixty years than to anyone else.

There was a strong religious life at the college when I was a student. Attendance at daily chapel was required and, looking back, I am glad that it was so. The YMCA and YWCA held weekly prayer meetings on Wednesday evenings. It was at one of these meetings that I ventured to pray aloud in the presence of others. This was such a big step that I made note of it in my diary entry for February 10, 1915.

Among those in the student body who exercised a great influence in my life was a senior, about ten years older than I, Walter O. Benthin. He also was a student for the ministry. One day he asked me: "Have you ever joined a church?" I replied that I had not. Again he asked: "Why did you not join the Methodist Church which you and your family attended while you were on the farm?" Nobody asked me," was my simple answer. Again he asked: "Do you believe in Christ? Are you a Christian?" I replied that I did believe and that I was a Christian. I had had no stirring emotional experience in a revival meeting. For me, to believe in Christ was the natural thing to do. This was the result of my mother's training.

Benthin urged me to make a public confession of my faith and join a church and this I decided to do. The question then arose, which church? Although I had come out of a Methodist home, I decided to become a Presbyterian. I had two good reasons for making this decision. To begin with, I wanted to have fellowship on Sundays with my schoolmates. We were then attending the Lakeside Presbyterian Church of Storm Lake at least four hours each Sunday. This program included Sunday School and worship service in the morning and then Christian Endeavor and another worship service in the evening. This was a perfectly valid reason for changing from being a Methodist to that of being a Presbyterian — I wanted to be with my friends.

I knew little of the doctrinal differences which separated these two denominations. I knew in a vague way that the Methodists followed the teachings of John Wesley while the Presbyterians preferred those of John Calvin. To me at the time, the important difference between the two churches lay in the field of polity or their respective forms of government. I remembered how the Methodist Bishop would change the pastors of my country church every year or so and I noted that the ministers of the Presbyterian churches could stay as long in one particular parish as the individual minister wished or as long as his congregation was satisfied.

One of my earliest memories was that of my mother tucking me in bed as a small boy and then kneeling by the bed to pray for me. She prayed aloud so I was able to hear her. There was one petition which must have been repeated many times for it left an indelible impression on my mind and that was that I, her son, might grow up to be a minister. I have never forgotten that prayer.

Thus when I was thinking about joining a church, I was attracted by the polity of the Presbyterian Church. Although I had not as yet decided to study for the ministry, I had accepted this as a possibility. I did not want to be in a denomination where the Bishop might tell me to come hither or go yonder. For these two reasons, I decided to join the Presbyterian church.

I met with the session of the Lakeside Presbyterian Church and when inquiry was made as to whether I had been baptized, I replied that I had. I remember my sister Blanche telling me that my mother arranged to have the Methodist minister then serving the Pleasant Hill Church, the Rev. George Wareham, come to our home and baptize all the children beginning with Blanche, the eldest at home, and going down the line chronologically to Sarah, the youngest. I made my public confession of faith on Sunday morning, February 28, 1915. This has proved to have been one of the cardinal decisions of my life. In later years, several members of my family followed my example and also became Presbyterians.

Several years later, after I had made known my intention of entering the Presbyterian ministry, my sister Clara, who is a loyal and devout member of the Methodist Church, asked me why I had deserted the Methodist to become a Presbyterian. After explaining to her that in the Presbyterian Church when a minister is called to a particular church, he is always referred to in official documents as the bishop of that church. So I told Clara: "You see, it was this way. The Methodists never promised to make me a bishop, while the Presbyterians do so as soon as I am called to a church."

My first months at Buena Vista were such happy ones that I began to be concerned about the possibility of remaining for the second semester. This, to my great joy, my father permitted me to do. I registered as a freshman at the beginning of the second semester, on January 20, 1915. My next concern was whether I could return in the fall of that year.

My father expected me to do odd jobs and earn such money as I could. And so I did. I shoveled snow, did typing, and beat rugs.

My diary for December 5, 1914, carries the information that on that day I worked 7½ hours beating rugs for 25¢ an hour. According to this notation, I beat "20 rugs, 2 hall carpets, and 5 large rugs." I earned $1.75 and my right arm was sore that evening.

College closed on Friday, December 19, for the Christmas vacation. Although Early was only fifteen miles south of Storm Lake, it often took me five hours to go there by train.

During my Christmas vacation, I helped harvest ice from the Boyer River. According to my diary, the weather was bitterly cold for several days, the thermometer dropping to fifteen and then twenty-two degrees below zero. On New Year's day, I went hunting with some neighbor friends and we bagged twenty-three small rabbits and one jack rabbit. I cleaned and dressed my share and took some back to Storm Lake when vacation was over and gave the frozen carcasses to Mrs. Foote where I boarded.

On Christmas eve, the family attended the Christmas program at the country church. Although I then did not realize it, this was to be the last time I would ever attend such a service in that church. I made no note of it in my diary, but my father was then thinking of leaving the farm and moving to Early. On Christmas day, I wrote: "We had lots of company today and a turkey dinner." My father was a gregarious and hospitable person. He loved to have company, especially for a Sunday dinner. He reveled in having his older married children return home with their spouses and children. Often we would have to have two sittings at our table which was large enough for twelve. On those occasions, we younger children would have to wait for the second servings. When surrounded by his guests, my father loved to discuss politics and to tell jokes.

I remember one such occasion when I took advantage of his high spirits. I was about to be taken back to Storm Lake in our auto to be driven by one of my brothers. I needed at least $15.00 to pay some board bills. I decided to write out a check payable to me for this amount and then wait until he had told a good story and was laughing, then I would lay the unsigned check with a pen before him and ask for his signature. Finally, the appropriate time came. I quickly laid the unsigned check on the table before him and asked him to sign it. He took one look at the amount and handed the check back to me with the remark, "Go, write another." I knew what he meant. He wanted me to write a check for a lesser amount but he had not been specific. I rewrote the check but raised the amount to $25.00 and laid it before him. He glanced again at the amount and gave a hearty laugh and signed the check.

When I became a full-fledged freshman at the beginning of the second semester, I was soon involved in a number of extra-curricular activities. Looking back now, I feel that this was a good thing. As a small college we carried on most of the student activities in larger institutions. This meant that peer pressure was brought to bear on all students to take part in several of these extra-curricular activities as drama, athletics, YMCA and YWCA, oratorical and debating contests, and in the so-called "literary societies" which met twice a month. Before my college experience was over, I was manager of the student paper, called the TACK, for two years and for one year was manager of the college annual. I was on the student council and one year was manager of the lecture course which we had contracted for with the Redpath Lecture Company, and during my senior year, I served as president of the student body. In reviewing my college years, I feel that I gained as much from participating in these activities as I did from my studies. I was not an "A" but rather a "B" student.

The social life of the students who were at Buena Vista during my years there was restricted by certain puritanical standards then commonly accepted by the Presbyterian, Methodist, and other Protestant denominations. Dancing, for instance, was considered sinful and was, therefore, forbidden on the campus or at off-campus college functions. A young couple in love, or who were even known to be engaged, dared not show any signs of their affection in a public way. It was unthinkable that they should put their arms around each other in a public place.

No one on the faculty was more vigilant in correcting the least infraction of proper conduct between boys and girls than Miss Alice Wilcox, then Dean of Women and Professor of English. Miss Wilcox was a superb teacher of English and I owe much to her. At the same time I remember some of the rebukes I received from her for being too familiar with the girls.

Once while coming down the main stairway, I saw a young lady sitting on the lower step. I put my hand on her head, as though it were a newell post, swung around to continue my descent down the side stairway, and then I ran into Miss Wilcox who happened to be coming up that stairway and had seen what I had done. I was immediately given a stern lecture on good manners and proper decorum. A young man was to keep his hands off of young women!

During my college years, there was a growing anti-liquor sentiment throughout the nation which resulted in the final approval of the 18th amendment on January 16, 1919. The attempt to regulate drinking by law was a failure and this amendment was repealed in 1933. As a part of the intense propaganda leading up to the adoption of the 18th amendment, oratorical contests were sponsored in colleges. Such a contest was held in Buena Vista College for several years. I entered the contest at Buena Vista held on April 7, 1915, and won first place, together with a $15.00 prize. A state contest was held on March 31, 1916, at Cornell College, Mt. Vernon, Iowa, which I entered. Although I was awarded third place on thought and composition of my essay, other contestants won the honors in public speaking.

Perhaps the discipline of reading extensively on the evils of excessive drinking while gathering material for my essay, confirmed in me my determination not to touch alcoholic beverages. The first time I tasted wine was at a communion service in a Presbyterian church in Edinburgh, Scotland. When I was a student in high school and not more than thirteen or fourteen years old, a visitor came one day to address the student body on the dangers of smoking cigarettes. After giving a very forceful presentation, he handed out pledge cards which bound the student on his or her honor not to smoke until he or she was twenty-one. I signed such a card and I kept the pledge faithfully. Then when I passed my twenty-first birthday, and when I was still in the army in World War I, I tried smoking. I didn't like it, so I have never thereafter smoked. I think my faithfulness in abstaining from alcoholic drinks and from smoking has been beneficial to my health. And incidentally it has saved me a lot of money.

I returned home for a visit on Saturday, May 15, anxious about the possibility of returning to college in the fall of 1915. During the next day I inquired of my father and to my joy, he consented and that gave me the assurance that I would be able to return to college that fall. Perhaps it was then that my father told me of his plan to retire from farming and move to Early. He had purchased a grain elevator in Early which he planned to operate. He had also purchased a lot in town on which he planned to build a house. Although he was then in his 53rd year, he was not in rugged health. This may have been the main reason why he wanted to leave the farm.

I returned home for the summer vacation on Wednesday, June 15. This was to be my last summer that I was to work on the home farm. An important era in my life was drawing to a close. In addition to the usual farm duties as plowing corn, harvesting crops, and caring for the animals, I spent several days hauling gravel for the county to spread on the dirt roads. Often after a heavy rain, the dirt roads became impassable. With an increasing number of farmers owning automobiles, there was likewise an increasing demand for graveled roads which would permit travel in rainy weather. Paved roads were still in the future.

There was a gravel pit about a mile from our home. I would drive my wagon into the pit and shovel the gravel onto it. The wagon had one foot planks for its sides, and 2 x 4" lumber for the bottom. When loaded, the wagon would hold about one and one-half tons of gravel. When driven to the site where the gravel was to be dumped, all that was needed to unload was to move some of the two-by-fours and the gravel would drop to the earth. The county paid 50¢ for every load delivered to the dirt road. I was often able to haul eight loads a day, four in the morning and four in the afternoon. It was very hard work, but the pay was good.

Our new house was being built in Early during the summer of 1915. It was to have five bedrooms, a full basement, central heating, and electric lights! As compared with the farm house where the Drury family had lived under crowded conditions, the new house promised luxurious living. A large screened porch was on the east and south sides of the house. This was necessary in the days before air conditioning. People would sit out in the evening to get cool.

Although I willingly accepted my assigned duties during those summer months, yet I was eagerly looking forward to my return to college. I began counting the days before I could return. On July 25, I noted in my diary: "43 more days," and on August 24: "Only 18 more days." Because of rainy weather, my departure for Storm Lake was delayed. Finally, I left on Monday, September 13, going by train from Early, first to Sac City, and then to Storm Lake. With the exception of three short visits to the farm in the fall of 1915, my life on the farm was over.

Although I felt great relief in knowing that I would not be called back to the farm to do manual labor, yet now I realize that the years I spent in my youth on the farm were of inestimable value to me. I appreciate my farm heritage. I learned the value of work. I learned self-reliance, and I developed a consuming desire to achieve. Looking back over the intervening seventy-five years, I feel a deep sense of gratitude that I was privileged to spend the early years of my youth on a farm.

CHAPTER FOUR

Buena Vista College, 1915-1916

The academic year, 1915-16, was for me a year of transition and also a time when vital decisions had to be made which would affect my whole life. My father died on February 9, 1916, when I was a few months beyond my 18th birthday. Since by law I was still a minor, D. D. Carlton, an Early merchant, was appointed my guardian but, so far as I can remember, he never once advised me as to what I should or should not do. Suddenly, I was very much on my own.

Midway through the academic year, I decided to enter the Presbyterian ministry. I made this decision a few weeks before my father passed away. Looking back on those days, I realize that I was strongly influenced by my college friends. The class of 1918, of which I was a member, had six men and two women. Five of the men became Presbyterian ministers. One of the two women, Florence Mitchall, married a seminary classmate, Harry Wylie, and the two went out to India as Presbyterian missionaries. Our class set a record at Buena Vista which has never been equaled.

I enrolled at the college on Tuesday, September 14. I wrote in my diary: "This is one of the happiest days of my life." Actually I was still a freshman as I did not have enough college credits to be classified as a sophomore. I took as many courses as the faculty would permit as I wanted to make up for what I had missed. In the background of my mind, I was debating whether I should study for the ministry or prepare myself to be a medical doctor. So I took beginner's Greek, along with several classmates, and at the same time several science courses.

Football practice began during the first week of college. We had no football field as such, nothing more than the grassy lawn in front of Old Main.

The spirit of the college was such that nearly all the able bodied men turned out for football practice. This included me even though I did not weigh much more than 140 pounds. Two teams were formed. The first team played other small colleges. The second team, nicknamed the "scrubs," played high schools. I played center on this second team.

I returned home on Friday, November 5, to spend my 18th birthday with my family. Saturday night was the last night I slept in the old farm house before the family moved to the new home in Early. This move was made on Wednesday, November 24, the day before

Thanksgiving. Fifty-three years later, or on November 25, 1968, drawn by nostalgic memories, I returned to the farm and spent the night as a guest of Reuben and Emma Hokkanson, who were then renting the former Drury farm. A flood of memories came rushing back as I walked about the farmyard and went from room to room in the old house, then about 100 years old. I slept that night in what we used to call the "spare room," off of the parlor. I had been born in that room seventy-one years before my return.

My diary shows that my studies and my extra-curricular activities, including being manager of the school paper, kept me very busy. I was involved in so many activities outside of my studies that I was unable to do my best in the classrooms, although my grades show that I maintained a "B" average. I did not go home for Thanksgiving. The weather turned cold so that by December 3rd, some of us were skating on the lake. On the 7th, when skating near the shore with Russell Ensign, we suddenly heard the frantic cries for help coming from a spot several hundred yards to the west of us. We started at once for the open hole in the ice which we could see but were careful to stay some twenty-five or more feet apart. I remember that the ice was so thin that it swayed under my feet. When we came to the spot, all we could see was the hat which belonged to our football coach, Edward Ball, and the muff which Miss Fern Benedict, his skating companion, had been carrying. We called for help and after some time the bodies were recovered. Had the rescuers then known what is available today to resuscitate a drowned person, perhaps both lives could have been saved.

When I returned to Early on December 23rd for my Christmas vacation, I discovered that I had a new baby brother — Dean Allison, born on December 16th. This was the first night that I spent in the new Drury home. Christmas day was a happy day for all.

During the previous school year, the college YMCA had sponsored a gospel team of five of its members which visited a nearby church and held revival meetings over the New Year's weekend. The venture proved so helpful, not only to the church itself but also to the five who participated in the services that the "Y" decided to sponsor a similar project for the New Year's weekend, 1916. A Methodist church in Lavinia, a small town near Rockwell City, Iowa, invited the "Y" to send a gospel team there. This time seven were selected, including me.

According to my diary, the members of the team began making preparations for their visit to Lavinia by holding meetings each Sunday afternoon beginning December 5th. We planned to arrive at Lavinia on Friday and give a program of music and readings that evening. Saturday would be spent in visiting homes in the community. Special religious services were held on Saturday evening, and twice on Sunday. We planned to return to Storm Lake on Monday.

In making plans, I was selected to give the main talk on Sunday evening, January 2, 1916. I chose for my subject and text the words from Joshua 28:15: "Choose you this day whom you will serve." In preparing for my talk, I began a practice which I followed for over twenty years or throughout my preaching ministry. I would write out my sermons and then make an outline which I would take with me into the pulpit. I never read my sermons. I had my sermons bound in volumes, and these volumes are now deposited in the Presbyterian Historical Society in Philadelphia.

The first manuscript in the first volume of the series of my manuscript sermons is a revised copy of my Lavinia talk. As I re-read those words spoken on the theme, "Choose you this day," I realize that I was preaching to myself that evening. How could I ask others to surrender themselves completely to Christ and follow Him when I was not willing to do so? I felt somewhat hypocritical. I was troubled. Why was I holding back from making a decision to enter the ministry when I felt in my heart that this was what God wanted me to do?

It so happened in the providence of God that a letter from Walter Benthin came a few days after we had returned to the college. Benthin was then studying for the minitsry in the Presbyterian seminary at Auburn, New York. He put the challenge directly to me: "What are you going to do with your life?" In my diary entry for January 8, I referred to Benthin's letter and then wrote: "I am troubled. What am I going to be?" I wrote to my father and told him that I was seriously thinking of going into the ministry. In one of his last letters to me, he commented: "Your gospel team experience may have appealed to you but the life of a poor paid preacher is not very enticing."

Even though my father did not give me direct encouragement to become a minister, still I have evidence that he was proud of my decision. My brother Billy told me that one Sunday in January, my father said to him: "Come, let us go to the Presbyterian Church this morning. We should stand behind Cliff." And my sister Sarah remembers how shortly before he died, he told her that he was thinking of joining the church because I was planning to be a minister. After he had died, I found a small folder in his coat pocket which had been sent to him by the Presbyterian Board of Christian Education which dealt with the training required to be a Presbyterian minister. Evidently he had written to the Board for that information.

On February 2, I wrote in my diary: "Today had a long talk with Miss Conquist in regard to the ministry. She is undoubtedly one of the best friends that I have."

On Wednesday, February 9, I received an early morning telephone
call which gave me the news that my father was very sick and for
me to return home at once. I got back to Early about noon. My father
was then in a coma and passed away about 2:00 p.m. He was then
in his 54th year. An autopsy showed that he had a cancerous pan-
creas. The funeral was held in the Methodist church of Early on
Saturday morning, February 12, with the Rev. George Wareham, who
had conducted my mother's funeral, officiating. Although it was a
severely cold day, yet mourners from all over the country came to
pay their last respects.

The Chicago and Northwestern railroad provided a special train
to Odebolt and return for the many relatives and friends who wished
to be present for the burial which took place in the Drury plot in
the Odebolt cemetery.

A great feeling of loneliness swept over me when I realized that
my father was gone. With both parents deceased, I, then at the age
of eighteen, was entirely on my own. Following the funeral, I wrote
in my diary: "I am glad that I had decided to enter the ministry and,
although I did not have a chance to speak to my father about it, he
knew what I was planning to do."

I returned to the college on Monday, February 14, and threw myself
into making up the work I had missed. My major emphasis had to be
put on getting ready for my first inter-collegiate debate which was
scheduled for the following Friday evening, the 18th. We were debating the question as to whether or not the United States should
build and man a merchant marine. Our three-man team went to
Central College at Pella, Iowa, to meet their negative side, while
our affirmative team, of which I was a member, met their team from
Pella at Buena Vista. We won by an unanimous decision of the three
judges, as did the team that went to Pella.

At this time, several of the YMCA men were taking turns conducting Sunday morning services in a Presbyterian church at Eldora,
Iowa. At one time there was a flourishing Presbyterian congregation
there, but the church fell on hard times. It should have been dissolved
but a devout old Scottish lady, a Mrs. Boyd, insisted on keeping a
semblance of life alive by paying a modest honorarium to some minister to hold a Sunday afternoon service.

Evidently running out of supply ministers in Eldora and vicinity,
Mrs. Boyd appealed to the president of Buena Vista College who
turned the request over to the YMCA. Several of the members, who
were candidates for the ministry, responded and took turns going to
Eldora. Since I had been on the gospel team with them and had
declared my intention to become a minister, I was persuaded to take
the services in the Eldora church on Sunday, March 19. I knew that

this would be the first time I would ever conduct a church service all by myself.

I worked hard on my sermon. I took for my text I Cor. 3:23: "And ye are Christ's and Christ is God's." It is sermon No. 2 in the first volume of my series of sermon manuscripts. As I read it now, I realize that I had much to learn about how to marshal thoughts and illustrations for a good sermon. It was more of my personal witness as a Christian, than a theological discourse.

There were no good rail connections between Storm Lake and Eldora and still worse for the return trip. I left Storm Lake on Saturday morning at 9:00 a.m. for Iowa Falls where I had to change cars. I had to wait 2½ hours for the train to Eldora. I was met at the station by the son of my hostess, Howell Boyd, who was a bachelor and about thirty-five years old. Mrs. Boyd was a dear little old lady, a staunch Presbyterian. Her home was furnished with antique furniture which deserved to be in a museum. I slept that night on a featherbed so large that it almost enveloped me.

I attended a Baptist church that Sunday morning and then after a Sunday dinner, Howell took me to the Presbyterian church. His mother was too infirm to attend. The Presbyterian church was an old brick building large enough, if I recall correctly, to seat about 300 people. Howell warned me that the congregation would be small, and it was. I wrote in my diary that night: "There were eight people present, 6 men and 2 women." An elderly man who was once a professor of music played the reed organ. I noted in my diary: "The singing was awful," and added: "This is a day which I shall never forget."

Having decided to study for the Presbyterian ministry, I had to follow the procedure outlined in the church's government. I appeared before the session of the Lakeside Presbyterian Church in Storm Lake on April 16, 1916, and was taken under its care as a candidate for the ministry. The Presbytery of Sioux City met in Storm Lake on April 18 and I was then taken under its care. Elleroy Smith, who was soon to be married to Mabelle Conquist was ordained into the ministry that same evening. They were under appointment by the Presbyterian Board of Foreign Missions to go out to China during the coming August.

One of the songs that we frequently sang during the college chapel period had the chorus:

> I'll go where you want me to go, dear Lord,
> Over mountain, or plain, or sea;
> I'll say what you want me to say, dear Lord,
> I'll be what you want me to be.

After being taken under care of the Presbytery as a candidate for the ministry, I felt that I could not sing those words unless I meant them. We had in Buena Vista College then a small group of Student Volunteers who were planning to go out as foreign missionaries should the way open. On April 20, two days after the Presbytery had taken me under its care, I joined this little band of Student Volunteers.

Having once served as a pulpit supply, other calls came before the school year closed. I was called back to Eldora on April 2 and on June 11. Each time only a few were in my audience. On the latter date, I noted that six were present. On May 7, I was called to Meriden for both services. This time I cleared $9.00 over expenses.

On Saturday, April 24, while on a weekend visit to Early, I signed up for a $2,000.00 20-year pay life insurance policy with Bankers Life Insurance Company of Des Moines. During World War I, I took out another 20-year life insurance policy, this time for $10,000.00. The cash reserves on these two policies bailed me out of my financial difficulties when I was a graduate student at the University of Edinburgh, 1927-28.

My financial records show that my father gave me $165.00 from September 13, 1915, to January 24, 1916. After his death, I was able to draw upon my share of the estate.

Since I had missed the first semester of my freshman year at Buena Vista, and since I wanted to be graduated with the class of 1918, I felt it necessary to go to a summer school to gain some of the needed credits. Upon the recommendation of my Professor of Biology at Buena Vista, I made application to attend the six-week summer school of the University of Iowa at its biological camp on Lake Okoboji. I registered at the school on Monday, June 19, for three courses which would give me five college credits.

We lived in tents and most of the class work was out-of-doors. If I remember aright, about forty students were in attendance. Our professors came from several institutions in Iowa. The dean was Dr. Bohumil Shimek of Bohemian ancestry and who was on the faculty of the University of Iowa. He was a devout Christian and conducted services for the camp each Sunday.

The summer school closed on Friday, July 28, and I left for Early the next day. My brother Millard was then renting a farm about four miles to the northeast of Early. The harvest season for small grain was at hand and he needed help. I accpted his offer of working for him for a month for $35.00. Thrashing oats began the following Tuesday, August 1st. One of the highlights of the summer was seeing the silent movie, "The Birth of a Nation," on Monday evening, August 14, at Chautauqua Park in Storm Lake. The admission charge was

$1.00, a sum that was about equivalent to what I was earning in a full day's work on my brother's farm.

Another unforgetable event of the summer was the wedding of Mabelle Conquist and Elleroy Smith at her home near Kiron, a few miles to the southwest of Odebolt on August 30. Mabelle asked me if I could get the use of my father's touring car, an Overland, and then drive to Storm Lake and pick up four of her favorite women students and then drive to Kiron. My brother gave me permission to use the car.

The wedding was held about 3:00 o'clock in the afternoon on the lawn in front of the farm house. The event was filled with mixed emotions. There was the joy of the wedding and then the sadness which came with the realization that the young couple was to leave within a few days for their mission field in China.

BUENA VISTA COLLEGE
As it appeared in July, 1957

CHAPTER FIVE

My Junior Year at Buena Vista, 1916-1917

My month's engagement working on my brother Millard's farm came to an end on Wednesday, September 6. This ended my career as a farmer. My brother Billy drove me to Storm Lake on the following Sunday. Three of my closest friends — Harvey Hood, Stewart Brown, and Arthur Riedesel — and I had made arrangements to room together in the residence of the Rev. T. A. Ambler, pastor of Lakeside Presbyterian Church. We rented two rooms, one of which contained two double beds and the other four small desks. There we stayed until the end of the semester when we moved to another corner of the campus, where we got similar accommodations.

On September 12, I enrolled as a junior in the college, though I still lacked five or six credits for full junior standing. My classes included Greek, chemistry, biology, English, and physiology. Since Buena Vista was a church sponsored college, all students in the college department were required to take a one-hour-a-week Bible course which was continued through all four years. I noted in my diary that my schedule called for twenty-four hours of class and laboratory attendance each week. This was a heavy schedule. I was still considering the possibility of studying medicine and going out to a foreign field as a medical missionary, instead of studying for the ministry.

According to my diary, my involvement in extra-curricular activities was heavy. During this school year, I served as manager of the college paper and also of its annual. For my work on the college paper, I received a credit of $27.00 on my tuition, which was one-half of the total for the year. I was secretary of the YMCA and a member of the gospel team which, that year-end, held services in the Presbyterian Church of Alta. Although I did not like the roughness involved in football, yet out of a sense of loyalty to the college, I went out for practice and played center on the "scrub" team. I was an active member of the Franklin Literary Society which met on Friday evenings twice a month, and also was a member of the Student Volunteer band. This was a small group of both men and women who had declared their intention, God willing, to go out to some foreign field as missionaries. On Wednesday, September 20, I wrote in my diary: "I am so busy that I can barely find time to wind my watch."

Two other important activities demanded time and attention. One was conducting Sunday services in nearby churches and the second was participation in both inter-society and inter-collegiate debates. I was invited to take the Sunday services at five churches during the fall of 1916. Three times I went to Eldora, once to Auburn, and once to Cleghorn. A new development arose at Eldora when those from the college who went there were invited to take a morning service in a country church called Mount Pleasant about eight miles distant from Eldora. The attendance at the services I conducted there ranged from 75 to 100, but the honorarium was very low — usually less than $5.00. My audience in Eldora rose to fifteen one Sunday afternoon.

During the first years after I started preaching, I found it difficult to face an audience when members of my family were present. I became self-conscious. The first time that this happened was on Sunday, October 22, 1916, when I was conducting the morning service in the Presbyterian Church of Cleghorn, Iowa. My sister, Blanche, and her husband Fred Hobbs were living on a farm a few miles to the west of Cleghorn and near the town of Marcus. The service had started that morning before my sister entered. Seeing me in the pulpit brought tears to her eyes. It was also an emotional experience for me for I, like her, began thinking of my mother. Blanche took me to her home after the service and that evening both she and Fred attended. I spent the night with them before returning to Storm Lake.

A more trying and more emotional experience for me came in the following April when I occupied the pulpit of the Presbyterian Church in Early at which time members of my family and relatives filled two pews in the front part of the church. Then I was really self-conscious.

How did this happen to come to pass? Why did I volunteer to preach in my home community knowing that members of my family, some of my former schoolmates, and my neighbors, who knew me from earliest infancy, would be present? The answer is that circumstances forced me to do it.

During the winter of 1916-17, I was looking forward to the summer of 1917. I still needed five or six credits beyond what I could earn at Buena Vista to qualify me for graduation with the class of 1918. I, therefore, felt the necessity of going to a summer school in the summer of 1917. When my older brother, Millard, heard of my plans, he sought to dissuade me. He wanted me to work for him on his farm. He felt that I had gone to college long enough. He needed me. He offered to give the standard wage for a farm hand — $35.00 a month and keep. Even though my father's estate had not yet been settled, I knew that I could draw upon that share which some day would be mine for my continued school expense. I did not have to work on the farm for money with which to continue going to college. Moreover, I felt the need of completing my college course and then go on either to a medical school or a theological seminary. I felt that I must go to a summer school in the summer of 1917.

I felt that the only way by which I could convince Millard that I was in earnest about qualifying for my B.A. degree would be to ask the pastor of the Presbyterian Church in Early for the privilege of speaking from his pulpit some time in April. I knew that if such an arrangement could be made, all of the members of my family and all of the collateral branch would be there if physically able. I was asking for something which I dreaded doing. If the presence of my sister Blanche at the Cleghorn church made me self-conscious, how would I feel with several pews filled with relatives sitting in front of me? Who was I, at the age of nineteen, to be preaching to them?

I wrote to the Rev. Thomas Hughes, then pastor of the Early church, and asked for the opportunity to speak from his pulpit some Sunday in April. Arrangements were made for me to speak on Sunday morning, April 29, 1917. I returned home from college on the preceding Saturday. Before church the next morning, I wrote in my diary: "The fatal day has come. I would rather talk before a thousand people than the congregation in the Early Presbyterian Church today. May God help me."

The sanctuary of the church was packed that day and there, seated on front pews, was the Drury family and my guardian, D. D. Carlton, and his wife. By this date, I had written several sermons which I had delivered in various churches. These are now bound in volume one of my sermon manuscripts, but I failed to indicate which one of these I used that day. I believe it was the one which developed the text: "Follow me and I will make you fishers of men." In the closing paragraph of this sermon is the statement: "Follow me is a command I cannot escape. I shall try to follow Him regardless of where he leads me." Thus I gave my witness and stated my commitment.

At the close of the service, Mr. Hughes ushered me to the main entrance where I had a chance to greet those who were present. I wrote that evening in my diary: "More than one woman had tears in their eyes when they shook hands with me. Some said they wished my father and mother could have been there. I think I accomplished all that I came for. Millard can see my viewpoint and now I can go to summer school." As will be stated later, I selected the biological camp of the University of Michigan at Lake Douglas at the northern end of the southern peninsula for my summer's study.

Even though I followed a busy schedule in both the classrooms and in extra-curricular activities, I still had time for social events. Out-of-town students were often invited to the homes of local students and often there would be taffy pulls, or oyster stews, or boat rides on the lake. During the spring of 1917 I bought a canoe for $10.00 which I kept for a year.

I suffered through a painful experience in late November 1916 when my middle right ear became infected. My diary entry for November 13 carries this notation: "Today I didn't feel well and then after an explosion of bromine in the lab, I breathed too much bromine. Staggered around all day. Went to bed for a couple of hours this afternoon." Even though I felt miserable, I worked that evening with my Franklin colleagues getting ready for the inter-society debate. On Wednesday, the 15th, my ear pained me so much that I went to a doctor that afternoon who, after examining the ear, told me that the inner ear was infected.

On Thursday, the 16th, I wrote in my diary: "Slept only one hour last night because my ear hurt so badly. Went to the doctor twice today. Can't sleep, can't study, can't do anything except just bear the pain." The doctor gave me morphine to ease the pain, but even so I spent two more restless nights with but little sleep. Then during Saturday night, the 18th, the infection broke through the ear drum and drained onto my pillow. I slept the sleep of the exhausted. I felt much better when the inner pressure was released. For several weeks, I had to pay frequent visits to my ear doctor to have the ear channel washed out — always a painful experience, but my hearing was saved.

My total expenses for the academic year 1916-1917 came to $615.00. Of this amount $525.00 came from the Drury estate through Millard, who was the executor, and $90.00 were earned. Board and room for nine months amounted to $189.00, or a little more than $20.00 a month. I did not itemize my doctor's bills, except to make note of one payment of $65.00. There may have been others.

The Darkening Clouds of War

When war broke out in Europe it made but little impression on me. The battlefields of Europe were far, far away. But the world was shrinking. Even the sinking of the *Lusitania* on May 7, 1915, seemed to be such an isolated event that it would never affect me. Through the following month, a series of events took place which steadily pushed the United States closer to war. On April 6, 1917, a joint resolution of Congress declaring that the state of war with the Central powers of Europe existed was signed by President Woodrow Wilson.

The first entry in my diary which indicates that I was aware of the threatening situation was on March 30, 1917. I then wrote: "Dean Parkhill gave a very stirring talk today in chapel in regard to the threatening war between the United States and Germany. I might have to go."

I recall how my roommates and I had long talks about the threatening future. How would the European war affect us? The newspapers reported that the Government would soon require all young men twenty-one years old and older to register for the draft. I recall how, in one of our discussions, I asked the question: "Would the Government draft college students?" Hood replied immediately: "Most certainly. We would be among the first to go." And so it was. Although a number of the college men volunteered before being drafted, Hood was the first to be drafted. He left on September 5th for duty in the army and saw service in France. Since I was only nineteen then, I was not required to register.

A strong patriotic fervor swept the country. We male students at the college took the situation seriously. We began drilling on the lawn in front of Old Main, using broomsticks for rifles, for some forty-five minutes before breakfast. One of our number had attended a military academy and knew the drill manual. According to a notation in my diary, twelve men turned out for drill on April 14. This number grew to twenty-six by May 15.

Among the closing events of the academic year was the presentation of debate medals to some who had taken part in several inter-collegiate debates. I was one thus honored. This was the first college letter I ever received and I was proud of it. I had the medal fastened to my watch fob for my gold watch which I carried in the small pocket in the waistband of my trousers.

Commencement exercises were held on Thursday, June 14, and that evening six of the YMCA men, including myself, took the night train for Geneva, Wisconsin, where we were to attend the large midwest conference sponsored by the national Y for college men. This conference began its ten-day session on Friday, the 15th. About 500 from colleges and universities scattered through the midwest were in attendance. Here for the first time I met some foreign students, including several Chinese. The speakers at this conference were nationally known and their messages were most inspiring. Each of the ten days I spent there was a thrilling experience for me.

Several of my schoolmates and I left for Chicago on Monday morning. Since I was planning to leave on a lake steamer for Mackinac Island, at the northern end of Lake Michigan, on the following Friday evening, I had four days to see the sights of the city. My diary shows that my college friends and I got rooms at the YMCA hotel. We visited the Art Institute and the Field Museum. We went to a movie and to an amusement park. This was the first real extended vacation that I ever enjoyed.

I boarded the lake steamer, the *Manitou*, at 6:30 Friday afternoon for my twenty-four hour voyage up the lake. Since there were times we were out of sight of land, this was like an ocean voyage. This was a new experience for me and I reveled in it. The ship arrived at Mackinac Island about 6:30 on Saturday afternoon, June 30. I registered at one of the tourist hotels. On Sunday morning, after attending a church service, I hired a driver who had a horse and buggy for a tour of the island. No automobiles were allowed on the island. That afternoon I took a ferry for Mackinaw City, which is located on the tip of the northern peninsula. From there, by various stages by train, bus, and boat, I finally arrived at the biological camp on Lake Douglas.

This camp, sponsored by the University of Michigan, was located in an abandoned lumber camp. Two good sized log cabins, evidently once used as a bunk house and as a mess hall, had been converted into laboratories. Our dining facilities were all under canvas and all of the students, who numbered at least forty, slept in tents under mosquito nets. The country had been logged over and then burnt over. I heard my first whip-poor-will that night and soon discovered gorgeous orchids growing in the swampy marshlands near us.

I enrolled for three classes in zoology for a total of eight credits, which were more than enough to make up what I still lacked to give me full senior standing at Buena Vista. Most of the class work at the camp took place out-of-doors. We were often required to walk ten miles to and from some particular site under study. The weather was often extremely hot with the thermometer going above 100° F. My diary records the fact that one day we were working in a sandy pit where the sand registered 140°. We were looking for insects which could live in such an inhospitable environment.

We sometimes saw marvelous displays of northern lights. On the 15th of August I noted in my diary: "Last night I saw a most wonderful display of northern lights. They shot up from all parts of the horizon, meeting in a big corona directly overhead. Some were colored. Some streaks seem to hang overhead, out over the lake and these seemed to dance in half circles. This was a night to remember."

I continued my side interest in collecting land snails which I had started the year before at Lake Okaboji. Each specimen was classified and placed in a small box. My collection grew to more than forty different specimens. Several years later, I presented this snail collection to the zoological department of the University of California at Berkeley.

Having just come from the exhilerating spiritual experiences I had had at the YMCA camp, I missed Sunday services. Most of the students worked in the laboratories on Sundays, as I, too, did sometimes.

But, in addition, I would seek some secluded spot in the surrounding brush where I would hold my individual worship service.

I learned one important lesson at this camp from which I profited throughout my literary career. In describing a certain stream which we were studying, I wrote in my report in general terms that the water was clear and flowed swiftly. I had for my professor a man of German parentage who laid great emphasis on accuracy in descriptive writing. He wrote "Bosh" on my report.

I went to him and asked how I had failed. I insisted that the stream was clear. "How clear?" he asked. And he told me how to indicate the clarity of the water. "Take a silver dollar and drop it into the stream. Measure the depth of the water at that point and then tell me if you can read the date on the dollar." We then were still using silver dollars. I conducted this test and found that I could read the date through ten inches of water. That proved that the stream was clear.

Regarding the speed of the flow, my professor told me to put a stick in the water and then note how many seconds it took to move fifty yards. I rewrote my report and was careful to be accurate and precise. I learned that day an important lesson which was remembered when I began writing my history books. I was to be exact in my descriptions and not mix imagination with facts.

The summer school closed on August 22nd and I left the next day for Chicago and Storm Lake. On Saturday, the 25th, I wrote in my diary: "Never did Storm Lake look so beautiful or more attractive than it did when I arrived this morning." I spent the intervening two weeks before college opened visiting relatives and friends and doing odd jobs. Now that I had fully made up all of the work I had missed in the fall of 1914, I knew that I could be enrolled that fall as a senior and thus could qualify for graduation the next spring.

CHAPTER SIX

My Senior Year at Buena Vista, 1917-1918

The effects of our nation's involvement in World War I were felt at Buena Vista College in the fall of 1917. The student enrollment took a 30% drop over what it had been the previous year. Whereas there were eighteen freshmen in the fall of 1916, only ten were thus enrolled in 1917. The total enrollment in all departments in 1917 was only seventy-five, of which number only forty-one were in the college classes. There was a noticeable decline in the number of men students.

Buena Vista College has often faced financial crises. The tuition charged paid only a small fraction of the current expenses. During my years in college, the income from the endowment was pitifully small. The president and others in the administration had to be constantly on the alert seeking gifts from churches and individuals in order to keep the institution going. One of the most faithful of the trustees was W. C. Edson, who will enter again into my story.

Great credit is due to some of the older members of the faculty who remained in spite of the fact that they were given low salaries which were not always paid on time. These included Dean J. W. Parkhill, Dr. George Fracker, and Miss Alice Wilcox. Each excelled as a teacher. One advantage which came to us students who were there when the enrollment was small was that we received individual attention.

When I registered for classes in the fall of 1917, I signed up for first year German and first year French, second year chemistry, physics, and Bible. This gave me fifteen units of credit. In addition I expected to earn another two units in inter-collegiate debate.

When the school year opened, we had no professor of chemistry. For some reason, the one selected did not come. After consulting with the dean, I volunteered to teach the freshman class in chemistry until someone was found. I taught this class for two weeks which was then taken over by Dr. Fracker. I was asked to take charge of all laboratory work for the freshmen for which I received a stipend of $4.00 a week. This experience proved to be of prime importance to me a few months later when I applied to be enrolled in the Chemical Warfare Service of the U.S. Army as a chemist. By the beginning of the second semester, the administration was able to secure the services of Professor E. H. Cummins to teach chemistry. I continued as his assistant in the laboratory.

We had a change in the presidency of the college during the sum-

mer of 1917. Dr. R. D. Echlin, who served as president for about
five years, resigned in the spring of 1917 in order to accept a call to
a church at Rolfe, Iowa. The trustees then selected Dr. Stanton
Olinger, also a Presbyterian minister, to be his successor.

Because of the smaller student body in the fall of 1917, some of
the former activities had to be discontinued as the inter-society
debate, the gospel team, and drama. The major activities, however,
continued. I was no longer responsible for the management of the
college paper or annual, but was made president of the student
council. This entailed managing the annual lecture course which had
been contracted through the Redpath Company by the previous
student council. Thus, I inherited the responsibility of promoting
the sale of tickets, meeting the incoming talent at the train and es-
corting them to the hotel, and then introducing them to their evening
audiences.

It so happened that one of the lectures scheduled for the 1917-18
season was to be given by a German woman, Miss Marie Mayer, who
had played the part of Mary Magdalene in the 1910 Oberammergau
Passion Play. The contract for her coming was signed before the
United States had declared war on Germany. When the announcement was made in Storm Lake that a German woman was to speak,
I found an amazing amount of opposition. Some advocated boycot-
ting the program, claiming that she would be sending money she
would earn back to Germany. All of this gave me great concern as
the student body was responsible for the payment of the contractual
honorarium.

Miss Mayer arrived in Storm Lake on Thursday, December 6. I
met her at the train depot and was able to visit with her in the hotel
for about an hour. I found her to be a charming person. She spoke
excellent English. The program that evening was held in the Lakeside
Presbyterian Church. The audience was small, not large enough to
cover expenses. The Redpath Company tried to make up the loss
by sending another speaker at a later date at no charge to us. If
I remember aright, the proceeds of that program enabled us to balance our budget.

I passed my 20th birthday on November 7th, and, according to my
diary, a few days later wrote to the War Department offering my
services to the army's chemical warfare branch as a chemist. This led
to my call to active duty during the following April.

Another matter which gave me concern during my senior year was
our football schedule. According to the college annual of that year,
there were only fifteen men who turned out for football. I was one
and I played center. Practically all of our first team players, includ-

ing our star, big John Fulton, had left for military service. We who used to play on the second, or "scrub," team were now on the varsity team. Our football record for the previous year had been excellent. We had won five games out of nine. Among the teams which beat us was the University of Dubuque, then known as Dubuque German as it was sponsored by the people of German descent who lived in central and eastern Iowa. Dubuque beat us in the fall of 1916 by a score of 39-0, yet Dubuque wanted a return engagement in 1917 at Dubuque. They promised to pay all travel costs and to provide hotel and meal expenses. Buena Vista, on the other hand, agreed to pay a $50.00 forfeit if we did not go.

Our football season opened rather auspiciously. We beat the team from Ellsworth on October 11 by a score of 14-6. We lost to Yankton College on October 20 by 41 to 15. Then came the big game with Dubuque scheduled for November 16th. Disturbing news from Dubuque reached our ears. Practically all of their last year's team were back in school. It is possible that the men in Buena Vista were more patriotic than were those of German descent at Dubuque. Among those still in college at Dubuque was their star player, a negro, Sol Butler, who was very fast on his feet. Moreover, we heard that the Dubuque team outweighed our team by twenty pounds per man. All of this was most discouraging news but there was nothing for us to do but to go. For one thing, we did not have the $50.00 to pay the forfeit if we did not go.

We travelled by train to Dubuque on Thursday. Early the next morning we inspected the football field which was located on the bank of the Mississippi River. It had rained the day before and the field was littered with frozen clods of mud. There was no grass turf. The game started at 2:30 p.m. and we got the ball by the flip of a coin. I was at center and Stewie Brown was quarterback.

We started the game by using some silent signals, which may not be legal today, by which I flipped the ball to Stewie who carried it through their line for several yards gain before they knew that we were playing. We tried this trick a second time and they got the ball and we never had it thereafter through the entire game. Sol Butler would get the ball and race for a touchdown and none of us could catch him. The ball would then be taken to the center of the field and often Butler would kick it over our goal post. It would be then brought out to the twenty-yard line and in four minutes Dubuque would get another touchdown. There was nothing we could do to stop him.

I remember the crowd, numbering about 200, shouting, "We want a hundred." They got their hundred and an additional twenty-five.

The final score was 125 to 0 in their favor! In the last five minutes of the game, I tackled Butler and he fell on top of me knocking me unconscious. I came to about forty-five minutes later when a doctor was examining me for fracture of the skull. My chief regret then was — why was I not knocked out in the first five minutes rather than the last five minutes of the game. The only kind words the Dubuque newspaper said of us was that we had the fortitude to stick it out through all four fifteen minute quarters. Even though we were beaten and battered, we did not give up. I played in one other game at Buena Vista against Trinity College. We were beaten 27 to 0. That ended my football career and I was glad that it was over.

During the Christmas vacation, I returned to my home in Early. Word then came that Homer, one of the twins who was afflicted with epilepsy and who had been placed in a state institution at Woodward, Iowa, near Des Moines, was very ill. Consequently, Laura, my step-mother, Howard, and I took the train for Des Moines on Saturday, December 22nd. We spent the night at a hotel in Des Moines and left the next morning on the interurban for Woodward. We found Homer sick in bed. The twins were then about 9½ years old. Homer's condition was always a burden on the whole family and putting him in a state hospital was the best possible solution. On Monday, Mother and Howard returned to Early while I remained for another day. Finally, the doctor said that I ought to return home for there was nothing I could do. Always in the background of our thinking was the age-old question, why do the innocent suffer? I rejoined the family in Early for our Christmas festivities.

Sometime following the 1917 football season, the Army Air Force sent out application blanks to all who had taken part in college athletics inviting them to join the Air Force. This was before there was a separate air command. We who had played football at Buena Vista received such applications and two of our number responded — Stewart Brown and John Parkhill. They received notice of their acceptance on January 11, 1918, but actually were not called to duty until several months later. They were then sent to Kelly Field in Texas where they took their flight training using the old Jenny planes and without parachutes. The war ended before they were sent overseas.

Before the Christmas vacation, our negative and affirmative debating teams were selected to meet with the teams from Ellsworth College on February 15. I was captain of the team which took the negative position on the question — "Resolved that the United States should adopt a system of compulsory military training as a government policy." Seemingly, I and my colleagues were on the unpopular side for that day, but we argued that what the nation needed was a strong navy instead of a standing army.

On February 7th, just eight days before he was to take part in the debate with Ellsworth, Art Riedesel, my best qualified colleague, received his call to report for military duty. He and I were very close friends and I was strongly tempted to go with him to Vancouver Barracks, Washington. In desperation, as captain of the negative debating team, I had to draft John Parkhill to take Art's place, even though John had not been working with us in preparation for the debate. He was given Art's speech and told to memorize it. Also, I wrote out on 4 x 5 cards, answers to every possible point that the other team could advance. These were carefully indexed. During the debate, I selected cards for John to read in rebuttal for I did not trust him to speak extemporaneously on any aspect of the subject. Thus we managed to win, as did the affirmative team at Buena Vista. This ended my debating career at Buena Vista. Looking back, I realize that I gained much from these debates and it was satisfying to realize that I was always on the winning team.

An interesting entry appears in my diary for February 6th. It states: "The nation is now on rations. Pure wheat bread is now unknown, only rye and corn meal. Prices of food now at unheard of prices." My board bill went up from $4.00 a week to $4.75.

Our new professor of chemistry, E. H. Cummins, had some wild ideas which he thought might help some of his men students who were facing military service. One such idea was to teach them how to make explosives. On March 8, I wrote in my diary: "Helped John Parkhill set off a little nitro glycerin bomb." John put the bomb in the ash pile back of the building. The explosion scattered ashes all over that part of the campus. That one experience was enough for me. I dropped out of this project.

A few days later, on March 11th, I entered the chemical lab just as John was mixing up another big nitro glycerin compound. When I saw smoke coming from the beaker, I started for the stairway for I remembered the warning — if the mixture starts to smoke, put the beaker under cold water. I saw John carry the beaker to the sink, turn on the cold water but there was no water. Someone in the basement had turned it off. It was then that I began to run. John hurried into the adjoining room where luckily he found a five gallon stone jar filled with water. He plunged the beaker with its plume of smoke into the water and cooled it down. I am sure that the trustees never knew what their professor of chemistry was encouraging some of his students to do.

On March 18, I learned that my application for the Chemical

Warfare Service had been approved by some Iowa authorities and had been forwarded to Washington. "I am glad," I wrote that day in my diary, "and yet what a mixture of emotions. Joy, anticipation, hating to leave college, home and friends. I have been beside myself all day."

Because of a continued delay in getting final word, I went to Des Moines on April 1 and called on a Lieutenant McFaul at Drake University. The lieutenant advised me to write to one of our state senators, A. B. Cummings, who was a friend of my father's, and ask for his intercession. Lieutenant McFaul assured me that I would receive my call within three weeks.

Marousek, my classmate, received his notice to report for duty in the army on April 9th and my notification came a few days later on the 15th. To make sure that I could pass the physical, I was requested to go to a recruiting officer in Fort Dodge on the 16th and take the examination. I made the trip and easily passed. Then I returned to Storm Lake to clear out my room. My brother Billy drove up from Early on Wednesday morning, the 17th, to take me home to say my goodbys to the family. My departure from the Olson home left only Stewie of the original four still there, and his orders were soon to come. One by one the men were leaving and Buena Vista was becoming a girls college.

My last day at home was filled with emotion. Blanche came down from Marcus to say goodby. I packed a suitcase to take with me and members of the family and some of the neighbors gave gifts. I remember getting a bag for my toilet articles with my initials embroidered on one side. Blanche gave me a five-pound box of chocolates. Someone gave me a wrist watch so that I could leave my good gold watch at home. Finally the hour came when I had to leave. Billy and Sarah were to take me to Storm Lake to catch the 7:30 evening train for Fort Dodge. I wrote in my diary: "The parting was rather sad. The women were brave and did their best not to break down." The women included Laura, my stepmother, and my three older sisters, Maud, Blanche and Clara.

I remember that there were no tears, only brave smiles, until after I got back into the car and we had started. I then looked back and saw all four using their aprons to catch their tears. Billy drove me back to the college to get a few things and then to the depot where a small crowd of students had gathered to say goodby.

My college days at Buena Vista were over. Even though I had left nearly two months before commencement, the college followed the common practice for men leaving for military service of granting me my B.A. degree in absentia.

CHAPTER SEVEN

Eight Months in the U.S. Army, 1918

Knowing that I would not have to report to the army recruiting office in Fort Dodge until late the next morning, I got a room in a hotel and slept the sleep of the exhausted. The strain of saying goodby to my family and my college friends for an unknown future had taken its toll. I slept late the next morning, April 18, 1918, and then reported to the recruiting officer.

From Fort Dodge, I was sent to Omaha where I arrived in the afternoon of the 18th. There I was given another physical examination. I left that evening by train for St. Louis from whence I would go to Jefferson Barracks. My diary shows that I had mixed emotions. I wanted to go and yet I hated to go. I wrote in my diary: "I know I won't get back until the war ends. This is my duty and with God helping me, I'll do my duty as long as I see it."

I arrived at Jefferson Barracks in company with fifty other recruits, or "rookies" as we were called, in mid-morning of Friday, April 19. It was raining, cold, and miserable. Since I had been informed that I was to be sent to Yale University in New Haven, Connecticut, where I was to work with others on some chemical project, I had left home wearing my best suit. That was a mistake. I should have worn my oldest suit. We were marched to the basement of a barracks which was "full of men and smoke." I noted in my diary: "Men of all types were there, of all classes and colors." I remember that as we were marched to the barracks, some of the recruits who had arrived a few days before us and who had received their uniforms, called out to us as we passed: "You'll be sorry. You'll be sorry."

I had barely arrived in the smoke filled basement before a call came for thirty men. Later I wrote in my diary: "Thinking that my chance had come to get my vaccinations. I stepped up like a good fellow. I was marched with the others to put up tents and to pile bricks in the rain." And I was wearing my best suit! I spent that evening in the YMCA. This was, as advertised, a "home away from home."

On Saturday, the next day I took still another physical and was vaccinated and innoculated. I remember seeing some of the recruits faint and fall to the floor when they saw the doctor with the needle. The doctor then calmly innoculated and vaccinated those who were down before they were revived. I took the oath of allegiance to the U.S. Government that morning and had my fingerprints taken.

On that Saturday afternoon, I learned that Lestern Yerrington, who had spent two terms in the commercial department of Buena Vista College when I was there, was in the camp. I looked him up. He told me that he had just gotten out of the hospital where he had spent several weeks with scarlet fever. Within ten days, I became a patient with scarlet fever in a New Haven, Connecticut hospital. Whether I caught the disease from Yerrington or from someone else at Jefferson Barracks, I do not know. I do remember that my visit with Yerrington saved me from being assigned to scrubbing a barrack's floor.

My diary refers to the fact that the sergeants, who had the responsiblity of giving us rookies the full indoctrination into the army, mixed a rich flow of profanity with every order. I was not accustomed to such treatment and this deeply offended me, but there was nothing that I could do except to be as alert as possible and avoid the displeasure of any sergeant who had authority over me.

Looking back, I feel that some of those sergeants had a sense of humor. Once when a hundred or more of us rookies were lined up, the sergeant asked if any had played tennis. "If so," he shouted, "hold up your right hand." Several did, but I did not. Those who responded were then ordered to the kitchen, given fly swatters, and ordered to swat flies.

On another occasion, some of us were asked if we had had our fingerprints taken. Those who did were ordered to a barracks, and told the put their fingerprints on a mop handle and get busy and scrub the floor.

On Sunday, April 21, I wrote in my diary: "A most disagreeable & unpleasant day. Had to sleep in a tent last night without enough blankets — cold, wet, no floor. I nearly froze. This morning it snowed." One bright spot in the day was the good food which was served. I mentioned having chicken pie and ice cream for dinner. I spent the morning working, helping move file cabinets from one barracks to another. By army orders, we were forbidden to go to the YMCA during the day, but in the afternoon I ventured to walk past the guard at the main entrance and find refuge in the railroad depot near the camp where it was warm. I bought a Sunday paper which, for the lack of something better, I read from page one to the last page of the advertisements. Since I was still wearing civilian clothes, I was not stopped at the main gate leaving or returning.

On Monday, April 22, I got my uniform. This included woolen trousers and a cotton jacket. The woolen trousers were totally unsuited for summer wear and I had to buy a new uniform after I got to New Haven. Soldiers then wore canvas puttees. The pair given to me was so large that after I had both laced up as tight as possible, I could still put my fist down on the inside of each. I was also given two blankets, an overcoat, shirts, underwear, shoes and socks, a broad brimed hat, and a duffle bag. Throughout my eight months in the army, I was never issued another uniform, so thereafter I had to buy what was needed.

After we had changed from our civilian clothing into our uniforms, a sergeant then announced: "If you want to send anything back to your homes, take it to this desk and we will mail it for you. If you want to give any of your civilian clothing to charity, then throw the items into these containers," and he pointed to a number of large packing cases. I sent most of my clothes back home in my suitcase, but I did discard several items in the containers. I found that when I had my duffle bag packed with my blankets, including the five-pound box of chocolates, from which I was eating very sparingly, it weighed about fifty pounds.

We also were given our dog-tags, which were about the size of a silver dollar, on which was stamped our name, blood type, and number. My number was 474-475. These tags we were supposed to wear round our neck suspended on a string.

After putting on our uniforms, we were ordered to line up out-of-doors and then the sergeant called on all who had put any clothing in the boxes for charity to step forward. I was suspicious, due to past experiences with these sergeants, that some unpleasant duty would be required of us, but, nevertheless, I stepped forward. Then came a second order: "All of you who put some clothing in the charity boxes, hold out your right hand." Rather mysterious. Why hold out our right hand? Then another non-commissioned officer, with a bag of dimes walked down the line and dropped a ten-cent piece into each outstretched hand. This, we were told, was a token payment for the clothing donated. I never heard of this being done at any other military base. I have often wished I had kept that dime as a keepsake of my rookie days at Jefferson Barracks.

On Tuesday, the 23rd, I was assigned to the office of the 16th Recruit Company, of which I was then a member, to assist in typing applications for government insurance. My knowledge of touch typing was paying dividends, for this duty was so much better than the manual labor that other members of my company were forced to do. On Wednesday night, one of my new friends and I got passes to go to St. Louis in order to attend a theater where the famed actress, Sarah Bernhardt, was playing the leading role. She was then known as the queen of the French stage in romance and classic tragedy. Even though one leg had been amputated in 1915, she still continued her acting career.

On Friday, April 26, I received my orders for detached duty to work with other chemists at the Yale Medical School, New Haven, where we were to seek a cure for men who had been gassed on the front lines in Germany. I later learned that I was to receive $30.00 a month as a private in the army, and then an additional $57.00 a month for my living expenses. After reporting for duty in New Haven, I never had to turn out for drill a single day. I lived a civilian's life while in uniform.

I left St. Louis by train for New York on Saturday evening, April 27. Some girls were at the depot giving candy, cake, and cookies to the men in uniform. This was typical of the generosity of the people all along the way to New York. If the train stopped for a few minutes at some station, there would always be a welcoming committee, usually women and girls, to hand out refreshments. On Sunday, I noted in my diary. "At the towns where we stopped, people would wave at us soldiers, cheer and shout 'Good luck.'"

I arrived in Grand Central Terminal, New York, at 11:15 a.m. and boarded a 12:00 o'clock train for New Haven. By this time I was feeling ill. My right ear ached and my throat was sore. Although I did not then know it, I was coming down with scarlet fever. I remember that while waiting for my next train in the Terminal, a kindly gentleman talked with me and suggested that, since I had never been in New York before, I check my duffle bag and spend some time sight seeing. I explained that I would very much like to do this, but I was too sick.

Upon my arrival in New Haven on April 29, I reported to my commanding officer who had a room reserved for me in one of the dormitories, called Kent Hall at 333 York St. I had a roommate, a fellow by the name of Gwinn. He also was a member of the Chemical Warfare unit working at Yale. According to my diary, the pain in my ear and throat increased during the following night.

On Tuesday, April 30, I wrote in my diary: "Felt worse this morning. Reported for duty but left at 1:00 o'clock because my right ear hurt so. I am afraid I am having another infection of the middle ear. From past experience I know the intense pain that this can cause."

I reported for duty and was assigned to a small group of five other men who were working in a laboratory at 150 York St. Incidentally, the beautiful library at Yale, which was begun when I was on duty there, occupies the sites on which Kent Hall and the biological laboratory once stood. The pain in my ear became so intense that morning, that I was forced to report to my commanding officer. He then told me to take a street car to a U.S. military hospital located a couple of miles to the west of New Haven.

The entry for that day includes the following: "The pain was so intense that I rolled on the bed and cried, and wrapped my head in a pillow. A Red Cross nurse brought a hot water bottle and comforted me in every way she could." A Dr. Blake, who was on the staff of the hospital, examined my ear and noted that the ear drum showed that there was an infection in the middle ear. He placed me on a stool and then with a scalpel pierced the ear drum. The pain was excruciating, but it brought immediate relief as the pus gradually drained out. Later I wrote in my diary: "The ear was washed out every hour day and night."

Later I learned that this hospital majored in taking care of tuberculosis patients. No doctor ever examined me to see what was really wrong with me. They didn't discover that I had scarlet fever. I was given the same heavy diet that the t.b. patients received — pancakes for breakfast, steak for dinner, etc., all of which I vomited up. Later I wrote in my diary for Wednesday, May 1, "Sick with a high fever. Nothing to do but to lie in bed."

The next day, after the commanding officer learned that I did not have t.b., I was discharged. I should have been sent to another hospital in an ambulance for I had a high fever. Instead, a nurse simply bound up my head with a white bandage and ushered me to the exit door. I remember that I felt so weak when I got to the place where a street car would stop that I had to sit on the curb. I remember also that some women passed and asked if I had been wounded in France. Finally a car came and I got on and told the conductor to put me off at the first hospital. I recall how the grinding of the car wheels on the iron rails sharply increased the pain in my head. It so happened that the car passed the New Haven General Hospital. There I left the street car and entered the hospital. Looking back, I censure those in charge of my case at the army hospital for grave negligence in the discharge of their professional duties. The lack of proper care at the army hospital almost cost me my life.

In the providence of God, I could not have gone to a better place for treatment of my illness than to the General Hospital of New Haven. I was first put in a general ward where there were several other beds. I was there for only a short time before a doctor came and examined me. He discovered that I had scarlet fever. I was immediately placed in a private room in the isolation ward. The doctor said that I would be with them for some time, and I was. I was kept in bed for the next nineteen day with a fever that registered 104 shortly after I was admitted.

I made a few notes later on the back of an envelope. Thus I know that on May 10 the glands in my neck were so swollen for five days that ice packs had to be placed on either side of the neck. "How I hated them," I wrote. "It was so hard to sleep with them packed by me." After the war was over, I found letters from Miss Case, the head hurse, addressed to my sister Blanche, saying that for a time I was on the "danger list."

I was highly favored in the personal attention given me in this hospital by the doctors, nurses, and other members of the staff. My doctor was a Dr. Reynolds who was as a father to me. After I was released from the hospital, he and his wife often entertained me in their home and included me in their car when taking their children for long auto rides along the coast. Miss Case, the head nurse, was most solicitous as to my welfare. Through her, I ordered a daily paper which I eagerly read each morning. And it was Miss Case who taught me four games of solitaire to help kill time.

I did not get into my uniform again until May 29. Up to that time I had only the short hospital gown, that was tied in the back, to wear. I remember the fine group of young women student nurses who were getting their training while I was a patient. One evening a number of them came into my room when I was still confined to my bed and sang a verse of the Star Spangled Banner. They then chided me for not being patriotic and standing up when the national anthem was sung.

Time did hang heavy on my hands. My only visitor was my room-mate of one night, Gwinn, who came once or twice a week with any mail that had been sent to my street address. Since he was not per-mitted to visit me in my room, he stood outside of my window when he came. Incidentally, he ate all of the chocolates which my sister Blanche had given me when I left home.

There was a twelve-year-old girl in isolation when I was there who also had scarlet fever. We played many games of checkers together to help kill time. Also in isolation were two young men who had leprosy. In that day this affliction was thought to be very contagious. Anyway, one of the lepers would often sneak out of the hospital in the evenings and go to a motion picture theater. I now wonder what the people who sat next to him would have thought had they known that they were seated next to a leper.

When the news of my being in the hospital was announced at Buena Vista College, it prompted a shower of get-well cards and letters, which were greatly appreciated. The 1918 commencement at the college came on Thursday, May 16. Since Harvey Hood had left for the army in the fall of 1917, only seven received the A.B. degree. The commencement program indicated that three of us — Stewart Brown, Ralph Marten, and myself — were already "with the colors." I was still confined to my bed on that day, but in spirit and imagination I was back at Buena Vista College.

I was kept on a liquid diet for about two weeks during which time I lost sixteen pounds. After I began eating solid food, I rapidly regained my lost weight. On May 31, just a month after I had gone out to the army hospital, I was permitted to leave the hospital and go to my room to get a few personal effects. The walk of a few blocks left me exhausted. On Monday, June 3, I noted in my diary that the hearing in my right ear had almost fully recovered. Today, even though the ear drum has been punctured twice, the hearing is normal.

Since summer was at hand, I knew that the heavy pair of woolen trousers, which had been issued to me at Jefferson Barracks, would be unsuitable, so I purchased two new uniforms. One of light weight for daily use in the laboratory. This cost $20.00. The other was a dress serge uniform for which I paid $25.00. Since I was embarrassed to wear the loose fitting canvas leggings issued to me at Jefferson Barracks, I bought a pair of wrap around leggings.

After being a patient in the isolation ward of the New Haven General Hospital for six weeks, I was discharged on June 12 and returned to my room in Kent Hall. Although I was glad to be out of the hospital, yet I was lonely and even at times felt homesick for it. Upon the suggestion of some of my army comrades, I requested a four-day leave for the purpose of visiting New York and vicinity. My request was granted. I had a cousin on my mother's side of the family, Gordon Dell, who was living with his family at Rutherford, New Jersey, a few miles out of New York. I sent a telegram to him asking if it were convenient for me to call. I received a cordial invitation to come.

I had not seen my cousin, Gordon Dell, since my mother took me and my younger brothers and sister to Niagara Falls, her pre-marriage home, in the fall of 1907. Gordon and his wife, Clara, were most hospitable. They had a daughter, Doris, then a little girl, who years later often entertained me in her home at Clifton, New Jersey.

On Saturday, I returned to New York with my cousin for more sightseeing and I returned to New Haven on Sunday afternoon, refreshed and eager to begin my work in the laboratory for which I had enlisted. Shortly after being returned to duty, my unit was transferred to Osborn Laboratory on Hillhouse Avenue.

SEEKING A CURE FOR PHOSGENE GAS POISONING

The Germans in World War I, for the first time in modern warfare, used several kinds of poisonous gas against the Allied troops on the western front. The gas was released at a time when the prevailing winds were blowing toward the Allied lines. Later, the Germans discovered that most of the winds blew towards them rather than towards the Allied lines. Even though the Allied forces were soon provided with gas masks, still a major problem remained. How were the doctors to treat one who had been gassed? We who had enlisted as chemists and who were sent to be a part of the Chemical Warfare unit at Yale University were commissioned to find a cure for gassed men.

I was assigned to a small unit of four or five men who worked under the direction of Dr. Henry Laurens, one of the professors of the Yale Medical School. Before the war ended, this Chemical Warfare unit at Yale had at least sixty men. We were scattered throughout the campus of Yale University and rarely got together as a unit.

Those with whom I worked had the responsibility of analyzing the effect of phosgene gas ($CoC12$) on dogs. Dogs were secured from the dog pound in New Haven and from surrounding cities. Individual animals would then be given the same dosage of phosgene gas as the troops on the western front were receiving. Our task was two-fold — first we were to ascertain the effects of the gas on the vital organs, and secondly, we were to find some method of treatment.

After the war was over, the results of our researches were published by one of the doctors of the medical school. I learned that our findings were of great value in the treatment of men who had been gassed in mine disasters.

AFTER DUTY ACTIVITIES

Surely few men in the military during the first World War had more pleasant duty than that which I had in New Haven. Being on detached duty gave me a great deal of freedom. I lived in quarters of my own choosing and took my meals in restaurants. I found that $57.00 a month allowed for living expenses were sufficient if I took reasonable care. My evenings and week-ends could be spent as I pleased, only I could not leave the city without permission.

But there was one unpleasant exception to this otherwise most agreeable situation and that was the necessity of associating with a few men with whom I worked in the laboratory. On June 26, I wrote in my diary: "I get heart sick at times to hear the fellows in my unit talk about girls as they do. No regard for virtue. No ideals, no faith in a God of love." One of my associates, whom I will call Jack, took fiendish delight in telling the most filthy stories and in boasting of his sexual adventures with girls. There was no escaping him after we started our daily work for our desks were adjoining each other. Any protest from me only made matters worse, so I just had to bear with it.

The climax of our association with each other came a few weeks after I reported for duty following my hospital experience. Jack planned a party to which I was given a special invitation. I hesitated to go but on second thought, felt it was better to do so than to stay away. Jack did his best to get me to drink, but he failed. I noted in my diary that night that for the first time in my life I saw girls drinking and smoking. After seeing couples drawing aside into a bedroom, I realized that the party had degenerated into a sexual orgy and I slipped away.

With a heavy heart, I started walking, not caring where I was going. After walking for some time, I happened to meet Jack and his girl friend. They stopped me and Jack said: "You got away this time, but some day we will get you." Then I had a chance to tell about my mother, and about the kind of a girl I hoped to marry, and my Christian ideals. Something that I said touched the heart of the girl. She turned to Jack and said: "Let him alone." She then turned to me and said: "Boy, live up to those ideals and some day some girl will be proud of you." That evening's experience seemed to have been a climax in my associations with Jack for after that he ceased to harass me as he had done.

The Lawn Club of New Haven, a rather exclusive social club, opened its facilities to men in uniform. Dances were held there from time to time. Although I came out of a home where dancing was considered sinful, and also so considered at college, I did go to some of the dances at the Lawn Club, but I never became very proficient in the art.

My roommate, Billy Schoonwatter, and I got passes for a weekend trip to New York leaving Friday evening July 19th. We took an overnight steamer from New Haven and found the short ocean voyage most enjoyable. We arrived at New York at 7:00 a.m., Saturday morning. After visiting Chinatown and St. Patrick's cathedral, we paused at the canteen run by a group of wealthy women on a site in front of the public library on 42nd street. All manner of light refreshments were served to men in uniform without charge. A one-day boat trip up the Hudson past West Point to Newburgh was for me an unforgettable experience.

Two new men joined our unit during the summer of 1918 with whom I became very friendly. They were Armin Hemberger and George Harley. Armin was an artist. Before the days of color photography, color reproductions of diseased tissues in the body had to be hand-painted from slides containing the tissue. After the war was over, Armin stayed on in New Haven illustrating medical textbooks. George became a medical missionary under the Methodist Church in Liberia where he received some high awards for his notable services.

Both Armin and George loved to take long walks. Several of the other men in our unit, including myself, joined them. We often walked ten miles or more on Saturdays or on Sunday afternoons. We tramped over the two high projections of rock, each about 400 feet high on either side of the city, called East Rock and West Rock. We also hiked along the ocean beaches. Hemberger rented a two-room apartment in anticipation of getting married, which he did in October, and a group of six or eight of us had the custom of meeting there once or twice a week to play cards.

Beginning with entries for October 1, references to the ravages of Spanish influenza became more frequent. Many people were dying. The hospitals were full of patients. Hemberger came down with the flu on October 12. He didn't want to go to a hospital and insisted that he was able to take care of himself in his apartment. I asked for permission to stay with him for a couple of days and permission was granted. On the 14th, I wrote in my diary: "I wore a mask, but still of course, ran a little risk." Hemberger soon improved and I suffered no ill effects from my nursing duties. Hemberger was married soon afterwards, and their home continued to be a meeting place for four or five of us to play cards.

I celebrated my 21st birthday on Thursday, November 7. This was the day when a false rumor of Germany surrendering spread like wild fire through the country. New Haven went wild with excitement.

The real armistice came on Monday, November 11. Following are extracts from my diary: "Peace is declared. I was awakened this morning at 4 o'clock by the whistles, bells, and even auto horns. I put on my clothes with my big overcoat and hurried to the green in the center of the city. In the dim flickering street light, I saw others hurrying in the same direction . . . I reached the intersection of Church and Chapel streets about 4:30. A motley crowd was beginning to assemble & the newspaper boys were selling their papers fast, and at twice the normal cost.

"The crowd grew. Parades began — spontaneous and short lived. Anyone with a flag or a drum or a horn was assured of a following . . . Gradually the crowd grew . . . The parades with their flags, torches, and music were but demonstrations of years of pent up feelings. An ecstacy of joy seized all. It was contagious . . . Men in uniform were popular. Many came up to shake my hand just because I was in uniform . . . This is the birth of a great national holiday and the beginning of a new world era.

"The celebration continued all day — a mad outburst of joy." I reported for duty in the laboratory that morning but all were excused from duty in the afternoon. That evening I returned to the green and found it "a seething mass of people."

Knowing that my unit would soon be discharged, I obtained a pass to visit Boston for the weekend of November 23. I arrived in Boston that Saturday afternoon and secured a bed for 25¢ in a hostess center which had been established in the basement of a church located at one corner of the commons. Then I was off on my sight-seeing tour which included a visit to Harvard University and to Longfellow's home. That evening I attended a theater where the famed actress Ethel Barrymore appeared.

On Sunday, more sight seeing including Bunker Hill, both Old North and Old South churches — attended a service in one of these. In the afternoon took a sight seeing bus out to Lexington and Concord, and other historical places. I arrived back in New Haven at midnight.

Toward the end of November, the long awaited promotions came through. I got the minimum possible — promoted to Private First Class. Realizing that our unit would soon be discharged, I spent my last days on duty writing a summary of the findings of the experiments that I and those working with me had carried on.

I noted in my diary on Sunday, December 8, that Hemberger had begun to draw my portrait. I sat for this several times during the following week. He drew entirely without the help of any mechanical device to outline my features on the paper. The result was excellent. This portrait is now in the Presbyterian Historical Society in Philadelphia.

When the announcement was made that all members of my unit would be sent to Camp Devens in Massachusetts on Tuesday, December 17, where we would be processed for discharge, I hastened to send home several boxes of items I did not want to carry with me. And then I began to say goodby to many of my civilian friends. On Monday evening, before we left for Camp Devens, I called on Dr. Reynolds. Dr. Reynolds urged me that if ever I returned to New Haven, I was to make their home my home. I was never able to meet those lovely people again.

On Tuesday, December 17, I wrote in my diary: "We left New Haven, Yale University, our friends and acquaintances, and the dogs at 10:20 a.m. for Camp Devens." I had mixed emotions. I was eager to return to civilian life and to visit my loved ones in Early, Iowa, yet at the same time I hated to leave so many friends in New Haven. We arrived in Camp Devens early that evening. First we had to go

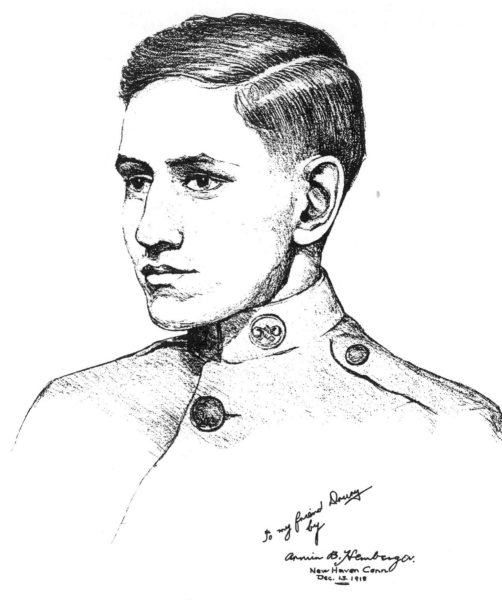

To my friend Drury
by

Armin B. Hemberger.
New Haven Conn.
Dec. 13. 1918

CLIFFORD DRURY, 1918
A portrait drawn by Armin Hemberger while he was stationed
with Clifford Drury in New Haven, Connecticut
with The Army Chemical Warfare Unit.

through cootie inspection as though we had just come from the louse infected trenchs of the western front. We were then quartered in one of the army barracks.

I was awakened the next morning by a bugler playing reveille, a strange sound for one who had spent his army life of eight months in a city. The whole day was spent in filling out forms, taking the final physical examination, and in making plans for my travel back to Iowa. Two alternatives were given to me. First, I could wait at Camp Devens until a group of Iowans had gathered large enough for the army to send them as a unit rather than as individuals. The second alternative was to accept my discharge at Camp Devens and then pay my own way home. Discharged soldiers could travel by rail at the special rate of two cents a mile. I quickly agreed on the second alternative as I very much wanted to visit my mother's relatives in Niagara Falls, New York, and then be home before Christmas.

I received my discharge on Thursday afternoon, December 19. I wrote that evening in my diary: "I was as glad to get out of the army as I had been to get in." I got paid up to the last day of service and no more. The men who served in World War I did not receive the special financial benefits made available to veterans of World War II as special severance pay and educational benefits. During the days of the depression in the 1930's, Congress approved the payment of a bonus of $1.00 a day to veterans of World War I for every day of active duty. Since I had served for eight months, I received about $245.00 which came at a time when such was much needed.

I took a night train for Buffalo where I arrived at 10:00 a.m. the next morning. From there I went to Niagara Falls where my mother's relatives lived. I was welcomed by her brother and his wife, Hamilton and Catherine Dell, another sister, Lilly Dell, and three of the children of Uncle Hamilton. Of course, I spent time seeing the wonders of Niagara Falls. I took an early morning train on Sunday, the 22nd, for Chicago and home. I wore a red chevron on one of my uniform sleeves which was a sign that I had been discharged.

When I got off the train at Early on Tuesday, December 24th, I was greeted by three of my brothers, Grover, Billy, and Howard, and by my sister Clara. It was a joyous and exciting time for all of us. My brother Grover had been in the Students' Army Training Corps at the University of Iowa, so he too was in uniform.

The first week after my return, I spent in visiting all of my relatives in Early and my sister Blanche and her family in Marcus, Iowa. I returned to Storm Lake and called on my former professors and such schoolmates as were in town. I began the transition back to civilian life by buying some civilian clothes.

I soon had to face the problem — what was I to do? I did get in touch with Rush Medical School in Chicago but learned that I needed a course in inorganic chemistry before I could be admitted. I thought of teaching school but could find no opening, nor did I feel really qualified for such work. Thus the year 1918 closed on an indecisive note. I was not sure what I should do.

CHAPTER EIGHT

Eight Months in Des Moines, Iowa, 1919

I spent eight months of 1919 in Des Moines, the first two months as head file clerk in the House of Representatives in the Iowa State Legislature and then six months as a Red Cross worker in the Fort Des Moines military hospital. It was there that I decided to study theology and become an ordained minister in the Presbytrian Church and then, if God were willing, I would go as a missionary to some foreign field.

I grew increasingly restless during the first week of January when I had nothing to do. On January 2, I noted in my diary: "I hate this lying around." A few days later, while in Storm Lake, I called on Willis C. Edson, a lawyer and a member of the Board of Trustees of Buena Vista College. Edson was also a member of the Iowa State Legislature and was planning to go to Des Moines on Thursday, January 9. He suggested that I go with him and apply for the position of file clerk in the House of Representatives. I accepted the suggestion without a moment's hesitation and I accompanied him on the train to Des Moines on the 9th.

Edson coached me as to what I should do to get appointed. I had some calling cards printed with my name and the position to which I aspired to be appointed. Many of the members of the Legislature had rooms in the Chamberlain Hotel where Edson was staying, and I was active meeting them, handing out my cards, and asking them to vote for me when the appointments were made. "My uniform helps out a lot," I wrote in my diary. We were then permitted to wear our uniforms for several months after discharge with the discharge red chevron. The selection of the staff members of the Legislature was made on Saturday, the 11th, and I got the appointment that I sought. The pay was four dollars a day. The work was not hard. Usually I could do all the filing needed within five hours and the rest of the time was my own. I found a private room in a home east of the capitol.

Several of my former schoolmates from Buena Vista who had served in the army were sent to Camp Dodge to be processed for discharge; among them was my classmate, Ed Marousek. I went out to the camp to see him on January 22. On my first trip to Camp Dodge, I was instrumental in saving the life of a fifteen-year-old Negro girl. We were both standing on the platform next to the rails shortly before the train was due. It was dark and the girl got confused and fell onto the tracks but had one hand grasping the edge of the platform.

The train was then only a few feet away and would surely have run over her had I not grabbed her arm and pulled her to safety. As the train moved past she said to me: "Boy, you sure saved my life."

On Monday, February 3, after finishing my work at the capitol, I went out to Drake University where I enrolled for a course in organic chemistry and also for one in German. The classes were held at hours which were adjustable to those I had to spend at the capitol.

Since some of the army units which had seen action on the western front were being sent to Camp Dodge for discharge, they were often marched through the streets of Des Moines and given a hero's welcome. My diary shows that I became sensitive, and somewhat apologetic over the fact that I had not gotten to France. I read in the newspapers about the Red Cross needing men who would serve aboard transports which were bringing back the troops from France. On Saturday, February 22, I wrote in my diary: "I am restless and dissatisfied. I wrote to the Red Cross and if they can use me, I'll go. Maybe yet I'll be able to say, I got across."

On Wednesday, February 26, after making arrangements for someone to take care of my filing duties at the capitol, I took the train for Iowa City to inspect the medical school there. I met my brother Billy, who was then a student at the University of Iowa.

Having previously made application to join the Masonic Lodge in Early, I received word from its secretary that the Lodge was ready to give me the first degree on Saturday evening, March 1, and, if I could memorize the required ritual, the second degree on Monday evening, the 3rd. My brother-in-law, Ferry Smith, was Senior Warden in the Lodge and he had promised to coach me.

After making arrangements for someone to take care of my duties in the state house, I took an afternoon train on Friday, February 28th, for Storm Lake. Hearing that my college classmate, Stewie Brown, had been discharged from the air force with the rank of lieutenant, I telegraphed him to meet me in Storm Lake. I was a bit envious of him in that he won an officer's commission while I attained only to the rank of Private, First Class.

Stewie met me at the train in Storm Lake. Our meeting was a joyous one for we had not seen each other for nearly a year. We stayed that night in a hotel in Storm Lake and talked until long after midnight. I urged him to make application for the Red Cross and join me at Fort Des Moines. This he later did.

I took the train for Early on Saturday morning and that evening I took my first degree in Masonry. I felt a sentimental tie to this fraternal order because my father had been active in several of its branches and the Masons were very helpful to the Drury family at the time of my father's funeral. I attended the Early Presbyterian Church on Sunday morning and was called upon, unexpectedly, to speak. In that day considerable discussion was being carried on throughout the nation regarding the supposed conflict between science and religion. To me, there was no conflict. So when I was asked to speak, I stated my position regarding the harmony which existed between the Biblical account of creation and scientific findings. I spoke for about one-half hour, of course without notes.

"I received many compliments," I wrote in my diary that evening, "the best of which were some tears in the eyes of some men." Mr. D. D. Carlton, my former guardian, said as he grasped my hand at the door: "Merrill, I repeat it. I am proud of you." I am frank to admit that such expressions of appreciation for something I had done or some expression of faith in what I could do always came as a shot of adrenalin to my ego. I wanted to be worthy of the faith that people had in me.

I spent part of Sunday afternoon and nearly all day Monday memorizing the Masonic ritual. On Monday evening, having passed my examination, I took my second degree in Masonry. Some people have the mistaken idea that Masonry is a religion. Not so. The ritual is a drama based on Old Testament stories in which the initiate unwittingly plays the leading role. The ritual stresses the importance of keeping high moral ideals.

I did not take the third degree until June 19 of that year. I have kept up my Masonic interest until my retirement at the end of 1963, moving from St. Elmo Lodge in Early, to Sinim Lodge in Shanghai, China, to Paradise Lodge in Moscow, Idaho, to Marin Lodge in San Rafael, California, and finally back to the Early Lodge. I received my 50-year pin from my home lodge in 1969. Through the years I have found my Masonic connections to be very helpful. I served as Master of the lodge in Moscow, Idaho, for one year and also as High Priest of the Royal Arch Chapter in Moscow, for another year.

I returned to Des Moines on Tuesday, March 4, and at once plunged into my appointed duties as file clerk at the capitol and as a student at Drake University.

Six Months with the American Red Cross

On Saturday, March 8, I noted in my diary: "I received another letter from the Red Cross and I am to have an interview with the Associate Director of the Red Cross from Chicago tomorrow." On Sunday afternoon, I met Mr. Van Tyle, a representative of the Central Division of the National Red Cross, who told me that all of the positions connected with overseas and transport work of the Red

Cross were filled, "but there was great need of men in some of the camps in this country, and just now at the army hospital at Fort Des Moines." He urged me to accept a position which was then open at Fort Des Moines.

Circumstances over which seemingly I had little or no control were guiding my steps. Looking back on those months, I realize now that had I not gone out to work with the Red Cross, I probably would not have gone to San Francisco Theological Seminary that fall. "I considered that it would be selfish indeed for me to turn down this needed work just because I could not get across," I wrote in my diary. "I will try to make arrangements so as not to jeopardize my medical course."

Fort Des Moines, an old military post located about five miles south of Des Moines, had been converted into a military hospital to which the sick and wounded veterans from France were being sent for further care and final discharge. I visited the Fort on Monday, March 10, and met Mr. Henry who was in charge of all Red Cross work. I found that if I accepted the call to be a Red Cross worker there, my opportunities for helping the soldier patients were so much more challenging than filing papers in the capitol building that I decided to accept. I called on Mr. Van Tyle that afternoon and accepted the offer.

My pay was to be $100.00 a month, plus uniform, a room on the grounds, and my meals in the officers mess. I was to have the status of a first lieutenant in the army.

I had to give up my classes at Drake, but was given two units credit for my class in German. I received no credit for the incompleted course in organic chemistry. My first day of duty as a Red Cross man at the Fort came on Wednesday, March 12. I was given the responsibility of visiting about 400 convalescent patients several times a week. Most of the men were recovering from wounds or the effects of being gassed. Some had lost a limb and a few had lost both legs. I visited one locked ward with mental patients.

I carried a small suitcase filled with items which I could give away, such as stationery, cigarettes, pencils, and a few toilet articles. Sometimes I was asked to write letters for patients, a few of whom I found to be illiterate. In my diary I mention getting claims started to locate missing Liberty bonds which had been purchased through monthly deductions of a soldier's pay. During my first two days on duty, I started tracers for some $600.00 worth of bonds.

During my first week on duty, one of the patients came to me with a telegram telling of the serious illness of his mother and requesting him to return home at once. The soldier tried to get a pass but failed.

His last appeal was to the Commanding Officer. It so happened that the C.O. was attending a movie in the Red Cross building but he was held in such awesome respect that no one dared to approach him at that time and ask for his signature on a pass. In my naivete, I had the boldness to stop the movie and call the Commanding Officer out of the audience and asked him to sign the pass. I explained that this was an emergency for the soldier as his mother was seriously ill, and that there was no other officer who was authorized to do so. The C.O. signed the pass and I went with the soldier to the railroad station in the city and made sure that he got on the right train.

To my joy, Stewie Brown joined the Red Cross staff on March 18. He was given the responsibility of providing movies and talent for the evening programs in the Red Cross hut. Again we were roommates. Another who joined the staff was a theological student, Chester Dunham, a graduate of Yale Divinity School, 1916, who was six years older than I. We had many serious discussions over the great issues of life. I was still struggling with the question of deciding between a medical career or the ministry. Dunham repeatedly urged me to go into the ministry. His words carried great weight with me because of my admiration for him.

I became increasingly aware in the spring of 1919 that I would have to decide between medicine and ministry before schools opened in September. My college classmates, Ed Marousek and Harvey Hood, were urging me to go with them to Princeton. I felt the need to stand in a pulpit again.

Feeling that another appearance in Early or vicinity was important to help me decide what to do, I got in touch with the Methodist minister at Lake View who was in charge of the afternoon service on Sundays at Pleasant Hill church and offered to speak on Easter Sunday, April 20, 1919. A cordial invitation to do so was immediately forthcoming. I returned to Early on Saturday, the 19th, and attended the Methodist Church in Early on Easter morning.

The prospect of a son of Pleasant Hill preaching here on Easter Sunday attracted considerable attention. According to an entry in my diary: "Five auto loads of people from Early drove to the church to hear me." Most of these were Drury relatives. The church was packed. A host of memories came flooding back. I saw again in my imagination my mother kneeling at the altar for communion, and I remembered the exciting Christmas eve programs. "I did my best," I wrote in my diary that evening, "but yet I felt that there was much I did not say."

That evening I wrote in my diary: "I have never received heartier congratulations or warmer praise than from those old neighbors,

former acquaintances, and friends." Th experience reenforced my
growing conviclion that God wanted me to be a minister.

I returned to Early about two months later to serve as toastmaster
for the annual banquet of the Early High School Alumni Association
scheduled for Thursday evening, June 18th. At that time when I was
back in Early, I took my third degree in Masonry on the 19th. Again
I played an unwitting role in a drama based on an Old Testament
story in which Hiram Abif Boaz, who is reputed to have been one of
the builders of King Solomon's temple, was a principal character. I
had some surprises during the ritual of which I wrote that evening in
my diary: "If I had not known the men who were giving the degree,
I would have run out on them."

My Decision to Go to California

Shakespeare wrote in Hamlet: "There's a divinity that shapes our
ends, rough-hew them how we will." I am convinced of that as I
review the circumstances which surrounded me in the late spring and
summer of 1919. By July 27, I noted in my diary of my intention to
enter a theological seminary in Los Angeles. Then on September 11,
my plans were suddenly changed and I went instead to the San Francisco Theological Seminary, a Presbyterian institution in San Anselmo,
Marin County, California.

I continued a special interest in ornithology ever since I took a
summer school course in that subject at the biological camp of the
University of Iowa at Lake Okoboji in 1916. Then here at Fort Des
Moines, I found a splendid opportunity to continue the study of
identifying birds and their songs. I bought a fine pair of binoculars,
and I also bought an illustrated guide of mid-western birds and a
small notebook to list my finds.

On May 11, a few days after I bought the binoculars, I hiked into
the meadow land and woods just east of the Fort in company with
Lieutenant Young, one of the doctors on duty at the Fort. That day
we identified twenty-three different species.

Bird hunting became increasingly a prime recreational activity
for me in the late afternoon and early evening hours. I would often
skip the evening meal at the officers mess and get a small bottle of
milk, sandwiches, and other snack items at the canteen bar in the
Red Cross hut and head for the woods. I would spend hours looking
for birds. Before the summer ended, I had identified, and listed in my
note book, sixty-seven species, all found in the vicinity of Fort Des
Moines.

A notation in my notebook for May 18 lists the name of Captain
Charles Warner, one of the doctors on duty at the Fort. He was an

avid ornithologist and we quickly became warm friends. He was about ten years older than I, a devout Methodist, and somewhat of a philosopher. Often while we were seated in some shady spot waiting for birds to come to us, he would discourse on the issues of life. I discussed with him my problem — should I study medicine or theology? He strongly urged me to study theology.

Captain Warner and I were together for only a month for he was released from active duty on June 21 when he returned to Los Angeles. During that month, he made repeated references to a theological seminary under Methodist sponsorship which was connected with the University of Southern California. One of the Captain's brothers was dean of this school. The Captain urged me to attend there and, for a time, I thought that this was a good idea. This school later moved to Claremont, California, and is now called the Claremont School of Theology.

My brief association with Captain Warner initiated a chain of events which led me to the San Francisco Theological Seminary at San Anselmo, California. How different would have been my life and others of my family had I not gone to San Anselmo.

My Last Months in the Red Cross

Even though Captain Warner was gone, I kept in touch with him through the mails. On July 27, I wrote in my diary saying that Captain Warner had opened an office in Los Angeles, and that "I expect to go there to school this fall." Had I done so I might have become a Methodist again.

My close friend, Stewie Brown, left on July 4th. One by one my closest friends were leaving — first, Dunham, then Captain Warner, and now Brown. My usual duties continued. I noted in my diary that I was supposed to visit seven or eight wards which had a total of 475 patients. Patients were still arriving. Often I was the only Red Cross worker free to meet them at the trains and get the necessary data from each which would enable the Associate Director to write a letter to the nearest of kin.

Personal Finances

My father left an estate of $75,000.00 or $80,000.00, a handsome sum for that day and especially when we remember that he was only eighteen years old when he bought a farm in Clinton Township of Sac County. He was then able to make a $200.00 down payment on his first farm. He was only fifty-three years and four months old when he died in 1916.

I do not have the exact figures as to how the estate was divided, but my impression is that Laura, my stepmother, got $15,000.00 and each of the twelve children received about $4,500.00. This would account for $69,000.00. Then would come medical and funeral expenses, executor's fee, and court costs. My brother, Millard, served as executor.

I do not have exact figures to show how much I drew upon my share of the estate for my last two years in college, but this must have amounted to $500.00 a year including the cost of a summer school. This would have reduced my balance to $3,500.00. I put this money in a savings account in the Citizen's State Bank of Early, which was then being managed by my guardian, D. D. Carlton. I received 5% interest. While in the army and during my eight months at Des Moines, I rarely drew upon this account so there was a little increase in capital because of the interest.

According to entries in my diary, Millard urged me to turn over to him about $3,000.00 early in 1919 which he needed to complete the purchase of a farm. I was hesitant and cautious, so I turned down the opportunity. On June 19, 1919, I wrote in my diary: "Grover accepted Millard's offer to go farming which I turned down & cleared about $8,000.00."

During the latter part of July, Millard, my older brother, wrote to me saying that he had another opportunity to buy a farm but needed $3,000.00 from me to complete the deal. The fact that Grover had made about $8,000.00 in a land deal with Millard, a deal that I had turned down, put me in a receptive mood. By this time Millard was living on a farm he had recently purchased near Everly, Iowa, which had a fine large house. According to my diary, I visited Millard, arriving there on Sunday, July 20.

Millard took me that Sunday afternoon to see the farm that he was planning to buy. The owner of the 160 acre farm was asking $325.00 an acre which meant a total investment of $52,000.00. Millard had $20,000.00 but needed my $3,000.00 to complete the deal. I realized that I had a three-year seminary course facing me and that I would have no more than $600.00 from my father's estate if I turned $3,000.00 over to Millard, yet, remembering Grover's experience, I consented. The farm was bought with the expectation that farm prices would continue to rise.

No papers were drawn up. My records include a cancelled check for $3,000.00 made out to Millard on February 28, 1920. I was then in the seminary at San Anselmo. Years later I wrote across the check in red ink: "Lost it all." Land values had gone down and Millard lost his $20,000.00. In following years, I could have spent that $3,000.00 in many ways, especially to help out with wedding expenses, travel costs from Shanghai to Edinburgh, etc. But, looking back, I am grateful that I received from my father's estate enough money to pay for my last two years in college and had about $600.00 for my seminary expenses.

DESTINATION — SAN ANSELMO

On September 10, I wrote in my diary: "Six months service in the Red Cross is up. To tell the truth, I am very desirous to get back to my studies." The next day I wrote: "Today heard from the Presbyterian Board of Education in Philadelphia. They strongly recommended that I go to the San Francisco Theological Seminary at San Anselmo, California. This means a radical change in my plans."

Since I had been taken under care of the Presbytery of Sioux City as a candidate for the Presbyterian ministry, and since I had received some scholarship aid from the church during my last two years in college, I felt obligated to follow the advice of the Board of Christian Education. I sent a telegram to the President of the Seminary at San Anselmo asking if I could be enrolled at a late date. An answer soon came saying that I could be enrolled even though I would be a few days late.

My last day on duty as a Red Cross worker was on Saturday, September 13th. In many ways this was a sad day for me for I had made many friends, and I had enjoyed my work. I wrote in my diary: "This was a day of goodbys." I arrived back in Early late Saturday afternoon. The pastor of the Presbyterian Church learned of my presence and persuaded me to speak in his church the next day.

I spent six days saying my goodbys to relatives and friends and in packing. My younger brothers, Grover and Billy, came down from Everly where they had been working for my older brother Millard. I left Thursday evening, the 18th, for Storm Lake. I was not to return to Early until after I had completed my seminary course and was ordained — that was in the summer of 1922. This meant an absence of about three years.

I saw my former roommates, Harvey Hood and Art Riedesel, in Storm Lake on the 19th. Hood and Marousek were soon to leave for Princeton Theological Seminary and Hood urged me to go with them. However, I felt that I had to go to San Anselmo. "I believe that the west will give me much more than the east," I wrote in my diary.

I left Storm Lake early on Friday morning, September 19, on what was called the "Flyer" of the Illinois Central line. Hood and Riedesel were at the depot to see me off. I stopped off at Marcus a few hours to see my sisters, Blanche and Sarah. Late that afternoon I took another train to Sioux City where I changed for one that carried me to Omaha. I left Omaha at midnight for California.

My railroad trip over the Rockies to California gave me one thrill after another for I had never seen such high mountains and deep canyons before. Train travel was slow for I did not arrive at Oakland until late Tuesday afternoon, September 23. I crossed the bay on a ferry, the first of hundreds of such trips I was to take in following years. I arrived in San Francisco's historic ferry building at seven o'clock and there changed to another ferry which took me to Sausalito, in Marin County, across the bay to the north of San Francisco. At Sausalito, I boarded an electric interurban train for a half hour's ride to San Anselmo. It was dark when I got off the train at Bolinas Avenue. Upon inquiry I learned that the seminary buildings were about two blocks down Bolinas Avenue.

Carrying my suitcase, I walked down Bolinas Avenue in the dark and rang the door bell of the first house on the campus that I came to. This happened to be the home of my Professor of Theology, Dr. Thomas V. Moore. A telephone call to Montgomery Hall, the men's dormitory at the top of the hill, brought one of the seniors down to meet me. He was John Murdock, a Canadian, who had seen action on the western front during the World War. He led me up a steep path to the hall and ushered me into a room on the third floor. Everything there was in readiness for my coming.

I arrived at nine o'clock that night and yet in reality, it was the dawn of three happy years that I spent at San Anselmo.

CHAPTER NINE

At San Anselmo

When I awoke on Wednesday morning, September 24, 1919, and looked out of my window, I was impressed with the park-like surroundings. Everything was so beautiful. I saw palm trees, eucalyptus, and off across the valley to the southwest, a range of mountains. Later I learned that the highest point was called Mt. Talampais and that it had an elevation of 2,400 feet, the same as Jerusalem. Indeed the climate of Marin County, in which San Anselmo was located, was so similar to that of the Holy Land that many of the plants mentioned in the Bible were growing there in San Anselmo.

I took breakfast that morning in the dining room which was then located in the basement of Montgomery Hall. There I met most of the members of my class of 1922, among whom was Lloyd Carrick who has been one of my life-long friends. The three classes in seminary were known as the Juniors, the Middlers, and the Seniors. At the time of my graduation in April 1922, my class had eighteen members.

I spent most of the next day getting unpacked and enrolling. There was practically no choice in what courses I was to take — these were prescribed and included Greek, Hebrew, Church History, Theology, New Testament Interpretation, Public Speaking, and Homiletics (sermon preparation). In some of these courses, all I had to do was to attend and listen to my own classmates practice preaching. Since I remembered some of my shorthand, I was able to take voluminous notes which I typed onto note paper after I returned to my room. Later I had these classroom notes bound together into one volume, now in the rare book room of San Francisco Theological Seminary.

San Francisco Theological Seminary at San Anselmo, California, bears its name and address reference to two Roman Catholic saints — Saint Francis of Assisi, Italy (1182?-1226), the gentle and lovable founder of the Franciscan Order, and Saint Anselm, an Italian monk (1034?-1109), who became Archbishop of Canterbury in 1093 and is known as a great theologian. The leading spirit of its organization was a local Presbyterian minister, Dr. William A. Scott, whose biography I was privileged to write and which was published in 1967. The Seminary, founded in 1871, struggled along in San Francisco under adverse conditions for twenty years. A major difficulty was the absence of Presbyterian colleges west of the Rocky Mountains which could feed students into the Seminary. During the first twenty years

of its history, the Seminary had only twenty-four graduates, plus
a few students who entered the ministry without being graduated.

Two important gifts came to the Seminary in 1889 which completely
changed its future destiny. The first was a site of seventeen acres
of land in San Anselmo, given by A. W. Foster, a son-in-law of Dr.
Scott. This had been a part of a dairy farm and included a farm
house which was still standing when I first arrived on the campus.
In the center of the acreage was a mound, about one-half mile in
circumference and about sixty-five feet high.

The second was a princely gift of $250,000.00 from a San Francisco
merchant, Alexander Montgomery. This money provided for the
erection of two castle-like buildings on top of the mound on the new
campus — one a men's dormitory called Montgomery Hall, and the
other a classroom and library building, called Scott Hall. Out of the
initial gift came funds for the erection of three faculty residences on
Bolinas Avenue which marked the southern boundary of the campus
and the endowment for two professorships. Later from the Montgomery estate came funds for the erection of the Memorial Chapel at
the foot of the hill. The Seminary began its work on its new campus
in September 1892. Thus it had been on its new location only twenty-
seven years when I enrolled in September 1919. The Seminary was
still in its infancy.

Growth on the San Anselmo campus was slow during its first twenty-
five years. The outbreak of World War I naturally cut down on student
enrollment. A new era in the Seminary's history began when veterans
from World War I were able to enroll. The first of these veterans came
in the late fall of 1918. About one-half of the entering class, which
enrolled in the fall of 1919, of which I was one, were veterans. The
Government then made no provisions to help veterans in their continuing education. The Y.M.C.A. which had carried on an extensive
work with the military during the war, granted scholarship aid to
the extent of $50.00 to all who applied and who were qualified. I
received one of these scholarships. Several of the veterans in my
class continued to wear their military uniforms, stripped of insignia,
as an economy measure.

The Junior class of 1919, which numbered twenty-four, was the
largest class ever to enroll in the history of the seminary up to that
time. The total enrollment during the academic year of 1919-20 was
fifty-eight, which number included the wife of one of the students
and three single women students in the Junior class. As I recall, only
one student, a Senior, had a car.

There were seven on the faculty when I arrived, all men of high
caliber. Dr. Warren H. Landon was President. The others were Wil-

liam H. Oxtoby, Hebrew and Old Testament; Edward A. Wicher, Greek and New Testament; Thomas V. Moore, Theology; Remsen D. Bird, Church History; Edwin F. Hallenbeck, Practical Theology; and Charles G. Buck, a layman, Vocal Culture. Later during my Junior year, Lynn T. White, formerly pastor of the First Presbyterian Church of San Rafael, joined the faculty as the first occupant of the Chair of Christian Sociology. This had been endowed by Robert Dollar, the shipping magnate and an elder in the San Rafael church.

Several of my professors had a profound influence on my life. Dr. Moore gave me a theological basis for my preaching. He was a strict Calvinist and a firm believer in the substitutionary theory of atonement, such as was held by Anselm of Canterbury. This has become the heart of my preaching — each sin we commit places us further in debt to God, and we have nothing wherewith to pay. Christ, who was without sin and therefore not in debt, did for us in his death on the cross what we could not do for ourselves. To me, that is the very heart of the gospel.

Dr. Bird awakened in me a love for church history. He remained at the Seminary only two years while I was a student and then accepted a call to become President of Occidental College. He was the youngest member of the faculty at that time, innovative and enthusiastic. He wrote in blank verse the script for a pageant which centered about the life of John Knox which, under his direction, the students presented in the spring of 1921 on the fiftieth anniversary of the founding of the Seminary. I had a minor role in this pageant. But when the seventy-fifth anniversary came in the fall of 1946, I was asked to write and present a pageant celebrating that occasion. Then when the 100th anniversary came in 1971, I was honored to be asked to give the principal address on the life of the Seminary's founder, Dr. W. A. Scott.

As a part of the semi-centennial celebration, Dr. Bird wrote a seminary hymn consisting of four stanzas. One stanza described the beauty of San Anselmo in the morning light and another when the valley was covered with darkness. The first line of this stanza read: "When the night thy beauty foldeth." It became my duty to cut a stencil so that sufficient copies could be made for all in the student body. The big day came when the hymn was to be introduced. The pages were distributed and then suddenly I became aware that inadvertently I had put a "y" after the word night so that the line read: "When the nighty thy beauty foldeth." Of course this one extra letter threw in an extra syllable which made the line unsingable. I remember Dr. Bird jumping to his feet and crying out that he had not written that line that way.

Another of the faculty members who had a great influence in my life was Dr. Wicher. He made me believe that I could be a great Greek scholar, which never came to be. But he did inspire in me the desire to achieve. He urged me to plan to get my Ph.D. degree.

About half of the student body served churches in surrounding communities in various capacities. To accommodate them, no classes were held on Saturday afternoons or on Mondays. The only Sunday assignment I had during my Junior year was to be Superintendent of a Sunday School in the Presbyterian Orphanage in San Anselmo. Nine other students from the Seminary assisted me. At that time, most of the children were either orphans or half-orphans. We had no problem about attendance as the children were eager to attend the sessions which were held in the mid-afternoon.

On Saturday afternoon, September 21, after morning classes, I made a trip to see San Francisco. In those days, an electric train carried us to Sausalito — a half-hour ride — where we boarded a ferry for the city. This was another half-hour ride, and to me always a delightful experience. The opening of the Golden Gate bridge in 1937 put these ferries out of business. Walking the streets of San Francisco for the first time was a thrilling experience. Market Street, a wide thoroughfare which began at the ferry building and ran up to the hills known as Twin Peaks, carried four street car tracks for two separate lines. Two tracks led to a circle at the ferry building where passengers disembarked for the ferries and incoming passengers boarded for city destinations. These tracks have long since been removed. Today a subway stretches under Market Street.

As the days passed, I took long exploratory walks. To the west of the campus was Mt. Baldy, well named as it was devoid of trees, about 1,500 feet high. To the southwest was Mt. Tamalpais, 2,400 feet high. In company with other students, I climbed both within a few days of my arrival. At the foot of Mt. Tamalpais, on its other side, was Muir Woods National Park with its magnificent grove of redwood trees, some towering 200 feet high. A narrow gauge railroad, which claimed to be the crookedest railroad in the world, carried passengers from Mill Valley to the top of the mountain. Sometimes we from the Seminary would climb up the northern slope and then return by the railroad. This railroad has long since been removed.

My diary shows that on December 21, 1919, I attended Trinity Presbyterian Church in San Francisco where I met again the Rev. Stanton Salisbury, who was serving as an assistant pastor. Stanton had visited Early High School when I was a student there and remembered me. Later he entered the Naval Chaplaincy and was serving aboard the U.S.S. Pennsylvania at Pearl Harbor. Shortly after the

Japanese attack on Pearl Harbor, I was called to active duty in the Navy and in the spring of 1941 was called to Washington where, as will be told, I had close contacts with Chaplain Salisbury.

I revelled in my studies. In college, I was a "B" student, whereas in seminary I was an "A." For one thing, I did not have the extra-curricular activities in the seminary that I had in college. In seminary, I had a single room to myself whereas in college I was one of four who had two rooms. We did have a full-sized football field at San Anselmo and had a soccer team. I had never played soccer before but quickly learned and played a half-back position. We played against the University of California and Leland Stanford, and sometimes won.

Being invited by Captain Warner, who was practicing medicine in Los Angeles, to be their guest over New Years and join them in driving to Pasadena to see the Rose Parade on January 1, 1920, I secured passage on a coast freighter. The ship sailed from San Francisco at 3:30 p.m. on Saturday, December 29, and docked at San Pedro on the following Monday morning. Before calling on Captain Warner, I called on Florence Mitchell, who was a member of my class at Buena Vista and who was taking a nurse's training course in a Los Angeles hospital. In the fall of 1921 Florence enrolled at San Anselmo. She married Harry Wylie, one of my seminary classmates, and the two went out to India as Presbyterian missionaries.

I was with Captain Warner late that afternoon and again we went on a bird walk. We saw a Hermit Thrush and other species which were new to me. New Year's day fell on a Thursday and I accompanied the Warner family in their car to Pasadena to see the 1920 Rose Parade. That was my first visit to Pasadena. Little did I then think that I would some day be living in a retirement home in Pasadena. I made no mention of the Rose Parade in my diary, but did comment on the large number of cars. "I have never seen so many before in my life," I wrote.

On my return trip, I rode by auto stage to Bakersfield and then took the train to San Francisco. I was back in San Anselmo on Monday, January 5th.

During the second half of my Junior year, I took a special interest in the cults and non-Christian religions which advertised their services in the San Francisco papers. I visited a Buddhist temple on February 12th and wrote an article on "'Buddhism in the United States" which appeared in the July 6, 1920, issue of the Presbyterian weekly called *The Continent*. This was the first of my articles which appeared in national publications during the following fifty and more years. I made a study of Hinduism and wrote an article on "Hinduism in the United States" which appeared in the April 1921 issue of *The Missionary Review of the World,* for which I received an honorarium of $5.00. Through the years I have had more than fifty articles published in church and historical magazines, most of which were printed without giving me an honorarium (*See* Appendix A).

As time permitted, I continued my bird studies. By February 9, 1920, according to my diary, I had identified forty-four species. The birds found west of the Rockies are quite different from those east of the mountains.

I had an interesting experience one evning in the early spring of 1920 when I was invited to accompany one of the Senior students, John Murdock, who had been invited to preach in a Gospel Mission Hall in San Francisco. John was a Scotsman and had served in the Canadian army during World War I. For a time he served at Ypres, a Flemish town in Belgium, which became the center of one of the most hotly contested places in World War I.

The Superintendent of the Gospel Mission was accustomed to do some street preaching before the service began in his hall. He took John and me with him. We stood at the intersection of a busy corner where a parade of men flowed back and forth before us. I was not cut out to be a street preacher and felt uncomfortable even though I was not called upon to say anything. As I recall, the hall could seat nearly 100 and was well filled — all men. Many of these were derelicts. I wonder now how they managed to live before Social Security was started.

John Murdock gave the principal talk of the evening and he was good. Seated on the front row was a stockily built Swede who seemed to take a special interest in John. Following the service, he approached John and said: "I have seen you before." The two compared notes. Both had been in the Canadian army and both had been in one of the battles which swirled around Ypres, but John had no memory of ever seeing the Swede before. I overheard the following conversation:

The Swede: "I remember now. Do you remember when in battle two Germans came after you? One had a fixed bayonet and was lunging at you; the other was swinging his gun around his head like a club."

"I remember," said John. "I got the one with the bayonet but the other fellow hit me and knocked me unconscious."

"I got him," said the Swede, "and then I picked you up and carried you to a dressing station."

The two had never met again until they met there in that Gospel Mission Hall. John was such a mild-spirited fellow that it was hard to imagine him shooting another human being even in battle and in order to save his life.

My diary shows that on Sunday, March 28, 1920, a group of about eighty Student Volunteers (i.e., those who were planning to go out as foreign missionaries if the way opened) from various Presbyterian churches of the Bay Area paid a visit to the Seminary at San Anselmo. I was a member of the reception committee to guide them around the grounds. Among the visitors was Miss Miriam Leyrer, who in November 1922 became my wife. Neither of us have any clear memory of meeting the other on this occasioon. It was only months later that on comparing notes, I learned that she was one of the group that visited San Anselmo.

What about my expenses? I kept detailed financial records for the first two years in seminary. According to these records, my total cost from the time I arrived in San Anselmo in September 1919 to the following April was $312.00. The seminary then did not charge tuition but did ask for a $25.00 a year payment for room rent. We students had a cooperative dining club which provided board which averaged about $20.00 a month. We hired our own cook. The earthquake of 1906 had damaged the fireplace flues, so the seminary had installed small heating stoves in each room. Each student had to go to the basement and carry coal to his room. I spent $180.00 for books during my first year.

I began the school year with about $200.00. My income included a $50.00 scholarship from the Army YMCA, and two $100.00 scholarships, one from the Seminary and one from the Board of Christian Education. I drew $190.00 from the balance left in my father's estate which had come to me, after I had paid my brother $3,000.00 for an investment in land. The balance came from a variety of sources. The fact that I was always skirting the very edge of personal bankruptcy, somehow, did not give me any great concern. Financially, I believe that I was somewhat better off than most of my fellow students.

A Lumber Camp Missionary — Summer, 1920

Even as medical students serve an internship before being licensed to practice their profession, so Presbyterian theological students of my generation had to spend their summer vacations in some church activity. A few of the students of the seminary when I was there served small churches; others worked under the direction of senior pastors in larger churches; and a few, including myself during the summer of 1920, were assigned to some special mission project under the Board of National Missions. During the month of March, the Seminary received a request from the Synod of Washington for two students for summer work. The Board of Missions promised to pay all travel expenses and give a salary of $125.00 a month out of which the students were to pay their own living expenses. Rex Louch, a member of my class in the Seminary, and I volunteered to go.

The Seminary held its commencement on Thursday, April 29, and I left by train for Portland, Oregon, that evening. Having been invited by my college friend, Walter Benthin, who was then serving as pastor of the Presbyterian Church at Parkdale, near Hood River, in central Oregon, to spend a weekend with him and his wife, I made the excursion to Parkdale before reporting at Seattle. It was Benthin who, in my first year at Buena Vista, when he was a senior and I a freshman, presented the challenge of the ministry to me. His wife, Ada, was also a graduate of Buena Vista.

I spent three days with them and preached for Benthin at one of his several services on Sunday, May 2. Benthin took me to see one of the great lava flows which had poured out of Mt. Hood when it had erupted long ago. We took hikes through the tall timber and ate lunches by a rushing mountain stream. All in all, this was a delightful four-day vacation.

I was back in Portland by noon, May 4, and the next morning Louch and I took the train for Seattle. There we reported to Mr. Keeeler, the Synod's representative of the Presbyterian Board of National Missions. He then told us where each of us was to serve. Louch was to go to Cle Elum where he was to take charge of a small church which at the time had no pastor. I was assigned to a field in the Skagit River Valley where I was to itinerate among some nine lumber and construction camps which employed about 400 men. My field stretched for nearly sixty miles along the Skagit River and some of its tributaries. My main mode of transportation was walking.

The city of Seattle was then constructing Diablo Dam on the Skagit near the mouth of Ruby Creek. This was to supply the city with hydro-electric power. The new dam was located about sixty miles, as the crow would fly, east of Bellingham, Washington. When I arrived on the field, a construction crew was busy building a road to the site. The only means of access was over a trail that skirted the river bank.

On Thursday afternoon, May 6, I met the Rev. Hugh Armstrong, pastor of the Presbyterian Church at Concrete located near the end of the railroad that led up through the Skagit River Valley. Armstrong was to give me further indoctrination as to my field and my duties. Mr. Armstrong and I left by train for Concrete on Friday afternoon at 5:00 p.m., arriving there at 9:00 o'clock. I noted in my diary that for the last twenty minutes of our ride we could see forest fires burning to the north of us.

I spent the weekend with the Armstrongs, gradually being informed as to the nature of my work. On Sunday afternoon we took the train to Rockport, which was the end of the line and about eight miles from Concrete. Armstrong had been holding services in a schoolhouse there from time to time. On this day I delivered the sermon. About twenty-five were present. I repeated the sermon that evening in the log church in Concrete.

I gradually became aware that my field would include two groups — first the men in the lumber and construction camps, and then the scattered communities which consisted largely of men who worked in the lumber industry with their families. Armstrong warned me about the men in the larger construction camps who might belong to the International Workers of the World, then usually referred to as I.W.W.s or Wobblies. They were communistic in their outlook and anti-Christian. They had small red backed song books which contained parodies on gospel songs and were sung to gospel tunes. To a Christian, such songs were often blasphemous in their contents.

Armstrong told me how in one camp in another area, when a missionary handed out a copy of the Gospel of John, one Wobbly tore it into pieces and exclaimed: "If I were present at the crucifixion of Christ, I would have driven in another nail." In another instance, when a missionary was leading a worship service late one evening when he needed a light, one of the men drew his revolver and shot out the light. Such stories put me on my guard, although I never met such pronounced opposition in any of the camps I visited.

On Tuesday, May 11, Mr. Armstrong took me to find a place where I could stay. Either by private or hired conveyance, we went six miles beyond the end of the railroad at Rockport and called at the farm home of Mr. and Mrs. Oliver Trudell. Mr. Trudell was a French-Canadian and a Catholic. His wife was a New England woman and a Protestant. They had one son, Fred, about twenty years old. The Trudells lived on a small farm which included an orchard of cherry trees and berry bushes. At first they were reluctant to receive me into their home for the summer months but finally consented. I was to pay for only the meals when I was present and my records show that I was away about one-half of the time. I used a small upstairs room where I had complete privacy.

My baggage consisted of a steamer trunk which contained some books and an army pup tent which I had gotten from the surplus army supply depot while at Ft. Des Moines; two army blankets; an army mess kit; and a small portable typewriter. My diary shows that I kept up my Greek studies during available time, often reading forty or fifty verses from my Greek New Testament at one time. There were days when Mr. Trudell needed help in the fields, especially during the threshing season, and I turned to. I also helped his wife by picking bing cherries and berries. I could not have found a more congenial place to live and a strong bond of affection grew up between us so that when I left on September 3rd to return to my seminary, I found it hard to say goodby.

On Friday, I began my work by walking the four miles to Marblemount and calling on the few scattered homes in that settlement. I invited all to attend a church service I intended to conduct the following Sunday in the local schoolhouse. On Saturday I walked another ten miles calling on homes in the general area, inviting them to the church service. On Sunday, only five children came to the Sunday School. I persisted and the next week, the attendance rose to twelve and then in the week following to twenty-one. The knowledge that these children had of the basic facts of Christianity was zero.

I started out on my first trip up the Skagit River on Tuesday, May 18th. Since I planned to be away two days and not knowing whether I would have a bed in some camp that night, I took with me in my knapsack, my pup tent, two army blankets, my mess kit and a few items of food. My pack weighed 30 pounds, far too heavy for a hike of thirty or forty miles. After this experience, I never took my pup tent with me again but did take my blankets for I never knew if I could get vermin free blankets in the camps where I might spend the night.

I visited seven camps on this trip but had only two opportunities to speak with a total attendance of 45. Sometimes I was able to hold a service in the mess hall following the evening meal. At other times we met out-of-doors with the men sitting on logs. I always had to speak without notes. On the whole, I was given a good reception on this, my first, attempt to preach to the men in the construction camps. I noted in my diary on Saturday, May 22: "I walked 86 miles, minus a few where I got a ride, during my first nine days here." I also noted that the work in the camp worried me for it was so difficult to get the men together for a religious service.

On Friday, May 21, I visited the Clark settlement, across the Skagit River and on the Cascade River, a tributary of the Skagit. I was able to cross the Skagit at Marblemount by ferry but then had to walk up a trail along the Cascade to where a large tree had fallen across the river which was used as a bridge, and then down the other side. This meant a three-mile detour. The Clark settlement consisted of three cabins with some seventeen residents covering three generations. It was so remote that the children had not been to school for two years. I heard that Mr. Clark, the patriarch of the clan, was a moonshiner. He hailed from North Carolina.

Here I remember, I was given a royal welcome. They rarely had visitors. I was served fresh trout from the mountain stream which flowed nearby. The cabin was made out of bare boards — floor, walls, and ceiling. In the evening, Mr. Clark called his ten children and their children together. My coming was a great event in their lives. That evening I told the story of Jesus Christ in as simple terms as possible. After the service, Mr. Clark kept me up rather late telling me "bar" stories. I returned to the Trudells the next day after promising that I would return to the Clarks.

On Tuesday, May 24th, I packed my blankets and mess outfit for my trip to a shingle bolt camp on Bacon Creek located about eight miles from one of the construction camps on the Skagit. The shingle bolts were cut out of cedar trees about thirty inches long. These then were put in the creek and carried by the stream into the Skagit and thence to a sawmill at Sauk, a community about two miles below Rockport. There the cedar bolts would be cut into cedar shake shingles.

I caught a ride with the mailman as far as Marblemount and then hiked the remaining five miles to a construction camp which I had visited the week before. I was invited to take my noon meal there, after which I was able to give a short talk with about twenty-five men in my audience.

I then started the long eight mile walk up the trail along Bacon Creek to the shingle bolt camp. I wrote in my diary: "It was certainly a long and lonely tramp. The scenery was beautiful and woods grand. But it got lonesome and the pack grew heavier and heavier."

When I arrived at the camp, the foreman greeted me civilly but explained that the men in the camp were not much interested in religion. At least five of them had their wives and children with them, each living in a small cabin. That evening I had twenty men present and five women. There were no I.W.W.s in this camp and I was treated kindly. I wrote that evening in my diary: "I felt greatly encouraged and believe that my message fell on good ground." I was given a cordial invitation to return.

While in this camp, I became aware that the woods were full of bears and that sometimes a mother bear with a cub could be very dangerous. One large old she-bear had chased several of the men of the camp back into the camp. The stories of their experiences made me nervous. For over a week I had tramped the trails of the area without fear, but now I began to be fearful. During my months in the field, I never carried a gun.

After hearing so many bear stories, I felt hesitant to make the long eight-mile hike back to the main trail alone. Instead I waited until a pack train was ready to go and then I went with it. This gave me an opportunity to ride a horse most of the way.

Since I had promised to return to the Clark settlement on Friday, May 28, I started about 3:00 p.m. on Friday to make my seven mile hike to that place. First I had to go to Marblemount and then take a small ferry across the swiftly flowing Skagit River to the other side. I recall having some feelings of apprehension as I stepped ashore on the other side and watched the ferryman return. I knew that there was no chance to return by ferry that day as the ferryman would not be on duty. Ahead of me was a three mile walk through the "bar" country so vividly described by Mr. Clark on my former visit. I also recalled the bear stories I had heard a few days earlier at the shingle bolt camp on Bacon Creek. I dreaded my three mile hike which lay before me but there was no alternative.

I hastened up the trail that followed the Cascade River. I passed the point where I could see the roofs of the buildings in the Clark settlement. About one-quarter of a mile beyond that point, I was startled to hear what I described in my diary to be "some snarling and growling in the woods" behind some bushes a little ahead of me. I froze in my tracks. I listened to make sure that I was not mistaken. When the growling was repeated, I turned and began running down the trail as fast as I could.

I remember asking some old timers what I should do if I met an angry bear and was told to climb a small tree. A bear cannot climb a tree when it has to overlap its paws. So as I went down the trail, I looked for a small tree. I never saw one. The forest was full of big trees.

I ran until I came to the place where I could see the roofs of the Clark buildings. I then sat down and contemplated my predicament. I dared not go up the trail again on my way to the tree that spanned the river, for there was a bear or something there which I did not want to meet. I could not cross the Skagit. I was stranded. Ahead of me was the Cascade River, about thirty feet wide, which carried the ice-cold waters from the melting snows in the high Cascade Mountains. There was nothing for me to do but to wade the river. I picked out what I thought was a shallow place but it turned out that the center of the river was nearly hip deep. I removed my shoes and slung them around my neck. That was a mistake for my feet got so cold that I could not find footing on the slippery stones. I made another mistake in not finding a stick to help me keep my balance.

Finally, I mustered up courage and entered the river. Later I wrote in my diary: "The clearness of the water deceived me as to its depth, and where I didn't think it would reach my knees, I found that it went over them. And the water was swift. Only a few steps taken and I realized the size of my task. The stones were slippery and round.

The water was so cold that my feet became numb. The swiftness of the water was too much for me for it swept me off my feet. Down I went and I began using my hands."

With not more than my head sticking out of the rushing water, I heard a shout from the bank I had just left. "Looking up hastily," I later wrote in my diary, "wondering who could be there, I saw a man on horseback watching me." He was a forest ranger who just happened to be riding by. My diary account continues: "I climbed out on the other side, my feet bleeding in a couple of places. I felt rather chagrined that any should have seen me in such a predicament."

The ranger wanted to know if I was all right and I assured him that I was. I didn't want to admit that I had tried wading the Cascade River because I thought there was a bear on my trail ahead of me.

Almost — there was no autobiography.

I made my way to the Clark home and, after taking off as many articles of clothing as was decent and putting them out to dry, I stood near a heating stove and gradually dried out. I was treated to another trout dinner that evening and, as usual, had most of the Clark family out to hear me read from the Bible and explain the Christian story. I spent the night there and returned without incident to Trudell's the next day.

Upon my return, Fred Trudell asked me: "I heard that you tried to swim the Cascade."

"Who told you?" I asked.

According to my diary, Fred then replied: "Oh, the forest ranger. He saw you when you were in the water up to your chin. He said that if you were the preacher and had nerve enough to wade that river, that he guessed he'd like to hear you preach."

One of the old timers at Marblemount told me: "Jesus walked on the water but you had better not try it."

When I explained what I heard to Mr. Clark and to Mr. Trudell, both, according to my diary, said "the growling was no doubt that of an old she-bear." According to my first monthly report submitted to the Board of National Missions, I traveled 163 miles during the last half of May, most of which I walked.

My monthly reports show that June was my busiest month for in that month I visited ten camps, and traveled 274 miles, most of this by walking. On June 9, I returned to the shingle bolt camp on Bacon Creek. The camp was not large, less than 30 men but all were out for my service. "They paid me the most respectful attention," I wrote in my diary, "and I felt greatly encouraged." On my return trip to the main trail which led to the construction camps, I noted how I had been followed on my way to the camp by a cougar or mountain lion.

I had walked across a marshy place on my way back, I noted that a cougar's tracks had been superimposed on my tracks of the day before. This was not a dangerous situation for a cougar would not attack a human being unless in self-defense.

I met with some antagonism in one of the construction camps I visited on June 17. I knew the attitude of the men and dreaded going there. I made my announcement to about 80 men who were at supper. About fifty men came out to hear me. I gave my talk which lasted for about thirty minutes and then I was heckled. I quote now from my diary. "One said, 'The Bible is the rottenest book God ever wrote.'" Another asked: "Who was Christ's father?" They asked me how much I was making and if the rich capitalists were paying me. I quote from my diary: "They brought up all of the mistakes of the Catholic Church. They were ready to laugh if they thought they had me puzzled. For an hour and a half they kept me." After it was over, a young man came to me and said: "Don't let those fellows worry you. They are foreigners and don't know what they believe." I noted in my diary that many of the men in the construction camps were Swedes and Serbians. The latter group came out of an Eastern Catholic background and were anti-church.

At the end of this day, I was ready to go back to San Anselmo. I was convinced that no converts were ever won to Christianity through arguments.

With the exception of the shingle bolt camp on Bacon Creek, where I was always given a warm welcome, I found that my services were most appreciated in the scattered mill towns where I could meet not only with the mill hands themselves but also with their wives and children. On Saturday, June 26, I visited the sawmill town of Sauk where I was invited to supper in one of the homes. Everything was neat and clean but it was evident that the family was poor. They had only two chairs. The children sat on soap boxes. I was given one of the chairs at supper time.

On Sunday, June 27, I conducted a service in the hotel at Sauk with twenty-six present. Afterwards, I walked five and one-half miles to Van Horn where I conducted another worship service. And after that, I walked to Concrete and stayed with the Armstrongs over the weekend. That evening I attended Armstrong's church and noted in my diary that it was the first sermon I had heard for two months.

On Thursday, July 1, I left for a sawmill camp on the Skagit River, eighteen miles from Trudell's. This camp had about 90 men. I walked the entire distance except for a ride that I got for the last two miles. I arrived at 5:00 p.m. I made the announcement for a service at the evening meal and thirty men stayed for that. Here for the first time in my summer's experience, several volunteered to take charge of the singing. I am not a singer and usually had to conduct services without the benefit of music. But now I had some singers who wanted to help out. I had with me copies of some gospel songs. "It was a great inspiration to me," I wrote in my diary, "to hear those big rough men sing the songs I knew and loved." I met several in this camp who were Christians and they expressed appreciation for my coming. This made me feel that my ministry there was indeed worthwhile.

I returned to the Clark settlement on July 6 and several times later before going back to the Seminary, fortunately without any more bear scares. In these visits to that isolated family, I am sure that I gave some of them instructions into the Christian faith that they otherwise would never have had.

The big event of the summer for me was the chance to attend a conference of lumber camp missionaries which met at Spokane, July 10-11, with sixteen in attendance. This was followed by a meeting of the Synod of Washington at Coeur d'Alene, Idaho, July 13-17. The Synod paid the expenses of both Rex Louch and myself to attend. Only five of the sixteen were giving full time to the lumber camp work. The others were pastors who gave part time. I was the youngest of those present and was made secretary.

The lumber camp missionary conference met on Saturday afternoon and again on Sunday afternoon. Each person told of his work and we shared our problems. I learned that 70% of the lumber camp missionaries of the Presbyterian Church were working in the Synod of Washington. This phase of national missions work now seems to have been discontinued. The introduction of good roads and automobiles seem to have eliminated the isolated lumber camps.

The Synod of Washington, which included northern Idaho, met in the First Presbyterian Church of Coeur d' Alene on Tuesday, July 13. I was asked to present the work of the lumber camp missionaries before Synod and was allowed fifteen minutes for this. I was introduced as the "kid lumber-jack." Just before speaking, Mr. Armstrong put me on the spot by crying out: "Tell about how you swam the Cascade River." I majored on the humorous aspects of that experience. "One moment I had all laughing," I wrote that evening in my diary, "and then I quickly changed and told of my visit to the camp which was filled with I.W.W.s who were opposed to Christianity."

Since northern Idaho was then included within the bounds of the Synod of Washington, there would have been some representatives from the Nez Perce churches present, including several of the Nez Perce Presbyterian pastors. At that time, I knew practically nothing of the Presbyterian mission work among the Nez Perces. It was not until 1928, when I became pastor of the First Presbyterian Church of Moscow, Idaho, that I really became interested in the Nez Perce history. I do remember that when Synod met at Coeur d'Alene, we were told that the eldest daughter of Henry and Eliza Spalding, also called Eliza, who was born at Lapwai on November 15, 1837, had died at Coeur d'Alene on June 21, 1919, just about a year and a month before the Synod met in the same city.

I returned to Trudells on Saturday afternoon, July 17, and I noted in my diary: "It was a relief to land in my little room again." On Sunday I returned to Marblemount to conduct the Sunday School. Ten were present including three adults. On Wednesday, I left for the shingle bolt camp on Bacon Creek and, although I went with the pack train, I had to walk — altogether — eighteen miles from Trudells. The people in the camp had come to know me and were genuinely glad to see me. "Why were you not here long before?" they asked. I had 100% attendance that night for my service. The next morning when I left, I was asked: "When are you coming back?" The cordial reception given me at this camp made me feel good. My work was worthwhile.

The day after I had returned from the shingle bolt camp, or on July 22, I set out for a railroad construction camp about eight miles distant. I went out of a sense of duty for I dreaded trying to preach the gospel to an antagonistic audience. I got to the camp in time to eat supper with them and at the tables I made the announcement of the service. There were forty men in the camp; twenty-six attended the service. Several days previous, when I made the arrangments to speak there, some of the men asked me to speak on "The Wage System and the Teachings of Christ." I did not feel competent to discuss the inequities of the economic system which then existed, so spoke only briefly about the Biblical statement that the laborer was worthy of his hire. I then turned to the spiritual aspects of the subject using the text found in Romans 6:23: "The wages of sin is death." Some of the men, evidently dissatisfied, got up and left the meeting.

After I had finished speaking, I was bombarded with questions: "Who made God?" "Convert the capitalists and then we will join your religion." "Why does God permit suffering?" When I urged the importance of applying Christian principles to settle labor disputes, one man said: "We'll use a gun first and then talk religion."

After the meeting was over, I happened to meet a lad, perhaps in his late teens, who was washing his face in the river. We had privacy and there we talked about the importance of accepting Christ. I asked him if he were a Christian. That evening, when summarizing the events of the day in my diary, I wrote that he said to me: "No one ever asked me that question before." I felt that although I may have made no impression upon the twenty-six men who heard me speak in the mess hall, perhaps the opportunity of bringing that young man face to face with the decision of being a Christian was the big event of the day. I will never know until the judgment day if that conversation with the lad on the river bank resulted in a decision on his part or not.

When I got back to Trudell's that day, I felt nervous and, as I noted in my diary, "limp as a dish rag." I also noted, "Through the grace of God, I did not falter while I faced those men for that long hour. But when I reached my room, I felt weak. My landlady fixed me a cup of tea and a little cake that took the place of the supper I had missed. Her kindness touched me."

This was the last camp I visited in July. The rest of the month was spent in visiting the sawmill communities. In each of these, I was received with cordiality, even affection. Private homes vied with one another for the privilege of entertaining me over night. During the last week of July, I joined a party of friends who went on a fishing expedition up the Skagit. In a way, this was my vacation. My report to the Board of National Missions for July shows that I traveled 135 miles on the field, most of which I walked. The total was reduced because of the week's trip to Spokane and Coeur d'Alene.

During the month of August, my last on the field, I reported traveling 249 miles, again practically all the way on foot. I often walked eighteen miles a day, and sometimes in the rain. I held services in three camps during August. On the 3rd, I visited the Gorge Creek camp where fourteen men out of twenty attended my service. That day I covered twenty-two miles, seventeen of which I walked, carrying a ten-pound pack.

The next day I visited the Seattle city's sawmill camp where twenty-five out of eighty men attended. I noted in my diary that "Mr. Udhen and some of the big bosses from the city were present and I hesitated to hold a service but went ahead anyway." This was the camp where I had the assistance of some young men to lead the singing, among whom were some students from the University of Washington. They expressed real regret when told that this was my last visit to that camp.

Here is my diary entry for Thursday, August 5: "Today was a hard day. I covered twenty-four miles on foot and the day was warm as any that they have up here. I was on the trail at 6:40 and made eighteen miles before dinner at Trudells. I failed to get any breakfast along the line and had only four cookies to go on. My feet were both tired and sore when I reached Trudells." I had promised to go to the Clark settlement that evening. "This was to be my last visit and I felt that I had to go, so after resting for two hours I started out on my seven mile hike to the Clark settlement." I continued telling them the story of Christ. I spent the night there, returning to Trudells the next morning.

About three weeks later, I met one of the young men from the Clark settlement. Of this meeting I noted in my diary: "Met Dolph Clark. He was somewhat under the influence of moonshine — but still sober enough to wish me success. 'I hope to meet you in the land to come,' he said. 'We have sure appreciated your coming over to us.'" Such words of appreciation meant much to me.

After returning from the Clark settlement on Friday morning, August 6th, I stayed at Trudells only long enough to make preparations to spend the weekend at Sauk with the Armstrongs. Looking back, I feel that my work with the community people was one of the most rewarding aspects of my summer's work. Saturday was given over to a Sunday School picnic at Sauk. I was a guest in one of the homes there that night and on Sunday conducted a worship service in the schoolhouse. I noted that about thirty attended. I then took charge of the service at Rockport in the afternoon, after which I went by train to Concrete where I was entertained by the Armstrongs.

On Monday morning, August 9, I was ready to return to Trudells, but Mr. Armstrong persuaded me to accompany him, his wife, and young son, perhaps eight years old, on an excursion to Baker Lake, eighteen miles up Baker River from its mouth on Skagit River. I had never hiked this trail before. We took a lunch with us and arrived at a shingle bolt camp, nine miles from our starting point, in time for supper. Mr. Armstrong led a worship service for men of the camp that evening. It was a unique experience for me to be one of the audience. After the service, an old man who said he was 75 years old, called me to his cabin. He claimed that he was the only Christian in the camp and was overjoyed to talk with another who was also a Christian.

The next day we hiked the remaining nine miles to Baker Lake where there was a U.S. fish hatchery. We arrived before noon and were invited to stay for dinner. Mt. Baker, 11,000 feet high, shown in all its glory and spendor. We moved on from the fish hatchery to another lumber camp where we spent the night. Near the camp was a hot spring with water about 110°. I ventured to take a bath in it. I was told that the temperature remains about the same winter and summer. Mr. Armstrong led in a worship service at the lumber camp that evening, and I spoke briefly.

Although the Armstrongs urged me to stay with them, I felt an urgency to return. So on Wednesday morning, August 11, I mounted one of the pack horses and went down with the pack train. We took lunch at the nine-mile camp and again I met the old Christian lumber-jack. He was delighted to see me, and again we knelt in prayer by the side of the soapbox chairs in his rude cabin. I finished my eighteen-mile trip late in the afternoon in time to take the evening train from Concrete to Sauk where I spent the night with one of the families which had entertained me before.

After breakfast the next morning, I started out on foot for Trudells, nine miles distant. I slept in my bed for the first time in ten nights. A forest fire was burning nearby leaving a pall of smoke in the valley so thick one could not see the distant mountains.

Sunday, August 15, was a busy day. It began with my Sunday School in Marblemount with fourteen present. This was the largest attendance of the summer. I then walked back to Trudells and on to Rockport where I had an audience of fifteen. Altogether I walked twenty miles that day. I was counting the days when I could return to San Anselmo.

On Wednesday, August 18, I made another visit to the shingle bolt camp on Bacon Creek. I missed the pack train and had to walk the full nine miles. When I first visited this camp on May 14, the foreman gave me little encouragement. He said that the men there were not interested in religion, and yet it was in that camp where I always received my warmest welcome. On this, my last visit, all eighteen men in the camp were present.

Since I was planning to leave for San Anselmo about September 1, the secretaries of the National Missions office in Seattle selected a Rev. Mr. Peterson to carry on the work I had started. Peterson came to Rockport on August 20 and I took him over part of the field. I was pleased to know that my work would be continued but time proved that he was not able to do what I had been doing.

I conducted three services on Sunday, August 22 — at Sauk with twenty present; then at Van Horn with the same number; and lastly at Concrete when I preached for Mr. Armstrong in the evening.

I spent the following week at Trudells, working on my farewell sermon. I also assisted Mr. Trudell several days with his threshing. On Friday, August 27, I noted in my diary that Mr. Trudell expressed his regret at the thought of my leaving. "You're all right," he said. "You did the right thing up here. Some of the folks on this flat wished now that they had come out and listened to you. They all respect you now and if you came back, they would turn out. I have never heard anyone speak ill of you."

On Sunday, August 29, I visited Marblemount for the last time and held a service for the eight people who attended. Had to walk the four and one-half miles each way in the rain. I said goodby to the Trudells on Friday, September 3, and left for Concrete.

I sponsored a picnic at Sauk on Saturday, the 4th. Forty-eight were present — everybody in the community except the men at work in the mills. My last Sunday on the field was spent at Sauk. Twenty-five attended my service. I then walked six miles to Van Horn where I held a service in the afternoon with only a few present. Then on to Concrete where I preached my farewell service that Sunday evening.

On Monday, I bade the Armstrongs goodby and took the 10:00 o'clock morning train for Bellingham. My "tour of duty" as a lumber camp missionary was over. It was a hard assignment. My monthly reports show that for the four months on duty, I covered 819 miles, almost entirely by foot. By the time my service was over, I was eager to return to San Anselmo.

Having been in touch with my classmate, Rex Louch, we decided to return to sea. We boarded the S.S. Queen at Seattle on September 9 which brought us into San Francisco Bay late Saturday evening, the 11th. On Sunday morning, Rex and I returned to San Anselmo. I wrote in my diary that the place looked like "a little paradise" to me. With a heart full of gratitude, I settled myself in my room.

My Second Year at San Anselmo, 1920-1921

San Francisco Theological Seminary entered its semi-centennial year with the largest enrollment if its history which totaled seventy-eight, an increase of nineteen over that of the previous year. Many of the Juniors were veterans of World War I. Among the Juniors were several men of great promise with whom I formed a lifelong friendship. These included Harold Clark, Henry McFadden, and Donald G. Stewart. Stewart, best known to his friends by his initials, D.G., is now one of my neighbors here at Monte Vista Grove Homes where we both live in retirement.

Classes began on Friday, September 17. I signed up for nineteen hours. By this time I was aware that the faculty each year selected the top student of the Senior class to receive the Alumni Fellowship, consisting of $600.00, with the expectation that this student would use the money to go to some foreign school, as the University of Edinburgh, for advanced studies. I resolved to work to get that scholarship. I threw myself into my studies with enthusiasm.

After returning from the summer's field work, I quickly resumed the routine of the Seminary. I got out for soccer football and played full-back in the games.

The most important extra-curricular activity in which I was engaged during my second year in Seminary was the teaching of a Bible class in San Quentin prison. This prison was located about six miles from the Seminary. I could take the electric train to San Rafael and would then walk the remaining two or three miles to the prison.

I was invited by the chaplain of the prison to teach a class which met in the prison's library each Saturday afternoon. The chaplain was not able to offer any remuneration. I accepted the invitation feeling that this experience would be valuable and that perhaps I could give some spiritual help to the prisoners. The chaplain emphasized to me that he wanted me to major on instruction rather than on preaching. This was agreeable to me for I have always felt that in my sermons I was more of a teacher than a preacher.

I held my first class on Saturday afternoon, October 16. I still remember the chill which spiraled up and down my spine when the big steel gates clanked shut behind me on my first entrance into the prison. Only twenty-five were present for that first class, but by December, up to 200 were in attendance. The average attendance for the six months period was about 60. The attendance would be larger on rainy days for then the men could not play baseball.

One of the members of the class was a cartoonist and often he would illustrate a verse or passage which would be in the following week's lesson. Once knowing that I was to give an exposition of Matthew 7, my cartoonist friend majored on the 14th verse which, in the King James version, reads: "Because strait is the gate and narrow the way which leadeth to life and few there be that find it." The cartoonist drew a fanciful picture of the path a Christian must follow.

The cartoon began on the left side of the paper with a narrow gate. Leading from it was a crooked path that wound up and down hills and around obstacles until it finally ended at a beautiful city on a hill, placed on the right side of the picture.

One of the members of the class, after seeing the picture, said: "The Bible says that we must follow a straight and narrow path and you have made it a crooked one." Actually, the verse in Matthew says that the gate was "strait" and the way "narrow." My cartoonist friend then replied pointing out the fact that there are two words in the English language which are pronounced alike but have very different meanings. These words are "strait" and "straight." The first word is used in "strait-jacket," and my audience knew the meaning of that. The second word describes the shortest distance between two points. According to the text from Matthew, we enter the Christian life through a "strait" gate which calls for repentance and faith. Our pathway then is often crooked, winding in and out of the difficulties of life but it must follow a "strait" channel. I learned a lesson that day which I have never forgotten.

The time came after six months for me to give up the class. By that time I had come to know and respect many of the prisoners. I remember one middle-aged man who one day arose in my class and said: "I thank God for the day I was sent to San Quentin for it was here that I found my Savior, my Christ."

Before leaving my class, I distributed 4 x 5 inch cards to those present and requested each to write a short message to young men which I could use in my church work. I remember that several wrote to the effect: "Tell the young people to learn how to say NO!" One wrote: "If I had known how to say NO to the temptations which friends presented to me, I would not be here today."

When the day came to say goodby, I found it hard to do so. Through the six months that I had been going to the prison, I formed some strong bonds of affection for some of the men.

On New Year's Day, 1921, I called on my New Testament professor, Dr. E. A. Wicher at his cottage located on a bluff overlooking the Pacific Ocean at Bolinas in Marin County. I quote from my diary: "We sat on a bench overlooking the ocean and I brought up some of my hopes. His words of advice helped me to crystalize my dreams. I resolve now to aim for a chair in the Seminary such as that which he now occupies." Dr. Wicher warned me that this would mean postgraduate study at some European University. "God willing," I wrote in my diary, "I am going to work for that."

I never had a teacher who inspired me as much as Dr. Wicher. He led me to dream dreams and see visions. He wanted me to become a Greek scholar, but I was no linguist. Church history captured my attention, but his dream of me becoming a member of the Seminary faculty at San Anselmo came true. When I began my professorship of Church History at San Anselmo in the fall of 1938, Dr. Wicher was still active on the faculty.

In those days, the Presbyterian Church required its candidates for the ministry to be licensed near or at the end of their second year in seminary and then ordination came the following year. Wishing to be licensed and ordained by the Presbytery of San Francisco, I found that it was necessary for me to change my church membership from the church in Storm Lake, Iowa, to one within the bounds of San Francisco Presbytery. After some investigation, I selected the First Presbyterian Church of Berkeley, over which Dr. Lapsley McAfee then served as pastor. This was one of the best decisions I ever made in my life. Among the members of this church was Miriam Leyrer who became my wife in November 1922. As will be explained, the fact that I became the assistant pastor of this church in April 1922 qualified me to be called to be pastor of the American Community Church in Shanghai, China, in the early weeks of 1923.

Having become a member of a church within the bounds of San

Francisco Presbytery, and having fulfilled other requirements, I was licensed by the Presbytery of San Francisco at a meeting held in Old First Church in San Francisco on March 8, 1921. I wrote in my diary: "The ceremony was simple, but deeply impressive. How I wish that my Mother could have been present."

A few days after I was licensed, Dr. Wicher asked me if I would be willing to serve as supply minister for the Bolinas Presbyterian Church during the coming summer. This was a small church with only about 20 members and the stipend was only $70.00 a month. Dr. Wicher said that if I accepted the call, I could use a small room in the church for my bedroom and since it had a stove, I could cook my meals there. In addition to the local resident members, many who spent the summer in Bolinas likewise attended the church.

Dr. Wicher stressed the point that if I accepted the call, he would tutor me in the Greek New Testament. He dangled before my eyes the possibility of a special archaeological scholarship given by a society of which he was a member. I was still mindful of the annual Alumni scholarship granted by the Seminary each year to one member of the Senior class which had a stipend of $600.00. A second scholarship would have permitted me to spend two years abroad in study. The prospect of being tutored by Dr. Wicher for the archaeological scholarship was so alluring that I told Dr. Wicher I would take the Bolinas church for the summer of 1921.

This was the year that the Seminary celebrated its semi-centennial. Dr. Bird wrote the script for a pageant which told the story of John Knox. Plans were made to present this pageant at commencement week in April 1921. All of the students were involved in one way or another. I was given the responsibility of renting costumes from a theatrical firm in San Francisco. Also, I became the business manager of a Seminary Year Book which was sponsored by the student body. Because of the excessive amount of practicing needed to prepare the pageant for presentation, the faculty on April 12 voted to eliminate all examinations. The pageant was presented on Saturday, April 23. According to my diary about 2,000 people were present. Commencement exercises were held on the following Thursday, April 28.

I kept a detailed record of all expenditures and receipts during my second year in seminary. The total expense for the months September to May, inclusive, came to $715.14.

The money spent included board, books, transportation, etc. I noted in my diary for February 2, 1921, that I bought a suit of clothes which cost $58.50, and I noted that "this was the highest price I had ever paid for a suit of clothes." My receipts included scholarships for $250.00 and $419.17 from my father's estate. This closed the estate account. I made nearly $60.00 as honorariums in preaching.

With the exhaustion of my share of my father's estate, I had no assured income for my Senior year than the $250.00 in scholarships provided by the Board of Christian Education and the Seminary. I knew that I could not save much if anything if I took the Bolinas Church for $70.00 a month. And yet, I have no recollection that I was alarmed over this lack of finances. I had faith to believe that somehow I would find the necessary funds, and I did.

CHAPTER TEN

A Time for Major Decisions

Between April 1921 and the end of January 1923, I had to make more major decisions which affected all of my following years more than in any other comparable period of my life. In April 1921, I accepted the call to be assistant pastor of the First Presbyterian Church of Berkeley, California; in July, when on a short vacation in the Yosemite National Park, I met Miriam Leyrer who became my wife on November 17, 1922; I was ordained into the Presbyterian ministry on March 19, 1922; and on January 30, 1923, I learned that the American Community Church of Shanghai, China, had extended a call to me to be its pastor.

On Wednesday, April 13, 1921, about two weeks before the seminary's commencement, I learned that the prestigious First Presbyterian Church of Berkeley, over which Dr. Lapsley McAfee presided as pastor, was considering asking me to be its assistant pastor. The possibility of receiving such a call put me in a quandry. I had already promised Dr. Wicher that I would take the small Bolinas church for the coming summer. "Unless I can be honorably released from that commitment," I wrote in my diary, "I cannot go to Berkeley."

I called on Dr. Wicher and asked if I could be released from my promise to take the Bolinas church. He recognized the fact that the Berkeley position was much bigger than that at Bolinas, yet he did not feel free to release me until I found someone to take my place. I canvassed the student body and finally found a fellow student who agreed to go to Bolinas. I was then free to accept the call from the Berkeley church. Looking back, I now realize that I would never have been called to the Shanghai church if I had not had nearly two years experience in the large Berkeley church.

On Sunday, April 17, I attended the morning service in the Berkeley church. I wrote that day in my diary: "I looked out over the audience and thought of myself standing there in the pulpit. At the very thought of such an opportunity and responsibility, cold shivers ran up and down my spine." The possibility of being the assistant pastor in that large church seemed somewhat overwhelming. I was then only 23 years old and had one more year's work in the seminary.

The sanctuary of First Church, now replaced by a modern building, then seated about 800 with accommodations for another 300 in the balcony which like a large "U" partly encircled the lower floor. Dr. McAfee was more of a pastor than a preacher. He was conservative in his theology and greatly loved by his people. Two services were held on Sunday, one at 11:00 in the morning and the other at 7:30 in the evening.

In those days before the construction of three bridges which now span the Bay, I had to spend at least two hours to make the trip from San Anselmo to Berkeley. I first took the electric train from San Anselmo to Sausalito; then the ferry to San Francisco; then another ferry to Oakland; and then a street car to the heart of Berkeley. This meant a four-hour round trip.

On Sunday, April 24, the day after the presentation of the John Knox pageant, I returned to First Church, Berkeley, to be indoctrinated into my coming duties by my predecessor, the Rev. Earle Cochran, who had been called to the pulpit of the First Presbyterian Church of Alameda, California. In the course of my indoctrination, I learned that I was to be the Superintendent of a departmentalized Sunday School which had an average attendance of four or five hundred. I was ill prepared for such responsibility. I found that it was staffed by a fine group of competent and devoted people.

Earle Cochran also told me that I would be expected to conduct a Daily Vacation Bible School for several weeks during the summer. Again, this was something entirely new, for I had never seen such a school in action. Fortunately, the Presbyterian headquarters in San Francisco conducted some training sessions for those who expected to teach in such a school.

Earle also gave me advice regarding pulpit dress. The clergy in those days in First Church did not wear gowns, nor did the choir. Dr. McAfee wore a Prince Albert coat which came down to his knees. Earle wore a cut-away while in the pulpit and advised me to do likewise. Certainly I did not want to wear a Prince Albert. Even so, wearing a cut-away with striped trousers made me very self-conscious, especially when I left the church and appeared in the street. It became my custom to change clothes as soon as possible after the morning service.

As previously stated, the Seminary conducted its Commencement ceremonies on Thursday, April 28th. Dr. McAfee attended and sought me out for a private interview. We met in my dormitory room. I was so impressed by what he said to me that I took time to write a rather full account of our conversation in my diary. I quote now from that account.

Dr. McAfee probed into my dreams for my future. "Are you willing to be a little man?" he asked. I replied: "If I can best forward the Kingdom of God by occupying some humble position, then I am willing."

"No, that is not what I mean," he said. "Are you willing always to serve in a small capacity?" I then admitted that I aspired to make a mark in the world; to do big things for Christ and humanity.

Then in a fatherly manner, Dr. McAfee said: "Listen, my boy. There are one talent men and two talent men and five talent men. Now if what the students and faculty say about you is true — and they all seem to agree — then you are a five talent young man. Did you ever think of the fact that the Lord has made an investment in you and that you are to return dividends to Him on that investment? It is not conceit to strive for high places."

He then gave me some good advice regarding my position as the assistant pastor in his church. "When you come over this summer," he said, "the people will think of you as the assistant pastor even if technically you are not yet ordained. Don't try to correct any such opinions. If you think little of yourself, the people will think the same way. You are not to be my errand boy. I am going to leave you very much to your own initiative."

All through the nearly two years that I served with Dr. McAfee, he was a constant inspiration to me. I learned more pastoral theology from him than I had learned in the seminary. It was he who taught me how to visit the sick; how to conduct a funeral or a wedding, and how to work with the session and other church bodies. He taught me the fundamental principles of ministerial ethics. Repeatedly, in various ways, he stimulated me to believe in my own abilities and to dare to attempt great things for Christ and the church.

My Ministry in the Berkeley Church

My classmate, Rex Louch, who had served with me in a National Mission field in the State of Washington during the summer of 1920, was called to be pastor of Faith Chapel in West Berkeley. We decided to be roommates. We found agreeable accommodations in the home of Mrs. Harvey Chapman, who lived near First Church. Our room cost each of us $10.00 a month. Mrs. Chapman also provided board which came to about $25.00 a month. First Church paid me a salary of $124.00 a month with no allowance for travel. I had no car then but depended on street cars to do my calling. As I recall, Dr. McAfee's salary was only $5,000.00 a year out of which he paid his own house rent. Of course, he received many fees for funerals and weddings. He never accepted a funeral fee when the deceased was a member of his congregation.

My duties began on Sunday, May 1. The choir entered the sanctuary from two sides. Dr. McAfee led the procession for one side, and I from the other. I wrote that day in my diary: "What a wonderful day for me! As I mounted the pulpit platform and looked for the first time into the faces of that big congregation, a distinct thrill passed through me. How happy would I have been had my Mother been spared to see this day."

The average morning attendance, during the months I was with First Church, was about 1,100 and about 350 for the evening service. Included in these figures were several hundred University students who came to Berkeley from all over the state. A Christian Endeavor society for the college age young people, called the Calvin Club, met each Sunday evening with an average attendance of about 150. For the first time since my college days, I had opportunity to meet Christian young women of my age or a few years younger. After leaving college, I often had dates with girls but I had found no one whom I felt was the one I needed for a wife. Having completed my second year in seminary, I was becoming more and more aware of the need to find a life partner.

On Mother's Day, May 8, Dr. McAfee told me that he would like to have me take both services the following Sunday. I had a week to prepare. For the morning service, I preached on the atonement using for my subject: "The Gospel According to Christ." In the evening I told about the repentent David using for my text, Psalm 51:3; "For I know my transgressions and my sin is ever before me." About 1,200 were present for the morning service, and about 400 for the evening. The response I received at both services was most generous and this encouraged me. On June 26, I also took both services.

I started a Christian Endeavor Society for high school young people which began with about twenty members but soon we had fifty. Among the members were the Lawrence girls, ages about 15 and 16. Their father was an elder in the church. A friendship developed between us which has continued to this day. In adult life, both became active workers in the church. My Daily Vacation Bible School began on June 13 with seventy-five pupils. The attendance doubled within a week.

I was immersed with many activities. Sunday was the busy day with Sunday School, two church services, social hour at 5:00 p.m. for the college young people, and then two Christian Endeavor societies. The mid-week prayer meeting came on Wednesday evening. Friday evenings and sometimes Saturdays were given over to socials and picnics for various groups of young people. Then in addition was the calling on the sick and possible new members — there was no end to this. I had little time for study.

A Two Weeks Vacation in Yosemite

The Presbyterian Synod of California held its annual meeting in

First Church, Berkeley. The meetings began on Thursday evening, July 21, and ended Thursday morning, July 28. I worked closely with Dr. McAfee in making arrangements for the entertainment of the delegates.

I was granted a two weeks vacation beginning the day that Synod closed. My roommate, Rex Louch, whose vacation coincided with mine, and I decided that we would take advantage of the time and visit Yosemite National Park. In order to conserve on expenses, we decided to camp out. I had a pup tent and army blankets which I had purchased from the surplus army store while serving with the Red Cross. One of the elder delegates to Synod offered to give us a ride in his car to Merced, which marked the end of the railroad line which led into the park.

We left Berkeley about 2:00 p.m. and arrived at Merced just as it was getting dark. Although we both preferred spending the night in a hotel, we felt that since we had our camping equipment with us, we should sleep out-of-doors. After walking out of town for about a mile, we came to a likely spot on the bank of a ditch which was lined with heavy brush. We leveled off a spot and spread out our blankets and settled in for a good night's rest. Shortly afterwards, we were startled to find that someone had lit a fire in the brush and we had to move out as quickly as possible. We then started walking back towards the town. The night was very dark. Finally we came to a hay stack in what appeared to be a vacant lot. Without further ado, we spread out our blankets and went to sleep. I noted the next day in my diary: "Spiders, mosquitoes, spear grass, freight trains and the crackling of the fire burning over our previous location contributed to the sleeplessness of the night." I wished that we had gone to a hotel.

When dawn broke, we found that we had camped in a vacant lot surrounded by houses. We managed to shave with the water I carried in my canteen. After getting breakfast in a restaurant, we took the first train to El Portal. An auto stage met us there and carried us into the magnificent Yosemite Valley. We located Stuart Seaton, one of the members of Calvin Club, and we put up our pup tent next to his. We gathered armfuls of pine needles over which we spread our blankets.

After getting settled, Louch and I hunted up Henry McFadden, who was serving as Park Chaplain for the summer. Henry was a member of the seminary class after mine and we became close friends. He was the best man at my wedding. Henry gave us a cordial welcome and invited us to join a small group, mostly from Calvin Club of First Church, that evening in his tent for a taffy pull. Among those present was Miriam Leyrer who was working as cashier for the cafeteria at

Camp Currie that summer. I no doubt had seen her in Calvin Club on previous occasions, but that night I felt a special interest in her.

Saturday was spent in seeing the wonders of the park. In the evening Louch and I went to Camp Currie to see the famous fire fall from Glacier Point, one-half mile above us.

On Sunday, July 31, Louch and I attended the morning service in the beautiful chapel in the Park. Henry McFadden preached and Miriam Leyrer played the organ. Following the service Miriam and I dined at Camp Currie's cafeteria and then, in the afternoon, hiked to Happy Isles and Mirror Lake. After supper we went together to Yosemite Lodge to see a program. This day marked the beginning of our courtship.

As would be expected, we told each other of our background. Her parents, Otto and Edith Leyrer, were Salvation Army workers. Miriam had been born in Santa Ana, California, and was a couple of years younger than I. She had one brother, Leonard, and three sisters, Lois, Alice, and Muriel. Miriam was the eldest. Miriam had completed her third year at the University of California and was planning to enter her senior year that fall. She was musical and played both the piano and the pipe organ in the Congregational Church in Pacific Grove where she spent her high school years. After the family moved to Berkeley, she joined the First Presbyterian Church and became an active member in the Calvin Club.

Miriam and I were together at least once nearly every day of my two-weeks vacation. We took long hikes. We attended nature lectures. We dined together at the cafeteria, and we joined with others from Calvin Club in evening socials.

On Monday, August 1, Louch and I climbed to Glacier Point, which was about one-half mile high and at the top of a large overhanging rock. One could stand on this projection and look straight down to the floor of the valley. By previous arrangement, Miriam agreed to stand in a vacant lot near the cafeteria at 10:30 at which time I would be at the top of Glacier Point. Then, if we saw each other, we would wave. We had no difficulty in seeing each other.

On Wednesday, August 3, Louch and I climbed Half Dome, one of the most spectacular peaks in Yosemite with an elevation of 8,852 feet. We were told that the round trip from Camp Currie was nineteen miles. Having secured a box lunch the night before, we were up early and on the trail by 5:00 a.m. I noted in my diary after our return, that the climbing was hard "but the higher we climbed the greater the view." We entered sunshine about 8:30 o'clock. As we circled the rear of Half Dome, it looked most formidable. The hardest part of the climb was the last five or six hundred feet when we had to climb up the steep and smooth surface of the rock. The Park authorities had inserted a series of steel rods into the rock in pairs with a loop on the top of each through which a cable had been strung. There were parallel cables. At the bottom of the climb were belts with a clasp at the end which could be hooked onto the cable. Thus, if perchance a climber slipped on the smooth rock, the belt would prevent him from falling to the bottom. We did have to stop at each rod and move the clasp to the other side. I noted in my diary that the ascent was so steep in places that one had to lift himself by the strength in his arms to move from one pair of rods to another.

The view from the top was magnificent but I was so concerned about making the descent that I had no appetite for my lunch. We walked to the edge and looked down. The valley floor was about a mile below us. The view was both beautiful and frightening. How could I descend that cabled pathway leading downward? We stayed on the top for about an hour. Years later, I learned a new word — acrophobia — which is a morbid fear of high places. That describes my feeling that day when on top of Half Dome I looked down to the valley below, one mile down!

Descending the cable pathway was more nerve-racking than the ascent. I was looking upward when making the ascent, but when going down backwards, I was obliged to look down. This meant that I was seeing the long expanse of steep smooth rock, stretching for hundreds of feet. If for some reason, my safety belt which was attached to one of the cables, failed me, I would fall to the bottom. With thanks we arrived safely back in camp about 4:00 o'clock.

On Saturday evening, Miriam and I saw the spectacular fire fall from the top of Half Dome. This, like the fire fall from Glacier Point, is now discontinued. Upon McFadden's invitation, I had the privilege of giving the sermon in the chapel on Sunday, August 7. Miriam played the organ.

I started back on Tuesday. Miriam returned that day also as she had to get back in Berkeley to enroll. We traveled by bus to El Portal and from there by train to Merced where we got lunch. Then on another train to Oakland where Miriam's mother met us at the depot. I resumed my duties at the church the next day. As time permitted, Miriam and I took hikes in the Berkeley hills, or went to Chinatown in San Francisco to dine in a Chinese restaurant, or went to a movie. The better we became acquainted with each other, the stronger became the ties that bound us together.

At a meeting of the session held on Tuesday, August 16, my status for the coming school year at First Church was discussed. Was my work with the church to be discontinued when I returned for my third year at the seminary, or could I continue on a part-time basis? The church needed a full-time ordained man as Dr. McAfee's assistant. I knew that he was pleased with my work for one day he told me: "Drury, you are making good." No doubt Dr. McAfee recommended that I be kept on on a part-time basis. "To my great joy," I wrote in my diary the next day, "the elders said that they wanted to keep me. It is now certain that I will remain in this position throughout this year, working weekends. My salary of $125.00 a month is to continue. Then, after being ordained and graduated, I will be expected to give full-time work." This action of the session was providential for I then had no other available means to pay my seminary expenses through my Senior year.

On Sunday, September 4, Elder A. L. Munger asked me to take his Buick roadster and perform an errand for him. He told me that I could return the car following the evening church service. I was delighted to drive a car again for I had not done so since arriving in California about two years previously. Following the evening service, I invited Miriam to go with me when I returned the car. Mr. Munger, seeing us together, asked if I had any special plans for the next day, which was Labor Day. I said that I had none. Monday was my usual day off in my church work. He then offered me the use of the car on Monday and outlined a trip of over 100 miles in the east Bay area for us to take. We made the trip as he planned — a most enjoyable day.

My Third Year at the Seminary

The Seminary opened its fall term on Thursday, September 15, 1921 with the enrollment about 100 — the largest in its history. Among the new students was Florence Mitchell, a member of my class of 1918 in Buena Vista College. After her college graduation, she had gone to Los Angeles to take her nurse's training course and then decided to go to the seminary for Bible training. At the seminary, she met my classmate, Harry Wylie. The two fell in love and were married in the spring of 1922 after Harry had been graduated and ordained. Our paths crossed several times in later years.

I carried a full schedule of courses at the seminary during my senior year. I was still hoping that I would win the $600.00 Alumni Scholarship as I was still dreaming of taking postgraduate work abroad, hopefully at Edinburgh. My extra-curricular activities included playing soccer and being manager of the school paper which was mimeographed. Looking back on my seminary work, I feel that I received a fine preparation for my ministry. The only lack in the curriculum of that day was its failure to provide courses in pastoral counseling. When I was serving as chaplain in the Navy in World War II, I found that counseling was a most important aspect of my work, and I had had no professional training in that field.

During my last year in Seminary, two prizes of $50.00 each were offered for the best essays written by a student on assigned topics. The subject of one was, "The value for the minister of the discourses of Jesus found in Matthew's Gospel." The second subject was, "The status of women in the New Testament." Feeling the need for another $100.00, I wrote on both subjects in October. Only one other student entered the contest. During the chapel service held on December 7, the announcement was made that I had won both prizes. I noted in my diary that I went to San Francisco that afternoon and "bought myself a fine overcoat which I needed very much for $50.00." I spent the other fifty on my board bill. Through this year, I worked on my senior thesis which then was required of all graduates.

On Sunday afternoon, November 13, I got the use of Mr. Munger's car and then called on Miriam. I noted in my diary that I drove to a hill. I wrote that evening in my diary: "There overlooking San Francisco Bay, I told her that I loved her, and she filled my heart with joy when she said she loved me." It was then that I proposed marriage. The thought of becoming a minister's wife frightened her. She asked for a few days to consider my proposal. I was called back to Berkeley on Thursday, the 17th, to attend a church dinner. As soon as I was able to get away from the dinner, I hastened to her home. "She was waiting for me," I wrote in my diary. "Had only a few minutes with her, but she told me she would!" Another of the great decisions of my life had been made.

Our great joy on becoming engaged was tempered with concern over Miriam's declining health. She suffered from severe headaches and was obliged to give up her university work. She entered the university's infirmary on December 21 for a check-up. The doctors discovered that her left inner ear was infected. The eardrum was lanced on February 8 and on the 11th, she underwent an operation for acute mastoiditis. Today the use of antibiotics would make such an operation unnecessary. She made a good recovery and was back in her home by the 15th.

On March 8, the faculty announced that Harry Wylie had won the Alumni Scholarship. I noted in my diary that day: "I felt keenly disappointed at first for I knew that I was under consideration and I did want to win. My average grade was 95.2 while Harry's was two percent higher." At that time the faculty made its decision almost entirely on grade points. Looking back, I realize now that it was well I did not win, for had I been chosen, I would not have gone to Shanghai.

The spring of 1922 was an exceedingly busy one for me. I had to write a senior thesis before being graduated. On Friday, March 17, Miriam and I announced our engagement to our friends in Calvin Club. We also mailed engraved cards with our names and the one word "Betrothed" to our relatives and friends who did not live in Berkeley. The announcement also appeared in the Berkeley *Gazette.*

Dr. and Mrs. McAfee left on February 20 for a five month trip to the Holy Land and other Near East countries. Dr. McAfee's absence meant more work for me at First Church. My records show that I had four morning and five evening services after he left before the end of May.

I was ordained in First Church along with two of my classmates, Harry Wylie and Paul Goss, by the Presbytery of San Francisco on Sunday morning, March 19, 1922. According to Presbyterian custom, we three knelt when the hands of the members of Presbytery were laid on our heads during the ordaining prayer. According to my diary, the church was filled to capacity with about 1,300 being present. Both Wylie and Paul Goss are now deceased.

Again according to Presbyterian custom, the newly ordained minister is asked to pronounce the benediction. Since I was the assistant pastor of the church, I was the one selected. Up to the time of ordination, the candidate for ordination is supposed to use the plural pronoun in the benediction which uses the words: "May the Lord bless us and keep us . . ." After being ordained, the minister can separate himself from his congregation and use the second person plural pronoun: "May the Lord bless you and keep you . . ." This is the last remaining vestige of the priestly functions which were in the pre-Reformation church. By the change of pronoun, the minister stands alone in praying for the people.

The announcement of our engagement appeared in the church's bulletin for that day. After the service, Miriam and I stood at the front of the sanctuary. Scores of our friends came down to congratulate us. This was a happy day for both of us.

After being ordained, I was qualified to administer the sacraments and to officiate at weddings. I had my first baptism on April 12 and had a total of seventeen before Dr. McAfee returned in August. My first wedding came on April 16. I had a total of ten before August. The fees were either $5.00 or $10.00. My first funeral was on April 3. I officiated at my first communion on April 27 in First Church.

One of my closest friends and a leader in the Calvin Club, Silas Mack, timed my prayers. He then informed me: "Dr. McAfee prays for eight minutes. Drury comes along and goes ten and one-half." I recorded this in my diary and then wrote: "I promised him that I would cut it shorter and really felt that I had done so. Imagine my surprise when I learned that I had gone eleven minutes this morning." I did not write out my prayers but did follow an outline. I was taught in seminary that a good pastoral prayer should have the following outline — adoration, thanksgiving, confession, and then intercession for one's self and for others.

Thursday, April 27, was commencement day at the Seminary. There were eighteen of us in the graduating class, most of whom received the Bachelor of Divinity degree. The degree system of the Protestant seminaries in the United States was then archaic. A student received the B.A. degree after four years in college, and then another bachelor's degree after three years in seminary. This has now been changed. Most seminaries now give a Doctor of Ministry degree in place of the former B.D.

FULL-TIME SERVICE AS ASSISTANT PASTOR

I began my full-time service as Assistant Pastor of First Church, Berkeley, on May 1. My salary was then $175.00 a month, or $2,100.00 a year. I paid my own room rent. The Presbyterian Church then had no required pension plan. I received no travel allowances or any other emoluments except the occasional wedding or funeral fees. I rented a furnished apartment in Lafayette Apartments within two blocks of the church for $35.00 a month, which included all utilities except the telephone. I moved into this apartment on May 3. I wrote in my diary that day: "It is wonderful to have a home of my own."

On Tuesday evening, when Mr. Munger introduced me to a meeting of the Men's Club, he said: "Clifford Drury has been busy lately. The church work was enough to take all of his time. Then the work at the seminary demanded attention, and on top of that he has been winning the love of Miriam Leyrer."

After starting my duties as a fully ordained minister, I felt the urgent need of an automobile. It was most inefficient for me to do pastoral calling in such a large parish when dependent on street cars for transportation. I knew that an item had been included in the budget for $600.00 for the purchase of a car. However, the budget of $25,000.00 had not been raised. Only $14,600.00 had been received in pledges. Another $4,000.00 was expected in the loose plate offerings.

I met with the church's trustees on May 31 and asked if somehow a car could be purchased. The answer was that they had no money. Finally a compromise was worked out. I agreed to pay the initial $200.00 on the cost of a Model T Ford touring car and would keep up the monthly installments of $38.75 if the church would pay $17.00 for monthly upkeep and then later reimburse me for what I had

paid. The trustees agreed to this plan and on June 22 I wrote in my
diary in capital letters: "GOT THE CAR THIS AFTERNOON." Before
leaving for Shanghai, the church repaid me what I had advanced.

The car had no trunk and no storage battery. The lights were connected directly with the generator which meant that while the engine
was running slowly, the front lights would nearly go out. There were
running boards on each side. The top could be lowered and then, if
needed in case of rain, raised and side curtains could be snapped on.
The gasoline tank was under the front seat. There was no fuel gauge
on the dashboard. Instead, I used a foot long school ruler to measure
the amount of gasoline in the tank. Even though it was only a Ford,
I wrote in my diary on that memorable June 22nd: "To me it looks
like a Pierce Arrow."

A BROTHER AND SISTER VISIT ME

Sometime early in February, 1922, I got the idea of inviting my
brother Billy and my sister Sarah to spend the summer with me. Both
were then in Morningside College at Sioux City, Iowa. The idea
appealed to them and they notified me that they would arrive by
train at Oakland on Wednesday, June 14. Fortunately I was able to
rent a two-bedroom apartment in the same building where I was
living. This cost $60.00 a month and I moved in on the 12th.

Since they were to arrive late on a Wednesday afternoon, I made
arrangements with one of Miriam's sisters, Lois, to have a dinner ready
for us. Miriam was still at the sanatorium in Livermore. I was at the
Oakland depot when their train arrived at about 6:00 p.m. For the
first time in three years, I was with members of my family again. My
cup of joy was overflowing. Being able to borrow Mr. Munger's car,
we four drove out to Livermore the next day to see Miriam. I wrote
in my diary that we found her "feeling much better" and she joined
us in a picnic lunch.

Billy located a clerking job with Skagg's grocery store, which later
became a part of the Safeway Store chain. Sarah kept house for us.
We did as much sight-seeing of the San Francisco Bay area as possible,
especially after I got my own car. I noted in my diary for July 17
that the head doctor of the Arroyo Sanitorium told me he saw no
reason why Miriam and I should not make our plans to be married
at least by December. This was good news for both of us.

Since the Presbyterian Synod of California was scheduled to open
its meetings in the Pasadena Presbyterian Church on Thursday evening, July 20, Billy decided to give up his job and ride down with
Sarah and me. We left on Tuesday, the 18th, and drove to King City
the first day. We spent the second night at Ventura, and on Thursday

morning we arrived at the home of our cousin, Roy Dell, in Los Angeles. I attended the first meeting of Synod in Pasadena that night.

During the week that Synod met in Pasadena, I had opportunity to call on my bird-loving friend of Fort Des Moines days, Dr. Charles Warner. It was he who was largely responsible for me going to California, only he wanted me to attend the Methodist Theological Seminary at the University of Southern California. Instead, being a Presbyterian, I went to San Anselmo. But it was exciting to go with him on another bird hunting excursion.

We started on our return trip on Thursday morning, July 27, taking the Ridge Route road. We spent the night at Bakersfield and arrived back in Berkeley about 5:00 p.m. the next day. I had to give two sermons on the following Sunday. On Wednesday I drove out to Livermore to see Miriam and found her in good spirits. We shared in a picnic lunch that I had taken. A few days later, Miriam returned to her home in Berkeley.

Through the late spring and summer of 1922, Miriam and I were discussing our future. Both of us had been members of the Student Volunteers which meant that we were ready to go to some foreign field as missionaries if the way opened. Our correspondence shows that we were thinking of going to Persia (present-day Iran). Of course, any appointment would depend on her passing a physical examination. In one of my letters to Miriam, I quoted Dr. W. H. Oxtoby, one of my seminary professors, as saying: "Drury, I think you should stay in this country. You have so many talents that we need you here in this land, but of course every man has to decide for himself."

Billy and Sarah left on August 15 to return to Iowa. My month's vacation was to begin about a week later, on the 21st. I thought it would be exciting if I arrived without giving prior notice, and they pledged secrecy. Billy agreed to meet me at the Illinois Central depot in Wall Lake on the 24th. No matter how much I have traveled and how long I have lived in other places, I have always thought of Early, Iowa, as being home. Since I had been away from home for three years, I was eagerly looking forward to my return visit.

Before leaving, Billy expressed his intention to return to Berkeley following his graduation from college in the spring of 1923. He had fallen in love with California. In the spring of 1923, he bought a Ford and drove out to Berkeley and renewed fellowship with friends he had made in First Church the previous year. One of these friends was Elder Donald Cone, an employee of the Telephone Company in San Francisco who was instrumental in getting Billy placed in that company. Billy remained with the Telephone Company for forty-three years or until he retired in 1966. At that time he was serving as Division Sales Manager.

Billy also found in First Church Elinor Davis who became his wife. His whole life had been changed because I had induced him and Sarah to spend a few weeks with me in the summer of 1922.

A RETURN VISIT TO IOWA — SUMMER, 1922

After making arrangements with a friend to take care of my car during my absence, I left by train for Wall Lake, Iowa, on Monday, August 21. My diary shows that I paid $86.00 for a round trip ticket which took me to Chicago, New Orleans, and then back to Oakland. This included the cost of an upper berth in the Pullman. I was glad to be able to go to New Orleans, without any extra cost, since I then had a chance to visit my Aunt Nettie, a sister of my father's, who lived at Hammond not far from New Orleans.

Billy met me at Wall Lake on Thursday, the 24th. My arrival was a complete and joyous surprise to all members of my family. My step-mother, Laura, was so surprised that she was speechless for a time. She quickly rose to the occasion and at once planned a Sunday reunion for all of our relatives within driving distance. A covered dish dinner was planned for Sunday, after the church service, for my brothers and sisters and their families. Then plans were made for other relatives to come in the middle of the afternoon.

On Friday and Saturday I called on relatives and friends. I borrowed a car and drove out to the old homeplace. The old country schoolhouse and the country church were still standing and being used. I called on the family which was living in our old home and was able to see the inside again. What a flood of memories came sweeping back.

Sunday, August 27, was a Drury family reunion day. For the first time since our father's funeral in February 1916, all of his twelve children were together. There was a span of thirty-one years between the birth of Maude, his first-born, and that of Dean, the last of the twelve. According to my diary, twenty-eight of the immediate family partook of the dinner after the Sunday morning service. During the afternoon, twenty-two more relatives came. A group picture of the fifty was taken and also several of the twelve children and Laura, the mother of .the last two. The twelve children of Will Drury were never able to get together again in the same place and at the same time.

My recent ordination brought requests from the pastors of the Methodist and the Presbyterian churches in Early to speak. I spoke in the Methodist Church on Sunday evening, the day of the family reunion. My records show that 100 were present, twenty-five of whom were members of my family. On the following Sunday, while visiting

THE DRURY FAMILY, 1922
Standing, left to right: Laura, Blanche, Clara, Millard, Maud.
Kneeling: Homer, Sarah, William, Grover, Clifford.
Front row: Dean and Joyce. Howard is not shown.

my brother Millard and his family at Early, Iowa, I spoke in the Methodist Church there.

On my last Sunday, September 10, I spoke three times. First at the morning service of the Presbyterian Church in Early where 125 were present. Then in the afternoon, I occupied the pulpit of the Pleasant Hill Methodist Church which I had attended in my youth. I noted in my diary: "Many of the older members who had retired to Sac City drove out to hear me. I met many of my old neighbors. I must say that I had a big lump in my throat." The church was packed with about 125 being present. This was the second time I had preached in that church. That evening I spoke in Lakeside Presbyterian Church of Storm Lake, with about eighty being present. This was the church which I joined on confession of faith when I was a student at Buena Vista College. I gave the same sermon on all three occasions.

On Tuesday, August 29, I visited Buena Vista College and called on several of the faculty members and old friends. Again nostalgic memories of my student days swept over me as I visited familiar scenes. In 1980 my Alma Mater received an anonymous gift of $18,000,-000 which is to be matched by a $9,000,000 amount from other givers during the next nine years. For years this college struggled along with a student body of less than 100 and with a very limited budget. Now a most promising future for it has opened up.

After spending about three weeks in Iowa, I left by train for Chicago on September 12. There I changed trains and took the Illinois Central for Hammond, Louisiana, where I arrived on the 14th.

I spent three days visiting my aunt and her family. The people in the South were still living in the reconstruction days. Negroes were "niggers." No matter how well educated a Negro might be, he was not permitted to enter a white man's home through the front door. He would have to enter through a rear door. I remember that, when walking down a narrow sidewalk, if I met one or more Negroes, all would step into the gutter to let me pass. All of this discrimination made me feel unhappy. It wasn't right.

I visited my cousin Ruth Bates Campbell one day in Baton Rouge where Ruth worked as a librarian in the State University. She arranged for me to meet an old Negro who was a janitor at the University who was called Uncle Cornelius. The old Negro had been born a slave and probably never attended a school for a single day in his life. Yet, during the Reconstruction period, Uncle Cornelius served for a time as a District Court judge. No doubt much of the discrimination against the Negroes, which I saw when I visited my relatives in 1922, was rooted in the Reconstruction period following the Civil War.

Following my return to Hammond, my aunt took me to see her pastor, Mr. Taylor, who was ill. Mr. Taylor had been a Roman Catholic priest but had left that church to become a Methodist pastor. I wrote in my diary: "There by his bedside, the old man who had been educated for the Catholic priesthood, had me kneel and he gave me his blessing." I remember how during his prayer, he placed his hands on my head.

According to Roman Catholic doctrine, ordination is a sacrament performed by a bishop who, by the laying on of his hands on the head of the candidate being ordained, passes on the right and the power to perform the sacraments. The Roman Catholic Church teaches that this power has come down from the days of the Apostles through an unbroken series of ordinations. This theory is referred to as Apostolic Succession and the special power bestowed upon the newly ordained priest is called sacerdotalism — that is, "to give sacredness." There is one exception, the Catholic Church recognizes the baptism of Protestant ministers.

After being blessed by the ex-Roman Catholic priest, with the laying on of his hands, I might be considered by some to have been given all of the mystic powers inherent in the Catholic doctrine of Apostolic Succession. Beginning with Luther, Calvin, and other Reformers, ordination became nothing more than an initiation rite into the ministry. For me, the experience of kneeling at the bedside of the kindly old ex-Catholic priest, now a Methodist minister, for his blessing was a spiritual experience I have never forgotten.

I left for San Francisco on Tuesday, September 17. According to my diary, when the train rolled through Imperial Valley, the temperature in the Pullman rose to 105°. There was no air conditioning to make us comfortable. I noted that day in my diary: "We were shut up for about five hours, as it was much hotter outside."

I arrived in air-conditioned San Francisco at noon on Wednesday, September 20, glad to be back but also very glad for my visit with relatives and old friends in Iowa. The next day I drove out to Livermore to see Miriam and found her much improved.

MARRIAGE — RECOMMENDED TO COMMUNITY CHURCH, SHANGHAI, CHINA

After my return from my trip to Iowa, Miriam and I began to make plans for our marriage in November. Although she had not fully regained her former robust health, her doctor felt that there was no good reason why we should not get married. Although I could remain for the time being an Assistant Pastor in the First Presbyterian Church of Berkeley, I was beginning to look around for a church of my own.

On October 7, I attended the annual Grape Festival held in Kentfield, Marin County, California. This was a charitable event sponsored by the Presbyterian orphanage of San Anselmo for the purpose of raising funds for its current expenses. There occurred that day an event which changed the whole course of my future life.

During the afternoon of that day, Captain Robert Dollar, the shipping magnate and head of the Dollar Steamship Line and President of the Seminary's Board of Trustees, hunted up Dr. E. A. Wicher, one of my seminary professors, for a private conference. Later Dr. Wicher summarized for me the substance of their conversation.

Captain Dollar explained that he had been requested by the American Community Church of Shanghai to recommend some young minister who would be qualified to serve as its pastor. Captain Dollar mentioned the fact that he had a special interest in the welfare of the American community in Shanghai, which numbered between 2,500 and 3,000 people, because he maintained one of his principal overseas offices in that city. He explained how a group of missionaries and business people had started a song service in 1917 which met at first in private homes and then in the Masonic Hall. The song service was so successful that a church was organized in October 1920 with a membership of about 250 members. The church was interdenominational with no property but with a great potential of growth.

The newly organized church extended a call to Dr. Luther Freeman, a Methodist minister then serving a church in Pittsburgh, to be its first pastor. He and his wife arrived in Shanghai in November 1920. However, Dr. Freeman resigned in the spring of 1922 and returned to the States. The Governing Board of the church then canvassed some of the American missionaries, but without success. The Board then appealed to Captain Dollar, who had been a liberal contributor to the church, asking if he could recommend a suitable young minister.

After giving this brief review of the situation, Captain Dollar then asked Dr. Wicher: "Whom would you recommend?" Just at that opportune moment, I happened to walk in front of the two men who were seated on the ground beneath a tree. Dr. Wicher, pointing to me, replied "There is your man."

Captain Dollar, who knew me, then called for me to come to him. He asked if I would be interested in going to Shanghai, China, to be pastor of this infant church. I knew nothing of the financial arrangements which were to be made, but the idea appealed to me and I answered in the affirmative. I told him that I would be glad to have my name submitted. Captain Dollar then said that he would send a cable to Shanghai recommending me as soon as he returned to his office in San Francisco. This he did.

The idea of spending five years as pastor of the American Church in Shanghai was intriguing. I quickly saw the possibility of going on around the world and spending some time in post-graduate study at the University of Edinburgh. I wrote in my diary that evening: "This appointment would fit in wonderfully with my plans. It would give travel, experience of living in a foreign land, perhaps an opportunity to encircle the globe, and maybe an opportunity to spend a year in Scotland, then back to this country." As will be told, this dream came true.

After receiving Captain Dollar's cablegram, the Shanghai church sent word to Milton Stauffer of the International Y.M.C.A. with an office in New York City, requesting him to investigate my qualifications. Stauffer had spent some time in China with the "Y" and knew the situation in Shanghai. Dr. Wicher encouraged me to have hope by saying that with Captain Dollar's endorsement, my chance of being called was 80% certain. I realized the truth of the old saying — it is not what you know but whom you know that counts. Since it took two months or more for a letter to go by ship from the States to Shanghai and for a reply to be received, the proceedings moved slowly.

In the meantime Miriam and I continued to plan for our wedding. After consulting with Dr. McAfee, we set the date for Friday evening, November 17, for a public wedding in First Church. On Sunday, October 29, Dr. McAfee announced this date from his pulpit and invited all to attend. On November 13, Miriam and I got our wedding license. I was a few days past my 25th birthday and she was about two and one-half months before her 23rd birthday.

In order to cover expenses, I found it necessary to borrow $400.00 on one of my insurance policies. Our wedding invitations were mailed to friends and relatives who lived outside of Berkeley by the last of October. Miriam's friends in the church gave her two showers. At one she was given a 45-piece set of dishes. We had more dinner invitations than we could accept.

We chose the members of our wedding party. Miriam selected five bridesmaids with her sister, Lois, as maid-of-honor. I selected five ushers of whom Henry McFadden was to be my best man.

I was able to rent an apartment for $60.00 a month in Lafayette Apartments. This cost, plus the $38.75 which I was paying monthly on the cost of the car, took a big chunk out of my monthly pay of $175.00. The people of the church were most generous in the gifts which were showered upon us. The most unusual gift of all came from Mr. Munger who paid the cost of our week's honeymoon at the Highlands Inn at Carmel. I told him that such a gift would give us memories that no thief could ever take away.

Knowing that many from Calvin Club would want to shower us

with rice when we left for our hotel, I made plans to elude them. I took our baggage down to Hotel Oakland in advance and parked the car there in a garage. I got a friend to park his car outside the main entrance of the prayer-meeting room as a decoy. Dr. L. B. Hillis, the Presbyterian student pastor, agreed to drive us to the hotel. His car was to be on the outside of the basement entrance on the other side of the church. Stuart Seaton and Myrle Foster, both members of our wedding party, planned to announce their engagement at the time of the reception. A slide projector was placed in the prayer-meeting room and at a signal from me, the lights would be turned out and a slide bearing the announcement of their engagement would be shown. At that time, Miriam and I planned to escape going down through the basement and out the side door to the Hillis car.

I knew it would be too exhausting for both of us to stand in a reception line to be greeted by all who would want to congratulate us, so we planned to leave after receiving one hundred or more of the guests. Among those in line was the wife of my theology professor at the Seminary, Mrs. T. V. Moore. She asked me if I had any relatives present. I replied no. "Then," she said, "I want to kiss you for the sake of your relatives who are not present," and this she did. Among those present was Elinor Davis, who, a few years later, became the wife of my brother Billy.

All worked according to plan. We spent the night at the Oakland Hotel and the next day drove to historic Monterey; then to Pacific Grove where Miriam had spent her youth; and then to the Highlands Inn. This was a magnificently beautiful place. The Inn was located on a hill overlooking the Pacific Ocean. Back of it were the foothills of mountains. Scattered through the pine forest surrounding the Inn were a number of cabins for the guests. The dining room, where we took our meals, was in the main building. No more beautiful or romantic place could have been found for a honeymoon and we thoroughly enjoyed every day. We made a number of calls on Miriam's former schoolmates and friends in Pacific Grove.

We returned to Berkeley on Saturday, November 25, and got settled in our first apartment-home. I returned to my church work the next day. On Thanksgiving day, we had the Leyrer family dine with us.

On November 26, Dr. Wicher forwarded to me a copy of a telegram which Milton Stauffer had sent to Captain Dollar who, in turn, had sent a copy to Dr. Wicher. This was the first definite word I had received which indicated that I was being seriously considered for the Shanghai church. The telegram read:

New York, November 20, 1922. To Robert Dollar, San Francisco. Can you confer with prominent citizens regarding Clifford Drury, preaching ability, dignity, tact, energy, ability to appeal to mature Shanghai business residents, and carry heavy burdens connected with growth of church and eventual building program. We fear youthfulness and inexperience. Is his bride equally capable and devoted in meeting responsibilities of so large a church? Hope this can have your personal attention . . .

A letter from Stauffer to me, dated the same day carried the following: "Splendid recommendations have been received from Warren H. Landon (President of the San Francisco Theological Seminary), Lewis B. Hillis (Presbyterian student pastor at the University of California), and Robert Dollar." Stauffer also stated that they were waiting to hear from some others but he hoped that a final decision could be made before the end of the year. It appeared that there was some hesitancy to extend the call to me because of my youth and relative inexperience. The fact that I had carried the burden of the pastoral duties of First Church for five months during the absence of Dr. McAfee when he and his wife were on their Mediterranean tour, proved to be a strong point in my favor.

In this letter of December 8, Stauffer sent me a summary of the financial arrangements that the church was prepared to pay. "The salary to be at the rate of five hundred Mexican dollars or approximately two hundred and fifty gold dollars per month." I later learned that Mexico had exported a huge number of its silver dollars which were used in China as·currency. Each dollar was worth the value of the silver that it contained, usually about 50¢ of U.S. currency. Since the United States was then on the gold standard, its currency was often referred to as "gold."

The allowances included all travel expenses for a man and his wife to and from Shanghai. The salary was to begin one week before sailing. The new minister was expected to sign up for a five-year term but if either party wished to terminate this length of time, six months notice was to be given. The church was to pay house rent and all medical expenses except for surgery and confinement. The church had a model T two-door Ford sedan (no locks on the doors) for the use of the pastor and an allowance of $50M dollars a month for upkeep. The church would also make a contribution of 1,000 Mexican dollars for furniture for the use of the pastor. It would also pay the telephone bill.

On the whole the financial compensation offered was at least double that I had been receiving from First Church, but, as I later learned,

it was necessary for me to hire from two to four servants and this
sometimes amounted to $40M a month. Also, we were expected to do
far more entertaining than was ever expected of a pastor in this
country. But, on the whole, the salary and allowances offered appeared
to us to be most generous.

The next important development came on Thursday, December 7,
when Dr. Luther Freeman, who served as the first pastor of Community Church and who was at this time pastor of the Methodist
Church in Pomona, California, called on us in our Lafayette apartment in Berkeley. He had been asked by the Shanghai church to make
the visit in order to interview me personally and to talk with people
of the San Francisco area who knew me. One of the first questions
he asked was: "Are you a pre-millinarian?" In that day there was a
strong group of Christians in most denominations who believed in
the imminent return of Christ who would rule for one thousand years.
I assured Dr. Freeman that I was not. He replied: "If you were, I
would never recommend you for the Shanghai church."

Dr. Freeman reported the results of his inquiry in a letter dated
December 12 to Milton Stauffer, who forwarded a copy to me. I now
copy, with some eliminations, the contents of that letter.

> I first saw Captain Dollar. I found him interested in the church
> and favourably disposed towards Mr. Drury. He, however, mod-
> estly expressed his lack of confidence in himself to pass judgment
> upon such a matter.
>
> I had a long talk with both Mr. and Mrs. Drury. I probed him
> thoroughly. I got his theological attitude, social reaction and life
> vision.
>
> Conclusions:
>
> 1. Clifford Drury is a young man of unusually attractive, win-
> some personality. He is modest, reserved, but cordial, and im-
> presses me with his genuine devotion. He is scholarly. He reads
> the best. He has not wearied of thinking and so has not "settled"
> things. His school reports that he is one of the very best minds
> they have ever had there. He is a Student Volunteer and tells me
> that he plans, if this work does not come to him, to offer himself
> for foreign service. His heart is warm for real usefulness. He is
> alive at the top.
>
> 2. Mrs. Drury is a remarkably attractive young woman. She is
> delightfully gracious and cordial, but has herself well in hand
> and impressed me with her poise. I would risk her anywhere.
>
> 3. Every report I could get on Mr. Drury was pronouncedly
> favorable. Dr. McAfee spoke without reservation, especially com-
> mending his mental poise, his genius in getting on with all sorts

and conditions of men, his toleration while possessing strong personal convictions. During the Pastor's five month absence, Mr. Drury carried the entire responsibility of the pastoral work and preached about half of the time. He met the demands of this large church, just off the campus of the University of California, splendidly. Every report of his preaching ability was complimentary. I searched carefully and must report that I could not find one unfavorable judgment.

4. Mr. Drury is young. That is a fault he is certain to correct in time. He is mature and steady beyond his years. He has had no experience in handling a church as a pastor, but he acquitted himself well in conducting a large church during the Pastor's absence.

I believe we would be safe in recommending him to the Shanghai committee. He will grow with the church. The young life, the business and school life, will be attracted by him. He and Mrs. Drury will be a strong, constructive religious force wherever they go. I am confident that this young man, if sent to the Orient, will make good.

Faithfully yours (Signed—Luther Freeman)

According to my diary, Dr. McAfee informed the session (a body consisting of the active elders of the church) on December 20 "that it was practically certain that I would go to Shanghai." However, a few days later, I received a letter from Stauffer dated December 26, which stated: "I learned two days ago that the Shanghai Committee recently called a missionary to the pastorate. No official notice of this has been received by us. The person called has not accepted." This was disturbing news. I was comforted by the thought that the Shanghai committee had not as yet received Dr. Freeman's report.

Waiting was hard. On January 11 and again on the 17th, I noted in my diary: "No word from China." Then on January 30 came the confirming news in a telegram from Stauffer: "Following cablegram received this morning. The Board unanimous to ask you to call Drury pastor." I was instructed to apply to Captain Dollar for traveling expenses and to "come without delay." Stauffer also stated: "Congratulations on one of the greatest opportunities that could come to any young man I know. I know you'll like Shanghai and be a blessing."

The next day I called on Captain Dollar to make steamship reservations. Captain Dollar felt that we should sail before March 1st, and since there was no ship of his line sailing before that date, he recommended that we take passage on the Japanese ship, Shinyo Maru, due to leave San Francisco on February 20. This I did. Captain Dollar advanced $940.00 to cover expenses.

Applications were made for our passports, and we began receiving injections and innoculations for various diseases we might meet in the Orient. I had boards cut for a number of boxes to hold the 400 books I planned to take. I had the boxes built so that after taking off the lids, they could be used as book shelves. Upon the advice of Dr. Wicher, I bought both a tuxedo and a dress suit. I found, after arriving in Shanghai, that I really did not need the dress suit but the tuxedo was much used.

On Sunday morning, February 11, I preached my last sermon as Assistant Pastor in First Church. The audience numbered over 1,100 people. During those last few days in Berkeley, Miriam and I were invited out to dinner many times. I settled accounts with the trustees regarding the car. During the six months that I had it, I drove over 6,000 miles. The trustees agreed to reimburse me for all that I had paid on the Ford except $130.00. This was most satisfactory for me. On February 19, the day before we sailed, I noted in my diary that after paying all expenses, I had but $160.00 on hand. Dr. McAfee kindly gave me a letter of credit for $500.00 which sum I paid back within a few months after arriving in Shanghai.

My diary shows that I had eleven boxes of books, three barrels of dishes and other items, one cedar chest crated, one large trunk and two steamer trunks, and several other boxes. One of the elders of the church kindly took out an insurance policy of $2,500.00 for all of these goods. I reserved for our stateroom several suitcases and my portable typewriter.

Finally, the big day came — Tuesday, February 20, 1923. The truck came for our baggage at 7:45 a.m. and arrived at the pier where the Shinyo Maru was docked a little after nine o'clock. Miriam and I were already aboard. We were surprised to have so many friends come to see us off. Drs. Landon and Wicher came from San Anselmo, Dr. McAfee and several of the elders from Berkeley. All of Miriam's family came except her father who was out of town, and also a score or more of our friends from Calvin Club. Many presents of flowers, candy, and books were left in our cabin. Finally the signal was sounded for all visitors to go ashore. About 12:30 the ship cast off, and we were on our way to China, not to set foot again on United States soil for over five and one-third years.

Our great adventure had begun.

CHAPTER ELEVEN

Community Church, Shanghai

We were called to lunch just as the ship moved out through the Golden Gate. After lunch, we went out on deck. The fading shores of California were slipping over the eastern horizon. We had started our voyage to China which would take twenty-six days, including one day in Honolulu and six days in Japan.

The Shinyo Maru had a passenger list of seventy-nine after receiving twelve more at Honolulu. About one-half of the passengers were Japanese. Among those aboard were the Rev. and Mrs. M. B. Palmer, Presbyterian missionaries returning to their work in Siam. They had with them their three young sons. The very writing of their names calls to mind a story which Mr. Palmer told us. One day he overheard his two younger sons, ages four and six, discussing the profound question — where is God? One said to the other: "I looked in the bathtub to see if God was there, but he wasn't. Then I looked in the sugar bowl, and there he was."

After living through the last hectic days in Berkeley when we were busy packing and saying our farewells, I luxuriated in the leisurely life aboard ship. The cuisine was excellent. Weather permitting, Miriam and I encircled the deck seven times, which was supposed to make a mile, before breakfast.

Knowing that I would be under scrutiny by my congregation in Shanghai, especially for my first sermons, I worked on my sermon notes. I decided that for my first sermon I would take one I had preached in Berkeley and revise it. I called it a study in the salutations of Paul. Paul had the custom of signing his name at the beginning of his letters rather than, as we do, at the end. After studying the salutations when the letters were arranged in their chronological order, I noted that at first Paul simply mentioned his name; then he boasted of the fact that he was called to be an apostle; then came a further spiritual development when he referred to himself as a servant or slave of Jesus Christ; and finally, "Paul, a prisoner of Jesus Christ." My theme was that we should emulate Paul's spiritual experiences until we, too, could claim to be a prisoner of Jesus Christ.

We arrived at Honolulu early Monday, February 26. In company with three other passengers, we rented a car to drive to the Pali, a high cliff in the mountains. It seems that a strong wind is always blowing inland at that point. An old timer resident of the islands told me the wind was so strong that one day when a man tried to commit suicide by jumping off the Pali, he was blown back. We visited

Waikiki Beach and tried using a surf board but soon learned that this demanded a skill we did not have.

Our ship sailed from Honolulu late in the afternoon of February 26th. We crossed the international date line on March 2nd, and that day was dropped from our calendars. We arrived at Yokohama early on the morning of March 9. I wrote in my diary: "In company with a few others, we rented a car and drove out to Kamakura to see the big Diabutsu Buddha. The statue was about fifty feet high and hollow. We climbed up on the inside into the head."

At Yokohama we received a number of letters from members of Community Church, each bidding us welcome. One wrote: "We have wanted you and do need you so badly. We can scarcely wait another week for you to arrive." Another wrote: "We are thrilled. Your coming has already put a new fire of enthusiasm into us which for a long time has been but smoldering." And another wrote: "You will find a warm welcome in all our hearts for good religious guidance . . . We hope you can serve here for many years." And still another: "We eagerly await your coming and trust we may all work together to advance the Kingdom."

Among the letters was one from Dr. J. B. Fearn, Superintendent of the Shanghai General Hospital who had formerly been a missionary under the Southern Methodist Church. He wrote: "We need you very much, especially those who have been carrying the burdens of our Church, and we feel ready to pass on to you those phases of the work for which we feel you are so much better fitted . . . You are coming to friends, and we want you to feel it."

A letter from Charles Boynton contained the following: "We are looking forward with expectation to your coming into our midst for service and welcome you with open arms to Shanghai. By agreement with the Governing Board of Community Church, Mrs. Boynton and I are to have the privilege of having you live with us during the period while you are looking for a permanent home." Boynton explained that he and his family were living temporarily in a spacious house while the owners were in America.

And finally there was a short note from Mrs. Elleroy Smith. Her maiden name was Mabelle Conquist. She was my "Professor of Oratory" in college. Since she was about five years older than I, she was more of a big sister to me than a mother. I turned to her for advice and comfort when my father died in February 1916. She and Roy left that day for their mission station at Ningpo, China, which was about one overnight voyage by ocean steamer to the south of Shanghai. We had been corresponding with each other, but I had refrained from telling her of the possibility of my being called to the Shanghai church because for a time everything was uncertain. For some reason, I had failed to tell her of my marriage.

Later I learned that when the *North China Daily News*, the leading English daily newspaper in Shanghai, carried the announcement of my call along with a picture of myself, Roy received the paper before Mabelle had seen it. He then took it to her and said: "Here is the picture of the new pastor of the Shanghai Community Church."

"Why did they send it to us?" Mabelle asked. Then she saw my picture and name. In amazement, she cried out: "Merrill Drury called to the Shanghai church! How wonderful!"

There at Yokohama along with the other letters we received was a brief note from Mabelle: "I'm standing on my head ever since the paper came this morning saying that you are to be the next pastor of Community Church, Shanghai! . . . You will find a big work awaiting you in that church — people both good and otherwise. Don't be afraid to speak out, give them *meat*." Mabelle also stated that she and Roy were leaving on June 30th for the States having been in China for seven years. She wanted us to visit them in Ningpo as soon as we could. This I resolved to do.

We also received at Yokohama an urgent invitation from Gordon and Katherine Chapman, former members of First Church, Berkeley, who were serving as Presbyterian missionaries at Kanazawa, about an overnight's train ride from Yokohama, to visit them. Learning that we could meet our ship at Kobe before it left for Shanghai on March 14, we decided to accept their invitation. We boarded a night train on Saturday evening, March 10th, and arrived at Kanazawa the next morning. We got berths in a Pullman car but, according to my diary, my upper berth had only a thin mattress over boards. Miriam's lower berth was the same. We spent two days with the Chapmans. These were thrilling days for us. I noted in my diary: "Kanazawa is far enough out of the way of tourist travel for us to be objects of curiosity. Once we had no less than seventy-five Japanese children following us."

Here in the Chapman home, we had our introduction to a Japanese bath tub. It was oval with a stove at the large end. The bather would sit down in the narrow end and straddle the hot stove. When I took my bath, a maid came in to scrub my back, but I quickly indicated that I had no need for her. Gordon told us a story of a Methodist bishop coming out from the States to hold a conference with a group of Japanese Methodist ministers. The meeting was held in a Japanese inn which contained a communal pool where both sexes bathed without swim suits. The American bishop was shocked and insisted that the innkeeper should separate the sexes. The Japanese innkeeper politely bowed and said this could easily be arranged. He then stretched a rope across the middle of the pool — on one side were the men, on the other, the women.

On the 13th we went by train to Kyoto where we were met by a Y.W.C.A. secretary who was a former member of First Church, Berkeley. We spent an unforgettable half-day visiting the magnificent shrines and temples of Kyoto. We left for Kobe by train at 9:00 p.m. and by 1:30 a.m. we were back in our stateroom aboard the Shinyo Maru. Our ship left the next day for Nagasake and Shanghai.

I began my China diary on March 17, 1923, writing it on my type-writer, with these words in capital letters: TODAY WE ARRIVED IN SHANGHAI. The day was the first anniversary of my ordination. Our ship had entered the Whangpoo River, a tributary of the mighty Yangtze River, and before noon had anchored at Woosung, perhaps six or eight miles below Shanghai. After lunch we saw a tug boat drawing near, and then a banner appeared with the words — COMMUNITY CHURCH. On board was a welcoming committee of four consisting of Mrs. Carleton Lacy, Mrs. Ray Christy, Mrs. George Kerr, and the Rev. Charles Boynton. These four with their spouses were among our closest friends as long as we lived in Shanghai. We watched our baggage being loaded on the tug boat.

Finally, we were able to climb down into the tug boat where we exchanged greetings, and then we were going up the river to the jetty on the Bund where another welcoming party was awaiting us. The Bund was the waterfront street of Shanghai, lined on the land side with foreign style office buildings, hotels, and business blocks. On this trip up the river, Mr. Boynton told me that I was expected to preach at both services to be held the next day, which was Sunday. He pointed out the Masonic Temple on the Bund where the afternoon service was scheduled to be held. The morning service would be held in the Columbia Country Club located five or six miles to the west of the Bund.

As we drew near the jetty, we saw another large sign: WELCOME DRURYS, COMMUNITY CHURCH. About sixty-five were in the crowd awaiting our arrival. As we drew nearer, I was overjoyed to see Roy and Mabelle Smith waving frantically to us. Here in a foreign land were old friends from Iowa and Buena Vista College.

I am sure that I was the first one off the tug boat when the gang plank was placed. Mabelle and I rushed into each other's arms. One of those present asked: "Mabelle, if I got away and then return, will you greet me with such an embrace and kisses?" She explained that I was one who was very special in her life, as she was in mine. While Boynton took charge of clearing our baggage through customs and seeing that it was transported to his home at 89 Rue Pichon in the French Concession, Miriam and I were being greeted by each one of the larger welcoming committee. An hour passed before we were able to leave with the Boyntons for their home which was, for the time being, to be our home also.

The Boyntons had been in Shanghai for fifteen years and were "old China hands." He was a secretary with the Interdenominational National Christian Council and also business manager of the Shanghai American School which enrolled about 400 students. We could not have had better teachers than Charles and Leila Boynton to introduce us to the complexities of our new life in China. They explained the intricacies of the local currency, the superstitions and customs of the natives, and how to manage servants.

As we rode out to the Boynton home, they pointed out to us many items of interest. We noticed coolies with their long pigtails hanging down their backs. Charles explained that at the time of the Sun Yat Sen rebellion in 1911, cutting off the pigtails was a sign of sympathy for the revolution. However, some of the coolies, fearful of the return of the Manchus to power, refused to cut off their pigtails. We also saw many Chinese women with bound feet, a cruel custom which for centuries was inflicted on the Chinese women by the Manchu rulers. We saw a dozen or more coolies pulling on individual ropes hauling heavily loaded wagons through the streets. Human life was cheap. Charles explained to us that the very word "coolie" meant "to sell labor." They were at the bottom of the social scale and had nothing else to sell but their labor.

Having read about the history of Shanghai before our arrival, I knew that there were two foreign concessions — the International in which the Americans joined with the British in its government, and the French. There was no accurate census to show how many Chinese lived in these two concessions and in the surrounding areas. Some claimed one million, and others said twice that number. Today's estimates vary between nine and ten million.

Charles pointed out the fact that over 3,000 Americans were registered in the American Consulate, making this the largest American community outside of the United States. The missionary community numbered about 800, counting wives and children. Shanghai was then a headquarters for many missionary groups which accounted for the large number of missionaries in the city.

Our baggage arrived at the Boynton home before we did. We found that the house in which the Boyntons were living was owned by a missionary on furlough in the States. The house was spacious, having five bedrooms. We were given a fine room with a private bath.

My first sermon in Shanghai was delivered Sunday morning, March 18, 1923, in the ballroom of the Columbia Country Club in the western section of the International Settlement. All of the 160 who attended had to pass the bar near the entrance. Never before had so many attended the morning service. Of course, many came out of curiosity to see what kind of person I was. I spoke on the "Salutations of Paul." Among those present was Miss Ruth Benedict, a reporter for the *North China Daily News*. Her account ran to thirteen inches in the Monday paper. Among her comments was the following: "Mr. Drury's manner is direct and sincere, and his delivery is unmarred by oratorical bombast."

The afternoon service was held at 5:00 p.m. in the Masonic Hall located on the second floor of a business building, No. 30 The Bund. The hall had a seating capacity of 400 and was filled. People came to see and hear me, the new pastor of Community Church. I used as my text Paul's words as recorded in Acts 19:21: "I must also see Rome." My theme was the driving power of a great ideal. While standing at the main entrance greeting people, a woman slipped a $5.00 bill into my hands. It was Chinese currency worth about $2.50 in American money. The next Sunday I tried to pick out the woman who was so kind in order to thank her, but I made a mistake and thanked the wrong person. She felt so badly that she had not been the one to give me the $5.00 that the next Sunday she gave me $5.00.

I wore the cutaway coat and striped trousers as my pulpit dress all through my Shanghai ministry. A pulpit robe would not have been suitable for that congregation. Following the Sunday service, Roy and Mabelle Smith called on us at the Baynton home, and Mabelle and I did most of the talking. She wanted to know how the miracle happened that I was called to Shanghai. The Smiths gave us a cordial invitation to visit them in Ningpo as soon as possible. An overnight steamer from Shanghai would deliver us in Ningpo the next morning. We agreed on a tentative date — Monday, April 2, the day after Easter. I saw the Smiths twice during the next two days.

Several years later, Mabelle in a letter to me commented on her feelings as she and Roy sat on one of the front seats in the Masonic Hall to hear me. She remembered how excited she was. She was so eager, she wrote, that I would make good. She wrote that she was praying for me all through the service.

My experience with Dr. McAfee in the Berkeley church was most helpful to me as I used some of his methods. Shortly after my arrival, I introduced the custom of having the hymn "Near to the Heart of God" sung after the pastoral prayer, as he had done. It met with an immediate and favorable response. I had over 1,000 copies printed, a copy pasted in each of our hymn books, and the others for popular distribution.

An announcement was made in each of the services on Sunday, March 18th, that a reception and tea would be held in our honor on the following Wednesday between 4:30 and 7:00 p.m. in the Old Carlton Hotel. Over 200 attended.

Miriam and I were overwhelmed with the number of invitations extended to us for lunch, called tiffin in Shanghai, or for an evening dinner. It was customary for the men to wear a tuxedo for the dinner parties. I remember that for one two-week period, we were out every evening except one. Within a few months, I became aware that I had gained weight. I soon learned that the Americans in Shanghai felt it necessary to have these frequent social gatherings in order to keep up their morale. Being constantly immersed in a Chinese city became trying. We needed social fellowship with our own. Having servants made it fairly easy to give a dinner party for ten or twelve guests.

The contrast between our manner of life in the States and that of the Chinese was so striking that it took us weeks to feel acclimated. We were foreigners, a tiny minority in the midst of a great metropolis of Chinese. For centuries China had been a sealed land. The war with England in 1842 opened up five treaty ports for foreign residence and trade. Other wars and treaties followed which enlarged the privileges accorded the foreigners. The common Chinese word for a foreigner literally meant "foreign devil." A more polite term meant "outside country man," but most of the common people did not know this polite term. To them. we were "foreign devils."

Since all of my professional activities would be with the English-speaking people, Miriam and I did not feel the need to learn Chinese. However, on the advice of the Boyntons, we hired a Chinese teacher to teach us enough of the language to enable us to give directions to rickshaw coolies, to our servants, and to do shopping.

Most of our communication with servants and other Chinese was in "pidgin" English. This was a jargon consisting of English words, often corrupted in pronunciation, and arranged according to Chinese idiom. The Chinese often spoke in antithesis as "how pu how" literally "good or not good." Another example, "koi pu koi," which meant "can you do this or not do it." A word ending in a consonant sounded harsh to Chinese ears, so a vowel was usually added. "Wash" became a two syllable word, "wash-ee."

Upon the suggestion of Charles Boynton, I asked my Chinese teacher to give me a Chinese name. Since the Chinese do not use an alphabet, my teacher had to break down my last name into syllables and then select Chinese words which came the closest in sound to the syllables. I explained in a letter to my relatives in Iowa: "My Chinese name is Da Ru Li. In order, the words meant Intelligent, Polished manners, Scholar. Or, in other words, an intelligent scholar of polished manners." The name was flattering to say the least, but I was told that this was characteristic of all Chinese names. Since the Chinese used the first character as the "family" name, I was Mr. Intelligence. I had my calling card printed with my English name on one side and my Chinese on the other.

The currency in use when we were in Shanghai was complicated. Mexican dollars were still being used; therefore, when referring to money matters, I will use the code letters (M) for Mexican, and (G) for gold. The value of the Mexican dollar varied according to the price of silver on the world market. Ten dimes did not always make a dollar; sometimes twelve were needed. We never knew exactly how much money we received in our Sunday collections until we had the bank appraise our deposits. In addition to these two currencies, China had its own coinage which was roughly equivalent to the Mexican. And still, in addition, was the custom of dealing in taels, which was an ounce of silver. Large business transactions were usually figured in taels, each tael being worth about 75¢(G).

In addition to the annual salary of $6,000.00(M), the church was obligated to furnish us with living quarters, to pay for all medical expenses, and to give $75.00(M) a month for car expenses. No provisions were then made for a future pension. I had no secretary and paid my own utilities including telephone. Even so, my income was at least twice what I had been receiving in Berkeley, but the living expenses in Shanghai were much greater.

On March 19th, the first Monday after our arrival in Shanghai, George Kerr, a Methodist missionary and one of the officers of Community Church, delivered the church's Ford to me. This was a 1920 Model T Ford, two-door sedan. It had no trunk, no locks for the doors, and had a running board on either side. As was the case with the Ford I had in Berkeley, the gas tank was under the front seat. My tire pump was under the back seat, and was stolen by rickshaw coolies several times. England introduced the custom of driving on the left side. Thus when my car had the driver's seat on that side, it was sometimes awkward to admit passengers. Shanghai then had thousands of rickshaws and all motorists had to be extremely careful.

On March 31, I noted in my diary: "A tire went down and at the garage, I discovered that one of my wheels was bigger than the other three. A Chinese trick." When I took possession of the car, it had demountable rims, thus making it easier to change a tire than with the older clincher rim type. However, a thief got to my car one night and took all of the demountable rims with tires and left the old style clincher rims in their place. Another Chinese trick. Gasoline cost 50¢(M) a gallon. There were no service stations as we know them now in the United States.

Following the delivery of the car on March 19th, George Kerr gave us a guided tour of the old city of Shanghai. He took us through the western gate and drew our attention to four or five heads of executed robbers which were stuck on stakes atop a wall. This visible evidence of what happened to criminals was intended to serve as a warning to others.

Kerr took me to the heart of the old city and showed me the artistic tea house located in a large pond. The wooden bridge which led to the tea house was erected in a zig-zag manner. Kerr explained that this was in accordance with a Chinese superstition called fung-shuei, literally "wind-water." In other words, the Chinese believed that the elements surrounding us were filled with evil spirits just waiting to do us harm. Therefore, it became necessary to ward off the evil spirits through deception. Since evil spirits were supposed to travel in a straight line, streets were deliberately made crooked. Hence, the crooked bridge leading to the tea house in the center of Shanghai.

I recorded my impressions of my visit to old Shanghai in my diary entry for Monday, March 19: "I felt repelled by many of the sights there — the bound feet, the beggars, the smells, the dirty narrow streets and the superstitions. I am able to thank God for being born in a Christian country. I thought that all "pigtails" had been cut off, but this wasn't so. I thought that the feet of the little girls were no longer being bound, but I was wrong." Old customs die slowly. Today, the cruel custom of binding the feet of little girls is past, and the coolies no longer keep their pigtails. But back in 1923 we were still living in the old China.

Having the use of a car, I was ready to call on possible new members. Fortunately for me, this was one aspect of my church duties in which my wife joined enthusiastically. My diary shows that on Easter Sunday, April 1, we received twenty-nine new members into the church at the afternoon service. The services were crowded that Easter day. Among those who attended the afternoon service were many first-class passengers from a large liner which was in port. As they greeted me at the door after the service, they mentioned from whence they came. I wrote in my diary: "I can touch the whole world here."

By this time I had learned that the membership of Community Church was roughly divided into two groups — those of the missionary community and those from the business community. There were two noticeable age groups in our membership — the young people who were attending college in the States, and the older people. I noted that I had forty ordained ministers in my congregation and that about 70% of all adults were college graduates. About 25% of the membership was always on furlough or for some reason out of the city. At times I felt that I was preaching to a procession. Quoting from a copy of a letter dated May 5, sent to Dr. Freeman, I stated that fifty-two new members had been welcomed into the church since I had arrived. This brought the membership up to about 500.

More than twenty different denominations were represented in the membership of the church, ranging from Quakers to Unitarians. While most of the members were from the United States, we had some from England, Canada and Australia. Theological differences were more apparent than denominational. Looking back, I feel that most of my members were of the conservative persuasion, but there was a strong and sometimes vocal liberal element. In a letter dated April 2nd directed to one of the elders in First Church, Berkeley, I wrote: "There was considerable speculation as to my theology. Not knowing much about San Anselmo, they could make no deductions. If I were from Princeton, they would have classified me as a conservative. If I had come from Union Seminary in New York, I would be a liberal. But since I was from San Anselmo, they didn't know how to classify me, and of that I am glad, for I would rather build my own reputation than rest upon that of a seminary."

One of my largest constituencies were the 350 to 400 children in the American School. When we arrived in Shanghai an entirely new school plant was being erected, including dormitories, dining facility, and classrooms. About half of the children enrolled came from eleven different provinces in China and from missionary homes; the others came from the homes of American business families. Community Church became the church home for most of these young people. After the new buildings were ready for occupancy, I was asked to teach Bible courses in the school, a responsibility that I greatly enjoyed. For months I conducted a class of sixty or more at an early hour before breakfast. I also served as advisor for their Christian Endeavor societies.

On April 19, 1923, about a month after our arrival in Shanghai, I joined the Sinim Masonic Lodge in Shanghai. The certificate given me then shows that I paid $10.00(M) a year as dues. The name "Sinim" occurs in Isaiah 49:19: "These from the land of Sinim." Old Testament scholars usually agree that Sinim refers to China.

In addition to the ordained ministers who attended Community Church, often bishops were present. One Sunday I was surprised to meet a bishop of what was then the Southern Methodist Church who said that his name was Hiram Abif Boaz. In the Masonic ritual the legendary Hiram Abif Boaz helped Solomon build the Jewish temple in Jerusalem. Bishop Boaz explained to me that his family name was Boaz and that his father was a Mason and knew the significance of the name Hiram Abif. It so happened that Sinim Lodge had a dinner meeting when Bishop Boaz was in Shanghai. I arranged to take him to the dinner as my guest and with some enjoyment presented the real Hiram Abif Boaz to the assembled Masons.

I also joined the American Club which was largely supported by the leading American business men. This Club had a fine building on Nanking Road. I frequently took tiffin there. On Friday, March 23, I played my first game of golf with the Presbyterian missionary as my teacher. We played on a nine-hole course in the center of the race track in downtown Shanghai, International Settlement. I played a few times thereafter, but I hesitated to take the time for the game as I was usually too busy. I remember an incident which took place one day when I was on the golf course. A Chinese funeral was passing on the street which bordered the course. A number of coolies were carrying the coffin, followed by the mourners dressed in white (the sign of mourning in China), and then a Chinese band which was lustily playing an American song — "A Hot Time in the Old Town Tonight." The members of the band had no idea of the words which accompanied the music — they just liked the lively tune.

Easter Sunday, April 8, was crowded with activities. I spoke four times — first to the Sunday School, then at the morning service in the Columbia Country Club, then at the afternoon service in the Masonic Hall where there was standing room only, and finally in the evening before the Christian Endeavor society of the American School. I welcomed twenty-nine new members into the church at the afternoon service. My first weeks in Shanghai were so busy that I had little time to write new sermons. I was forced to draw upon a preacher's proverbial "barrel," using sermons I had written in Berkeley.

On the following Monday afternoon, Miriam and I boarded an English steamer for an overnight voyage to Ningpo, a city of about one-half million, located on the coast to the south of Shanghai. I recall that the first-class passengers had comfortable cabins on the main upper deck. Several hundred Chinese passengers were crowded into the lower decks where they rolled out their bed rolls and slept on the floor of the deck. A heavy iron grill separated the upper deck from the lower decks. This was to prevent any attempt on the part of would-be pirates to capture the ship. The first class passengers, of whom there would be only five or six on each voyage, dined with the captain and his officers. The ship made no effort to feed the Chinese passengers.

Roy and Mabelle Smith met us at the dock in Ningpo at 7:15 Tuesday morning. I remember that as we rode in rickshaws out to their home, Mabelle was able to shout above the hub-bub: "Riding in rickshaws is not conducive to carrying on a conversation." The Smith home was in a compound consisting of about one and one-half acres, surrounded by a high wall with a gate and gate-keeper. There were three missionary residences in the compound including the Smith home. Ningpo was one of five ports opened to foreign residence by the treaty with England in 1842. It was here that the Presbyterians began their first work in China.

In the afternoon following our arrival, the Smiths took us on a picnic. The main problem was where could we go to find any privacy. They decided to take us by train to a town about thirty miles distant. Describing this unusual outing to Elder Munger of the Berkeley church in a letter dated April 6, I wrote: "We were objects of great curiosity for we were being seen by country people who never before had seen foreigners." The only place we could find for our picnic was a Chinese cemetery. We then were told by the Smiths that the Chinese buried their dead above ground and then heaped earth over the coffin. The land was dotted with these mounds.

Our presence drew the attention of some forty or fifty Chinese, some of whom were seeing foreigners for the first time. Since there are no blondes among Chinese women, Miriam's blonde hair attracted much attention. It was a mystery to them why she should have such a young face and at the same time such old hair. Roy asked one of the Chinese men how old he thought Miriam would be. The man replied: "Seventy years or more."

The Smiths took us to the Presbyterian chapel where, at the time we were there, about 200 Chinese men were gathered. I found it a thrilling experience to hear them sing Christian songs in their own language. As we walked through the narrow streets of the ancient walled city, I noticed that some of the older Chinese would hold their noses when they passed us. Roy explained that they did so because they found the smell of foreigners offensive. They claimed that we smelled like sheep.

The Smiths took us to the small cemetery which had been set aside for foreign use. There we saw the gravestone of the Rev. E. C. Lord, a pioneer Baptist missionary who came to Ningpo with his wife shortly after the port had been opened by the treaty of 1842. In the same plot were the graves of his first wife and of the following four wives. Here was vivid evidence of the health hazards which all foreigners in that early day faced when living in China. For centuries the Chinese had used human night-soil, as they still do, to fertilize their gardens and fields. This meant that foreigners, who had not built up in their bodies the immunity to intestinal diseases which the natives evidently had acquired, often suffered from diarrhea and dysentery.

Roy told us that when Mr. Lord's first wife died, the Baptist Missionary Board in the States sent out a single woman to take her place. Soon the two were married, and a little later, the second wife died. A third single woman was sent out who also married Mr. Lord and then died. Two more came and the story was repeated. This earlier generation of China missionaries did not take the precautions of boiling their drinking water, nor did they have the benefit of modern medicines such as the sulfa drugs.

Mr. Lord's tombstone bore the inscription from I Corinthians 9:25: "Be temperate in all things." Since, undoubtedly, the tombstone was engraved following his death, it is reasonable to believe that he did not select that particular verse for his epitaph.

After spending two days in Ningpo, we left for Shanghai on the Wednesday afternoon steamer and were back home the next morning.

THE BUILDING CAMPAIGN

My coming to be pastor of Community Church focused attention on the necessity of the church raising funds to erect its own building. Enthusiasm for such a project was high. A group of twenty-four of the leading men of the church met for tiffin on the first Tuesday after our arrival to make plans to launch a building fund campaign and to select a proper location.

In the early part of 1921 or 1922 the Trustees of the American School had purchased about ten acres of open farm land in the southwestern part of the French Concession for a school campus. After the purchase of the land, the French authorities pushed a street through the area which was called Avenue Petain. The street cut off a triangular area of about two acres on the east side of the plot. On April 30, the Governing Board of the church voted to buy these two acres, for about $29,137.00(G). I remember how Boynton took me out to see the land which the church had bought. Across the street the buildings of the new American School were being erected. The location of the church so near the school was ideal. According to a contemporary statement, 80% of the constituency would be living within two miles of the church by June 1924.

Plans were made to conduct an intensive campaign for funds beginning on Friday, June 8, and ending on the following Thursday. The advertising materials which were issued for the campaign reflected the highly sanguine expectations of the officers of the church regarding the future growth of the American community in Shanghai. Therefore, they planned for big things for their church. They felt that the new church should have a sanctuary large enough to seat 1,000; that there should be an all-purpose social hall large enough to seat 600; and that these two units should be connected by a three-story Sunday School unit.

The Governing Board decided to set a goal of 65,000 taels, or about $48,750.00(G). According to the campaign literature, this sum was to cover the cost of buying the two acres; the balance of $19,620.00 was to be used to erect the first unit. Labor and materials were cheap as compared to modern prices, but I am now amazed to think that the Governing Board could dream of erecting the first unit for less than $20,000.00(G).

The advertising folder stated that the average morning attendance during the months of April and May, 1923, was 80 and the average for the afternoon service was 400. The membership of the church at that time was given as being 469.

The campaign was officially started at a tiffin held on Friday, June 8, when ninety canvassers were present. The announcement was then made that $9,175.00(G) had already been received in advance cash or pledges. Those present at the luncheon that day gave another $5,625.00, thus bringing the total to $15,000.00(G) or nearly one-third of the desired amount. The canvassers met every noon, except Sunday, to make their reports and to receive additional cards giving the names of prospective givers.

I was asked to serve as secretary of the campaign committee. Thus it became my duty to keep a record of all cards handed out and to tally the results. I noted in my diary on June 8: "I have been feeling punk lately and my doctor, Dr. Dunn, feels that I have dysentery; so he has been giving me injections of emetine. Must take seven. Am also on a diet." The Governing Board made arrangements for other ministers to take my two services on the Sunday of the campaign week.

About 100 were present at the last campaign luncheon held on June 14. The announcement was then made that about $31,500.00 had been received in cash or pledges. This was considerably short of our goal, but sufficient to enable the church to pay for the land and have a residue of about $2,360.00 left over to apply on the cost of erecting the first unit. In a quiet way, the solicitation of funds continued. As I recall, Captain Dollar gave $2,340.00 for the building fund. This was in addition to his annual contribution of $1,000.00 for our current expense budget.

On the whole, our campaign was a success. The missionary members of our church were unable to give any substantial amount since they were receiving such limited salaries. All of the American firms were canvassed. After the campaign, the Governing Board appointed a Building Committee and selected an architect. A folder was printed for distribution to possible givers living in the United States. Ground was broken for our new church by Dr. J. B. Fearn, Chairman of the Governing Board, on April 4, 1924 and the corner stone was laid on the following June 8, just one year after the building fund campaign was launched. Almost another year had to pass before the new building could be dedicated.

A Ten-Day Vacation at Tsingtao, Shantung

All through the week of the campaign, I felt unwell. I noted in my diary that I often had headaches and on several days had a little fever. After the campaign was over, my doctor recommended to the Governing Board that I be given a ten day rest leave to include two Sundays. The Board accepted his recommendations and made arrangements for me to go to Tsingtao, Shantung, about 400 miles to the north of Shanghai, to stay with Mr. and Mrs. C. D. Giauque (pronounced Gee-yoke) who were conducting the American Academy there for boys.

Upon inquiry regarding steamship accommodations, I learned that I could get one berth on a steamer leaving for Tsingtao on Saturday, June 16, but not two. I wanted to take Miriam with me, but under the circumstances, had to go alone. The steamer left Shanghai on Saturday afternoon, June 16. After sailing down the mighty Yangtze to its mouth, she turned north to cross the Yellow Sea. We arrived at Tsingtao on Monday morning, the 18th, where I was met by Mr. Giauque who escorted me to his house which had at least five bedrooms.

Two vivid first impressions remain fixed in my memory. The first concerned the appearance of the city itself — it was a foreign city with wide streets and foreign architecture. I was amazed. Giauque explained: "During the Boxer rebellion of 1899-1900, some German missionaries were killed. As a result, Germany seized a portion of Shantung peninsula and built here the same kind of city they would have known in Germany." Germany held this concession for some fifteen or more years or until World War I when Japan seized the port.

My second surprise was to see the northern Chinese as being much taller than the Chinese around Shanghai. They reminded me of the American Indians. Giauque then explained: "According to the theory of the anthropologists, some of the natives of this part of the world migrated across the Bering Straits and became the ancestors of the American Indians." To me, the resemblance was striking.

The Giauque home was one of the German houses, large and comfortable. The Giauques were gracious hosts, and I quickly felt at home. The Academy which they conducted consisted of about ten American boys ranging in ages from ten to fifteen. Both Mr. and Mrs. Giauque taught classes. Here I stayed for eight days, or until Monday, June 25. Here I was able to relax after the strenuous days of the financial campaign, and I quickly regained my normal good health.

Giauque showed me many points of interest in the city. We visited the massive fortifications which the Germans had built with their large guns pointing out to sea. But these proved ineffective when the Japanese attacked during World War I. The Japanese took over the German concession in Shantung. This marked the beginning of the Japanese occupation of a large part of eastern and northern China which continued until World War II.

One day when Giauque and I were taking a walk into the country, we passed through a Chinese village where we heard a child sobbing piteously. Looking in through an open door of a Chinese home, we saw an elderly woman, perhaps the grandmother, wrapping bandages tighter and tighter around the feet of a little girl. The child was having her feet bound. Sometimes the bindings caused the toes to be bent under the foot. This was a cruel custom which brought untold suffering to million of Chinese women, but which now is no longer practiced.

One day I noticed an unusual sign over the door of a tailor shop. It was "JELLY BELLY, TAILOR." Giauque laughingly explained: "The Chinese tailor wanted a good American name so he asked one of the American sailors who happened to be in port to suggest a name. The sailor, in a jocular mood, suggested 'Jelly Belly' and so it was."

It so happened that when I was in Tsingtao, seventy-five or eighty Presbyterian missionaries from all over the province of Shantung were holding their annual conference in the city. I was invited to preach at their Sunday service, June 24. I noted in my diary for that day that I had 115 in my audience, which included some of the English speaking Chinese of the city. I left on my return voyage to Shanghai on Tuesday, June 26, and was soon back in the old routine.

Knowing that our stay with the Boyntons was temporary, we began looking for a suitable house shortly after our arrival. Writing to relatives in Iowa on April 2, I mentioned the fact that we had found a new house being built at 7 Doumer Terrace in the French Concession which the church was able to rent for $95.00(G) a month. This was to be ready for occupancy by August 1st. This meant that we would be living with the Boyntons for a little more than four months. We were paying them $120.00(M) a month for our board.

Upon the advice of Boynton, I ordered eight white cotton suits which cost $7.50(M) each and one white serge for about $20.00. I was told that when the hot, humid days came during the summer, the foreign men in Shanghai often wore a freshly washed white suit each day. I also had to buy a pith helmet. Miriam, likewise, had to buy a new wardrobe for the coming summer. We sent our washable clothing, including my white suits, to a Chinese laundry. My records show that the laundry bill came to about $4.00(M) a month. The charge was 02¢(M) per piece whether this was one sock or a bed sheet.

I was concerned about how I would be able to furnish a six room house, plus servants quarters. We had shipped from the States a quantity of items as our dishes, kitchenware and bedding. The church gave us $1,000.00(M) to buy dining room and living room furniture. The church would retain ownership of such purchases.

We followed the local custom by cutting out a picture of the style of furniture we wanted from a furniture catalog and giving this to a Chinese carpenter, who made an amazingly accurate copy of the picture. The dining room furniture consisting of a table, six straight chairs and two armchairs, a china closet, and a sideboard, all made out of solid teak wood, cost about $400.00(M). We also had some furniture made for our living room. According to the *Encyclopedia Britannica:* "Teak is the most valuable of all known timbers. For use in tropical countries, it has no equal."

Fortunately for us, one of the church families was leaving on a year's furlough and offered to let us use some of their belongings, as drapes and bedroom furniture, during their absence. Another family, also going on furlough, offered us the use of their piano. Even with such aids, we still had to spend several hundreds of dollars to complete furnishing the house. The cost of buying summer wardrobes, getting settled in our new home, and sending about $500.00(M) to the States to cover insurance premiums took more money than I had. As a result, I had to take out a loan for $1,000.00(M) at the American Oriental Bank. It took me over a year to pay off this note.

Another problem was that of hiring servants. We needed a cook and a house-boy. The word "house-boy" referred to a position and not to the individual's age. About a week before we were to move into our new home, our two servants whom the Boyntons had secured for us, appeared at the Boynton home. We hired both, agreeing to pay Chang, the cook, $15.00(M) a month, and Lol Su, the house-boy $10.00(M). They were supposed to pay for their own food, but after we had moved into our house, we soon learned that they were helping themselves rather generously to our supplies.

Chang knew a little English, but Lol Su was fresh from the country. Literally, his name meant "number four." In the China that we knew, if you were to ask a Chinese man how many children he had, he would count only his sons. Girls didn't count. Evidently Lol Su, being the fourth son in the family, was not given any other name than that of being Number Four. Among the first words that Lol Su learned were "Master" and "Missy." I remember when we first met. He folded his arms over his breast, bowed deeply, and said: "Master." I felt somewhat embarrassed to be called Master but knew of no substitute.

We were very fortunate to have lived with the Boyntons for four months before trying to keep house by ourselves. During that time we learned much about Chinese customs. The owner of a grocery store was called a comprador. My wife could telephone in her order but when the monthly bill was paid, our cook got his fee. If we became suspicious that he was taking at least one egg out of each dozen ordered, we could tactfully ask: "Das-sa-fu, are you sure that the comprador delivers twelve eggs each time we order a dozen?" The cook then knew that we knew he was taking eggs. He would stop that and begin taking something else. The house-boy would collect his fee from the laundry man and from all tradesmen who made home deliveries.

I remember asking Boynton why we could not trade with a foreign comprador who would not give our cook his "cumshaw" or fee, which was naturally added to our monthly bill. "If you did that," said Boynton, "you might find some sand in your sugar. No, it is best to conform to Chinese customs and make the best adaptation possible." He then quoted a verse from Rudyard Kipling, who, out of his years spent in India, wrote the following advice:

> "Now it is not good for the Christian's health to hustle the Aryan brown,
> For the Christian riles, and the Aryan smiles, and it weareth the Christian down;
> And the end of the fight is a tombstone white with the name of the deceased,
> And the epitaph drear: "A fool lies here who tried to hustle the East."

I began moving some of our belongings into our new home on August 1, which happened to be the hottest day of the year. I noted in my diary: "Temperature about 99 with high humidity, but the truth is that I was so busy I did not mind the heat." The two-story house measured about thirty feet square and stood on a lot which had a frontage of about fifty feet with a depth of about sixty feet. Next to the house was a garage. A high bamboo fence surrounded the lot.

Our house had two bedrooms upstairs, each with a bath and a fire-place, and two smaller rooms, one of which I used for a study. Down-stairs we had a spacious living room, a dining room, hallway with the only closet in the house, a kitchen and the servant's quarters. There was no central heating. The living room had a fireplace which was not very efficient. I bought two small coal stoves, one for the study and one for the living room. I paid $13.00(M) for a ton of anthracite coal.

A missionary friend loaned me 300 books while he was on furlough. This brought my total to about 800. I had to be self-sufficient in my library as there was no other available library to which I could turn. I soon found preparing two sermons a Sunday demanded both much reading and writing. I wrote out all of my sermons which I preached in China and have sent the bound volumes to the Presbyterian His-torical Society in Philadelphia. I arranged my books according to subject matter. One time when I was away, the house-boy rearranged the books by the color of the binding.

I noted in my diary that we took our first tiffin in our new home on August 7, and that "it was like getting married all over again. I was extremely happy, and so was Miriam." We entertained our first guests, the Boyntons, on the 12th. One of my closest friends, Colonel George Stroebe, an engineer in the employ of the Chinese Govern-ment, advised me never to do any manual work which the servants could do. I should not even carry in packages from the car after I had been shopping. Once, feeling the need for some exercise, I mowed part of my lawn. I was advised not to do this, for in doing it, I would lose face.

U. S. NAVY AND THE NAVY Y.M.C.A.

Throughout the years we lived in China, extra-territoriality was still in effect. This meant that certain foreign governments, including the United States, imposed their laws above those of China. England and France had their concession in which their laws, and not Chinese, applied to their citizens. The United States did not have a concession but did join with England in the International Settlement at Shanghai. For a number of years these three foreign governments had their own post offices in the foreign concessions, and their own courts. The United States Navy patrolled the Yangtze River as far inland as Hangkow with the ostensible purpose of defending American lives and property. All of this was made possible by a weak central govern-ment at Peking. But, by the time I arrived in China, there was a grow-ing sense of nationalism and an increasing resentment for such foreign domination. Extra-territoriality was on its way out.

In order to support the extra-territorial rights of its citizens, the

United States maintained its Asiatic Fleet in the Far East. This fleet would spend its summers at Chefoo in Shantung Province, and the winters in Manila. Usually one or more of the ships were anchored off the Bund in Shanghai. Often in one day there were as many as 800 United States sailors in Shanghai. The moral conditions in the city were very bad.

As early as July 1920, the International Committee of the Y.M.C.A. purchased a lot at the corner of Szechuan Roads for $150,000.00 (G). The corner stone of a $165,000.00 building was laid by John R. Mott on May 6, 1922. This building was still in the process of being erected when my wife and I arrived in Shanghai the following March. Shortly after my arrival, I was made a member of the Board of Directors of this Navy "Y."

The new building was a home away from home for the American sailors. It contained four or five floors of dormitory rooms, a gymnasium, a dining room, and a room for writing and games. Even before it was dedicated on October 10, 1923, some parts of the new building were in use. According to my diary, the Governing Board of the church was holding its business meetings in the dining room as early as July 2.

For the first time in the history of the church, Sunday services were continued throughout the hot summer months; these still were held in the dance hall of the Columbia Country Club. Often the hall was decorated with garish signs making it difficult for anyone to imagine that this was the "House of the Lord."

Again turning to my diary, I noted that we held our afternoon service in the gymnasium of the "Y" on July 2. I recall that I had to speak above the noise of eight fans, six of which were placed on the window sills. We continued our afternoon service there until the new church was ready in the spring of 1925.

While clearing out my file of letters pertaining to my life in China, I came across one dated October 2, 1923, from a missionary in Changsha, Hunan. The writer told of attending one of my services and wrote: "I enjoyed the service and thought 'now Shanghai has a GOSPEL church.'" But then he penned this criticism: "I am appalled at now seeing your name in connection with the opening of a dance hall and billiard room for the sailors: I refer to the Young Men's Club, often called the Y.M.C.A. but why they retain the 'Christian,' some of us cannot see."

My correspondent was referring to the fact that following the formal opening of the Navy "Y," a dance was held in the gymnasium for the American sailors. A selected group of young American and English women, many of whom were working as secretaries in the business and missionary offices in the city, were invited to be the partners of the sailors at the dance. I replied to my critic on November 6 and quoted the following statement made by Admiral E. A. Anderson, then Commander in Chief of the U.S. Asiatic Fleet: "Recently I heard Admiral Anderson say that whereas there used to be a dozen or more cases of venereal disease reported each week among the sailors, that now, due to the work of the Navy Y.M.C.A., there were weeks passing without a single case being recorded." And then I added: "This is but one angle of the fine work that this institution is doing for our sailor boys."

I was occasionally asked to conduct divine services aboard one of the Navy ships. Sometimes church parties from these ships would attend one of my services. This was especially true after our new building was opened in March 1925.

I joined the American Club which shortly before my arrival had erected its fine club building on Nanking Road. This provided dormitory rooms for single men, an excellent dining room, and a reading room which contained the latest periodicals from the States. I often took tiffin at this club.

Miriam and I both joined a newly organized Short Story Club which met once a month in a member's home. The club was made up of aspiring authors who welcomed the chance to read their stories and get criticisms from others. During our four years in China, the club published two volumes of short stories which had been written by its members. The stories varied greatly in quality. Both Miriam and I had at least one story in each volume.

Living in a great Chinese city and being constantly associated with the Chinese, the Americans felt a great need for social contacts with their own. Following the example of other American men, I always wore my tuxedo on such occasions. Community Church was active in sponsoring dinners, outings of various kinds, and occasionally dinner aboard one of the President liners when such vessels were in port. Several tennis courts were available. Only two or three roads reached out more than ten miles into the surrounding country. We were very much confined to the city.

Shanghai was at the crossroads of the Far East. Distinguished visitors were constantly coming and going. With the encouragement of the Governing Board, I was free to invite available speakers whenever I could. One of the first of these visiting speakers was Miss Jane Addams, founder and director of the then famed Hull House in Chicago. She spoke on May 6, 1923. On Sunday, November 25, one of the best known evangelists in the United States, the Rev. W. E. Biderwolf, and his singer, Homer Rodeheaver, spoke at both services.

The combined attendance was estimated at 800, breaking all previous records.

The visiting speaker whom I most appreciated having was Captain Robert Dollar who, with his wife, visited his son, Harold Dollar who was manager of the Dollar Steamship office in Shanghai, for several weeks in November and December 1923. Captain Dollar spoke at the Sunday morning service held in the Columbia Country Club on December 2. According to my diary, we had a "full house." As I recall, the Country Club could seat about 250. Captain Dollar then told how he had read his Bible through thirteen times.

Miriam Goes to Foochow

During the late summer and fall of 1923, Miriam was afflicted with the same intestinal disorder which I had had in June and which had sent me to Tsingtao to recuperate. She, too, had to take seven shots of emetine which added to her discomfort. Since some Methodist missionaries from Foochow happened to be in Shanghai, and were planning to return to their mission station on November 8, she was invited to go with them and spend some time there recuperating. She was eager to go, and I was glad that this was possible.

Since I had had no vacation following my ten-day trip to Tsingtao, I decided to spend a few days with my missionary friends, the Shoemakers, at their mission station at Yu Yao, about fifty miles inland from Ningpo. Roy and Mabelle Smith were on furlough, so I could not stay with them. I took the evening steamer from Shanghai to Ningpo on Monday, October 29. The fare one way was $2.50(M) which included the evening dinner and a berth. I was met at Ningpo by one of my missionary friends, Rev. F. R. Millican, who took me to the train to Yu Yao where I was met by the Rev. Jonathan E. Shoemaker and taken to his home. Here in Yu Yao, a city of about 40,000, I was in old China.

I was deeply impressed with the success of Presbyterian mission work in this city. The oldest Presbyterian work in China was started at Ningpo shortly after the 1842 treaty was signed. Ningpo was one of the five treaty ports then opened to foreigners. At Yu Yao I learned about the Presbyterian church, with its third generation pastor, which was then self-supporting; also about the hospital with two Chinese doctors. The Shoemakers were assisted in their educational and evangelistic work by two single women missionaries.

I well remember the first night spent in the Shoemaker home. At regular intervals I heard someone coming down the street beating a gong. I made inquiry about this in the morning and learned that this was a watchman who, instead of carrying a gun, carried the gong.

Shoemaker explained: "By beating his gong, the watchman tells would-be thieves that he is coming and for them to get out of the way." Shoemaker also said that the watchman was self-appointed and collected a small monthly fee from the people of the neighborhood for this protection. The Presbyterians paid him ten cents, Mexican, a month. "The trouble is," commented Shoemaker, "that his month is always growing shorter and shorter."

The Shoemakers had another guest while I was there, James Howe, Jr., a single man of about my age who was on the faculty of the Presbyterian College at Hangchow. A friendship was started during that visit which has continued to this day. One day I borrowed a shotgun and walked out into the hills in search of the Chinese pheasants. I noted in a letter that I walked eight miles without seeing a single pheasant. This beautiful game bird was introduced into the United States in 1882 by Judge Owen N. Denny who served for a time as Consul General at Shanghai.

After a restful four-day visit with the Shoemakers, I returned to Shanghai on Saturday morning, November 3. In a letter to a seminary classmate, I gave the following account of an experience that J. Howe had when he ventured into a village which had never seen a foreigner before. "The whole village turned out to meet him," I wrote. "They felt his clothes; they asked innumerable questions; they watched him eat; and one of the white-haired fathers ventured to taste one of the foreigner's biscuits which was covered with butter. How strange this all seemed to the Chinese."

On November 9, Miriam left with her Methodist friends for Foochow where she stayed for six weeks. I found keeping house alone a lonesome experience. I was frequently invited out for meals, so much so that my cook found it difficult to serve the left-overs. One evening I planned a stag dinner and invited eight of the young business men of the church to dine with me. Only, I made a mistake when I invited eight, for I had only eight place servings. When all eight arrived and I realized my error, I hastily called on the cook to go to some neighbor's kitchen and borrow another place setting. This he did. J. Howe of Hangchow visited me on December 2nd. We spent some interesting hours over our respective stamp collections. This was but the first of many visits for "J" was able to come to Shanghai rather frequently and always was a welcome guest.

THE CLOSING WEEKS OF 1923

Community Church published a bulletin which was mailed weekly to its constituency. Shortly after my arrival in Shanghai, I was given the responsibility of editing this bulletin. The complete file issued during my pastorate in Shanghai is now in the archives of the Presbyterian Historical Society in Philadelphia. The December 7, 1923, issue carried the announcement that the Governing Board of the church had decided to accept the tudor style of architecture for the new church.

Writing to my wife, who was then still in Foochow, on December 10, I told the story of how our house-boy, Lol Su, had been called to a dispensary in the French Concession to take a physical examination. This was a new experience for him. He felt humiliated when the doctor ordered him to take off all of his clothes. Then when some small boys were brought into the same room for their examination, Lol Su was doubly humiliated. It so happened that a member of my church and a close friend, Dick Vanderburgh, called on me shortly after Lol Su was back home. Dick was able to speak the Chinese dialect of that area fluently, and Lol Su was eager to explain his experience. "I take off all my clothes," he said, "all little boys look see. I only big boy."

On December 11, I wrote a letter to my sister, Sarah, who was then taking her senior year's work at Morningside College, Sioux City, Iowa. She was then engaged to Hillis Lory, also in his senior year. They planned to get married after they were graduated. In this letter, I wrote: "I have just talked with the principal of the American School and learned that there will be seven vacancies next year and that they will be needing both a high school teacher of English and one of History."

The possibility of having Sarah and Hillis come to Shanghai was very exciting to me. They did make application for an appointment on the faculty of the American School but were not appointed. However, their names were on file in the Y.M.C.A. office in New York as possible candidates for an overseas assignment; so when a request came from the President of the Japanese Imperial University at Sapporo, Hokkaido, for someone to be head of its English Department in 1925, Hillis Lory got the appointment. There they remained for nearly four years and, because of that experience, Hillis in 1944 joined the Division of Japanese Affairs in the U.S. State Department.

Looking back on the events of 1922 and 1923, I now marvel how I, unknowingly at the time, shaped the future careers of my brother, Billy, and my sister, Sarah and her husband. The fact that Billy and Sarah visited me in Berkeley in the summer of 1922 brought Billy back to California in 1923 where he had a long and highly successful career, and the fact that my suggestion that Sarah and Hillis join the faculty of the American School in Shanghai led to Hillis's appointment to the faculty of the Japanese Imperial University at Sapporo and later to the Japanese Division of the U.S. State Department. A quotation from Shakespeare's Hamlet comes to mind: "There's a divinity that shapes our ends, rough-hew them as we will."

Miriam returned from Foochow on December 21. Although in some ways she was in better health than when she left, still she did not have that degree of good health which she enjoyed when I met her in Yosemite. It was a good thing that we had servants for she would have been unable to do the housework usually expected of a wife in the States.

Community Church reported having 469 members at the time it held its building fund campaign in June 1923. My records show that 97 new members were received before the end of the year, nineteen of whom came on confession of faith.

An unique feature of the weddings was that since there was no court house in Shanghai to grant wedding licenses, the certificate I gave was the only legal document the couple had to prove that they were married. I always asked the Americans whom I married to report their new status to the American Consul in Shanghai.

The main foreign cemetery in Shanghai was called the Bubbling Well Cemetery. Many of the funerals, perhaps one-third, were held with no relative or friend present, only a representative from the American Consulate if the deceased happened to be an American. Often these were American seamen who had jumped ship or some hapless drifter who happened to be in Shanghai when he died. When I first was called upon to conduct a funeral service when no one was present except the undertaker and the representative of the American Consulate, I was nonplussed to know what to say. There was no one to comfort. Then, learning that the American Consul always tried to pass on the news of the funeral to some relative in the States, I did offer a prayer for the living relatives, should such be found, and then gave the committal service. Of all such funerals that I conducted, I had only one response from the States. A mother wrote saying how grateful she was that her son had a Christian burial. That one experience made me feel that all the time I had given to such services was eminently worth while.

CHAPTER TWELVE

An Eventful Year, 1924

The normal human being is incurably gregarious. This instinct was especially noticeable among the Americans of Shanghai during my residence there. When one is immersed among people of a different culture and standards, speaking another language, it is natural to seek the fellowship of his own kind. This was the basic reason why the Americans in Shanghai had, so many private dinner parties.

Community Church sponsored a variety of social gatherings including picnics when weather permitted, swim parties in the large pool at the race course, dinners aboard one of the American liners when such were in port, excursions by train to nearby places of interest as Soochow, and dinners held in the gymnasium of the Navy Y.M.C.A.

Since we did not arrive in Shanghai until March of 1923, we took no vacation that year. As has been mentioned, both of us paid a short visit to Ningpo. I spent a little more than a week in Tsingtao, and in the fall of 1923 Miriam spent six weeks with Methodist friends in Foochow. With the coming of 1924, I had opportunities to take two short excursions into the mountains. The first came during the early weeks of February when I went on a hunting trip with five men of the church to the mountains in western Kiangsu province.

We spent nearly a week there but got little game except for one small deer, some Chinese pheasants, a few squirrels, and some quail. In those days the foreigners needed no hunting license. Few of the natives had guns; so it was always open season for foreigners to hunt. We were hoping to get a wild boar but failed. We did see tiger tracks. We were told that a Chinese hunting party, who somehow had secured some guns, had gone through the area shortly before we arrived and had cleaned out the available game.

About two months after going on the hunting trip, Dick Vanderburgh, the scoutmaster of the American School's Boy Scout troop, asked me to go with him and about twenty-five scouts on an outing into the mountains west of Nanking. I was glad to accept the invitation, as this gave me another chance to see more of old China. We travelled by train to Chinkiang, which is near Nanking, and then walked about seven miles to a Buddhist temple in the mountains. Dick had made previous arrangements for us to stay there with the sole priest, who took care of the temple.

A few weeks after I returned from the Boy Scout trip, I received a letter dated June 9, 1924, from Dr. E. L. Mattox, then President of the Presbyterian Hangchow College located at Zakow near Hangchow. Dr. Mattox, on behalf of the faculty, invited me to give the commencement address on June 21. He explained: "There will be in all probability 15 students to receive the degrees of B.A. or B.S. and about the same number graduating from the Senior Middle School. The address may be twenty or thirty minutes in length, and on the subject of your choosing." Dr. Mattox also stated that the students had a sufficient knowledge of English so that no interpreter would be needed.

I left Shanghai by train on Friday, June 20. The commencement took place in the college chapel beginning at 3:00 p.m. on Saturday. I returned to Shanghai by the evening train and was back in my home by midnight.

While in Hangchow, I was a dinner guest in the home of J. M. Wilson one evening. Jim Wilson was on the faculty of the college. In the course of our conversation, I learned that he owned a summer cottage at Mokanshan, a summer resort for some 500 missionaries, including their families, mostly from east central China. Mokanshan lay at an elevation of about 2,500 feet with an average daily temperature about 10° below what it would be in Shanghai. The Wilsons offered to rent me a room for $37.50 for one month for both Miriam and me, and for an extra month for Miriam. Board would be $2.40 a day, all in U.S. currency. This appeared to be high, but was truly reasonable since all of the food had to be carried up to the mission village by coolies. I quickly signed up for the month of July.

This was to be the first time in my life when I was to have a whole month for a vacation. I had only ten days in 1923 which was more of a sick leave than a vacation. Likewise, when I was associated with Dr. McAfee in Berkeley, I had only a two-week vacation. The possibility of spending a whole month at the mountain resort which had tennis courts, swimming pool, stone church, and miles of trails through bamboo forests was most alluring. An additional attraction would be the pleasure of having fellowship with many missionaries of various Protestant denominations. When I returned to Shanghai and told Miriam of this prospect, I found her enthusiastic for the experience. Both of us needed the change.

WE BUILD OUR CHURCH

Within a week after my arrival in Shanghai, the Governing Board of the church launched its building fund campaign. The time was ripe for such an effort. The need for a church building was long apparent. No matter who the new minister might have been, an effort to raise money for a church building would have been undertaken.

We now had held a fairly successful campaign, raising funds of over $30,000.00. This included several thousand dollars from friends in the United States, including a $2,500.00 contribution from John D. Rockefeller. We received no financial aid from any of the mission boards or any of the Protestant churches in the United States. We had purchased the land, which at one time had been a paddy field, and were eagerly looking forward to building.

Early in the fall of 1923, the Governing Board selected one of its members, Joel Black, who was also a member of the Methodist Mission in Shanghai, to be the church's architect. Black was eminently qualified as he had planned and supervised the erection of several important mission buildings in Shanghai. After some study, the Board adopted the Tudor style of architecture.

The Governing Board, believing that within a few years the American population in Shanghai would be several times larger than what it was in 1923, decided to plan for the erection of a sanctuary that would seat 1,000 and for a social hall large enough to accommodate 600, including space for 100 in the gallery. These two buildings were to be connected by a two-story unit which would provide Sunday School rooms.

The choir loft was large enough to accommodate at least forty people. Two rooms were planned, one on either side of the choir loft, each opening into the gallery. One of these rooms was to be my study. A passageway beneath the choir loft permitted half of the choir to enter from each side at the same time.

A concrete baptistry was built under the main platform for the use of those who wished to be baptized by immersion. The cost of this came from Charles Boynton as a memorial to his father. The time came when our Chinese contractor, Whay Chang Kee, wanted payment. However, the word "baptistry" was far beyond his limited knowledge of English. After trying to find a substitute name, he finally came up with the following: "To Community Church, one concrete cesspool, 200 dollar."

An annex, measuring about 20 x 40 feet, was planned for the south side of the building, with one-half protruding beyond the east wall of the social hall. The lower floor of this annex contained a church parlor, an entry way, and a kitchen. The two upper floors and a large attic were to be converted into an apartment for the pastor and his family. Since the church was paying $95.00(G) a month for rental of the house on Doumer Terrace, the church would be saving that expense by providing living quarters for its pastor in the new building.

As the Governing Board made plans for the building of the first unit, it was faced with the necessity of securing a loan. The church

had $10,000.00(G) or less to apply on the cost of erecting the social
hall which was expected to cost over $30,000.00(G). Dr. Fearn suc-
ceeded in negotiating a loan which made it possible for us to begin
construction. Dr. Fearn broke ground for the new building on April 4,
1924, and the corner stone was laid on June 8 by Joel Black and
Charles Boynton. I remember that the interest charges on our debt
during 1925 absorbed about 25% of our income.

Throughout the remainder of 1924, I made almost daily visits to the
site to note the progress of construction. I experienced one thrill after
another as I saw the walls rise and the building take shape. In the
true sense of ownership, this was the church of all its members, yet
in a special way, this was MY church.

Our Mokanshan Vacation

Summers in Shanghai were hot with the thermometer often going
above 100° and usually with high humidity. We used large floor fans,
and some homes had ceiling fans.

We were fortunate in being able to make arrangements for two
women from my congregation, a mother and a daughter, who needed
temporary living quarters, to live in our home during the month of
July. Thus, they were able to not only look after the house, but also to
keep the servants busy.

Although Mokanshan was about 125 miles from Shanghai, the journey there took over twelve hours. We traveled by train, canal boat,
and sedan chairs. We left Shanghai by train for Hangchow on Thursday, July 3, at 8:15 a.m. We took with us fifteen pieces of luggage.
This included our bedding, books, a portable typewriter, our lunches
for two meals, and bottled drinking water. We dared not drink the un-
boiled water available along the way. In Shanghai, during the hot and
humid days of summer, the foreign men usually wore a freshly laun-
dered white duck suit each day. My recollection is that I took seven
such suits with me to Mokanshan, just to be prepared if we had hot
humid weather there. Miriam, likewise, took an ample supply of
summer dresses.

In a letter that I wrote on July 5 to my brother Billy, I stated:
"At noon we left the train and moved onto a launch in which we rode
for five or six hours going up a large canal and then into a smaller one.
We passed under several beautifully arched bridges. We also passed
by fields of rice and through groves of mulberry trees. We left the
launch at six o'clock and got into sedan chairs for the six or seven
mile trip up the mountain." Each chair was carried by three coolies
and the cost was $3.00(M) for each of us.

It took us three hours to make the ascent. At times I felt sorry for the coolies who were carrying me. Hence, I walked about one-third of the way up the mountain, especially when we came to steep places in the trail. When darkness fell, a paper lantern, with a lighted candle inside, was given to each of us to hold so that none of the coolies would stumble. Miriam was in the chair just ahead of mine. I remember how at times her lantern disappeared as she was carried around a corner. Far below us on the trail that zig-zagged up the mountain, we saw the tiny lights of other travelers who were also on their way up the mountain.

We arrived at the Wilson cottage about nine o'clock where we were cordially welcomed. In my letter of July 5 to Billy I wrote: "Miriam was the first to rise the next morning and looking out across the valley from the veranda, she urged me to come and see the magnificent expanse of green covered mountains that extended as far as the eye could see." We spent the day, July 4, exploring our vacation community. Mohanshan was unique in many respects — no roads, no telephones, no electricity but with a variety of recreational facilities, including tennis, swimming, and hiking through magnificent bamboo forests. Individual bamboo stalks rose to twenty or thirty feet and were six or eight inches in diameter at the base. Of course, the main attraction was the privilege of meeting so many missionaries of various denominations.

One of the attractions of Mokanshan was a copious spring of excellent water which eliminated the need for filtering or boiling, so necessary in Shanghai. Indeed, the existence of this spring may have been the reason why Mokanshan was selected to be a summer resort for missionaries and their families.

Another great attraction at Mokanshan during the time I was there was Dr. Harrison Kirk, pastor of an influential Southern Presbyterian Church in Baltimore, who delivered a series of six lectures on the Bible. I found them to be very stimulating.

One of the most stimulating experiences that I had at Mokanshan was to take part in an informal discussion group, usually held in the evenings at one of the private homes. A subject of prime interest was extra-territoriality. This term referred to the imposition of foreign jurisdiction by England, France, and the United States upon citizens residing in China. It included the right of England and France to exclusive rule in certain designated areas in several of the port cities. In Shanghai, for instance, the English had the International Settlement while the French had a separate, but adjoining, concession. The total area had a circumference of about twenty-six miles.

This foreign occupation of China began with the Treaty of Nanking between Great Britain and China and signed at the end of the Opium

War (1839-1842). By this treaty, five ports including Canton, Amoy, Foochow, Ningpo, and Shanghai were opened to foreign trade and residence. This meant that both Protestant and Roman Catholic missionaries could live in these ports and propagate their religion. The foreign occupation of China had begun.

Other treaties with foreign powers followed which extended the rights previously granted. A French treaty in 1865, through an interpolated clause in the Chinese version, granted foreigners the right to travel and live in the interior provinces. Thus all of the foreign laws prevailed over Chinese laws in the various foreign concessions. In Shanghai, for instance, citizens of Great Britain, France, and America were subject to the laws of their respective homelands. Foreign police patrolled the city. We Americans had a district court in Shanghai. For many years, some of these foreign powers even had their own post offices in the concessions. Throughout my residence in Shanghai, I was subject to the laws of the United States and not those of China. This was extra-territoriality.

There at Mokanshan, I heard many discussions about extra-territoriality. Some of the missionaries claimed that the imposition of foreign concessions was an infringement on China's sovereignty. They said: "The United States would never permit any foreign power to have concessions in our country or to have foreign naval vessels patrol the Mississippi River. Why then should we impose such indignities on China?"

Those with contrary views replied: "Missionaries could never have penetrated into the interior of China were it not for these treaties. Foreigners in China still need the protection provided by foreign powers."

I made a notation in my diary for July 21 that Dr. Kirk, after listening to the arguments pro and con regarding extra-territoriality, stated that he believed extra-territoriality would be abolished within ten years and that the missionaries would have to turn all of their work over to the Chinese." I added: "I doubt this." Actually Dr. Kirk's prognostication was about fifteen years short, for the Communists took over Canton on October 1, 1949, and the process of abolishing all extra-territorial rights in China had begun.

By the end of July, both Miriam and I were looking ahead to the end of my five-year term with Community Church and were thinking of returning home via Europe and Scotland. I was then dreaming of the possibility of studying at the University of Edinburgh for a doctor's degree. A year or so later, when our plans began to take shape, I was advised by a friend who had studied at Edinburgh, that it would be very wise for me to pick out a subject for my doctoral dissertation before I arrived in Edinburgh. Since extra-territoriality was such a timely subject, I decided to write on the relationship of treaties with the introduction and spread of Christianity in China. Although I was unaware at the time of the importance of the discussions on this subject by the missionaries at Mokanshan, I later realized its relevancy. This was the beginning of my interest in the subject and also the beginning of my collecting source material for the doctor's thesis I hoped to write.

I was invited to take the Sunday service in the Mokanshan church on July 27th. According to a notation made on the first page of the manuscript of this sermon, 350 were present. This number probably included all of the adults then at Mokanshan.

After the church's annual report for 1923 appeared in the early part of 1924, I sent a copy to Captain Dollar. He wrote to me on June 20: "I was very pleased on my return home to find a copy of your annual report for your church and the work you are doing, which I consider to be very satisfactory. I wish to compliment you on the good work you have done and hope that you will be able to continue the improvement because it has been very great since you started. With kind regards. (Signed) Robert Dollar." This letter was forwarded to me at Mokanshan from Shanghai. I was greatly heartened to receive this commendation of my work for it was he, more than any other person, who was responsible for my being called to Community Church.

I started back to Shanghai on Wednesday morning, August 8, leaving Miriam to spend another month at Mokanshan. I noted in my diary that the ride in the sedan chair down the mountain was "perfectly delightful." The day was cool. I arrived in Shanghai about 7:00 o'clock that evening and was met at the depot by a friend with my car. It was good to be home again. Mrs. Sands and her daughter remained with me through August, or until Miriam was able to return. They then moved to their newly rented apartment. I found a stack of mail awaiting my return, including some thirty magazines. I plunged at once into the routine of my work.

During my month's absence, members of my congregation worshipped in the English Union Church. The English people had two main churches in Shanghai — the Anglican Cathedral which stood at the corner of the race course in the center of the city, and the nonconformist Protestant Church a few blocks away, called the Union Church. As far as I know, no Anglican bishop was ever seated in this cathedral during my residence in China, even though the word "cathedral" implies the presence of a bishop's chair. There was also a small English Baptist church in the Chapei district to the north of the International Settlement.

I had friendly relations with the Rev. A. N. Rowland, pastor of the Union Church. For the summer months, we agreed to hold joint services. He took the month of July, and I took August. The average attendance in August was 125. Conducting the services while standing in an elevated round pulpit was somewhat of a novelty for me.

Miriam returned from Mokanshan on Monday, September 1. About a week after her return, we entertained our first guests from the States. They were Dr. Stuart and Myrle Seaton, who were in our wedding party, and the Rev. and Mrs. Harry Wylie. The Seatons were assigned by the Presbyterian Board of Foreign Missions to the island of Hainan off the south-eastern China coast, while the Wylies were to go on to India. Harry was the honor student in my seminary class of 1922, while Florence was in my college class of 1918.

Roy and Mabelle Smith returned from their furlough on September 22 and soon left for their mission station in Ningpo. During the first week of November one of my college classmates, Russell Ensign and his wife, Martha, called. They were under appointment of the Presbyterian Board of Foreign Missions for work in Hainan. Then, on December 8, Miriam's only brother, Leonard Leyrer, arrived. He was the radio operator on a freighter.

One of the strangest meetings with a former acquaintance from Iowa took place one day on one of Shanghai's busiest streets when my car was involved in a minor accident with another car. Hastily getting out of my car to find out who the other driver was, I learned to my surprise that it was the Rev. William Manly, brother of A. L. Manly, our closest neighbor on the farm where I spent my youth. William Manly was a Methodist missionary to some place in the interior of China. He and I had worked together in the summer of 1915 hauling gravel for the roads. He was then on furlough. After recognizing each other and exchanging mutual apologies, we went our separate ways — but I marveled how we had happened to meet under such unusual circumstances in Shanghai so far from our Iowa homes!

On August 23, I wrote in my diary: "Each day I make a trip to see how the church is coming along." I took pleasure in seeing the walls rise, and the roof put on. The day came when the carpenters were to nail on the slate shingles. Each shingle had two holes at one end — each hole for one nail. The coolies doing the work decided that one nail was sufficient and put the second nail into their pockets for later sale. After more than 100 shingles had been laid, a strong wind arose, and each loosely attached shingle began to beat a tattoo on the boards beneath. The noise was intolerable. Joel Black, the architect, and Whay Ching Kee, the contractor, came, and the reason for the noise was soon discovered. All of the shingles had to be removed, and the coolies given strict orders to use two nails for each shingle.

An alarming conflict developed between the war lords of Kiangsu and Chekiang provinces. Actual fighting took place on September 19, 1924, just outside the boundaries of the French and International Settlements a few miles northwest of where my wife and I lived. I wrote that day in my diary: "All day we have been hearing the firing of guns . . . it is hard to write a sermon when you can hear the booming of guns which you know are meant to kill human beings." The Shanghai municipality mustered all of its police force; called the Shanghai Volunteers to duty; and also got all of the sailors and marines that could be spared from the foreign naval ships then in port. This force was stationed along the western and northern borders of the two foreign settlements, not to keep the refugees out who were fleeing to the protection of the foreign settlements, but to prevent the soldiers from entering the settlements.

A potentially dangerous situation arose towards the end of September when the leaders of one military faction abandoned their troops and fled to Japan. About 30,000 leaderless soldiers remained as a threat to the foreign settlements. Hence the need for the military force which the Shanghai authorities had been able to assemble to guard the boundary. On October 3, I wrote in my diary: "The war situation is quiet."

The outbreak of hostilities between two of China's war-lords on the edge of the foreign settlements in September 1924 was but a prelude to a far more serious situation which came in the spring of 1926 when Chiang Kai-Shek, then a Communist, was on his way with his army to Nanking.

Occasionally, the parents of some of the students, who were Baptists, would ask me to administer baptism by immersion for their children. In such cases I would take them to a small English Baptist church in the Chapei district. The baptistry tank there was in the floor immediately in front of the pulpit, with the cover being flush with the floor. According to my diary, I made arrangements with this church to baptize by immersion one of the boys in the American School, whose parents had requested me to do so. We arrived at the church just at the time the evening service had closed. The speaker that evening was Dr. Edwin Poteat, an elderly Baptist minister who had two sons on the faculty of the Shanghai Baptist College located on the Whangpoo River about fifteen miles below Shanghai.

When we arrived at the church that Sunday evening, September 28, Dr. Poteat was in a back room taking off his pulpit gown. The lad to be baptized, and I sat down on one of the front pews where we watched coolies remove the cover of the baptistry which was already

full of water. Suddenly Dr. Poteat entered from a side door. When
he saw us, he waved his notebook as a greeting as he said: "Hello,
Mr. Drury." The notebook happened to obscure his vision for he did
not see the open baptistry and, therefore, walked into it and went
completely out of sight. His note book floated on top of the water.
As I helped him climb out, I asked: "Dr. Poteat, do you still believe
in immersion?" "I certainly do," he replied.

Thinking ahead regarding Edinburgh, I realized a big problem was
money. I had no scholarship, nor did I have any relatives who would
have been able to subsidize me during a year when I would be off
salary. On October 20, 1924, I received a notice from the American
Oriental Bank, where I had my checking account, that I had over-
drawn my account. This necessitated me taking out a loan, and I wrote
that day in my diary: "We have been in a perpetual state of debt ever
since coming to Shanghai."

I was several hundreds of dollars in debt when we arrived in Shanghai. The cost of buying summer wardrobes and equipping a home,
even with the $1,000.00(M) received from the church, were two
reasons why my debt on October 20 amounted to $600.00(G). On
the brighter side was the fact that I had been keeping up payments
on my $2,000.00 20-pay life insurance held with the Bankers Life
Insurance Company of Des Moines, Iowa, and on my $10,000.00
20-pay life Government insurance taken when I was in the Army.
The combined annual premiums amounted to about $260.00(G). The
cash values of these two policies constituted my sole financial reserve
when we left for Edinburgh in June 1927.

Some friends helped me celebrate my 27th birthday on November
7th. About that time I was having some trouble with my eyes. My
doctor put some drops into the eyes which made it almost impossible
for me to read. Since the affliction continued into the next week, my
doctor advised me to take a short vacation to get away from my study.
I quickly arranged to visit my friends, the Smiths, at Ningpo. I left
on Monday, November 10th, and returned the following Friday.

APPROVAL AND DISAPPROVAL

Looking back on my experiences as pastor of the American Community Church of Shanghai, I realize that the responsibilities which
were thrust upon me were far greater than my qualifications to meet
them. I was only twenty-five years old when Miriam and I arrived
in Shanghai in March of 1923. I had been ordained for less than a
year, and my pastoral experience was limited to the two years I spent
as the Assistant Pastor of the First Presbyterian Church of Berkeley.

Community Church claimed to have had 469 members when I arrived, but nearly 100 of these were no longer living in the city. Many had returned to the States. The members came from over twenty different denominations. About one-half came from the city's business community while the others came from the various missionary groups. I was not long in Shanghai before I became aware of vast theological differences which divided the congregation. For the most part these theological differences were confined to the missionaries and not to those who came from the business community. Missionaries usually held deep theological convictions, or else they would not have been missionaries.

Even before my arrival in Shanghai, about 2,000 out of the 8,000 Protestant missionaries in China had formed the Bible Union of China in order to counteract the growing liberalism found among some of the missionaries. Many of the members of the Bible Union were also members of the Shanghai church. Since most of these were dissatisfied with my predecessor, Dr. Luther Freeman, whom they considered to be too liberal, they were much concerned about my theological views. Sometime early in 1924 the Rev. E. G. Tewksbury, a leader in the Bible Union and a member of the Community Church, in a letter to Elder Munger of the First Presbyterian Church of Berkeley, wrote the following about me:

"I cannot tell you how much we appreciate the coming of Drury and his wife to us. The situation in a community church such as Shanghai is one that is a very serious problem. Not only are half the church members missionaries, but the missionaries differ decidedly in their viewpoint of the Bible and its truths. The other half of the church members are business and community people whose thoughts along these lines are not deep, and their lives in a city like Shanghai are lived with temptations all about. It would have been difficult to find a man who could approve himself to all these elements better than Mr. Drury does. His strong evangelist purpose and firm evangelistic faith, and not least his modesty and youth, appeal to all alike."

For the first two years in Shanghai, I had to deliver two sermons each Sunday except when some distinguished visitor had been invited to take the morning service. I had with me the manuscripts of the sermons I had preached in Berkeley. I never read my sermons but did take with me into the pulpit a few notes. For the most part I had to write new sermons, and I did that which was easiest for me — I preached expository sermons. I drew heavily on my seminary notes, especially those from lectures given by Dr. Wicher, the Professor of Greek and the New Testament, and on the lectures of Dr. T. V. Moore, Professor of Systematic Theology.

Among my papers are copies of several sermons that were printed in *The China Press,* the American daily newspaper.Among these are two that deal with the doctrine of the deity of Christ. The first is dated Sunday, August 17, 1924, when I preached it before the combined congregations of the Community and the Union Churches of Shanghai. The subject was "Jesus, the Christ." On August 29, 1926, I preached on "The Deity of Christ," which was reprinted in pamphlet form.

My emphasis on the deity of Christ prompted one of my critics to say: "The trouble with Mr. Drury is that he preaches Christ too much." I accepted that as a compliment.

In October of 1924 I became aware that I had a few critics who were unhappy with my preaching. They were Harry Kingman and Dr. W. W. Peter, both laymen and both on the headquarters staff of the Y.M.C.A. in Shanghai. On October 18, following a dinner party with the Kingmans at which time Kingman made some critical comments about my work, he wrote to me. He said in part: "You have such a supremely difficult task that you should ordinarily be given encouragement rather than criticism. At the same time I suppose that a pastor should feel rather grateful to those who are frank, brutal, and interested enough to tell the truth as they see it."

Also in this letter was the following: "You face a great difficulty. To minister to the younger and less conservative element of your community, you are forced to alienate those who think that the religious message which was good enough fifty years ago is good enough today."

Kingman maintained that "there is a small but important minority group, numbering possibly a few score, whose members, although giving you credit for your fine spirit, loyalty, enthusiasm, and hard work, are tremendously dissatisfied; I have heard Community Church members who are in church every Sunday say that they attend the services merely to set a good example to their children. They have gone on to lament the fact that the presentation of Christianity which their children meet in Community Church and Sunday School cannot conceivably satisfy or challenge them when they have grown older."

Of course, the contents of the letter hurt. I could not help but feel that Kingman spoke for a small minority of my congregation. The statistics of attendance that I was keeping showed that the attendance at the morning service in October 1923 was about 330. I did not feel that I was alienating the young people. My early morning Bible class which met at 6:30 before breakfast in the American School was having an average attendance of about 70. No school credit was given for this class. All came voluntarily. Moreover, with the new church building nearing completion, there was a general spirit of enthusiasm in the church.

After reading Kingman's letter, I telephoned him and asked him to suggest some topics on which he wished me to speak. He replied the same day, and I quote from his second letter to me:

"I suggest that you preach a series of four or five sermons on Applied Christianity, using such subjects as the following: (1) What should it mean to be a Christian business man in Shanghai? (2) What should it mean to be an American Christian in China? (3) What should it mean to be a Christian in future war time? (4) What should it mean to be a Christian citizen of Shanghai? and (5) What should it mean to be a Christian factory owner in Shanghai?"

I felt appalled at the idea of preaching on such subjects. I had been in Shanghai for about one and one-half years. How could I analyze the social and economic ills of the city and then issue directions from the pulpit as to what should be done? I wrote a friendly letter to Kingman suggesting that we together review the manuscript of a sermon which I had preached a few weeks earlier when he was not present. The subject of the sermon was "The Function of the Church."

Kingman did not reply to my letter but did refer copies of his letters to me and mine to him to W. W. Peter. On October 22, Peter wrote to Dr. J. B. Fearn, then Chairman of the church's Governing Board. In this letter he stated: "It makes little difference to me what texts or subjects Mr. Drury chooses, for to me he was about as interesting and helpful on one subject as another — neither very much so. It surely would be taking a fish out of water to insist that Mr. Drury should attempt to deal with some of the subjects on Mr. Kingman's list . . .

"If more so called 'modern' preaching is desired, we had some of that under Mr. Freeman with the result that there was perhaps just as much objection to his preaching as there is to Mr. Drury's . . . In my opinion there is no preacher who would satisfy all in Community Church congregation from the very nature of our antecedents and present variety of beliefs."

Writing to me again on November 24, 1924, Dr. Peter stated that he had opposed the organization of Community Church. He wrote: "You may be interested in my point of view. Briefly stated it is this, that a very big mistake was made by us in attempting to convert an informal but effective Song Service operating at small cost . . . into something which is costly, stereotyped, and conventional. Shortly after Dr. Freeman came to be our first pastor, he took me to task for refusing to lead the singing or to assume any other responsibility. I felt it necessary to inform him that the reason was my belief that he was an expensive luxury, the natural result of a mistaken policy."

However, before closing this letter, Peter had the grace to write: "I owe it to you to say frankly that I admire you very much from what I have seen of you in action in other lines as your being interested in athletics . . . I have also had fine reports of the way you mix with the children in the school and how they love you. I do not know anything about your pastoral work, but from all sides I hear nothing except favorable comments about your faithfulness, your diligence and capacity for hard work."

This change of attitude was due to the good offices of Dr. J. B. Fearn, Chairman of the church's Governing Board, who held a luncheon meeting on October 28 to which Kingman, Peter, and a few of the leading men of the church had been invited. I knew nothing of this at the time. Later a friend, who had been at the meeting, told me what had happened. In a letter to Dr. Wicher, dated November 21, I summarized what I had learned.

The discussion centered about three aspects of my ministry — the pastoral, priestly, and prophetic. Evidently the letters of criticism which Kingman and Peter had written were read, together with my replies. Regarding my pastoral duties, there was no criticism, only praise. One present pointed out the fact that 60 or more of the American School young people would not get up before breakfast once a week to attend my Bible class because of their love for the Bible. He emphasized the point that it was my personal friendship with them which led them to attend.

Regarding the priestly aspect of my ministry, some felt that I should make my services more liturgical; others disagreed. Regarding the main criticism that Kingman had made regarding my preaching Christ too much, one of the ordained ministers present said: "They criticize Drury because he preaches Christ too much. I wish that they could say that of me."

Regarding my failure to preach on social issues, the concensus was that the subjects suggested by Kingman were unsuitable for me to use. On the whole the meeting proved to be most helpful to me. Both Kingman and Peter became more conciliatory. The meeting took one action which I greatly appreciated. It was suggested that I should feel free to invite some visiting minister, or even some member of my congregation, to take a morning service. Since I had no church secretary or assistant, I often found the task of preparing two sermons a week in addition to my other duties was too much. I was glad to have this promised relief.

Much to my satisfaction, the morning service was moved from the dance hall in the Columbia Country Club, where it had been held ever since I had arrived in Shanghai, to the assembly hall of the

American School during the first week of December 1924. We were then hoping to enter our new church before Christmas, but that was not to be. We continued to hold our morning service in the American School until the new church was dedicated March 8, 1925. The average attendance was about 375.

Although our main worship service was held in the morning, we cooperated with the Navy Y.M.C.A. in a Sunday vesper service held there in its gymnasium. When U.S. naval vessels were in port, we always had a number of the American sailors present. The secretaries of the "Y" sponsored a Japanese sukiyaki supper after the service. Those present were in groups of ten or more seated on the floor encircling the round tables which were only a few inches off the floor. This supper was cooked in Japanese style on a charcoal burner in the center of the table. This gave the American sailors a chance to have fellowship with their countrymen.

These contacts with the U.S. Navy had a profound effect on my later life for, during the time I was in Shanghai, I became acquainted with some of the senior members of the Navy's Chaplain Corps, including Thomas Kirkpatrick, Georg Rentz, Harry Peterson, and Syanton Salisbury. All of these were Presbyterians and each played a vital role in my ministry as a Navy Chaplain in World War II. But this is a story which belongs to a later chapter. Suffice it to say now that had I not gone to Shanghai, I probably would never have become a Navy Chaplain in World War II. After we had the use of our new church building, the chaplains, when in port, sponsored church parties for the sailors; they were also in my congregation. During most of my ministry in Shanghai, I served as a member of the Board of Directors of the Navy Y.M.C.A.

In a letter to relatives at home, I stated: "We had a delightful Christmas. We were invited to at least four different turkey dinners, besides having a turkey given to us . . ." We were glad to have Leonard Leyrer, Miriam's brother, with us again for several days. During the fall of 1924 we entertained five couples, mostly from First Church Berkeley and from the Seminary, who were en route to their respective mission fields. Shanghai was indeed an important crossroad of the Orient.

COMMUNITY CHURCH IN SHANGHAI, CHINA
The building was dedicated on March 8, 1925.

CHAPTER THIRTEEN

Another Eventful Year, 1925

The officers and members of Community Church throughout 1924 were hoping that the new church would be ready for occupancy by Christmas, but this was not to be. Although the building was fully enclosed by that time, with the exception of having the windows placed, much interior work remained to be done. On New Year's Day, 1925, about seventy-five of the members and friends of the church met in the unfinished building near the pulpit platform for a short service of praise and prayer. I remember how cold it was, but the prospect of being in the church for regular Sunday services within about two months warmed our hearts. Our dream for a church building of our own was coming true.

During the first part of January, 1925, Dr. John Timothy Stone, pastor of the prestigious Fourth Presbyterian Church of Chicago, was a Shanghai visitor. He occupied my pulpit for one of the Sunday morning services, then still being held in the American School. I noted in my diary that, following the service, I escorted him from the school to the new church across the street. He interlocked his arm with mine and said: "Drury, there isn't one young minister in a thousand in the United States that gets the chance that you have here. Let me give you one word of advice — be faithful in your prayer life." His fellowship and advice came to me as a shot of adrenalin. He made a contribution of $500.00(G) to our building fund.

On Wednesday evening, February 18, while trying to start my Ford engine, which was cold, I suffered a broken right arm at the elbow. Since the self-starter was not working, I had to use the crank which dangled below the radiator between the two front wheels. I was aware that it was dangerous to take hold of the crank when the handle was held between the thumb and the palm of the hand, for the Fords of that day had a tendency to backfire. I, therefore, was careful to put the handle of the crank in my palm, but that did not prevent a sudden and violent backfire which broke the head off of the radius of my right arm at the elbow. After an X-ray was taken, my doctor, Dr. Alfred Swan, decided that an operation was necessary to set the bone.

The operation took place in the Shanghai General Hospital the following day with a Chinese doctor in charge. For the first time in my life, I took ether. I later learned that patients coming out from the influence of ether will find their inhibitions freed from restraint; hence, some incoherent talk or laughter. When I was regaining consciousness, I began to cry. I remember a nurse leaning over and asking me: "Are you in pain?" "No," I replied, "I am just grateful that I could be under the influence of ether when the operation was being performed."

I was told by my doctors that I would have to carry my arm in a sling for about four weeks. Thus, on Sunday, March 8, when we dedicated the new church, I still had my right arm in a sling. I managed to drive my Ford with my left hand and even did some typing with that hand. I secured the services of a stenographer who helped with correspondence and wrote out a sermon that I dictated.

On September 25, 1925, I noted in my diary: "My arm, which was broken at the elbow last February, has given me a lot of trouble. I have had twelve weeks of massage and have been under ether three times because of it." The cast was removed shortly after the new church was dedicated, but the ligaments had tightened so that I could not straighten out the arm. After trying massage, I returned to my doctor and asked for an X-ray. This showed that the bones had not healed and that the head of the radius had separated from the main bone. During the first part of April I was again a patient in the General Hospital. About one and one-half inches of the head of the radius were removed. At that time I was unable to straighten my arm, having lost at least 25% of its flexibility. I renewed my massage treatments with but little effect. In August, I returned to the hospital, and while under ether, the doctor tried to pull the arm straight. I was then fastened to a splint to keep it as straight as he could make it. I remember how painful the arm was when I regained consciousness. I do not remember ever having any medicine to deaden the pain. Again I resumed my massage treatments, but with little effect. Gradually there was some improvement, but even to this day my arm cannot be straightened. I have lost at least 10% flexibility.

DEDICATION — MARCH 8, 1925

At last the great day came — Sunday, March 8, 1925 — when the first unit of Community Church was dedicated. I was still carrying my injured right arm in a sling. The building was filled to capacity, about 650 being present. Several important clergymen took part in the service, including Bishop L. J. Birney of the Methodist Church. The preacher for the day was the Rev. Cleland B. McAfee of McCormick Theological Seminary and a brother of Dr. Lapsley McAfee of Berkeley with whom I had been associated for about two years. Cleland McAfee was the one who had written both the words and music of the hymn, "Near to the Heart of God," the first stanza of which we were accustomed to sing after the pastoral prayer each Sunday morning.

At the time of the dedication, the church claimed a membership of 458, about one-fourth of whom were in the States. A $2,000.00(G) special thank offering was received that day to be applied on the building fund debt. According to the statistics given in the dedication folder, the total receipts of the church for current expenses, benevolences, and building fund came to $41,378.25(M). The total indebtedness on the church at the end of 1926 was $28,800.00(G). About 20% of our current expense budget was alloted for interest in 1926. The debt incurred, because of the loan taken out at a bank to complete payments to the contractors, added an item of about $4,000.00(M) to the budget which in 1927 came to about $26,000.00. The enthusiasm engendered by having our own building brought an increase in attendance and in giving; so we had no real problem in meeting our budget. The average attendance at the morning service was about 400, except for the summer months when it fell to about 120.

Through my contacts with the U.S. Navy, I became acquainted with two Presbyterian chaplains who were destined to play key roles in my future life. One was Thomas Kirkpatrick who, while in Asiatic waters, was Fleet Chaplain of the U.S. Asiatic Fleet during 1925-6. It was he who in 1933 induced me to apply for a chaplain's commission in the U.S. Naval Reserve. More about this later. The second was Harry M. Peterson, chaplain with the 4th Marines when they were stationed in Shanghai during the troubled days of 1927. When I was called to active duty in December 1941, following Pearl Harbor, I was assigned to Chaplain Peterson's office in San Francisco. Peterson was then District Chaplain of the 12th Naval District. Thus, my whole future life was changed by these contacts with the U.S. Navy when I was in Shanghai.

First Church in China to Broadcast

Radio broadcasting in China was in its infancy when our church was dedicated. The one broadcasting station in Shanghai claimed that there were 4,000 crystal receiving sets in its area, plus the ships at sea which came within the listening zone. In those days, we used the crystal set which consisted of a crystal fastened to the top of a box measuring about 6 x 8 x 4 inches. A swinging arm with a thin wire point was near the crystal. To this was attached a pair of ear phones, perhaps two could be used. The thin wire point, called a "cat's whisker" had to find a sensitive point on the crystal which would then convey sound into the ear phones. To me, this was indeed a miracle box.

The Governing Board of Community Church made arrangements with the broadcasting station to have our morning service broadcast. So far as I know, this was the first church in all of China to broadcast an English worship service. The enthusiastic response which came to me in the form of letters of appreciation was a delightful surprise. One of the first letters to be received came from a friend of mine, Charles Barkman, then on the faculty of the Hangchow Christian College, a Presbyterian institution at least 100 miles distant.

Following our first broadcast on March 8, 1925, Barkman wrote to me saying: "I just finished listening in on the Community Church service. It was all very plain, beyond expectations. Do you realize that we hear your voice here before those who sit in the back part of your church hears it? Sound waves travel some 1,100 feet per second while radio waves travel some 186,000 miles per second."

Barkman also added the following advice: "Also a little tip. If you don't want to be singing solos to an audience of some 2,000 people, don't stand too close to the microphone when you take part in the singing of hymns." While a student at Buena Vista College, my attempts at singing became a joke. One of my classmates said that I sang shortstop which, in baseball terms, meant being a little off second base.

Following our first broadcast on March 8, 1925, letters soon began to flow in from many widely separated places from Hangchow to Nanking to Tientsin, from an occasional ship at sea, and even some from English speaking Chinese. Without exception all expressed gratitude for this opportunity to hear a worship service in English. A missionary family could feel isolated even though the family was in the midst of a city of one-half million. Many sent in contributions to help pay the cost of the service, although I have no facts to show that the receipts met the expenditures.

One of the first letters received came from a construction worker at a lighthouse located on an island ten miles by sea from Ningpo. In a letter dated March 8, 1925, the day of our first broadcast, the writer commented: "I am carrying out some construction work on a lighthouse on this island . . . . so perhaps you can imagine how much it means to me to be able to listen to a service on Sunday morning. The smile was on my side when the collection was taken up; so I am enclosing $5.00 herewith and will consider it a favor if you will kindly drop it into the bag for me."

The following note, dated March 9, came from Mrs. Helen H. Goddard, the wife of a missionary at Shaihsing, near Hangchow, and the mother of a daughter and son who were boarding students at the Shanghai American School, located across the street from the Community Church. She wrote: "Dear Mr. Drury. Can you imagine the great pleasure it gave us to listen in yesterday and hear perfectly all the service in the Community Church, and while you welcomed those in Ningpo and Suchow, there were others in this smaller station hearing for the first time a sermon in English on the Sabbath day. And best of all, we had been able to attend the Chinese church service earlier in the morning. To feel that our two dear children were in that audience so far away, and yet we were worshipping together. Truly what wonderful things God hath wrought. We hunger after a service in English, and I think I never listened more attentively."

The incoming letters often mentioned the fact that small groups of missionaries had adjusted the hours for their Chinese church services so that they could listen in to the service from Community Church. One of the missionaries attached to the Chinese-American Hospital in Ningpo wrote on December 13, 1926, saying: "It may please those in charge of your broadcasting to know that our Sunday School hour has been changed so as to allow the foreign teachers and scholars to listen in on your morning service. You are very popular here. We expect to have twenty-five next Sunday at my house. I know of other radio sets in Ningpo but do not know how many are listening in."

Although we broadcasted our morning services, only rarely did we make arrangements to broadcast an evening service. When we did, it was usually because our choir was giving a program of religious music. On the evening of our dedication, our choir under the direction of Elam Anderson, then Principal of the Shanghai American School, presented a program of sacred music which was broadcast. Many who listened to that program sent in letters of appreciation.

One of the members of the choir was H. H. Cameron, a business man, who was gifted with an unusually fine tenor voice. After hearing him sing a solo at our Sunday morning service on December 19, 1926, W. B. Burke, who was serving as a missionary at Soochow University Bible School, Sungkiang, wrote to me: "I also heard that wonderful solo, 'Comfort Ye My People.' I did not know that anyone in your church could sing like that. I would like to hear him once a week. Who is he?"

Cameron returned to the States on furlough during the late fall of 1925. In a letter to me dated December 20 from Malden, Massachusetts, he wrote: "There are many things I would like to tell you. First, on the steamer coming home, the *President Madison,* the doctor is a great radio fan. He said that our church was giving the best musical programs of any church on the Pacific Coast. He did not then know that I was a church member. He also said that the preacher there is very good, and the doctor added: 'I always listen to these services if I am within hearing distance.'"

When Captain Robert Dollar was back in Shanghai during the first weeks of June, 1925, I took great pleasure in showing him our new

church, and I extended him an invitation to speak for the second time
before my morning congregation. He was reluctant to accept but
finally consented. Even though the American School was closed for
the summer, thus taking some 200 out of our congregation, we had 300
present to hear him on Sunday morning, June 14. He spoke on the
importance of the business people and missionaries cooperating. Being
so highly respected, his Christian testimony was most effective.

Our broadcast project proved to be one of the most fruitful activities sponsored by the church. We were never able to know how large
this invisible audience was, but the evidence indicated by letters
received led us to believe that our radio audience was larger than that
which gathered in the church. We continued broadcasting throughout
the remaining two and more years of my ministry, and this was
continued by my successors.

<h2 style="text-align:center">A POSTSCRIPT</h2>

Several pastors carried on the ministry of the church through the
years following my leaving in June 1927. The Rev. Emory Luccock,
a former Presbyterian missionary to Shanghai, became pastor in 1929
and remained for ten years. Gradually the policy of the Governing
Board changed to include Chinese as members. During the years of my
ministry, several Chinese asked to join the church, but the Governing
Board then felt that the Christian Chinese should be members of one
of the Chinese Protestant churches in the city. As the political conditions in China began to change, after the founding of the People's
Republic in 1949, the church was taken over by the Government and
then became an entirely Chinese church, administered by Chinese
pastors and supported by a Chinese congregation.

Christian activities in China were interrupted in 1966 with the
dominance of the Cultural Revolution. Community Church, along
with other Christian churches, was forced to close all of its activities,
and the buildings were taken over by the Government. With a change
in Government policy, Community Church was given back to the
Christians at Christmas time in 1980, and the name changed to the
International Church.

I have had the good fortune to be able to get in touch with one
of the three Chinese pastors, the Rev. I. F. Shen, who, in a letter
to me dated December 25, 1981, stated: "Within one year, more than
130 people, old and young, have been received, baptized and confirmed. Now we have two services every Sunday morning with a total
attendance of 2,000. As our church can seat only 700 people, there
is always an overflow and some have to stand throughout the service.
We do not receive any subsidy from the Government, and like all

other churches, we are well supported with the offerings of the congregation and some rents of church properties. I believe you will rejoice with us for the progress of Christian work in China in recent years."

Indeed, these developments have made me happy, and also the few of my former congregation who are still living. This is as it should be.

WE MOVE TO THE CHURCH'S APARTMENT

The church was paying $95.00(G) a month rental, or $1,140.00 annually, on the house on Doumer Terrace where my wife and I lived for about two years. In order to save this expense, an apartment was built for us in the annex of the new church building. We moved into the new apartment during the first week of April, 1925, about one month after the dedication of the church. In some ways we were better off in this new apartment than we had been in our home on Doumer Terrace. Our new quarters were more spacious. We had hardwood floors, furnace heat, some gas for cooking in addition to a coal stove, closets instead of wardrobes, and space for a vegetable garden. Since the Chinese farmers fertilize their fields and gardens with human excrement, we foreigners in Shanghai avoided eating such garden produce as lettuce and strawberries, for fear of getting dysentery. But now, with plenty of space for a garden and a coolie to do the work, I was able to grow a good variety of vegetables and strawberries.

Shortly after moving into our new apartment, I received an unusual telephone call, but first a little background.

When I was a student at the San Francisco Theological Seminary, my professor of Hebrew and the Old Testament was Dr. William H. Oxtoby. He had the gift of making even the study of Hebrew interesting. One day, when studying the meaning of certain Hebrew words, we came to the English words of blood and tabernacle. Very solemnly, he told the class that the Hebrew words for these two English words were never to be spoken aloud. Accordingly, he explained, he would have to whisper these two words into our ears. So the members of the class lined up, and one by one we stopped at his desk as he gave us the Hebrew words.

When my turn came, he whispered into my ear: "The Hebrew word for blood is 'damn,' and the Hebrew word for tabernacle is 'O hell.' Later I learned that actually the word was spelled with but one "l" — making it 'ohel.' After arriving in Shanghai, I discovered the Jewish Synagogue in the city was called the "Ohel Synagogue," which was just as logical for the Jewish people to choose that name as it would be for a congregation of Christians to call their church the "Tabernacle Church."

One Saturday morning I received a telephone call from a woman who said she was with a party of Jewish people on board a tourist ship then in port. Since Saturday was their Sabbath, they wanted to attend a Jewish service. "Is there a Jewish Synagogue in Shanghai?" she asked. "Yes," I replied. "What is its name?" she then asked. I replied, "O hell." The lady was shocked. Actually I then knew more Hebrew than she did. Her voice betrayed her disbelief — why should a Protestant minister be using such language to her? Perhaps, she thought, she had not heard aright. So she asked the second time: "What is the name of the Jewish Synagogue in Shanghai? Speak louder for I am not sure I heard you correctly." This time I did speak louder and cried out: "O hell."

My wife, who knew nothing of the essence of our conversation happened to be on the upstairs landing of our hall way. She was shocked at my language and, leaning over the banister, exclaimed in alarm: "Clifford! What's happened to you?"

CIVIL DISORDER IN SHANGHAI

I noticed that the Americans who lived in Shanghai were more inclined to take part in patriotic events than would have been the case if they were in the United States. Such days as Memorial Day, Fourth of July, and Thanksgiving, were enthusiastically observed. Memorial Day, May 30, 1925, was no exception.

According to my diary, about 500 of the American citizens gathered that day in Bubbling Well Cemetery for a program. The American Consul General was master of ceremonies. An American cavalry troop and the American Company of the Shanghai Volunteers were out in force, also units from American naval vessels in port. After an inspirational program of speeches and music, taps were sounded over the graves of some American soldiers and sailors who lay buried in the cemetery.

In the afternoon Miriam and I, with two friends, motored about five miles out into the country west of the International Settlement. This was one of the few roads around Shanghai which was opened to motor travel. On our way back, we called at the home of one of our doctors who invited us to visit.

While at our friend's home, we learned that a violent riot had taken place before a police station on Nanking Road. Most of the demonstrators were students from the non-Christian schools in the city. We later learned that there had been a disturbance at a Japanese factory the day before and that six students had been imprisoned. The demonstrators were demanding their release. The mood of the crowd became violent with such shouts as "kill the foreigners." Here was evidence that the agitation against the extraterritorial rights of the foreigners was becoming increasingly anti-foreign. As the result of the efforts of the mob to free the six prisoners, the foreign police found it necessary to fire on the crowd and as least six were killed. The psychological effect on the Chinese was tremendous. The crowd broke up and the students fled, but this was not the end of the trouble — only the beginning.

On Monday, June 1, another riot occurred on Nanking Road when the police again felt it necessary to fire on the crowd. Three more were killed, bringing the total killed during the disturbance to fourteen. The police turned water hoses on the crowd which infuriated the people. Windows of stores were smashed, cars overturned; all business was brought to a halt. Police on horseback patrolled Nanking Road. The grocery stores operated by Chinese merchants were forced to close. I found that we were low in provisions and went out to see if I could find an open market. I finally found one shop where I was able to buy some vegetables by entering a back door. Newspapers were not printed; our only news came from the radio. Some 2,000 marines and sailors from various foreign naval vessels then in port were landed to help the local police force keep order.

The city was paralyzed. On June 6th I noted in my diary that 250,000 workers were on strike. Bands of students roamed through the city demanding that all shops be closed. On the 7th I wrote: "Calls have been sent out for foreigners to milk the cows at the dairies, and to run the taxis. Servants working for foreigners were urged to leave them." One of our servants, Lol Su, had to attend a meeting. When asked if he worked for foreigners, he said "No." I replied, "Oh, Lol Su, you should not lie." He answered, "I greatly feared." One of the servants working for a neighbor was caught and tortured by having acid poured down his back. The unrest lasted for several weeks, during which time our first-born arrived.

The riots of June 1925 in Shanghai marked the beginning of the end of foreign domination. Two years later, in the spring of 1927, the situation became worse with the arrival of Sun Yat Sen's army on its march from Canton to Nanking. But this story belongs in the next chapter.

Unto Us a Son is Born

Anticipating the arrival of our first-born early in June, we hired a Chinese grandmother, who had had some training in a maternity hospital, to be our amah. I do not remember her Chinese name; to us she was Amah. We paid her $18.00(M) a month, which was nearly twice what we paid our cook or house boy. She shared the servant's quarters which were located over our garage. She belonged to an older generation for her feet had been bound when she was a small child. I rcall how she hobbled along as though she had peg legs, and I pitied her. Amah knew a little English, and we knew a little Chinese. Thus, with the use of pidgeon English, we were able to communicate quite well.

Mrs. J. B. Fearn, wife of Dr. Fearn, Chairman of the church's Governing Board, who was also an M.D., had rented a large mansion which was located about one-half mile from our apartment, which she had turned into a small hospital. Arrangements were made with her to have our baby born there. Our doctor was Dr. Alfred Sawn, a member of Community Church.

Robert Merrill arrived on Monday, June 8, 1925, weighing in at seven pounds. Our cup of joy overflowed. Unto us a son had been born. I doubt if there is any thrill equal to that which comes when a father holds his first-born in his arms for the first time. When I first held Bobby in my arms, the words of that song sung by the famed soprano soloist, Alma Gluck, in Des Moines in February of 1919 came to mind:

> Sweetest little fellow,
> Everybody knows,
> Don't know what to call him,
> But he's mighty like a rose.

In the eyes of the Chinese in that day, a son was much to be preferred over a daughter. I remember hearing our Amah telling one of our servants about the birth of our son. "Missy have go hospital side," she said, "catchee one piecey boy baby. Velly good. Velly good." Then referring to another woman who was in the same hospital and who had given birth to a daughter, Amah added: "Other Missy catchee one piecey girl baby. Velly bad. Velly bad."

Following the birth of our son, I was told that it was Chinese custom to order our cook to boil some eggs, dye them red, and give them to our closest friends. I asked what the color should be if the baby were a girl. "Oh," was the reply, "then you don't send any eggs at all."

Our 1925 Vacations

In August I found that I was afflicted again with dysentery. I needed to get away to recuperate. I decided to return to Mokanshan for a ten day vacation. Miriam agreed that it would not be wise to take the baby up the mountain; so I planned to go alone. She would stay home with the baby while I was away. I wrote to my friends, the Wilsons, with whom we had stayed the previous year, and asked if they could receive me for ten days, or, if not, if they could find a place for me. I soon received word that I could stay in the home of Dr. and Mrs. Nelson for $3.00(G) a day. The fact that all supplies had to be carried up the mountain made board this expensive.

I left for Mokanshan on August 17 where I spent the next ten days. I did little hiking. Instead, I rested. Mrs. Nelson's mother, a Mrs. Sperry, was also in the home, and she took delight in reading aloud stories from the *Saturday Evening Post*. I spent hours stretched out on a settee listening to her read. I returned to Shanghai on the 23th of the month much refreshed by this experience.

After my return, we agreed that Miriam should take the baby and the amah and go to Tsingtao for her vacation. One of our best friends, Clifford Petitt, a Y.M.C.A. secretary who was on the Governing Board of the church during my first year in Shanghai, had been transferred to Tsingtao. I wrote to him to ask if they could receive Miriam and the baby into their home. They happened to be living in one of the big houses built by the Germans when they had control of the city. Petitt answered that they had plenty of room and extended a cordial invitation for Miriam to stay with them. Miriam and the baby and the amah left by steamer for Tsingtao on October 1st and returned on the 25th.

Taking advantage of the time I would be alone and realizing that I still had vacation time at my disposal, I decided to pay another visit to the Smiths at Ningpo and, if possible, make an excursion to the famed Buddhist center on Pootoo Island about six hours ride by boat from Ningpo. After making arrangements for someone to take the Sunday service, I gave the servants a ten day vacation, closed the apartment and on October 12th took passage for Ningpo. The Smiths kindly made arrangements for a Baptist missionary stationed at Ningpo, a Mr. Adams, to go with me. Since he knew the language, he could serve as the interpreter.

We booked passage on a small boat no bigger than the average tug boat, which was scheduled to leave on October 17. We took with us a servant, our bed rolls, and some canned meat for we knew that on the island the monks would feed us only rice and vegetables. When we boarded the little vessel we found that over 100 yellow-robed Buddhist monks from Tibet were making the pilgrimage to Pootoo and had also booked passage. The boat was far over crowded. I saw no sign of a life preserver. Adams and I crawled to the top of the pilot house to find some privacy.

Upon arrival at the island, we were quickly surrounded by monks from various temples each vying for our patronage. Adams finally selected a genial looking monk, and the two agreed upon a price for

food and lodging. I have kept no record of the cost. We were led to
a nearby temple and shown a room which was adequate, but the beds
had no mattresses — only boards. Our meals were served in the room.
Being vegetarians, the monks did not even eat eggs or drink milk. We
were glad for the extra food we had taken with us and were careful
to take the empty cans back with us.

My records indicate that there were either 70 or 100 temples and
about 1,000 monks on the island. We saw no women. The island
was dedicated to Kwan Yin, the Buddhist goddess of mercy, and in
some temples we found her statue enshrined where that of Buddha
would usually be placed.

As I recall, the irregular shaped island contained less than one
square mile of land. Adams and I roamed from one end to the other
majoring on the most important temples. One incident stands out in
my memory. We went to one temple which claimed to have a bone
of Buddha. Upon our request, and with the payment of a one dollar
fee, a kindly monk showed us an iron pagoda about twelve or fifteen
inches high. He told us to peer through one of the openings and see
the clapper of a bell fastened to its top. That clapper, so he said,
was the bone of Buddha. I looked first and was able to see the bell
and a grayish object hanging on the inside. The monk asked me:
"What color is it?" And then I remembered an old Buddhist saying:
"He who sees a white bone has a good heart, but he who sees a
black bone has a bad heart." I stretched the truth when I replied to
the monk: "It looks white to me." The old monk beamed: "You have
a good heart."

Then Adams took a look. He was less informed and certainly more
honest when he replied: "It looks black to me." The monk's face fell
and he said sadly: "Some people do see black."

We returned to Ningpo on October 20th, and I was back in Shanghai on the 25th, the same day that Miriam, the amah, and the baby
returned from Tsingtao. Bobby then weighed nearly fourteen pounds,
having doubled his weight in about four months. He was a healthy,
happy child and brought us great joy.

Dreams for the Future

Ever since I aspired to win the Alumni Fellowship in my Seminary,
when I was graduated in 1922, and which I failed to get, I dreamed of
somehow being able to go to Edinburgh University and work for a
Ph.D. degree. Since Shanghai was nearly half-way around the world
between California and Scotland, I felt that it might be possible to
use such travel funds as would be available when it was time to
return to the States and continue our journey around the world to
Edinburgh.

Under the terms of my call to the pulpit of Community Church, I agreed to remain for five years or until, by mutual consent, a shorter period was agreeable. September 1925 marked the half-way point in my five year term. I then took stock of my assets and considered how it might be possible for the three of us to go to Edinburgh. The major problem would be financial. Since I had no fellowship, I would be entirely dependent on my own resources. Although my salary of $500.00(M) a month was more than the average missionary couple received, yet it did not always cover expenses. During my first two years in Shanghai I often had to get a loan from the bank in order to pay expenses.

When I took stock of our resources in September 1925, I found that my only savings had been the $260.00(G) annual premiums paid for insurance. I had been informed by friends of mine who had studied at Edinburgh that it would be possible for me to get a position as assistant pastor in one of the city's churches. I counted on that. Also, I knew that the church would give me the cost of our fare across the Pacific, which then amounted to about $400.00(G) per person. I would also be entitled to my pay for my last month, one month's travel pay to return to the States, and one month's vacation pay — making a total of $750.00(G).

I wrote to Miriam on October 3, 1925 saying: "We did not save a cent last month." I reminded her that we both would have to do more to save if we were to go to Scotland. Looking back, I now realize that this decision to go to Edinburgh and study for my doctor's degree was one of the most crucial in my life. My life after leaving China would have been far different from what it was if I had not gotten the Ph.D. degree.

Having renewed my dream of working for my Ph.D. degree at Edinburgh, I became more alert to gather source materials for my thesis. The civil disorders in Shanghai, Canton, and other cities; the increasing objection to the foreign treaties which infringed on the sovereign rights of China; and also the growing anti-foreign agitation made my proposed study of the relationships of Christian missions to foreign treaties all the more timely. I began to collect materials which I felt might be of value when I arrived in Edinburgh in the fall of 1927 and began work on my thesis.

When the American School began in September 1925, I was asked by the Principal to teach a one-hour per week Bible class for the pupils in the seventh grade and also another one-hour class for the eighth graders. School credit was given for these classes.

Writing to relatives in Iowa on November 5, 1925, I reported that up to that date, I had welcomed 311 new members into the church, but, at the same time, had dismissed 326. There was almost a 25% turnover each year. This was normal; but, after the civil disturbances broke out, the number of people leaving for the States increased. Even so, the average attendance that fall was about 350.

My wedding records show that about half of the weddings performed were for non-Americans. They came from Russia, Japan, Philippines, Korea, and also from several European countries. I averaged about twelve weddings a month.

I was honored in November when I was asked to deliver the annual Thanksgiving address which was held that year in the Anglican Cathedral located at the corner of the race track. The invitation came from the American Counsel General, E. S. Cunningham. The sanctuary could seat about 600, and was filled to capacity that day with many standing. I spoke on the theme: "Why Give Thanks." After tracing out the history of the observance of the day in the United States, I gave a list of reasons why we Americans should set aside one day in the year on which, as a people, we should render our thanks to God for the blessings we had received. I avoided making any reference to the unsettled political situation which had threatened the peace and tranquility of the city.

In his letter of appreciation, dated November 27, 1925, the day following the service, the Counsel General stated: "Perhaps you do not know that in one particular, your address was a relief in that it contained no reference to local conditions which would have proven embarrassing to Department of State officials. This is exceptional, and when one listens to an address which is not likely to carry unfavorable comment, it is a great relief." A sixty voice choir contributed special musical numbers which added much to the service.

The sermon was printed in full by the English *North China Daily News* and by the American *China Press*. One of these papers reprinted the sermon in pamphlet form.

In a letter to my sister, Joyce, dated December 20, 1925, I related the following experience which I had with a would-be thief. "I awoke at four o'clock Monday morning," I wrote, "when I heard the bamboo gate creak on its hinges. I jumped out of bed, looked out of the window and saw a man go into our yard in the dark. I slipped on my bathrobe and slippers and crept down stairs. The church parlor and kitchen were under our apartment. I went out on the small porch which was at the head of the stairway leading from the servant's quarters. I turned on the light which lit up the whole back yard. At first I couldn't see him, and then I spied him standing behind the screen door leading into the church's kitchen. Perhaps the would-be thief felt that the Sunday's collection would be in that room.

"How to catch him was the problem. If I started down the back stairs, he would run." At the time I had no thought of him having a knife. Guns then were hard for the natives to own; so I had no fear of being shot. Our cook used to sun himself on that porch by sitting on a heavy stool, about two and one-half feet high. I picked this up and, leaning over the railing, swung it at the prowler. It hit him on the shoulder. The heavy padded coat he was wearing probably saved him from injury. Later Miriam commented that I was lucky I did not hit him on the head for he would have suffered a serious injury. I summoned up my meager command of the Chinese language and told him to come up quickly. This he did. He had a big muffler wrapped around his neck. I grabbed this with my left hand and led him through the kitchen to the telephone in the hall.

I called the French police, for we lived in the French concession, and within ten minutes two policemen arrived. They arrested the man who was found carrying a large number of keys. Later I was told that he was an old offender.

The next day I overheard our amah saying that "Master has velly good joss," which was her way of saying God was watching over me. Afterwards, looking back on the incident, I felt that I had acted foolishly for the thief might have attacked me with a knife, but at the time I felt no fear.

Before the end of December 1925, my sister Sarah wrote saying she and her husband, Hillis Lory, were going to Japan. As has been stated, I tried to get Hillis and Sarah appointed to the faculty of the American School, but this effort failed because the school had no provision to have a married couple on their staff. However, their names were on file with an interdenominational committee in New York for a foreign appointment. When the Imperial University at Sapporo, on the northern island of Hokkaido, Japan, sent in a request for someone to head their English Department, the papers referring to Hillis and Sarah were already on hand. This resulted in a quick appointment. The Lorys arrived in Sapporo during the first part of January 1926. As later events proved, that appointment completely changed the future for the Lorys. Upon hearing this news, I at once dreamed of going to Sapporo the following spring to see them.

CHAPTER FOURTEEN

Our Closing Months in Shanghai

Our last eighteen months in Shanghai — January 1926 to June 1927 — were filled with more events of excitement and concern than in any comparable period during the previous three years. The first of these events was the coming to Japan of my sister Sarah and her husband, Hillis Lory. They arrived in Yokohama on January 9, 1926. We at once made plans to visit each other.

On March 1, 1926, after the church had received Captain Dollar's annual gift of $1,000.00(G) for our current expenses, I wrote him a letter of appreciation. After referring to the fact that I had completed three years of service as pastor of the church, I gave the following summary of our accomplishments: "Since being here, we have received 329 into the church of which number 84 came on their first confession of faith. During this period we have dismissed as many as we have received. The turnover is about 25% each year. This constitutes one of our major problems. One of our biggest accomplishments has been the erection of our new church building . . . During the last three years the church has raised about $135,000.00(M). This does not include the increased value of the land estimated to be about $29,000.00(G). Our debt is now $40,000.00(M)."

During the latter part of April, Miriam and I, with the baby and his amah, took a seven-hour train ride to Nanking where I was to speak at a Christian Endeavor convention. About thirty young people from the American School also made the trip. At the time of our visit to Nanking, the city was encircled by an ancient wall about twenty-three miles long. In some places the wall was fifty feet high and wide enough for the young people of the convention to play such games as three-deep on its top. The eastern gate was about fifty feet long. Going through it was like going through a tunnel. Nanking suffered widespread devastation during the Tai Ping rebellion which ravaged central China for about fifteen years beginning in 1850. I remember seeing extensive ruins when we visited Nanking which had been caused by the Tai Pings. At the close of the convention, I returned to Shanghai, while Miriam, the baby, and the amah remained in Nanking for another two weeks.

By the spring of 1926, Miriam and I had decided to ask to have my term of service as pastor of Community Church shortened by about eight months so that we could leave in June of 1927 for Edinburgh, Scotland, where I wanted to study for my Ph.D. degree. I wrote to one of my favorite seminary professors, Dr. E. A. Wicher, and asked for his advice. He replied on August 11, 1926, saying: "By all means go to Edinburgh and get a Ph.D. degree. If it is largely a financial question with you, let me tell you the value of your stock will be so much enhanced by this degree that you will get back dividends on the investment. This is putting it on the lowest level. On the highest, you would be a still greater man mentally for the rest of your days by reason of the experience of a year in Edinburgh."

Since I would have to depend entirely on my own resources during the year I would be off salary, I made inquiries of a few of my friends who had studied at Edinburgh regarding the chances of my getting a position in one of the Presbyterian churches in the city as an assistant pastor. The answers I received were most encouraging.

MY TRIP TO JAPAN

Upon the arrival of my sister Sarah and her husband, Hillis Lory, at Sapporo located on the northern island of Hokkaido, both she and I began to make plans to see each other. Sarah wrote that if I did not come to Sapporo, she would flood Japan with her tears. At first, after I made the decision to go to Japan, I wanted Miriam and the baby to go with me; but when I learned that the trip would involve a two-day voyage by steamer from Shanghai to Kobe and then a long train trip of over 1,000 miles from Kobe to Sapporo, Miriam felt that such a long trip was too much for us to take a year-old baby. Later, after making the journey, I realized how wise she was. So we decided that I should go alone, and she would remain with amah and Bobby.

By this time she was driving the car and thus could be quite independent of me. I recall that while away on a trip, one of my church members taught Miriam to drive; when I returned, I found her at the dock waiting for me with the car. I was rather amazed, for driving a car in Shanghai then, with its thousands of rickshaws, was no easy task; but she managed very well.

I left Shanghai on a Japanese steamer on July 7 and arrived at Kobe on the 9th. I stopped over at Tokyo that Friday night, and then left the next noon by train for Sapporo. I took a berth on the train which proved to be very uncomfortable. For one thing, it was too short, and I was unable to stretch out fully. I learned a few Japanese words in advance so that I could order lunch and tea. The box lunches provided for train passengers consisted largely of rice and raw fish, including octopus. The raw fish did not appeal to me. The train guards, usually young men, were eager to practice their English on me, so I often had one or two sitting with me. After crossing the straits by ferry, which separated the northern island of Hokkaido from the main island, I boarded another train for Sapporo where I arrived at 1:00 p.m. on Saturday, July 10.

Hillis and Sarah met me at the depot. I have no words to describe the ecstacy of our meeting. This was the first time I had seen Sarah since the summer of 1922, and the first time I had seen Hillis. They had ridden on their bicycles to the depot. They hired a rickshaw for me. This was much higher than the rickshaws used in Shanghai. I found Sapporo much like an American city with wide streets. The house provided by the University for the Lorys was round with the main room in the center. We stayed up until two o'clock the next morning visiting and sharing letters from relatives in the States.

I spent about three weeks with the Lorys and the time passed rapidly. Sarah invited the President of the Imperial University, Dr. Sato, and his wife, in for a dinner; and, in turn, they soon had us as their guests.

Among the interesting people I met were the Rev. and Mrs. William Idhe, Methodist missionaries. Idhe was an enterprising soul who had made contacts with curio dealers in Tokyo and Kyoto, from whom he was able to buy such Japanese products as imitation pearls, lacquered and painted salad plates, and richly embroidered items as kimonos and shawls at wholesale prices. Th imitation pearls were of superior quality. They were made by digging out a piece from the inside of a clam shell and then covering it with a pearly substance and baking it. Some of the pearls were baked a dozen times or more. These imitation pearls could be thrown on the floor and stepped on without damaging the pearl.

I bought several hundred dollars worth of these pearls in long strings or chokers which I sold, some to a curio store in Shanghai and others to friends in Edinburgh at a 100% profit. The necklace string, called a choker, I got for $2.50(G) and usually sold for $5.00.

One week in July we took an excursion of one hundred miles or more to Lake Toya where we were to live in a cottage owned by one of the Lory's missionary friends. On the way to the lake, we left the train to visit an Ainu village. The Ainu were the aborigines of Japan and were treated by the Imperial Government somewhat as the American Indians had been treated in America. The Ainu were of Caucasian descent, not Oriental. The men were hairy, and the women tatooed their lips and chins to make it appear that they had mustaches. Their language was unlike any other known language.

We called first on the Rev. Mr. Batchelor, an English Anglican who had spent many years as a missionary to the Ainu. He graciously received us and gave us much information about these people. He then acted as our guide and took us to an Ainu home. There we took pictures, especially of some of the women who had been tatooed on their faces.

Our next stop on our tour was at the popular Japanese health and vacation resort at Noboribitsu which was located near an old volcano. Here we got rooms in a Japanese inn and spent the night. After taking a tour of the hot springs area inside the volcano, I wrote to Miriam: "I have never seen such a magnificent mixture of color. Steam was escaping from thousands of horizontal and vertical vents." In some places little pools of water were boiling furiously. At times we were almost overcome by the hot sulphur fumes.

The town contained many bath houses where, according to Japanese custom, men and women bathed nude in the same pool. In our hotel we had private baths with large tubs through which hot sulphur water from the volcano flowed all the time. One could regulate the temperature by turning on the cold water.

I started back to Shanghai on August 8. On this return trip, I was able to do some sightseeing in Tokyo, Kyoto and Nara. I marvel now as to how I was able to do so much traveling without knowing the language. I always found someone who was able to speak some English. By August 16, I was gladly back in Shanghai. I found my son Bobby then weighing about twenty-five pounds and beginning to walk. Before leaving Sapporo, the Lorys and I made tentative plans for them to visit us in Shanghai in the spring of 1927.

Hillis and Sarah remained in Japan for almost three more years after I had visited them. During those years they had the prophetic insight to realize that eventually the Generals of Japan might some day challenge China and even the United States. So both began to collect information regarding the military power of the Japanese Empire. Hillis had opportunity to meet some of the leading political figures in Japan. He was able to gather a wealth of material regarding the strength of the various branches of the military and the possible threat that this posed for the entire Pacific basin.

In 1943 Hillis published his *Japan's Military Masters*. The former ambassador to Japan, Joseph Grew, who became Acting Secretary of State in the U.S., wrote the Foreword. The book ran through several editions in the United States and abroad. In May 1943 the U.S. Government ordered 250,000 paperback copies of the book for distribution to our military forces. Largely because of this book, Hillis received an appointment from Grew to a position in the State Department where he remained until his retirement in 1964.

ASKED TO RESIGN

Shortly after my return from Japan, Dr. J. C. McCracken, a member of the Governing Board, informed me that a few of my "closest friends" had approached him with the suggestion that I resign. Dr. McCracken did not tell me who these men were, but it appeared that they were dissatisfied with my preaching. I was stunned for I felt that the church was in excellent condition. As subsequent events proved, that which at the time seemed to be a great personal disaster turned out to be a blessing in disguise. In my distress, I turned to Colonel George S. Stroebe, an engineer in the employ of the Chinese Government and a member of the Governing Board of the church, for advice. Colonel Stroebe was incensed that Dr. McCracken should have passed on the suggestion that I resign without first consulting with the members of the Governing Board. He gave me encouragement to carry on.

After discussing the situation with my wife and making the decision that I should study for my Ph.D. degree at Edinburgh, I submitted my resignation to the Governing Board of Community Church on October 1, 1926. Dr. E. W. Wallace, then Chairman of the Board together with Clifford Pettit, the secretary, wrote to me on October 14 warmly commending my ministry in Community Church and also stated: "The ideal which draws you to Scotland is one which commends itself very strongly to the Governing Board." The Board accepted the date which I had suggested for the termination of my ministry. Public announcement of my decision appeared in the October 15 issue of Community Service, our weekly newsletter which was then being mailed to all of the church's constituency.

This would mean cutting my expected five-year term short by about eight months, and it would give us time to take a three-month trip through Europe and land in Edinburgh by October 1, in time for me to enroll in the fall term of New College, a part of Edinburgh University.

I began to plan our itinerary. I realized that if we left Shanghai in June 1927, we would be going through the Indian Ocean during the monsoon season, the worst time of the year for such a voyage. In those days the ships had no air conditioners. The weather would be stormy and hot. I wrote to Florence Mitchell Wylie, one of my college classmates who, with her husband Harry Wylie, were serving as Presbyterian missionaries at Lahore, India. Florence replied on October 6, 1926, saying: "You are taking a mighty big risk, not only for the baby, but also for Miriam and yourself."

I was disturbed over the necessity of making public my resignation some ten months before my family and I expected to leave Shanghai. I felt that my efficiency as the pastor of Community Church would be adversely affected, but such was not the case. Indeed there were some positive benefits to the early announcement. My critics were silenced. Moreover, I was able to interview members of my congregation who had traveled through Europe on a limited budget, as I knew we would have to do. I was able to secure the names of pensions, as small boarding houses were called, in the various cities we expected to visit.

There was no lessening of activities in the church's program during the closing months of 1926. I still taught Bible classes in the American School. My morning audiences ran from 340 to 450.

Shortly after we had dedicated our new building, I preached one morning on the text found in Romans 8:28: "We know that to them that love God all things work together for good." An hour or more after the service, I received a telephone call from a salesman who worked in an English clothing store. He asked me to call on him, which I did. I then heard a strange story of how he had been harassed by his co-workers and others who in subtle ways had led him to believe that he was going crazy. This so preyed on his mind that he had decided to commit suicide. He bought a revolver, but before actually killing himself, he decided to go to church. He did not want to go to one of the English churches in Shanghai; so came out to our Community Church. By the grace of God, that sermon changed his whole outlook on life. His whole attitude changed; he gave up the idea of suicide. I called on him several times thereafter in his store and found him happy and readjusted. He had discovered a new meaning to life.

OUR INFANT SON SERIOUSLY ILL

Almost without exception, all foreigners who went to China during the time we were there got dysentery. Both my wife and I suffered from this affliction and each of us had to undergo an operation for hemorrhoids. This was a price we had to pay for living in the Orient.

Our son, then eighteen months old, came down with a virulent form of dysentery the first of November 1926. Of course, we called our doctor, Dr. Alfred Swann, who used the best antidotes then available, but seemingly to no effect. He grew worse. Miriam and I took turns sitting up with him for more than a week; then on November 7th, we hired a Chinese nurse to take over the night duty. She stayed with us for two weeks. Bobby's fever would often rise to 103. When, in despair as to whether he would live, our doctor came with some new antibiotic serum which he had just received from the States. The treatment called for the injection of 50 c.c. of the medicine at a time with several days in between injections. I remember holding the baby in my arms when each injection was given and seeing a bulge arise under the skin of his abdomen where the injection was made. The medicine was effective, and soon our son was on the way to recovery. However, it was not until the middle of December that he felt strong enough to try to walk again. We almost lost him.

In a letter to one of my Iowa relatives, I wrote: "Our amah, who is a devout Buddhist, has been diligently burning her candles and doing her 'joss pigeon' for Bobby's recovery . . . 'Master,' she told me today, 'three times I talkee God make Bobby better.'" It so happened that her three visits to a Buddhist temple, where she made a cash donation out of her meager salary, coincided with the three visits of Dr. Swann who gave the three injections. When Bobby showed such marked improvement, no one could tell her that this was not the result of her prayers to Buddha, and I did not try. I was deeply grateful for her concern.

Our last six months in Shanghai were marked with some exciting events. The Communist forces under command of Chiang Kai-Shek, then a Communist, were on the march from Canton to Nanking. The anti-foreign attitudes of the Communists were so well known that the authorities at Shanghai called for troops to protect the settlements. England sent the Coldstream Guards; the United States sent the 4th Marines under command of General Smedley Butler; and the French sent some of their troops. I recall that we had about 26,000 foreign troops to guard the twenty-six mile perimeter of the two settlements. Barbed wire barricades were erected at strategic points. Some trenches were dug and mines were laid. Foreign war vessels were at anchor off the Bund, the waterfront street of Shanghai. Plans were made for the evacuation of all American citizens to Manila.

Writing to a relative in Early, Iowa, on January 21, 1927, I stated: "We don't know what a day will bring forth. The Chinese within the Settlements, sympathetic with the Communists, are threatening to discontinue light and water services. There is a possibility that servants for foreigners might be forced to strike." During those troubled days, our servants were afraid to go out at night. Thousands of Chinese, fleeing from the approaching Communist army, sought refuge within the international settlements at Shanghai but were refused admittance by the foreign troops.

An exciting event took place on Sunday evening, February 20, when I was conducting a vesper service in the social room of the church. When the church was erected in 1924-25, an annex measuring about 30 x 40 feet, three stories and an attic high, was built at the southeast corner of the sanctuary. About twenty-five feet of the annex was attached to the main building with the other fifteen feet extending beyond it. The ground floor contained a social hall and kitchen; the second and third floors provided living quarters for our family.

Shanghai was built on low land; one could not dig down more than three or four feet without striking water. Needing a furnace room, the architect planned a 10 x 10 foot room at the corner where the annex extended beyond the sanctuary. This room was sunk about three feet below the surface of the ground with the rest above ground. A slab of reinforced concrete, three or four inches thick, provided the roof. The furnace room contained two furnaces — a large one which could heat the entire structure, and a small one to be used only to heat the annex. A couple of valves were installed so that when the big furnace was burning, the small furnace would be shut off. Likewise when the small furnace was lit, the valve of the big furnace governing hot water pipes leading to the annex was closed, and the valves on the small furnace were opened.

On this particular Sunday evening, I instructed our Chinese gardener to build a fire in the small furnace in order to heat the social room, for the day was chilly. The gardener built a roaring fire but failed to open the valve which let the hot water flow into the radiators in the social hall. Just as our soloist, Mrs. Joel Black, was singing "Going Home" — home was heaven and not the United States — there came a thunderous roar, and the whole building shook.

Greatly alarmed, we all rushed out of the rear entrance of the annex to see what had happened. We saw a cloud of steam pouring out of the furnace room, not only from its only entrance but amazingly through a hole in the concrete roof. Later we discovered that the pent up steam forced an explosion which blew the top of the furnace through the reinforced concrete roof. If that furnace room had been under the social hall, not one of us would have survived. All of us would have been "going home."

We found pieces of the top of the furnace and discovered that a nut had been screwed into the hole where a safety valve should have been. At the time of the installation of the small furnace, one of the Chinese workmen had simply substituted a nut for the safety valve, and then, presumably, had sold the safety valve.

Another exciting incident took place three days later on the evening of February 23. I was putting our little boy, then some twenty months old, to bed when I heard a terrific explosion which sounded as though it was just outside of the bedroom window. I looked out and saw an inverted cone of dirt fly up in a vacant lot less than a block away. Then I heard the whizzing sound of a mortar shell going overhead, followed by another explosion several blocks away. And then came a third shell which also landed several blocks away. Later we learned that the firing of the three-inch shells came from a Chinese gunboat which was lying at anchor in the Whangpoo River a couple of miles distant. Fortunately the church and our apartment were not hit.

About the time of this random shooting, a skirmish took place on the western borders of the French Concession between some of the Communist soldiers and the anti-Communist troops. The fighting was close enough for some of the American School buildings and our church to be hit by stray bullets. The children at the school sought safety on the off-side of the dormitories. Later, one of the boys told me of the excitement they experienced by counting the splashes in a pond where stray bullets were landing. Again, no damage was done, but the incident added to our concern. What would happen next?

About three weeks after the furnace blew up, my sister Sarah and her husband, Hillis Lory, paid us a visit from their home in Japan. Having heard of the Chinese gunboat firing on the French Concession and about other disturbances, they had cabled me asking if it was safe for them to come. I cabled back: "Perfectly safe." They arrived on March 14.

At the time of their arrival, Chiang Kai-Shek's soldiers were clearing out pockets of resistance in the Chinese areas surrounding the International Settlements. We often could hear bursts of gunfire. Writing to my brother Billy of April 7, 1927, I reported that Hillis had said: "I'm glad to be in Shanghai at this time. The eyes of the world are on this city. This is where history is being made."

A few days after he had made that remark, I took him to downtown Shanghai, and we got to the top of a high building where "we listened to rifle fire a mile away in the Chapei district and saw great columns of smoke rising from a section of the burning Chinese city." The streets below us were packed with people. We could see some of the foreign troops marching to and fro. The whole situation was fraught with danger. Then Hillis made another remark which I passed on to my brother: "I've seen all the history-in-the-making that I want to. I would rather have the earthquakes of Japan than these wars of China. Let's get out of here." I confess that I was then also becoming nervous and was quite willing to go back to the quiet of the French Concession.

In this same letter to my brother, I told of a practical joke I had played on Sarah and Hillis which turned out to be more realistic than I had expected. We were surrounded with Chinese neighbors who, on special occasions such as a funeral or a wedding, would touch off large firecrackers which exploded twice — once on the ground and again some thirty or more feet in the air. I knew that my Chinese neighbors would think nothing of it should I explode a few such firecrackers myself. So, I sent one of our servants out to buy a dozen of the biggest firecrackers he could find.

On the evening selected for the firecracker barrage, Miriam put Bobby to bed rather early. She was in on the plot and cooperated wonderfully. I took the firecrackers to our gardener and showed him what I wanted him to do. I placed them a few feet apart on the sidewalk just under our dining room window. I then gave him some matches and told him to fire all of them when our cook would give him the signal that we had finished our dinner.

During the course of the meal, Hillis, not knowing what was about to happen, unknowingly set the stage by asking: "What shall we do if the war breaks out?" I then gave some elaborate directions, keeping as straight a face as possible. "Well," I said, "if there is fighting just to the west of us and bullets begin hitting the building, don't keep sitting in front of that large window, but get down behind the brick wall where you will be protected. But if the Chinese begin firing that three-inch gun, then run for the furnace room. Even if there is a hole in the ceiling, it is the safest place we have."

After making some elaborations on these directions, I let the cook know that it was time for him to signal the gardener to begin firing the firecrackers. With the first "boom," followed by a larger boom overhead, both Sarah and Hillis showed alarm. Then came another double explosion. Knowing that these were not rifle bullets, Hillis made no effort to get off his chair and hide behind the brick wall. With the third firecracker, I shouted: "To the furnace room," and Miriam added reality to the scene by crying out: "Get the baby."

Hillis and Sarah, dragging Miriam with them, tore down the stairs to the furnace room while I went upstairs intending to wrap a baby blanket around a pillow and then come down. Before I could get a pillow, I heard Miriam calling: "Clifford, come down. They are too scared for this to be funny." I hurried down. Just as I arrived at the outside door, the gardener came holding an unexploded firecracker and in his best pigeon English explained: "Master, this won't go off. The wick is too short." Hillis and Sarah were so relieved to know that it was all a joke that they were able to join us in laughter.

Several months later, Hillis attended a dinner party in Japan when the host told this story with some embellishment, not knowing that one of the victims of the practical joke was a guest at his table. Hillis endured the story in silence.

Although Sarah and Hillis had planned to spend three weeks with us, they found that the tension and excitement was too much. After ten days they decided to return to Japan. Better the earthquakes of Japan than the wars of China.

"WILLIAM IS SERIOUSLY ILL"

After securing the country around Shanghai, Chiang Kai-Shek moved his troops up along the Yangtze River to Nanking, a former capital of China which was surrounded by a twenty-six mile wall.

The city was quickly captured. Some of Chiang's troops got out of control and ran amuck through the city, pillaging and burning foreign properties. Several American missionaries were killed. Finally, the American gunboats, which were lying at anchor in the river, opened fire. This frightened the rampaging soldiers who permitted the American residents to flee to the river where they boarded the gunboats and were taken to Shanghai.

A few days after the Lorys had left for their home, I turned to my crystal set to get the evening news. Suddenly, interspersed with the news, came the cryptic message: "William is seriously ill." Then followed several short sentences, ending with, "Have cabled to America." I felt convinced that this was a code designed to warn Americans living in isolated towns and cities in the vicinity of Shanghai. I hastened to the home of a neighbor who was a Baptist secretary at the Missionary Headquarters. He was startled when I quoted the message to him for it was indeed a code with every short sentence having a different meaning. The first sentence: "William is seriously ill," meant that all Americans should be on the alert for the situation was getting worse. The last sentence, "Have cabled to America," meant that a dangerous situation had developed and all foreigners should leave at once for Shanghai. It was the original thought that the situation would develop gradually. Each of the short sentences gave instructions for another stage in the unfolding situation. When I gave the coded message to my Baptist friend, he said: "Something terrible has happened which prompted the full code to be given." Of course, we did not know what was taking place in Nanking, nor could the foreign authorities in Shanghai be specific. That would alert the anti-foreign elements and might have led to the death of some foreigners.

I do not know the reaction of other nationals, but the Americans moved quickly. They came to Shanghai by whatever means of transportation was available. They reached the safety of Shanghai's borders before the general Chinese public had learned what had happened at Nanking. Had not this warning been broadcast, no doubt many foreigners would have been killed in revenge for American gunboats firing on Nanking.

Our United States gunboats brought hundreds of refugees down the Yangtze River to Shanghai. We received two from Nanking — William H. Clark, a seminary schoolmate, and his mother. We also received two who came by ocean steamer from Ningpo — our friends Elleroy and Mabelle Smith. The Clarks stayed only a short time, but the Smiths spent about three months with us, leaving shortly before we sailed for Edinburgh.

On March 30, I called at the Navy Y.M.C.A. on North Sechuan Road; I was then serving as a member of its Board of Directors. To my surprise I found a company of forty-seven men, women and children of the Lutheran Augustana Synod Mission who had just arrived by steamer from the interior of China. There were twenty-two children. They had no place to go. Most were seated on their baggage wondering what would happen to them. Without taking time to check with any member of my Governing Board, I invited all to stay in Community Church. I explained that they would have to sleep on the floor but the church did have a social hall which would be their dining room, a kitchen, and toilet facilities. My invitation was accepted with alacrity. The group camped in the church from March 30 to April 9.

The influx of refugees, so many of whom were missionaries, was reflected in my church's attendance. My records show that on April 5, 1927, 600 were present; April 10, 550; and April 17, 625. On this latter date, General Smedley Butler and members of his staff were present. The seating capacity of the church was stretched to its utmost capacity.

Of course, there was an exodus of Americans and other nationals from Shanghai as fast as steamer accommodations were available. In a letter to Iowa relatives dated April 7, 1927, I wrote: "Thousands have been leaving Shanghai — 4,000 left in the last two weeks, and still many are here." On April 27th, I wrote to my brother, Billy: "The President Pierce of the Dollar Line leaves this morning with about 500 passengers, most of them being missionaries." Some were going to Japan, others to San Francisco.

General Chiang broke with the Communist party following his capture of Nanking and headed the Nationalist party. He also became a Christian.

PREPARING TO LEAVE SHANGHAI

During the winter and spring of 1926-27, Miriam and I were able to send some of our belongings to relatives in Berkeley, California, with friends who were on their way back to the States. These items included our table silver and some Chinese curios.

On June 10, 1927, I turned over to the Dollar Steamship Line twenty-seven boxes of household effects for shipment to San Francisco. According to the bill of lading, the shipment weighed more than three tons and occupied 218 cubic feet. The many boxes which contained the books made up a good portion of the weight.

By the first of January, 1927, my wife and I began to make definite plans for a three or four-month sightseeing trip from Shanghai to

Edinburgh. I wanted to be in Edinburgh about October 1, in time to enroll for the fall quarter at the University. We wanted to spend about a month in the Holy Land, if possible.

Early in January, I made reservations for the three of us to go second-class on the S.S. Angers of the French Messageries Maritimes line for our passage from Shanghai to Port Said, and then first-class from Beiruit to Brindisi, Italy. The cost in U.S. money was $503.76. According to the receipt which I received when I paid for our passage, the steamship company gave me a 20% "missionary reduction," which was most welcome.

The possibility of completing our journey around the world, of spending three terms at the University to fulfill residential requirements for the doctor's degree, all when I would have no salary coming in, was frightening. I had no scholarship for advanced studies. Upon inquiry, I learned that the church would pay me one month's salary for travel time to cross the Pacific, plus one month's vacation. This would give me $500.00. I would also have my last month's pay — another $250.00. The risks were great. Such an opportunity would never come again if we returned to the United States across the Pacific . . . but what if we became stranded in some foreign country without funds?

I preached my farewell sermon in Community Church on Sunday, June 12, with about 500 in my congregation. I took for my text II Timothy 2:8 — "Remember Jesus Christ." I used the same theme when I closed my ministry in the First Presbyterian Church of Moscow, Idaho, in July of 1938; and also when I completed my twenty-five years of service as Professor of Church History at San Francisco Theological Seminary in 1963.

During this service in Shanghai, I welcomed forty-three new members into the church, among whom were my old friends, Elleroy and Mabelle Smith. For less than a week I was their pastor. That evening I spoke to an audience of sailors and marines in the Navy Y.M.C.A. on North Sechaun Road in downtown Shanghai.

My last religious service was a prayer meeting held on Wednesday evening in the church. About seventy-five were present. At the close of this meeting, a farewell reception was held for my wife and myself when another group of about seventy-five joined those who had come earlier. Mr. George Stroebe, then Chairman of the Governing Board of the Church, presented us with a sterling silver bowl mounted on a carved blackwood stand. On one side of the bowl was an engraving of bamboo; on the other was our names and an inscription stating that this came as a gift from the church. The realization that my ministry of over four years was nearly over induced feelings of emotion too deep to be expressed. It was hard to say goodby to so many fine people, most of whom I was never to see again.

Thursday and Friday of that week were spent in packing, paying bills, buying American Express money orders, and paying off the servants. We were especially grateful for the amah who had taken such good care of Bobby for two years.

I had to buy an extra small trunk to take care of the boxed silver bowl and other gifts which came during those last few days. Knowing that we would be traveling in the summer weather, I packed a suit-Express at Lucerne, Switzerland. Our schedule indicated that we would arrive in Lucerne on September 12 when warmer clothing would be needed. Likewise, I packed a trunk with our winter clothing and other items which was to be sent ahead to London. I confined our luggage to three suitcases and a duffle bag for our European trip. For shipboard use, I took with us a folding cot and a wicker easy chair. These were much appreciated when we had to sleep on deck while going across the Indian Ocean. Such items were discarded when we reached Port Said.

During those last few days in Shanghai, we rarely had a meal by ourselves at home. Rather, we were the guests of close friends. Saturday morning, June 18, the day we left, the Smiths who had been living with us as refugees from Ningpo and who had moved into their own apartment, had us in for a waffle breakfast. I had previously made arrangements for a Chinese drayman to call for our baggage at 9:00 o'clock and take it to the ship. I had all the baggage aboard and stowed away by 10:10 a.m. Soon afterwards friends brought Miriam and the baby to the ship, and shortly after that the Stroebes and Miss Russell arrived.

Before noon, the Drury party of nine were all on board. As the only adult male, I was the one responsible for our itinerary and all shore arrangements. I had written ahead for pension reservations for Cairo and Jerusalem. Other reservations were made later, but always in advance. We knew where we were going to stay before we arrived at any of our sight-seeing points.

A crowd of about seventy-five were on the dock to see us and other passengers off. There was much noise and confusion as the last minute preparations for the ship's departure were being made. Bobby was very restless. Once, while carrying him, I came close enough for him to grab my hat which I had hung on a hook in the cabin. This he put on my head, an eloquent way of saying: "Take me home." But there was no turning back.

CHAPTER FIFTEEN

Shanghai to Edinburgh

Our journey from Shanghai to Edinburgh, Scotland, extended from June 18 to October 1, 1927. The journey was unique in several respects. In those days the ships were not air conditioned. When we crossed the Indian Ocean in July, the temperature in our cabin rose to 90°, and we had to keep our porthole closed because of the high waves. For a month while sailing from Shanghai to Egypt, we receive no mail or other communications until we arrived in Egypt.

Also unique was the fact that we had with us our two-year-old son, Bobby, whom I was frequently obliged to carry, with him sitting astride my neck through museums, art galleries, and churches without number. He then weighed from twenty-five to thirty pounds. We took with us four gallons of a powdered milk for which the brand name was Momilk. This supplemented his diet on shipboard before we arrived in Egypt. On the whole, Bobby was a good traveler and remained in excellent health throughout the long journey, as did his mother and I.

An amazing aspect of our journey of more than three months was the low cost as compared to modern day prices. My expense record shows that, after paying for our steamer passage to Port Said and then for passage from Beirut to Naples, I had only $996.64 to cover all other expenses. The cost of our passports and visas for Egypt, Palestine, Syria, Greece, Turkey, Italy, Switzerland, France, and England came to $51.50. Out of the balance of $915.00 had to come all of our travel expenses from Port Said to Edinburgh. The margin was extremely narrow, for I had less than $9.00 when we arrived in Edinburgh. This meant that the average daily cost, including hotels, railroad fares, entrance fees for museums, etc., came to $2.53 for the three Drurys. I marvel now at our faith.

Traveling with us as far as Switzerland were Mrs. George Stroebe and her three children — Helen, 18, Billy, 14, and Dickie, 10. Also in the party was Elizabeth Blaine, better known as Nono, the daughter of a missionary, and Miss Victoria Russell, a missionary on her way to the United States. Since I was the only man in the group, I had to make most of the travel arrangements.

Before leaving Shanghai we were given a large bag of feathers to deliver to Miss Hilda Anderson in Jerusalem. The feathers were a great nuisance, but Miss Anderson proved to be a great help to us when we were in Jerusalem.

The sources for this chapter include my abbreviated diary, a detailed record of all expenses, and copies of some twenty-five or more letters written en route on my portable typewriter to relatives and friends. I was also privileged to read a detailed diary kept by the eighteen-year-old Helen Stroebe who traveled with us as far as Switzerland. Helen became a physician and married a doctor, Fred Clark. The two called on us at our Pasadena home on Sunday, December 16, 1979. We viewed pictures taken on the trip and compared notes. Memories of incidents which had taken place fifty-two years before were quickened. Helen's diary, so rich in detail, was left with me and I have been free to draw upon it for facts which I had forgotten.

Thus, in the account which follows, I draw freely upon documented evidence plus memory, and not upon imagination.

One Month at Sea

A little after 12:30, the S.S. Angers, once a German vessel but taken over by the French after World War I, cast off and we moved down the Whangpoo River to the Yangtze and then out to sea. Our days in China had come to an end. Our cabin was small, having two berths and a padded bench fastened to the opposite wall. Miriam took the upper berth; Bobby had the lower; I took the bench. Although we were traveling second class, as were all of the other members of our party, we had use of the first class dining room at earlier hours, full use of the main promenade deck, and the first class reading room.

All of the Drury party were seated at the same table. There was one other American family aboard who came from Japan. Most of the other passengers were French. We had four meals a day. First, a light breakfast between seven and eight-thirty. Having been warned that we would not like the way the French brewed their coffee, we took with us some powdered coffee under the brand name of George Washington. Lunch was served at 10:30; tea at 3:30; and dinner at 6:00. The meals were excellent.

On Sunday, June 19th, I conducted a short worship service on deck for the members of our party and the Martin family from Japan. This I did each Sunday during our travels whenever possible. Miriam and I took turns watching our little boy so that the other person could have some privacy to read or walk. We rented a deck chair at a cost of $1.50 which we were able to use until we reached Port Said.

Our ship stopped at five ports before arriving at Port Said, the first of which was Hong Kong, where we arrived on Tuesday, June 21st. Meeting us at the dock was Dr. Stuart Seaton who, with his wife Myrle, were Presbyterian missionaries on the island of Hainan. They had come to Hong Kong so that Myrle could receive some medical treatment. Both had been in our wedding party.

One of the French customs which surprised and somewhat amused us was the fact that both men and women would come to the early breakfast tables wearing their pajamas and would then promenade on the decks until 10:30 a.m. Finally Helen and Nono, as typical eighteen-year-old American girls, thought it would be a daring thing if they, too, would promenade in their pajamas. I quote now from Helen's diary: "About six-thirty we came down in our pajamas and kimonos and paraded the deck. We dared to do it because there weren't many up. Then we had Bill take a picture of us sans kimonos. And we did it! We 'pajama paraded' the dining room and had our breakfast in a little unnoticeable corner. The strange thing about it was that we felt so embarrassed about having kimonos on. No one else did that morning."

The ship docked at Saigon at 8:30 on Saturday, June 25th. Since Saigon was then still under French control, there was much transferring of freight from and to the ship. The ship did not leave for Singapore until 1:00 p.m. on Monday. We spent the two days in port visiting the botanical gardens, the small zoo, and the Governor's house.

We reached Singapore on Wednesday afternoon, June 29th, for an overnight stop. A friend of Mrs. Stroebe's met us and took us on a sight-seeing tour into the Malay state of Johore which was then ruled by a Sultan. We saw the jungle with its monkeys and some rubber plantations. Soon after leaving Singapore, our ship steamed northwest along the coast of Sumatra through the straits of Malacca out towards the Indian Ocean. As we came to the end of Sumatra, the sea began to be rougher. At midnight on July 1st, we had to close the only porthole in our cabin as the sea was so rough.

July 2nd was a stormy day and we were told that we would have rough seas all the way to Colombo, our next port of call on the Island of Ceylon. We were in the monsoon season. Many of the passengers were seasick. I noted in my diary for July 2: "So far we haven't missed a meal, tho at times I must confess I have been a bit woozy." We took some pills which were supposed to counteract seasickness, and evidently they did. That night, and for many subsequent nights, all members of the Drury party slept on deck, for it was too hot to stay in our cabins with the portholes closed.

I quote from my diary: "All of the portholes on our side of the ship were closed. I got one of the stewards to open ours for a few minutes today. I stood there looking out. One moment the water came up nearly to the porthole, and then the next minute I had the impression of looking down from a three story window. It wasn't long before the top of a wave dashed in, sprinkling my bunk with salty water and washing my face. I hurriedly closed the porthole."

We arrived in Colombo on Tuesday morning, July 5th, at 6:00. Again my wife and I were favored in having a friend meet us who gave us a two-hour ride showing us the main points of interest. We visited some Buddhist temples and saw a street magician charm a cobra. The ship left at 5:00 o'clock that afternoon for Djibouti in French Somaliland.

On July 6th, the day after we left Colombo, Helen Stroebe wrote in her diary: "All the day the sea got rougher and rougher . . . big swells that made me feel that the deck was dropping away from under us . . . the boat is bucking like a bronco."

On Saturday, July 11th, the coast of Africa came within view. The weather became cooler and the sea smoother. We arrived at Djibouti on Monday, the 13th, at 5:00 a.m. We were there for only a few hours and left at noon. In a letter to relatives dated July 15th, I described Djibouti as being a "desolate place . . . on the edge of French Somaliland at the south end of the Red Sea." I remember that it was hot, dirty, and that there was a superabundance of flies. A dozen or so flies were seen crawling over the face of a little girl, and she made no effort to brush them off. Other children were likewise afflicted. The only bright event of our visit was that we were able there to get some muskmelons, the first that we had had for years, for we were unable to get these in China.

Djibouti was the terminal for the railroad which came down from Addis Ababa. After we left the port and started up the Red Sea, an Englishman, who had boarded the steamer at Djibouti, introduced himself to me as having been commissioned by Emperor Haile Selassie to find an American or an Englishman to go to Addis Ababa to head the English Department in Ethiopia's schools. This gentleman offered me court rank and a salary several times larger than that I had been getting if I would accept the position. My response was immediate; I was not interested. I was set on going to Edinburgh and getting my doctor's degree, and then returning to the States.

I began my sight-seeing of Biblical places at 5:30 Sunday morning, July 17th, when the ship was passing up through the Red Sea. I was told that about that time I could see Mt. Sinai off to the east. One of the ship's officers pointed out a high massive mountain as being Mt. Sinai, the mountain where Moses got the ten commandments. I hastily called Mrs. Stroebe to share the experience with me.

After passing through the Suez Canal, we arrived at Port Said at 3:30 a.m. on Monday, July 18th. Our long sea voyage from Shanghai, which had lasted just one month, came to an end. I made a final check to see that my suitcase would be sent on to Lucerne and that the trunk would go to London. We discarded the camp cot and the wicker chair. The Drury luggage was reduced to three suitcases, the portable typewriter, and a duffle bag which served as a catch-all. Those were the days before synthetic cloth which made washing easier and ironing unnecessary. Thus, all of us had to take more clothing than would be the case today. The total number of baggage pieces for the party was twenty, all of which had to be hand carried on and off trains as it was not feasible to check baggage on the trains.

Since I had made previous reservations for the party in the Bristol Hotel in Cairo, a man from that hotel met us at Port Said and helped us with our baggage. After a four and one-half hour train ride, we arrived in Cairo at 12:30 and were assigned our rooms. Helen wrote in her diary for that day: "This hotel has no class but it is comfortable and clean." The rates were very reasonable — $3.00 a day per person for room and board. The afternoon was spent in unpacking, washing, reading our mail, making plans for the next four days of sight-seeing, and in selecting a good guide.

Upon the recommendation of the French proprietor of the hotel where we were staying, I engaged an Egyptian guide by the name of Hasamein Omar who claimed that he had lived for several years in the United States. He spoke excellent English. We agreed on a price of $2.00 a day for our party. Omar proved to be an excellent guide. That evening Omar took six of us for a boat ride on the Nile which, so I wrote in my diary, "had a sail like the wing of a bird."

On the morning of the 19th, Helen wrote in her diary: "I found that the family had acquired the queerest little old man for a guide. He dresses in the long (white) flowing garment so common here, but wears a small turban on his head. He is a Christian, he says." Possibly Omar made that claim in order to win our favor. A couple of days later, being somewhat better informed, Helen wrote: "He is not a Christian but a Mohammedan." Helen was so impressed with all that she heard and saw in Cairo that she wrote at least 3,000 words in her diary describing her experiences.

WE CLIMB CHEOPS PYRAMID

On Tuesday, July 19th, Omar took us to the Cairo museum so rich in ancient Egyptian relics. The tomb of Tut-ankh-amen had been discovered in 1922, and the fabulous treasures were on display. I noted in my diary that the solid gold coffin was worth $250,000.00. With an ounce of gold now selling for more than $400.00, the gold in that casket would now be worth many millions. This was my first experience of trying to see the wonders of a great museum while carrying our two-year-old boy. I had to carry him across my neck most of the time. Even so he was very restless.

In the afternoon Omar took us to old Cairo. We traveled by tram. We visited a famous old Coptic Christian Church dedicated to the Virgin Mary. According to tradition, the church was built on the spot where Joseph, Mary, and the Babe Jesus stayed when they fled from Herod's wrath. We saw the island Rhoda in the Nile where the Egyptian princess is supposed to have lived when she found the baby Moses floating in a basket among the bulrushes. At least there were some bulrushes still growing at the edge of the island. We were told so many things based on age-old traditions that we came to be suspicious of everything.

I do not now recall when I got the idea of climbing the big Cheops pyramid at Giza, eating breakfast at the top, and watching the sun rise over Cairo. I knew that a few of the top layers of stone had been removed, leaving a level place about twenty feet square. I also knew that some tourists had climbed to the top at one of the corners, but I had never heard of anyone going up in the dark and eating their breakfast there while the sun rose over Cairo. The idea appealed to me as something romantic and daring.

I talked the idea over with Mrs. Stroebe and found her willing to make the climb. This was a brave decision for her to make, for she must have been in her early forties. I talked with my wife and found her willing. I talked with Omar and although he was surprised at trying such a thing, he felt that it could be done. He said that he would get a Bedouin who would carry our little boy. I knew that I did not have to persuade the young people for they would be eager to go.

I then went to the proprietor of the hotel and asked if he would put up our breakfast in lunch baskets. I remember that he said we were crazy to attempt such a thing, but he cooperated and promised to have the lunch baskets ready when we were to leave the hotel at 4:00 a.m. the next morning, July 20. Omar promised to have two cars ready for us, and four or five Bedouins at the pyramid to help us make the climb. Mrs. Stroebe and my wife each had a man to help them. Perhaps even the young people needed help to climb up the larger stones at the bottom which were at least five feet high.

Omar filled us in on some facts. The pyramid covered thirteen acres, was about 465 feet long at each of its four sides at the base, and was also the same distance high. The ascent was at an angle of 50°.

We arose at 3:30 on that Wednesday morning and left the hotel in the two automobiles at 4:00 a.m. "It was lovely and cool at that time of the night," wrote Helen in her diary. "The car with Omar, the Drurys, Dick and Miss Russell went on ahead with our precious lunch. We nearly froze in our sleeveless dresses . . . the streets were almost deserted at that time of the day." The women had to dress in

Bobby Drury on the
Cheops Pyramid with
the Arab guide who
carried him to the top.

July 20
1927

anticipation of the heat of the summer day which was sure to come.

It took us about an hour to drive to the pyramid, and there was barely a trace of light in the eastern sky. We started to climb at once. Helen wrote: "The path of ascent is certainly worn by countless tourists, climbing up and down through the centuries. The outside stones, mammoth tho they are, are made of limestone and are soft enough to be scratched easily. Hundreds of people's names are carved all the way up." After we got to the top, I remember seeing where King Edward VII of England had cut his name in 1882. According to the notes that I made, we made the ascent in twenty-five minutes.

Mrs. Stroebe and my wife found that their dresses, which reached almost to their ankles, impeded their climbing. Modesty had to be laid aside and adjustments made to realities. Helen wrote: "Mother and Mrs. Drury were sights with their dresses and petticoats knotted around their waists and three guides pushing and pulling them up. Bobby was carried by one of the Arabs, and the poor baby didn't quite make out what was happening to him. The guides said it was the first time in their experience that such a tiny baby had gone up and also the first time that anyone had eaten on top."

We reached the summit a few minutes before the sun rose at 5:21. Helen wrote: "We watched the glorious sun rise like a golden disk in the east." The scene which stretched out before us was magnificent and well worth the effort. I remember seeing carved in one of the stones at the summit what appeared to be a checker board of small holes. One of the guides told me that centuries ago some Roman soldiers had carved the design as it was used to play one of their games. We saw the same arrangement of holes in the floor of the praetorium in Jerusalem where, it is believed, Jesus was tried.

After eating our breakfast, we started the descent which was much easier than the ascent. The Egyptian Government now forbids tourists from making the climb to the summit as it is too dangerous. When we were almost down, I and some of the party turned aside to enter the pyramid. One passageway led to the king's chamber where there was a huge stone sarcophagus which was empty and which evidently had been placed while the pyramid was being erected. We also walked down another passageway to a smaller room called the queen's chamber.

After making the descent, we took a camel's ride around the pyramid to the sphinx and after inspecting the recently discovered temple there, which had been covered by the desert sands, we returned to Cairo. After taking our usual rest after lunch, we went sight-seeing again under Omar's guidance. He told us that there were 381 mosques in Cairo and that one of the most beautiful had been built by a sultan who stripped the facing from the Cheops pyramid. Only a small part of the original alabaster or limestone facing remains. Originally this covered up the layers of stone blocks on each side and gave the exterior a smooth appearance.

On Thursday, July 21st, all of the Drury party except my wife, our son, and Dickie Stroebe, motored to Memphis, the ancient capital of Egypt, to see the magnificent ruins which were there. Having dismissed Omar, we had to depend on our guidebooks. We left early in the morning so as to escape the heat, taking our breakfast with us. We were back before noon; and after our usual rest, visited the bazaars.

Friday, the 22nd, was our last day in Cairo, for we were to leave by train for Jerusalem that evening at 6:00 o'clock. We all traveled third class. The cost of tickets for myself and my wife was $7.20. We knew that it would be a hard all-night journey as we would have to sit on hard benches. The train from Cairo would take us to Qantara, on the Suez Canal, where we would cross the canal by ferryboat and then take another train to Jerusalem, where we were due to arrive about 9:00 a.m. Second class was twice as expensive as third class, and even there we would have had to sit up all night. Most of Friday afternoon was spent in resting and preparing ourselves for the ordeal which lay ahead of us.

In and Around Jerusalem

We were taken to the train at five o'clock in the afternoon by the bus owned by our hotel. All of our nineteen pieces of baggage were stowed away in the car we were to occupy. The train left at six o'clock. By that time, the car was comfortably filled. After several hours, I felt it was time for Bobby to get some sleep; so I spread out a steamer rug on the seat opposite where I sat and put Bobby down and told him to go to sleep. But there was too much excitement. He was too restless, kept raising his head to look around. I tried to quiet him, spoke firmly, but to no avail. Finally I resorted to some spanking, and each time I did, he cried out in the exclamations his amah would use when annoyed: "Oi, oi, oi." Helen, in her diary, interpreted the words as being "Oh yoy, oh, yoy."

Helen then added the following: "Then Mrs. Drury came, and it was the sweetest thing the way Bobbie put his baby arms around her neck. Soon he was asleep. All went well and we were quietly dozing when the train stopped at one big place and the people just streamed thru the windows and doors with all their goods. I was nearly swamped by all the luggage that came in over me."

My diary gives added details. At about 9:00 p.m. our train stopped at Ismailia, a city on the Suez Canal. Waiting there for the train was a crowd of several hundred Moslem pilgrims who had just returned from a three-week journey by camels across the desert to Mecca. Now they were returning home. They were not traveling first class or even second class, but third class as were we. When the train stopped, some of the men rushed aboard and opened the windows to permit those on the outside to push through their baggage — bed rolls, tents, personal belongings of all kinds. They filled up the aisles with their luggage. We hastily pulled our bags together into three double seats. Still the baggage came piling in until there was so much that the Moslem pilgrims, when seated on their baggage, could touch the ceiling of the car with their heads. The members of the Drury party were completely surrounded and walled in by this mass of baggage.

I remember how one English-speaking Arab crawled over to speak to me. Looking down and seeing two adult women and two teen-age girls, he asked: "Is this your harem?" Perhaps he spoke in jest, and in like manner, I replied: "No, one wife is enough."

Helen and Nono, being attractive American girls, were quickly the objects of attention from some English-speaking Moslems. The girls asked why the Moslem women hid their faces behind the black veils, with the exception of their eyes. One of the men, according to Helen's diary, gave the following specious explanation: "Our friend told us that the reason the women wear veils is that some are pretty and some ugly. Naturally all the men want the pretty ones; so they have to cover their faces so that they can marry them all off." Helen then added: "What a gamble marriage is in Oriental countries."

Within an hour after leaving Ismailia, we arrived at Qantara where we had to cross the Suez Canal and take the train waiting for us on the other side for Jerusalem. As soon as the train stopped, I helped Billy go out through one of the windows and then passed our baggage out to him. I remember that I pulled the handle off of one of our suitcases because it had become jammed under the pile of Arab's luggage. After all of the baggage was out, I handed Bobby out through the window to Billy. The women managed to crawl over the top of the pile of baggage to one of the end exits of the car. Finally, I was able to do likewise.

After crossing the canal, we boarded a third class car on the train waiting for us. This time we had the car almost entirely to ourselves. It had long benches on which we could stretch out and get some sleep. We had to change trains at Lydda (or Lud) and take a branch line that ran up to Jerusalem. Along our route, I recognized some places which were mentioned in the Bible. For instance, when we passed through Gaza, I read from Judges 16 the story of Samson carrying the gates of the city to a nearby mountain. Looking up out of the window, I was able to see that mountain. I noted in the margin of my Bible: "Passed thru Gaza 5 a.m. July 23, 1927. Saw the Mt." Whenever possible I read the appropriate passage describing an historic site when we visited it and noted the date in the margin of my Bible. I am still using that Bible, though it is now coming apart.

We arrived at the small railroad station in Jerusalem Saturday morning, July 23rd, at 9:00 a.m. Although years have passed since then, I still remember the thrill of that day. Miss Helda Anderson met us at the station, and I turned over to her the bag of feathers I had received from her mother in Shanghai. Such minor problems as I had experienced in taking this item with me was more than amply repaid by Miss Anderson's many kindnesses to us. It was good to find one person in Jerusalem whom we had known previously.

Miss Anderson helped me hire three carriages to take us and our baggage to the Swiss Pension where I had made reservations. While the others were resting, I hastened to the American Colony, which was within easy walking distance, to get any mail that might be there. To my delight, I did find some letters waiting for me.

Leaving our baby boy with the hostess of the pension, the others in the party went with me late in the afternoon to visit the Wailing Wall. When we got into the city, we were struck with the similarities with the old city of Shanghai. Helen wrote of this: "Really, at times one would think we were back in China, from the narrowness (of the streets), the filth, the crowds, the appearance of the shops, and everything. The streets were full of people, donkeys and fruit stands."

These similarities were so striking that we all felt that living in China for a few years was a splendid intróduction to visiting Palestine.

It is not my intention to describe our experiences in visiting the many historic and sacred sites in and around Jerusalem, but rather will comment on unusual experiences and show how we were able to see so much with so little expenditures. All of us felt the necessity to economize. For instance, the charge made by the Swiss Pension for my wife, our son, and myself for nine days was $23.93. Had we gone to the American Colony, we would have had to pay $72.00. Soon after arriving in Jerusalem, I hired a guide to show me where the principal sites were located. After that I acted as guide and all of us used our guide books. We had far more walking to do in Jerusalem than was the case in Cairo. This made it more difficult for my wife and myself, for it was too hard to carry Bobby for any extended distance. One day the Drury party decided to walk around the walls of the city of Jerusalem, which meant a hike of about three and one-half miles. I rented a donkey for Miriam to ride, holding Bobby, while I led the animal. The other members of the party were quick to liken us to the holy family on its way to Egypt — Joseph, Mary, and the Christ child. On Monday morning, July 25th, Miss Anderson baby-sat with Bobby, thus permitting Miriam and me unimpeded time to do sight-seeing.

On Sunday, July 24th, our first full day in the holy city, we spent the morning sight-seeing. We went first to the Garden Tomb and Gordon's Calvary, which was in easy walking distance from the pension where we were staying. In the afternoon we attended a worship service at the American Colony.

When we were in Jerusalem, there was a flourishing place called the American Colony, As I recall its history, a group of people from Kansas fixed a date when Jesus would return to earth and to the Mount of Olives. Wishing to be there when that big event happened, they sold their goods and migrated to Jerusalem. The day came when Jesus was to appear, but nothing happened. Instead of returning to the States, they settled down and opened a tourist center. When we were there, they had a hostel and a curio store, both of high quality.

While going down Via Dolorosa one day, we came to a convent near the Ecce Homo arch. This convent was reported to have included the praetorium where Pilate judged Jesus and finally turned him over to the Jews. Helen described what happened: "Our guide rang the heavy knocker, and a Sister opened the door a crack and then raised her hands in flat refusal to let us enter. Finally we found out that we were not dressed properly, respectfully; so we could not go in. We needed long sleeves and we had no sign of such. The men offered to loan us their coats, but, no, that would be worse yet. Bill, Mr. Drury and our guide were allowed to pass inspection, but the rest of us were too worldly dressed for such a sacred spot. Even Dickie (age 10) in his short sleeves couldn't enter. Men without coats were also refused entrance. So we poor outcasts sat on a step of the house opposite and waited and laughed. It was amusing to see the horror on that vigilant door-keeper Sister's face when she saw us. What would she think of our banquet dresses?"

As one who was privileged to enter, I saw the floor of the Roman praetorium and noticed that one of the "checker board" games, such as we had seen on top of the Cheops pyramid, had been cut into the floor of the praetorium. The rejection of the women because they wore dresses without sleeves was repeated on several subsequent occasions by Roman Catholic clergy when we sought admission to some of their churches or sacred places both in Palestine and also in Italy.

Before leaving Jerusalem, there were two short excursions we wanted to make. One was to the Dead Sea and Jericho; the other was to Bethlehem and Hebron. Upon the recommendation of the American Colony, I agreed to pay the owner of a garage $232.75 for the use of two Buick passenger cars for the two short excursions and then for the week of travel from Jerusalem to Mt. Tabor, Nazareth, Capernaum, Damascus, Baalbek, and ending up at Beirut by August 9th. My share of this cost was $32.50.

On Tuesday, July 26th, we left at 6:00 o'clock in the morning in order to avoid as much of the midday heat as possible for the Dead Sea and Jericho. Of course, the touring cars were not air conditioned. Upon our arrival at the Dead Sea, which is about 1,200 feet below sea level, several of us, including the girls, Billy, and myself, tried swimming. It was a most disagreeable experience. The water was so filled with minerals that if you put an egg into the water, two-thirds would remain above the water. When I came out, I wanted to wash off the oily film which covered my body. I had to pay 50¢ to a Bedouin for a small pail of water. On our return trip, we visited Bethany.

On Friday, the 29th, we took our second half-day excursion — this time to Bethlehem and Hebron. Bethlehem, we felt, was one place where the identification of it being the birthplace of Jesus was authentic. So many of the sites in Palestine pointed out to us as being the place where some Biblical event took place were evidently false.

In our closing days at Jerusalem, each of us did as we pleased. On Wednesday Miriam and I walked to the Garden of Gethsemane, nearly a mile from our pension. I had to carry Bobby, now weighing thirty pounds, each way. For the first time on the trip, I had a cold which lasted for several days and made me feel miserable. With this exception, all of us enjoyed excellent health throughout our journey.

We started on our week's trip through northern Galilee early on Tuesday morning, August 2nd, heading for Mt. Tabor where we had reservations in Casa Nova, a Franciscan hostel on the summit of Mt. Tabor. En route we stopped at Jacob's well near Nablus.

Through almost 2,000 years, the level of the ground had risen so that the top of the well was now in the basement of a church then being built over it. Here, without question, was the original well mentioned in John 4 which tells the story of the woman of Sychar coming to it to get water and finding Jesus there. In John's account, we read that the woman said: "The well is deep." Helen noted in her diary: "A priest there let a bucket down and down to get us some cold sparkling water. It seemed such a long time to pull it up that 80 feet. We had a drink all around, and it certainly was good and from Jacob's well!"

We arrived at the Franciscan monastery on the summit of Mt. Tabor, which was 1,843 feet high. The hostel where tourists were received was called Casa Nova. We were their only guests at the time and were given a warm welcome. The presence of our two-year-old son made quite a sensation for the monks. Helen wrote in her diary: "They say they hardly ever see a tiny child, and the one who brought him his early supper went up to him and kissed him. I suppose they do miss all young life like that up on a lonely mountain top like this." Here at Mt. Tabor we were served our first fresh figs, and they were delicious.

According to Roman Catholic tradition, the transfiguration of Jesus as recorded in Luke 9 took place on top of Mt. Tabor, whereas Protestants identify the site as being somewhere on the slopes of Mt. Hermon, which is over 9,000 feet high and is crowned with snow around the year. In Luke's account, Peter said: "Master, it is good for us to be here; and let us make three tabernacles; one for thee, and one for Moses and one for Elijah." Luke added that Peter was afraid and spoke "not knowing what he said."

The early church actually built three small tabernacles on top of Mt. Tabor, something that Jesus evidently did not want the disciples to do. Centuries passed and then the Franciscan fathers came and erected a beautiful church which incorporated the foundation stones of the early buildings. Helen described the church as being "the most beautiful, most impressive church I have ever been in."

We left Mt. Tabor at 8:30 in the morning of August 3rd and within an hour and one-half were registered at the Franciscan Casa Nova in Nazareth. I noted in my diary that Nazareth was "a beautiful village."

It is a city now. When we were there, most of the residents were Christian Arabs. We visited the well where Mary was supposed to have gotten water, and the home of Joseph and Mary was pointed out to us, but again was the identification accurate? We also saw a very old synagogue which may have been there when Jesus was a boy. One thing remained unchanged and that was the topography of the land. I climbed the hill back of the village and in my imagination thought of Jesus as a boy and young man doing the very same thing.

After lunch, we drove to Carmel, the hill which overlooks the Mediterranean Sea. Here we refreshed our minds with the story of Elijah's contest with the priests of Baal which took place there. We then drove to Haifa and several of us, including the Stroebes, Nono, and myself, went swimming. We returned to Nazareth before 7:30 and I wrote in my diary that day: "This has been another wonderful day."

The next day we drove to Tabgtha, a hospice kept by a German Lazarite friar located on the shore of the Sea of Galilee within walking distance of the ruins of a synagogue thought to be at Capernaum. Even though the Sea is 680 feet below sea level, and we were there in August, yet we did not find the heat of midday oppressive. The mornings and evenings were delightfully cool. Father Tappar had several fig trees on his grounds with an abundance of luscious figs just ready for eating.

Before us stretched a beautiful beach which could have been the place where Jesus in a post-resurrection appearance asked Peter three times: "Do you love me?" We had planned to spend only one day here, but the quiet and beauty of the place made us decide to stay two days. Helen Stroebe explained in her diary: "There is a certain calm and quiet which broods over this place, so much so that we can hardly leave it." We went swimming several times and also boat riding. On one unforgettable evening when we were all in the boat a little off shore, Mrs. Stroebe, who had a fine singing voice, sang for us one of the gospel songs which began with the words: "O Galilee, sweet Galilee." The inspiration of that hour lives in memory to this day. Other tourists have rushed through their sight-seeing tour of Palestine in only a fraction of the time we spent, but, I am sure, did not see as much. We saw some of the out-of-the-way places in a leisurely way.

SYRIA AND A MEDITERRANEAN CRUISE

The next ten days, from August 6th to 16th, we were in French Syria visiting such places as Damascus, Baalbek, and Beirut. We were scheduled to board a French ship at Beirut on August 12th, but had to wait until the 16th.

We crossed the Jordan River a few miles above the Sea of Galilee and entered French Syria. Following the road that Paul may have taken when he traveled to Damascus at which time he had his vision of Christ, we climbed to an elevation of more than 3,000 feet as we crossed the Anti-Lebanon mountains. To our left and north was the snow covered peak of Mt. Hermon, more than 9,000 feet high. We drove through that area of the country called Golan Heights, the scene of fighting between the Israelis and Syrians in June 1967.

The melting snow on the west side of Mt. Hermon gives rise to the Jordan River, while on the other side, the waters form the Barada River which flows out into the desert and forms the oasis of Damascus, reported to be one of the oldest cities in the world. We had reservations in the Palace Hotel, which Helen described as being "the cheapest one in town," and then added: "But we are traveling not for comfort, but to see things. But it is clean." Here we stayed for two days, and my bill came to $7.00, which included both room and board for the three of us.

We arrived in Damascus at noon. A good part of the afternoon was spent in visiting the bazaars, where we wished we had enough money to buy some Persian rugs. We found Damascus cleaner than Jerusalem. We walked down the street called Straight mentioned in Acts 9. We were shown the house where Ananias cured Paul's blindness, but again how can one today be sure of its identity?

Sunday, August 7th, we spent in sight-seeing. We looked for a Protestant church and found one, but no services were held during the summer. Damascus, like Cairo, is filled with mosques. Helen noted that there were about 300. The most ancient and largest was the Great Mosque, which we visited.

Our drivers took us for a ride that morning to a look-out on a nearby mountain where we were able to get a magnificent view of the city of Damascus. Helen wrote: "Damascus is queerly built in the shape of a spoon. The river Arbana (Barada) runs through the city and is divided into seven main parts. Each of these is again subdivided so that part flows through each house. I never saw a city so plentifully supplied with water." The result was that the city, consisting of scores of square miles, flourished as a green garden in a sea of desert sand. No wonder that green is the favorite color of Islamic peoples. Helen's simile of a spoon was most apt. The river was the handle, and the oasis itself the bowl of the spoon.

We left Damascus on Monday morning at 8:30 for Baalbek which lies in between the Anti-Lebanon and the Lebanon ranges of mountains. It was here that we learned to our disappointment that our ship had been delayed and would not leave Beirut until the 16th, rather than on the 12th. We found comfortable rooms near the Roman ruins. The ruins at Baalbek are magnificent. The huge Temple of Jupiter, erected by Antonius Pius and destroyed by an earthquake in 1759, is marked by six massive monolithic pillars, the tallest ever erected by man. We were amazed at the size of the foundation stones. According to the figures in Helen's diary, the dimension of one of these stones was 62 x 14 x 11 feet. Moreover, these great stones were fitted so closely together that I could not insert a blade of my pen knife at the joints. Of course, no mortar was used.

We left Baalbek on Tuesday, August 9th, and registered at the Metrople Hotel in Beirut after lunch. I checked at the steamship office and received confirmation about the delayed sailing of the S.S. Angkor. We would have four more days in Beirut than we had expected. I was told that the ship was due to sail on the 16th, but that we could go aboard in the late afternoon of the 15th. I also learned that, although we had made reservations to go second class, we would have to pay an extra $19.00 per person and go first class.

We visited the American University in Beirut. This was founded in 1866 by American philanthropy and is the largest educational institution in Lebanon. It is also co-educational. We visited the Near East Relief camps near Beirut which ministered largely to Armenian refugees who had been forced from their homes by the Turkish Government. One day we drove out about five miles to the mouth of Dog River where some famous signatures have been carved on a cliff. Included were the names of Rameses II, Nebuchadnezzar, and ending with General Allenby of World War I fame. Those signatures reminded us that we were standing on an ancient highway where for centuries conquering armies came and went. We had time for swimming, boating, hiking and reading.

We were able to board our ship on Monday afternoon at 5:00 o'clock, and spent the night on board, even though the ship lay at anchor. We found first class accommodations rather luxurious as compared with the second class on the S.S. Angers when we left Shanghai. The ship sailed on the 16th for Smyrna where it arrived on the 18th. Smyrna had been a Greek city but fell to the Turks in September 1922, and a few days later was ravaged by fire. It was not the city that I wanted to see, but, rather, the site of the stadium on Mt. Pagus, back of the city, where in 155 A.D. Polycarp, Bishop of Smyrna, was martyred. All of the members of the Drury party except my wife, who remained aboard with our little son, went ashore, and I led them to the site of the stadium on the side of the mountain. The stadium had long disappeared, but the large declivity clearly indicated where it was once located.

When we reached the historic spot, I told the story of how Polycarp was brought before some Roman judges who demanded that he curse Christ and worship the Emperor. Instead, Polycarp replied: "Eighty and six years have I served him, and he hath done me no wrong; how then can I blaspheme my king who saved me?" A small monument at the site of the stadium commemorates Polycarp's martyrdom. Having been a Christian for eighty-six years, he must have known John and perhaps others who had been with Jesus.

We arrived at Constantinople early in the morning of Saturday, August 20th. The passage through the narrow Dardenelles was most interesting. Here we were in a geographical setting which was saturated with history. The ship remained in port for over two nights; so we had one full day of sight-seeing. We rented cars and drove out to Roberts College, another American educational institution which ranks in importance next to the American College in Beirut. In a day packed with thrills, we saw the Hippodrome, the bazaars, several mosques including the beautiful Blue Mosque and the ancient church of St. Sophia, erected by Theodosius II in 415 and clearly the supreme masterpiece of Byzantine architecture.

Our ship sailed for Piraeus, the seaport of Athens, at 6:00 o'clock Monday morning, August 23rd. We arrived at our destination at 10:00 a.m. Having made arrangements in advance with the American Express, two cars and a guide were awaiting us. We had an unforgetable day of sight-seeing — the Parthenon, Mar's Hill, the Temple of Jupiter, and many other places. We became surfeited with history. Miriam and I took Bobby with us. There was no chance for him to take his usual afternoon nap, but he didn't complain. He was a perfect little traveler.

NAPLES TO SWITZERLAND

Our ship sailed from Pireaus on Wednesday morning, August 24th, and arrived at Naples at noon on the following Friday. Having made previous arrangements to stay at the Baker Pension, a porter met us at the pier and escorted us to the pension. After getting settled, Mrs. Stroebe and I met with a travel agent to make arrangements for an excursion to Pompeii the next morning. The cost for this trip was $5.00 per adult. We also purchased train tickets, second class, from Naples to Lugano, Switzerland, with stop overs in Rome, Florence, Venice and Milan. We were to arrive in Lugano on September 10th. This gave us fifteen days in Italy. The cost of train travel was $20.00 per person.

I checked on my finances the evening we arrived in Naples and found that the total expenses of the Drury family from Shanghai to

Naples came to $523.14, exclusive of steamer fares. This meant that out of the $996.64 that I had when we left Shanghai, there was a balance of only $473.50 for the remaining five weeks or one-third of our journey. I realized that our costs through Europe would be more per day than had been the case to this point. Realizing the need for some extra funds to reach me in Edinburgh, I mailed a request for a loan on my Government Life Insurance policy, taken out when I was in the service in World War I, and asked that the money be sent to me in Edinburgh.

Early on Saturday morning, August 27th, the Drury party, with our guide, drove out to Pompeii. Our guide told us how the city had been buried under clouds of hot ash from the erupting Vesuvius back in 79 A.D. Most of the inhabitants escaped, but many did not. For centuries the city lay buried until its existence was discovered in 1748. The city was still being excavated when we visited the site.

It so happened that when we were there, we were alone in the deserted and ruined city. I experienced an eerie feeling when walking the deserted streets which once were thronged with people, and entering the roofless houses where people once lived. We saw the ruts made in the pavement stones by the iron rims of the chariot wheels. We saw the bakery where bread was being baked when the catastrophe occurred. All about us were evidences of life that once was, but now the ruins were but the corpse of a dead city.

The Stroebes and Miss Russell left for Rome that afternoon, but Miriam and I remained in Naples for another day. We visited a large museum on Sunday. We took an afternoon train for Rome, arriving there at 8:00 o'clock in the evening, and took a taxi to the Pension American. There we remained for the next four days.

There was so much of interest to see in Rome that we decided to take a three-day Carrani tour at a cost of $17.50, and it was well worth it. Our guide, A.D. Tani, was the author of a "New Guide to Rome." He was a walking encyclopedia when it came to Roman history and ruins. On Monday, August 29th, we saw the coliseum, the arches of Titus and Constantine, and several churches. On Tuesday we visited several forums and some museums. On Wednesday, the 31st, we visited St. Peter's and the catacombs. These days spent in Rome meant much to me when, years later, I taught church history at San Francisco Theological Seminary. Several of the women in our party were not permitted to enter some Catholic churches, as St. Peter's, while wearing short sleeved dresses. Gentlemen often loaned them their jackets, and then all was well. We had to cut our visit to Rome short because of the unforseen delay in Beirut where we lost three days of our schedule.

We completed our sight-seeing of Rome on Thursday, September 1st, by visiting the Vatican and its marvelous museum and the Sistine Chapel. We left at 3:00 o'clock that afternoon for Florence and arrived there at 8:30. We registered at the Pension Crocini where we got fine accommodations, board and room, for $4.75 a day for the three of us.

We spent a full week in Florence and found it the most interesting city we had visited on our entire journey. We loved it. Our pension was centrally located so that we were able to walk to most places of interest. Miriam and I took turns baby-sitting with Bobby. Occasionally we hired a carriage as we did one day when we drove to the cemetery to see the grave of Elizabeth Barrett Browning. We were able to visit the great art galleries, as the Uffizi and Pitti Palaces, the Medici Chapel, the Cathedral and San Marco Monastery. We saw masterpieces of painting and sculpture by Michelangelo, deVinci, Raphael and Donatelle. We heard again the story of Savonorola and his martyrdom. The seven days spent there were unforgettable.

From Florence we went by train to Venice. Our transportation from the railroad station to our pension, Casa Petrarch, was by gondola. The pension was located on the Grand Canal. One memory stands out in sharp relief. One evening while at dinner with Bobby seated in a high chair at the table with us, one of the Italian waitresses pointed to him and said: "Grande bambino," i.e., beautiful baby. So few tourists traveled with young children that our little boy often drew special attention.

During our two days in Venice, we saw the major attractions —St. Mark's Cathedral, the Doge's Palace, and the art gallery with paintings by Titian and Tineretto. We did what other tourists did and bought corn to feed the large flocks of pigeons in the square. I noted in the diary that I looked forward to getting our suitcase with some winter clothing as we were still wearing our summer garments and it was getting colder.

We left for Milan on Friday, September 9th, where we stayed in the Bonini Pension which overlooked the cathedral square. The cathedral in Milan is noted for its many spires and statues. I noted in my diary that it was "a dream in stone." I climbed to the top and followed the walk over the roof where one could see many of the statues which crowned the spires. We also visited the refectory where we saw deVinci's famous painting — The Last Supper. My notes fail to indicate just how much we were with the Stroebes while traveling through Italy, but I do know that we were together in Milan and on the last segment of our travels from Italy into Switzerland.

On Saturday, September 10th, the reunited Drury party of nine left for Switzerland. We left Milan in the morning by train for Como where we boarded one of the lake steamers shortly after lunch for the trip across the lake to Menaggio. We arrived there at 3:30 and then got on a narrow gauge railroad train for Portlezza where we took another steamer on Lake Como for Lugano, Switzerland. While crossing the lake we also crossed the Italian-Switzerland border. I noted in my diary that the scenery through the lake district was gorgeous. We arrived in Lugano in the evening and took rooms in the Washington Hotel.

SWITZERLAND TO EDINBURGH

We left Lugano on Sunday afternoon, September 11th, for Lucerne. Helen, in a letter to me dated January 16, 1980, tells what happened: "I can remember that when the train pulled in, we entered the first compartment we could, and put all our many bags in that one. Then several of us walked further in the train and finally found seats . . . most of us were in one car. Rather than move all the baggage, we decided that we would take turns sitting back there, one hour at a time. I had my turn . . . then it was Billy's turn. About this time we entered the new country. We had been in the Simplon tunnel." This tunnel is the longest in the world, 12½ miles.

Helen's account continues: "I remember that various conductors had passed through the train giving information. But it was not in English; so we did not understand. Mother had shown the custom agent our family passport, but then he wanted Billy to have it when the customs officers got to him. So Mother gave the passport to Dicky to take to Bill. He was gone but a moment and came back saying: "Bill isn't there."

"Don't be silly," she said, "go find him!"

"But the car wasn't there! and that was true. The last cars had been disconnected and hitched to another engine to go to Berne."

When 16-year-old Billy discovered that he was alone with all of our baggage, he tried to explain his predicament to the conductor, who put him off at the next station with all the baggage. In the meantime the other eight members of the party left the train at Lucerne, without any baggage. Helen wrote: "Mother was naturally frantic and contacted something like the Traveller's Aid."

Billy had no money except a miscellaneous assortment of small coins collected from the countries through which we had traveled. Back at the station where he was with the baggage, he learned that another train was due soon which he could board for Lucerne. However, he had to carry all of the baggage down through a tunnel to another platform. Helen added: "It took quite a number of trips before he had all the baggage transferred." We at Lucerne were greatly relieved when his train pulled in with our missing Billy and all our baggage.

The Stroebes stayed in Switzerland for several months where the three children and Nono Blaine entered French schools. Before we parted, I found it necessary to get a loan of $50.00 from Mrs. Stroebe for my cash reserve was down to less than $200.00 and I still had to cover expenses of more than two weeks' travel in France and England before reaching Edinburgh. Looking back on those days, I am amazed at my boldness in venturing to take a wife and child on a three and one-half month tour through so many foreign countries during summer months when I had so little money. Evidently the good Lord was looking after us. My consuming desire was to get to Edinburgh and earn that Ph.D. degree.

At Lucerne, I took possession of a large suitcase which had been sent on ahead with some warmer clothing. We were glad to get it, for our light weight clothing was not sufficient for the cool weather. We still had a trunk with more clothing awaiting us in England.

Miriam and I said good-by to the Stroebes at Lausanne on Wednesday, September 14th. They had been our traveling companions for three months and a most cordial relationship had existed. After leaving them, we were on our own. We traveled to Geneva that afternoon and found most pleasant accommodations in the Christian hotel called Pension Des Familles. The cost was only $3.50 each. Those in charge held family prayers each evening to which we were invited. I noted in my diary: "This is the best place we have stayed during our entire journey."

We had only two days to see Geneva. Here was another city saturated with history, especially that which related to the Reformation, for here John Calvin and John Knox and other reformers had lived and worked.

The now defunct League of Nations was meeting in Geneva when we were in that city. I attended one of its business sessions on Thursday, September 15th, and wrote in my diary: "Saw Chamberlain (of England) and Stressman (of Germany) act as tellers. Also saw Briand (of France)." Looking back, I now wonder how different western history might have been if the United States had joined the League of Nations.

We left for Paris on Saturday morning, September 17th, traveling third class for the ten hour ride. We carried a luncheon provided by the pension where we had been staying. I had made reservations in Paris at a pension conducted by an English woman at 85 Rue d'Assas, opposite the Luxembourg Gardens. The accommodations cost $8.00 a day for the three of us.

Before leaving Shanghai, I learned that the 10th annual convention of the American Legion was to be held in Paris at the time we would be there. Being a member of the Shanghai Legion Post, I was appointed the official delegate from this Post to the Paris convention. As soon as possible after arriving in Paris, I contacted Legion headquarters and picked up my credentials for a number of events including tours of nearby battle fields of World War I, and especially for the banquet given by the French Government for all official delegates on Sunday evening, the 18th.

On Sunday morning, I attended the services of the American Church in Paris, which was the counterpart of the church I served in Shanghai. There I met Gurdon and Miriam Oxtoby from San Anselmo. Gurdon was the son of Dr. W. H. Oxtoby, Professor of Hebrew and Old Testament when I was a student at the Seminary, and beginning in the fall of 1938, he and I served together on the faculty of San Francisco Theological Seminary until I retired at the end of 1963. Miriam was able to attend the services of this church the following Sunday when I took care of Bobby.

On Sunday evening I attended the American Legion Banquet as a guest of the French Government, along with all other Legionnaires present. I still have the official invitation, the dinner program, and a copy of the address given by M. Poincare, French Prime Minister. Among the honored guests that evening were General Pershing, General Petain (whose name was attached to the street on which we lived in the French Concession in Shanghai), and Marshal Foch. The American Legion had been formed in Paris just ten years previously; so this was an important anniversary occasion.

The big Legion parade was held on Monday afternoon with about 20,000 taking part in the march. Legionnaires from all over the United States and from various parts of the world were there. I was the only one from China and, for some reason, was put at the very end of the parade and was given a banner, "CHINE," to carry. I do not recall just where the parade began, nor exactly where it ended. I do recall that we marched through the Arc de Triumphe and then down Avenue des Champ Elysees. Hundreds of thousands of spectators lined the parade route. Knowing that the parade would cross the Siene River, I asked Miriam to be at the bridge with Bobby. They were there, the only ones in that vast throng whom I knew and who knew me. I noted in my diary that this day was "unforgetable," and that "I was all in this evening."

Under the circumstances, sight-seeing was far more important than attending the meetings of the Legion. Miriam and I took turns taking care of Bobby while the other went to some art gallery, museum, or church. Each of us was able to spend several hours in the Louvre. We went to the top of Eiffel tower, saw Napoleon's tomb, and visited such famous churches as Notre Dame and Saint Chapelle. I was with a party of legionnaires to see the battlefields at Chateau Thierry and Belleau Wood. We found taxis most reasonable; so had no difficulty in getting around.

Before leaving Paris for London on Monday, September 26th, I noted that I had less than $100.00 on hand, which sum included the $50.00 I had borrowed from Mrs. Stroebe. We went by train to Dieppe where we boarded a small channel steamer for New Haven. The crossing was very rough. Both Miriam and I had been good sailors. We did not get seasick while crossing the Indian Ocean during the monsoon season, but that short ride across the English Channel was different. Each of us did our best going to the rail while our little boy got along fine. Miriam and I stretched out on empty benches and kept swallowing. At times Bobby needed attention, and it was hard for either of us to arise and take care of him. We were very glad to step on dry land again at New Haven.

After a short train ride, we arrived in London and went out to the Home for Christian Workers on Finchley Road, St. John's Wood, where we got room and board for the unbelievable cost of five shillings each per day, or for about $1.20. I remember that we had to make our own beds. Prayers were held each evening, and all guests were expected to attend. The Matron in charge was very strict. All guests were supposed to be in by 9:00 p.m. as the main door was then locked. I remember that there was a young and active missionary couple there who wanted to go out to some evening program, perhaps to a theater. They left by way of the fire escape which they called the prayer escape. My wife and I found the accommodations satisfactory and were grateful for the low cost.

On Tuesday, the day after we arrived in London, I called at the American Express where I expected to find the trunk I had forwarded from Shanghai. But the trunk was not there. Instead, it was being held at the British Customs office at Folkstone on the Channel as it had to be cleared through customs. I spent the day in going to Folkstone and in getting the trunk redirected to Edinburgh. Our two third-class tickets from London to Edinburgh cost me in English money 3/13/6 or about $17.60.

While in London, we visited Selfridge's department store and bought about $20.00 worth of clothing for our son, including winter underwear, shoes, and a suit of clothes. We had to prepare for the winter weather of Edinburgh. This reduced my balance to $57.00. Our room at the Missionary Home was heated by a coin operated gas heater.

One had to insert a few English pennies rather frequently in order to keep the room warm.

We had only four days in London. One day was taken when I had to go to Folkstone. We did manage to spend some time in the British Museum, Westminster Abbey, the Tower of London, and St. Paul's Cathedral. We left London with the hope that we would return, which we were able to do in 1966.

A few days after our arrival in England, I received a letter from one of the members of Community Church with a three-inch clipping from the *North China Daily News*, a Shanghai paper. The clipping stated that the Rev. C. M. Drury of Shanghai had spoken at Wimbleton on June 9 and that he had then "said some very hard things about his fellow country men who were exploiting the Chinese." My friend sent the clipping with a penned note at the bottom: "You oughtn't malign the poor Chinese like that."

The news was a mystery to me for I was not in England on June 9th, nor was I ever at Wimbleton. Some time later I discovered that a "Rev. C. M. Drury, an appointee of the English Church Missionary Society, served for a time as a missionary in Hangchow." It was he who had spoken at Wimbleton for which I was given the credit.

On Saturday morning, October 1st, we left by train for Edinburgh. In Edinburgh we stayed at a boarding house conducted by Mrs. Grant at 33 Castle Street. I noted in my expense account that, after paying the taxi, I had only £1/18/0 or about $9.00. I was facing a year's post-graduate study without a scholarship and without any assurance of a job. I remember calling for mail at the American Express office as soon as I was able. To my dismay, there was no letter for me from my Government Insurance — therefore, no check.

CHAPTER SIXTEEN

Eight Months in Edinburgh

We were in Edinburgh, one of the fountain heads of Presbyterianism. My dream had come true. I called at the registration office of New College, which was the United Free Presbyterian Church's seminary, on Monday morning, October 3rd. I matriculated for the fall term. While there, someone advised me to wear the clerical collar and be known by my dress that I was a minister. So, that day I bought both a dickey, which was a detachable false shirt-front, and a clerical collar which buttoned in the back. I soon found that this helped, because the Scottish people had such a great respect for "men of the cloth." For instance, if while calling I rang the doorbell, which was often at the gate some fifteen feet from the front door, the resident would look out and see who it was. If I had on my clerical collar, the gate would be immediately unlatched by remote control. If I did not have on the collar, I might not be admitted.

I remember going to my classes at the University on the street car or tram, as it was called. If all seats were taken and the passengers saw my clerical collar, one by one men, even those much older than I, would arise and beg me to take their seat. This always embarrassed me, so that I avoided wearing the collar when attending classes.

No mail from my insurance company came on Monday or Tuesday. By that time I did not have enough cash to pay our bill at our boarding house. I knew that it was necessary for me to locate an apartment where we could keep house. My expense record shows that on Tuesday, October 4th, I paid -2-4 (or about 55¢) to a rental agency which had been recommended to me by the Seminary registrar, to get a listing of apartments available to American students. Having secured the list, I set out to find a place.

At the very first place on the list, to my great surprise and delight, a former Seminary schoolmate, Clifford Jones, answered the doorbell. We were students together in San Francisco Theological Seminary during the year 1921-22. He and his wife, Mabel, had arrived in Edinburgh a few days before Miriam and I came. He had gone to the same rental agency, and they had picked out the first apartment on the list. He, too, was planning to spend the coming academic year at New College and at the University of Edinburgh in post-graduate study.

After exchanging basic information, I brought up the subject uppermost on my mind. I explained that a check which I had expected to

reach me at Edinburgh had not come and that I was financially embarrassed. I then asked the crucial question: "Could you lend me
fifty dollars?" This he kindly did. A few days later my insurance check
came, and I was able to repay both him and Mrs. Stroebe.

I continued my search for a suitable apartment, knowing that I
had enough money to pay my bill at Mrs. Grant's and to make a
down payment on rent. Within a couple of days, Miriam and I selected
a furnished apartment at 207 Dalkeith Road. Our landlady, Mrs.
Ferguson, a nurse, rented two rooms to us for our exclusive use — a
bedroom and a living room. We shared with her the use of the kitchen
and bath. The apartment was located on the second floor, as we
Americans classified floors, but on the first floor according to English
counting, since it was the first floor above the ground floor.

There was no central heating, only a fireplace in the living room
and the gas cooking stove, built into the wall, in the kitchen. There
was no heat in the bedroom or bath, and no electricity, only gas
lights, and no telephone. The cost was reasonable, about $30.00 a
month. We had to pay for the coal used in the fireplace. Coal was
delivered in gunny sacks and stored in a closet in the kitchen. The
price was about two shillings, or 50¢, a sack. We moved to our new
address on October 10th after paying Mrs. Grant £5 for the ten
nights we stayed there. This averaged out to about $2.37 a day for
the three of us.

After finding a place to live, my next immediate concern was to
find a job. Again the Lord smiled on me. Within three blocks of our
apartment was the Mayfield United Free Presbyterian Church where
the Rev. J. Lorimer Munro was pastor. He was planning to retire and
wanted an assistant to take the evening services, the young people's
Bible class, and help out with the midweek meetings. I was not expected to do pastoral calling or take funerals, except in emergencies.
Mr. Munro offered to pay £100 for six month's service, which was
very acceptable to me. This meant that I had an income of about
$50.00 a month which proved to be enough to pay rent, groceries,
and other incidental living expenses.

Out of the loan received from my insurance policy, I was able to
pay my registration fee at the University, buy textbooks and winter
clothing for the three of us. I noted in one of my letters to relatives
that the thermometer dropped to 19° on the morning of October 21st.
This was but a foretaste of what was to come. I was advised to buy
long underwear as the Scots acted on the premise that it was cheaper
to wear warm clothing than it was to buy coal. Looking back on those
days, I doubt if in the winter weather, the classrooms in either New
College or the University were ever warmer than 60° on the coldest

days. I remember that on some days I could see my breath when taking notes in class. I also recall 'how people kept their overcoats on when attending church during the cold weather.

I took with me to Edinburgh about $200.00 worth of Oriental curios, such as Chinese linens and Japanese artificial pearls, which I sold in Edinburgh for 100% profit. One curio store in Edinburgh took most of these items. Even so, our expenses were more than I had expected; so that I had to apply a second time for a loan on my Government insurance.

Since Miriam was musical, she enrolled in the music department of the University to take courses in music. Her classes met two evenings a week, also a few hours of private lessons, on Saturdays. We rented a piano which was needed in her courses in composition.

My associations with the Mayfield Church for six months were most enjoyable. The sanctuary was always well filled for both morning and evening services. When a Scotsman comes to this country, he soon discovers that people are attracted by his accent. So it was with me, an American preaching in a Scottish pulpit. My accent was different and therefore attractive. I brought with me some of the sermon notes I had used in Shanghai; so I did not have to spend much time on preparing my sermons. Likewise, when in Shanghai I had taught a Bible class for students in the American School and took with me to Edinburgh some of the notes used then. The average attendance of my classes for young people in the Mayfield Church was about fifty. I greatly enjoyed both my preaching and teaching in that church.

Writing to relatives in Early, Iowa, on November 16, 1927, I referred to the fact that after landing in Edinburgh with a cash reserve of about $9.00, I had found work which provided a sufficient income to cover living expenses. I then added: "I believe that God has a special providence for foolish men like me, or else this is a reward for faith." I like to believe that going to Edinburgh and getting my Ph.D. degree was all a part of God's plan for my life. Looking back, I realize that my future as a Seminary professor, as an author, and as the historian of the Chaplain Corps of the U.S. Navy all depended on having that doctor's degree.

After my six months' service as the assistant in the Mayfield Church was completed in April 1928, I was free to accept preaching appointments in various parts of Scotland until we left for the States on May 26th. This was a delightful experience for I got to see places in Scotland, with all expenses paid, not usually visited by tourists. I remember conducting services at Arbroath on the east coast; at Sterling in central Scotland; at Aviemore near Inverness in northern Scotland; and at Largs and Ayr in western Scotland. I would usually leave by train for these preaching appointments on Saturday. I would always be entertained in a private home and then return on Sunday afternoon. After paying expenses, I rarely received as much as two pounds for an honorarium.

In order to give Miriam a chance to see something of the country, I made arrangements for her to visit cousins on her mother's side at Seeham Harbor in Durham county in north England. She was able to make this trip during the second week of April in between the winter and spring terms at the University.

As I have stated, I picked out my thesis subject before leaving China and collected much source material which I took with me to Edinburgh. This proved to have been a very wise move. Shortly after arriving in Edinburgh, I met Dr. Hugh Watt who was to be my senior advisor and Professor of Church History. He advised me to submit my proposed subject — "Christian Missions and Foreign Relations in China, an Historical Study" — to a committee of the faculty which had the responsibility of approving the thesis subject. This I did, and the subject was approved. Dr. Watt urged me to spend as much time as possible in collecting materials bearing on my subject while in Edinburgh. He advised me to examine the holdings in the Advocates Library, which ranks second only to that in the British Museum, where I would find a fine collection of books dealing with the China question. Dr. Watt also warned me that only a small percentage of the American students who enroll for post-graduate study at Edinburgh ever completed writing their thesis, and, therefore, they never got the Ph.D. degree. In order to obtain as much time as possible for research, I took but twelve hours a week during the three terms I was in Edinburgh.

While gathering materials for my thesis, I had the good fortune to discover how some zealous French Jesuit missionaries in Peking, who had served as interpreters for the French-Chinese Treaty of 1865, had added a spurious clause to the Chinese version of the treaty which gave permission for French nationals to leave the treaty ports and reside and travel in the interior. Before going to Edinburgh, I was able to get an English translation of the Chinese version of this treaty. After arriving in Edinburgh, I wrote to the Foreign Office of the French Government and received a copy of the official French version. The interpolation in the Chinese version was clearly evident.

China had been a closed nation for centuries. The several wars with foreign powers beginning in 1842 had opened up five ports for foreign (including missionaries) residence, but now, in 1865, the Chinese were led to believe that they had to throw open the whole nation. Any rights granted to the French were also necessarily granted to other nations by a "most favored nation clause" in other treaties. The story of this treaty with its spurious Chinese clause became one of the most important chapters of my thesis. So far as I know, I was the first to compare the two treaties and to point out the consequences.

Although I had a portable typewriter with me in Edinburgh, I was unable to do much writing on my thesis. My church duties, my research studies, and my classroom work absorbed most of my time. However, I did complete my search for relevant materials in the Advocates Library and was ready to write up my dissertation by the time we left for the States.

The prospect of returning to the States after living abroad for over five years was exciting. I wanted my relatives to meet my wife, Miriam, whom they had not seen, and for our relatives in both Iowa and California to see our son. Also, and this was very important, I wanted to get located and back on a salary basis. The University of Edinburgh then required its doctoral candidates to spend three two-month terms in residence. Since I wanted to take passage on the S.S. Adriatic of the White Star Line, due to sail from Liverpool on Saturday, May 26, for New York, I asked permission to leave Edinburgh a few days before my third term ended. My request was granted. I reserved third class passage for the three of us at a cost of $235.25. This money was also part of a loan received from one of my insurance policies.

Early in January, 1928, I wrote to Dr. Lewis B. Hillis, who was serving as the Student Pastor for Presbyterian students enrolled at the University of California, asking if he knew of any openings in a similar field at other universities. He forwarded my letter to Dr. M. Willard Lampe, who was Student Pastor for Presbyterians at the University of Iowa and also Director of University Work for the whole Presbyterian Church. As will be told, this contact with Dr. Lampe led me to Moscow, Idaho, where I was both Student Pastor and Pastor of the First Presbyterian Church.

A second possibility attracted my attention and that was of going to San Anselmo to serve as Professor of Church History. The position was vacant. My beloved Professor of New Testament and Greek, Dr. E. A. Wicher, whose recommendation of me to Captain Dollar brought me the call to Shanghai, wrote me on November 28, 1927, saying that he had nominated me for the vacant Chair of Church History in the Seminary. He stated that the faculty had adopted a resolution "favoring the appointment of an alumnus."

Writing to me on December 31, 1927, Dr. Warren H. Landon, then President of San Francisco Theological Seminary, said: "There is no one among our Alumni at all available who would suit me better than yourself." However, a few weeks later, or on February 10, 1928,

Dr. Landon wrote that there was a feeling on the part of some members of the Board of Trustees that "we ought to have a man of larger experience." Even though the very thought of being considered for the Seminary's Chair of Church History was flattering, I realized that I was not yet ready for that position. I did not have my doctor's degree and had no experience in teaching. However, the very fact that my name had been under consideration in 1928 prepared the way for my appointment to the same Chair ten years later. I was then ready and qualified.

I followed up my contacts with Dr. Lampe and we made plans for me to call on him in Iowa City when I would be driving across the country. I was so confident that a position would open up on my return to the States that this no longer was a cause of concern.

Shortly before leaving for the States, I received a letter from Dr. Wicher dated May 3, 1928, which contained the following: "But recently the Burlingame Church became vacant. This is a new church, but the most promising opening there is about San Francisco Bay. It would afford you a field that can not be paralleled today in Northern California. The faculty are recommending you for this pastorate." I could make no decision about this while in Scotland; so had to wait until I was back in the States.

A second matter which gave me some concern, as we made plans to leave Scotland and return to the States, was that of negotiating a loan of about $1,000 from members of my family. I figured that I would need this much to buy a car and pay traveling expenses across the country. I appealed to my stepmother, Laura Drury, who in turn asked two of my brothers, Grover and Billy, and my sister Clara, each to contribute. The needed money was raised and sent to me in care of my wife's younger sister, Mrs. Jack (Alice) Glessner who then lived in Detroit.

We said goodby to Edinburgh on Friday, May 25th, after spending eight busy and happy months there. Our ship sailed for America the next day. We found our third class accommodations very comfortable. In a letter to my sister Sarah, I stated that we were more comfortable than we would have been going first class on the French ship which we took out of Shanghai. We arrived in New York Monday morning, June 4th. I then had $35.00 which included some money I had received when I sold some of our Chinese curios to fellow passengers.

We entered New York harbor early in the morning and I was out on deck as we passed the Statue of Liberty. I was so glad to be back in my home land that tears rolled down my cheeks. They were tears of thankfulness and gratitude. After an absence of five years and three months, I was home again.

CHAPTER SEVENTEEN

Called to Moscow, Idaho

Waiting to greet us in New York when our ship docked on Monday morning, June 4, 1928, was the Rev. William Idhe, a former missionary to Japan, now serving as pastor of a Methodist church at Branchville, New Jersey, about seventy-five miles from New York. I first met the Idhes in the spring of 1926 when I was visiting my sister Sarah in Japan.

It was heart-warming to arrive in New York, after spending more than five years abroad, to see one familiar face among the many people waiting to greet passengers. Idhe helped us go through customs and also aided me in arranging for the shipment of our two trunks to Early, Iowa. I had given Mr. Idhe's address to some friends and relatives; so we had mail waiting for us at his home.

Knowing that I would be with him for a few days, Idhe made plans for me to speak on my China experiences on Tuesday evening, June 5th, in his church. He called for a collection and about $18.00 were turned over to me. This was much appreciated as I had landed in New York with only $35.00. The new sum of $53.00 was to pay our train fare to Detroit where I expected to get the loans I had requested from members of my family.

About April 1, when still in Edinburgh, I received a letter from Dr. Lampe, who was in charge of Presbyterian college and university student work, telling me that the pulpit of the First Presbyterian Church of Moscow, Idaho, was vacant. The church was located about a mile from the campus of the University of Idaho which then had an enrollment of about 2,000 students, of whom about 300 gave a Presbyterian preference. Moscow then had a population of 5,000, and the church reported having 400 members. The idea of combining being pastor of a church with student work appealed to me. I felt the need of having a pulpit. But where was Moscow, Idaho? I remember that my wife and I had to turn to an atlas to get the location.

Among the letters awaiting me at the home of Mr. Idhe were two from former professors of mine at the San Anselmo Seminary, each of whom strongly recommended that I take the Burlingame Church. Dr. Oxtoby had been supplying the pulpit there and knew the situation very well. He reported that the church would pay $3,300.00 a year without manse. Dr. Wicher claimed that the Burlingame Church offered "the most promising opening in the San Francisco Bay area." Their prognostications proved to be correct. At the time of this writing, it has over 1,300 members and is one of the stronger churches in San Francisco Presbytery. Both Oxtoby and Wicher urged me not to make any decision to settle elsewhere before visiting Burlingame.

These letters made a strong appeal to me. I was still a member of San Francisco Presbytery where I had been ordained in March 1922. Both my wife and I had relatives living in the Bay area. And, finally, Burlingame was within easy driving distance of the seminary at San Anselmo with its fine library.

Counterbalancing the appeal of the Burlingame Church was the challenge of being a Presbyterian student pastor at some state university. Dr. Lampe in his correspondence with me had mentioned three such openings. The possibility of working with students at the University of Idaho while serving as pastor of the First Presbyterian Church of Moscow had a growing appeal. A letter from Dr. Lampe which reached me at the Idhe home urged me not to make any decision as to where I might settle before I had had the opportunity to see him in his office at Iowa City, Iowa. I followed his advice.

We took a night train for Detroit, Michigan, on Sunday evening, June 10th and were met at the depot in Detroit the next morning by Miriam's younger sister, Mrs. Jack (Alice) Glessner. She and Jack had been but recently married. Jack worked in one of the automobile factories in Detroit. I was greatly relieved to receive at the Glessner home about $1,000.00 from relatives which would enable me to pay cash for a new car and have some money left over for traveling expenses.

I went shopping for a car on Monday afternoon and, on my brother-in-law's advice, selected a Chevrolet two-door coach, the basic price of which was $610.00. It had no trunk. Strange as it now may seem, I had to pay extra for the spare tire and even for the bumpers. The total cost of these extras, and for a Michigan license and insurance, came to $82.51, bringing the total cost to $692.57.

We left the Glessners and Detroit after lunch on Tuesday, June 12th, and headed west towards Chicago, Iowa City, and Early. I still remember the thrill I experienced when I first sat behind the steering wheel of my new car. The future looked promising for I was confident that I would soon get a job. I looked forward with eagerness to meeting my Iowa relatives and friends whom I had not seen since the summer of 1922, six years earlier, and to have them meet Miriam and our three-year-old son, Bobby.

In those days the purchasers were advised not to drive a new car over twenty-five miles an hour for several hundred miles so that the engine could be "broken in." Thus, our first day on the road we made only about 100 miles before we stopped at a small town in south-western Michigan called White Pigeon.

On Wednesday, June 13th, we drove through Chicago to Oak Park where we were guests in the home of the Rev. and Mrs. Emory Luccock Emory and his wife, Lois, had been Presbyterian missionaries in Hunan province in China but were obliged to leave because of unsettled conditions. For a time they were connected with the South Gate Presbyterian mission in Shanghai; then they returned to the States, and in time settled in Oak Park, Illinois, where Emory served as assistant pastor in the First Presbyterian Church of which Dr. Roy Vale was pastor.

Since Emory was so well and favorably known by many of the members of Community Church, he was called in 1928 to be my successor. At the time Miriam and I called on them on that Wednes-day, June 13th, they were making preparations to leave soon for Shanghai. We talked late into the night about the problems and oppor-tunities of Community Church. I was pleased to know that one of such ability was to be my successor. The Luccocks served Community Church for almost ten years and were then obliged to leave China for a second time because of unsettled conditions. Emory's widow, Lois, is now my neighbor in Monte Vista Groves Homes.

While at Oak Park, Dr. Vale interviewed me and invited me to be his assistant and take the place that Emory was soon to vacate. I declined as I had promised Dr. Lampe I would make no decision about a position until I had seen him.

We left Oak Park the afternoon of Thursday, June 14th. The next day we reached Iowa City where I called on Dr. Lampe. After dis-cussing the various possible openings that I might fill, he strongly recommended that I go to Moscow, Idaho. He sent a wire to Dean J. G. Eldridge, one of the members of the pastor-seeking committee, suggesting that he communicate with me by writing or wiring me at Early, Iowa. After having this visit with Dr. Lampe, I felt con-vinced that God was leading me to Moscow.

After leaving Iowa City on Friday, we drove to Jefferson, Iowa, where we were overnight guests in the home of my college classmates, the Rev. and Mrs. Edmund Marousek. Ed was pastor of the First Presbyterian Church of Jefferson for many years and also Stated Clerk of the Synod of Iowa. He and I were members of Buena Vista's class of 1918 and there was no one outside of members of my family with whom I carried on so long a correspondence as with him. He passed away in 1978.

The nearer we got to Early, the more excited I became. This was my first visit there since the summer of 1922, six years ago. On the other hand, Miriam was somewhat apprehensive when she realized that suddenly she would be meeting my large family of relatives. Three of my sisters were married and lived in Early — Maud, Blanche, and Clara. My two brothers, Millard and Grover, also married, were farming at Everly, Iowa, about seventy miles north of Early. Billy was in California, and Sarah and her husband were still in Japan. Homer, one of the twins, who was epileptic, was in a state hospital at Woodward, Iowa. I have no record as to where the other twin, Howard, was at the time. The two children of my stepmother, Joyce and Dean, were at home. In addition to these were several Wilson families, relatives of my father's first wife. Even though there was no blood relationship for the children of my father's second and third wives, still the Wilsons were our uncles and aunts and cousins as much as they were for the first four children. They always joined in our larger family reunions. According to a picture taken at the reunion held on Sunday, the day after we arrived in Early, at least fifty were present. No wonder that Miriam felt apprehensive.

We arrived at the Drury home in Early about 5:00 p.m. on Saturday, June 16th, and were enthusiastically greeted. My stepmother, Laura, whom I will hereafter refer to as Mother, had a room ready for us. My sister Clara had prepared a bountiful supper for us and for all members of the Drury family in Early. This was but the beginning of a series of feasts spread out for us during the eighteen days we stayed in Early.

On Sunday, June 17th, I spoke at the morning service in the First Presbyterian Church of Early. Each time when I return to Early and am invited to speak at a church service, I am torn between speaking in the Presbyterian Church or the Methodist. Since I am a Presbyterian minister, I feel an obligation to my denomination, yet since all of my relatives in Early are Methodists; so also I feel an attachment to them. I solved this dilema by alternating. Of course, as many of my Early residents who were free were at the morning service on the 17th. The women folk were helping Mother get ready for the reunion dinner planned for the afternoon. When I returned home after the service, I met my brothers Millard and Grover and their families who had driven down from Everly.

One of the first things I did after our arrival in Early was to acquaint Miriam with the scenes of my youth. I took her out to the farm, six miles south of Early, where I was born and where I spent the first seventeen years of my life. I showed her the one-room country school, located near the farm house, where I receivd my grammar school education. I drove her two miles to the east and showed her the Methodist Pleasant Hill Church the Drury family attended. And then we visited the Odebolt cemetery, about nine miles southwest of the farm, where my parents and other members of the Drury family lay buried. That evening we went to Storm Lake and I showed her Buena Vista College, just one large building which housed everything from classrooms and library to chapel.

On Tuesday, the 19th, word came from Dean Eldridge of Moscow, Idaho, inviting me to stop off there on our way to California and asked which Sunday would be agreeable for me to speak. In my reply, I stated that I could be there on July 15th, but added that we wanted to see Yellowstone Park on our way. Dean Eldridge thoughtfully replied suggesting that I postpone my arrival in Moscow for one week so that we would have plenty of time to see Yellowstone.

About this time, my sister Clara asked me where we planned to settle. I replied: "In Moscow," not thinking to give the state. In simulated horror, she raised her hands and exclaimed: "Heavens! First it was China, then Scotland, and now it's Russia!"

On Sunday, June 24th, I spoke at the afternoon service at Pleasant Hill Church. This was the third time I had occupied the pulpit there. I was always self-conscious whenever I stood up to preach before an audience which contained some of my relations or former neighbors. I could not help but think that they would be asking themselves: "How does it happen that Merrill Drury became a preacher?"

I had several occasions while at Early to speak about my China experiences. Once arrangements were made for me to speak in the Opera House in Early. In those days every town in Iowa with a population of 500 or more had to have an Opera House. My records show that I received $14.50 as an honorarium after the rental fee for the hall was paid. I was called back to my Alma Mater on Friday, June 22nd, where I addressed a summer school chapel audience. On Sunday, July 1st, I spoke at the morning service at Lakeside Presbyterian Church in Storm Lake. I became a member of that church on confession of faith when a student at Buena Vista College.

I gave my China talk in the Methodist Church of Sac City that evening and received the offering of $8.55. According to my records, the total honorariums received when I spoke about my China experiences at Branchville, New Jersey, and in Early, and Sac City, came to $41.41.

The climax of our eighteen-day Iowa visit came in an outing at a resort on the shores of Lake Okoboji in northwest Iowa. My brother-in-law, Ferry Smith, took the lead in sponsoring the outing. He rented two cottages large enough to provide sleeping accommodations for the nineteen members of the Drury family. Miriam and I joined the party on Monday, July 2nd. There we enjoyed swimming, boating, fishing, and more visiting.

Eager to be on our way to Moscow, we left on the afternoon of July 4th and drove to Rock Rapids. Cross country motoring is far different today from what is was in the summer of 1928. We could get motels for $3.00 a night, and as low as $2.00 if we provided our own bedding, which we carried with us. We also had a two-burner gasoline camp stove and were able to cook some of our meals. We tried to make 300 miles a day. It took us two days to drive through the Bad Lands and the Black Hills to Speerfish near the Wyoming border. The roads were unpaved, but for the most part were gravelled. A heavy rain storm struck the area on Friday, the 6th. Even though I put on chains, my car could hardly move through the sticky mud. Each wheel turned into a large doughnut. Of necessity we had to seek refuge in Speerfish. We found accommodations in a private home where we stayed until the following Monday, waiting for the storm to pass and the roads to dry out.

Automobiles in those days had running boards on each side of the car. I was able to get a guard rail which I fastened to the running board on the left side. This permitted me to put two suitcases and some other items in this space. Even though this was helpful, at the same time it was dangerous, for it blocked the use of the left door.

Our three-year-old son was, on the whole, a good traveler, but at times he became restless. In our two-door Chevrolet, he was usually kept in the back seat. I remember once while making a long drive, he leaned over, put his little right hand on my chin, and said: "Go home, Daddy, go home." But we still had a long way to go.

On Monday we drove to Buffalo, Wyoming, and then the next day we crossed the Big Horn Mountain range. I remember how the road wound upward and upward until it reached an altitude of 9,666 feet. This is the Powder River Pass. That night we camped at Ten Sleep, within a day's drive of the west entrance of Yellowstone Park, and the next day we drove into the Park. Tourist travel was light then compared to modern times; so we had no difficulty in finding accommodations, even though we had no reservations.

While in Yellowstone, I heard from Jay G. Eldridge who gave me directions as to how to find him at a youth conference which would then be under way at Twin Lakes near Spokane. He suggested that we call on him before going to Moscow. We left on the last segment of our journey to Moscow Monday morning and met Dean Eldridge at Twin Lakes on Wednesday, the 18th. There began a friendship which ripened with the passing of years. He and his wife, Polly, were among God's saints on earth. Eldridge was dean of the faculty of the

University of Idaho and gave us much information about the church in Moscow. He told us that a room had been reserved for us in the Moscow Hotel and said we should get settled there before contacting a number of people whose names he gave us. We arrived in Moscow on Thursday morning, July 19th.

The Demand for an Immediate Decision

We had but five days in Moscow before leaving for Berkeley. These were days of heightened interest for me. Miriam was quite willing for me to make the decision to accept or reject a call, if it should come, as she realized that the responsibility would be mine. During those five days, we met many of the active members and officers of the church. We were invited out to a meal at least once, and sometimes twice, a day. The church had been without a pastor for eight months and I found the people eager to have this matter settled.

I had not been in Moscow long before I heard of the Rev. John J. Canoles who had graduated from the Seminary at San Anselmo in 1925 and had become pastor of the First Presbyterian Church of Sausalito in Marin County. This church was rather small, and he was eager for a larger field. In January, Dr. W. H. Landon, President of the Seminary, had strongly recommended him to the Moscow church and, as a result, he was asked to visit Moscow in February or March. He preached at least twice and made a very favorable impression.

The church extended him an unanimous call. Instead of giving a yes or no answer, Canoles requested time to return to his home in California and think it over. It seems possible that he had by that time learned that the pulpit of the First Presbyterian Church of San Rafael was vacant and that his name had been proposed to the pulpit seeking committee of that church. At that time the San Rafael church was the largest and most influential in Marin County and was located about five miles east of San Anselmo. The Moscow church, eager to get Canoles as its pastor, granted him the privilege of waiting a few weeks before giving a final answer to its call.

When Canoles got back in California, he found the attractions of the San Rafael church so inviting that he accepted its call. Several weeks had passed in the meantime before he notified the Moscow church of his decision. Thus, the Moscow church had to begin its search all over again. Just about that time, Dr. Lampe's letter telling about me came to the attention of its pulpit seeking committee. Thus, Canoles, who is now deceased, did me a great favor by causing a delay which gave me time to appear on the scene. I was told with emphasis that if the church extended a call to me, it would demand a yes or no answer right then and there. This meant that I would not be allowed to go to California and investigate the attractions of the Burlingame church. All of this was in the background of my mind as I investigated the possibilities of the Moscow field and appraised my abilities to meet the challenge it presented.

Being historically minded, I inquired about the history of the church and learned that it had been founded in December 1880, and that the first pastor was the Rev. Daniel Gamble who, with his wife, were both still living when I visited Moscow. Mr. Gamble died a few weeks after I had visited Moscow during the time when my wife and I were in California.

The oldest part of the church, as it was when I was in Moscow, was dedicated on April 19, 1885. This was a rectangular building with the apse at the west end for the organ, choir, and pulpit. Sometime during the 1890s, during the ministry of Dr. D. O. Ghormley, the church building was enlarged by having two additions added, one on each side of the original sanctuary. This doubled the seating capacity by raising it to about 250. On special occasions, chairs would be brought in which added another 100. Also during Dr. Ghormley's pastorate, a manse was built next door to the church.

Sometime about 1904 or 1907 a beautifully toned pipe organ was secured through a gift from Andrew Carnegie. This organ was operated by a water pump immediately below the organ chamber. The pump itself came to be located in the middle of the coal bin. In 1912 a two-story annex was erected on the west side of the church which provided a room measuring about thirty-three feet on each side on each level. Previous to this, the only Sunday School space available was two rooms in the basement. Perhaps in 1912 the kitchen and toilets were also added.

My wife and I inspected the manse. Compared with the modest apartment we had had in Edinburgh, this house with its four upstairs bedrooms, and a living room, dining room, kitchen and hall downstairs, seemed commodious. There was a furnace for hot water heating in the basement and a garage in the back. I remember writing to my sister, Sarah, and telling what a fine manse we would have.

During the few days we spent in Moscow before Sunday, when I was expected to preach twice, I checked the records of the church as reported to the General Assembly for 1927. The church then reported having 393 members and had spent $4,828.00 for current expenses and had contributed $2,084.07 to the denominational benevolences. After going to Moscow, I discovered that the church's rolls had not been cleared of absentees, etc. for years. During the first year of my pastorate there, we removed 95 names. I learned that one-half of my active elders were on the faculty of the University and the other half were business or professional men or farmers.

Moscow was located in what was called the Palouse country, named after a river of that name, where the principal crops were wheat and peas. It was a beautiful little city with the Thatuna Hills, also called Moscow Mountains, about five miles to the northeast.

Always when a church is examining a candidate for its pulpit to replace a minister who has just left, there is an inevitable comparison of personality traits and preaching style between the two. This is only natural. In the process of comparing me with my predecessor, who had served the Moscow church for ten years, I discovered that my method of preaching was in sharp contrast to his, and this proved to be of crucial importance for my candidacy.

When I first met Dean Eldridge at the Twin Lakes conference, he inquired as to my experiences in China and Scotland, the progress I had made towards getting a Ph.D. degree, and such related subjects. Then he asked the key question: "Do you read your sermons?" I replied "No. I always write out my sermons, but I never take this manuscript into the pulpit. Rather, I take a few notes. I always write out any quotations so that I can give them correctly. I want to look at the faces of my congregation rather than at a manuscript, so I never read my sermons."

Dean Eldridge was pleased with my reply and remarked that the church did not want another minister who read his sermons. I preached twice on Sunday, July 22nd. I took for my subject for the 11:00 o'clock service, "The Transfiguration of Jesus." The publicity of my appearance must have been excellent, for the church was filled. In my record book, I noted that 250 were present. Remembering what Dean Eldridge had said about my predecessor's habit of reading his sermons, I was careful not to look at my notes more than was necessary. I preached again at the 7:30 service that evening, using the text: "I am the way, the truth, and the life." Again the church was filled.

A congregational meeting was held in the upper room of the annex following the morning service. Judging by the cordial reception that my wife and I had received, I felt reasonably certain that a call would be extended, and I was ready to accept. This was the kind of a church in a university town that I had wanted. Only one question remained in my mind — would the church offer me a salary commensurate with what had been promised by the Burlingame church. If so, then this would have been several hundred dollars more than what the church had been paying.

The congregational meeting did not last long, for there was an unanimous vote in favor of extending a call to me. I was then asked to join those who had assembled in the upper room of the annex where one of the elders explained the terms offered — an annual salary of $3,000.00, free use of the manse, a month's vacation, participation in the recently inaugurated pension plan of the denomination, and cost of shipping my two trunks from Iowa to Moscow and also my household goods, which had been shipped across the Pacific and were being held in storage in San Francisco.

I was then asked: "Will you accept our call " I had no hesitancy to do so, but asked for a month's interlude so that my wife, son, and I could visit her relatives in Berkeley. She had not seen her parents for over five years. I am now not sure if the members of the Moscow church then knew that the Burlingame church was seeking my services or not, but they had clear memories of their experience with John Canoles, and they did not want that to happen a second time. The elders demanded a firm commitment. Would I definitely at that time accept their call? It was either Yes or No. I assured them that I would not consider any call from a California church but that, after visiting relatives, we would be back about August 21.

Nothing was said about giving an allowance for auto expense, or telephone costs, or even office expenses such as postage. But in that day these omissions were not unusual, for I knew of no Presbyterian ministers in churches of 400 members, or even more, who were being reimbursed by the church for such expenses.

I was concerned about how I was to notify Dr. Oxtoby, and the elders of the Burlingame church who had been writing to me, about my decision to take the Idaho church. When my wife and I did arrive in California, I did not visit Burlingame to see what the situation there was like.

Going to Moscow proved to be crucial in my later ministry. Had I not gone there, I would never have written my eleven books on the history of the Oregon Mission of the Board. Had I not written three books before the position of Professor of Church History at San Anselmo opened up, I probably would not have been called to the faculty. And had I not established a reputation as an historian, I would not have been made historian of the Navy's Chaplain Corps in World War II. Going to Moscow was the key event which opened several doors in my future career.

Shakespeare wrote in Hamlet: "There is a divinity that shapes our ends, rough-hew them as we will." So it was in my call to be pastor of the First Presbyterian Church of Moscow, Idaho; I was convinced that this was God's plan for me.

CHAPTER EIGHTEEN

My Ten-Year Pastorate at Moscow, Idaho

A great burden of concern rolled from my shoulders when the congregation of the First Presbyterian Church of Moscow extended an unanimous call to be their pastor. Our venture of faith had been vindicated. After being without a regular salary for over a year, I felt the urgency of having a steady income. The outlook was bright and we were very happy over developments.

We asked for permission to be gone for a month so that we could visit relatives in Berkeley. Our request was granted, and I promised to be back on or before August 25. I received two messages of special interest from Berkeley while at Moscow. The first was from my brother Billy, who informed me that my household goods, which I had sent to him more than a year earlier, were about to be put up for sale. I had been informed when the goods were shipped that I had two years before I needed to claim them; but I had been misinformed. The time limit was one year and had expired July 1, 1928. Billy could not clear them through customs because he did not know the contents of each box; but he was able to secure a month's delay. This meant that I had to clear the goods before August 1.

The second message came from Dr. Lapsley McAfee, with whom I had been associated in the First Presbyterian Church of Berkeley before going to China. He said that he was to attend the meeting of the Synod of California over the last Sunday in July, the 29th, and invited me to take the morning service in his church on that day, which I was delighted to do. So, on July 29th I stood again in the pulpit of this church. I received an enthusiastic welcome from those whom I had known when I was Assistant Pastor. I also had an opportunity to see Dr. McAfee the following week.

We began our 1,100 mile journey to Berkeley on Monday, July 23rd and spent the first night at Walla Walla. At that time I knew little or nothing about the Whitman-Spalding story, nor could I then imagine what an important place this would be in my future writings. Our road led us along the south bank of the Columbia River to Portland. After leaving Portland we took a side trip to Crater Lake, and then on to Berkeley, arriving there Thursday, July 26th. For the first time in six years Miriam saw her parents; and, for the first time, of course, the grandparents saw their first grandchild.

As soon as possible I visited the customs house in San Francisco where I cleared our household goods through customs and had them shipped to Moscow.

I had opportunity to spend two weeks working on my thesis before we started back to Moscow.

We left Berkeley on August 15th and arrived in Moscow on the 23rd. We found our goods from San Francisco had already arrived. We brought back with us from Berkeley Miriam's eighteen year old sister, Muriel. Having lived in cramped quarters in Scotland, we were delighted to have a manse with four bedrooms, one of which I used for a study. However, when winter came, we found that the manse was poorly insulated, and we had to put on storm doors and windows. The hot water furnace was in the basement and was very inefficient. In really cold weather I often had to get up in the night to shovel in coal. There was an electric range in the kitchen which did not help to heat the room. After using it a year or so, we discarded it and got an old fashioned cooking range that burned both wood and coal. That did much to make us comfortable.

We found, upon our return, that the ladies of the church had presented us with a collection of jams, jellies, and canned fruit, which was very much appreciated.

One of our first responsibilities was to furnish the house. We shopped at David's Department Store where credit was extended, and we bought the necessary furniture, such as beds and living room furniture. My cash reserve was zero when we got back to Moscow, so I got an advance of half a month's salary to see us through September.

My first sermon in the pulpit in Moscow, after our return from California, was on August 26th with an attendance of 175. In those days there were no motion pictures on Sunday. Television was not yet born; we did have radio. People were willing to keep up a Sunday evening service, and we continued this for about five years with an average attendance of about 60. I had not great difficulty preparing two sermons for each Sunday because I had saved the sermon manuscripts that I used in China. From these I made notes and took only the notes into the pulpit.

At that time the University had about 1,500 students, of whom 300 stated a preference for the Presbyterian Church. Since there was no Congregational Church in the city, the Congregationalists came to us. But the church was one mile from the University, so that the students living on campus had to walk a mile each way in order to attend. Even so, I often had as many as 100 students in my audience.

Some interesting contrasts and parallels could be drawn between the Shanghai church and that in Moscow. The two churches had about the same number of members. The Shanghai parish was about equally divided between the missionary and the non-missionary families. In Moscow the division was between "town and gown," i.e. between the University and the non-University people.

The church had the usual list of activities, including two, and sometimes three,Boy Scout troops, two Christian Endeavor societies, and a large Sunday School. The enthusiasm engendered by my coming increased activity in all the departments. When the attendance at Sunday School rose to about 300, we had to rent an empty house across the street to take care of the overflow.

BORN TO US — A DAUGHTER AND A SON

Sunday, March 17, 1929, was a trying day for me. We were momentarily expecting the birth of our second child. I took Miriam to the nursing home early that morning and then returned for my usual Sunday morning duties. I remember asking myself: "Why should a baby be born to a minister's wife on Sunday, the most important day in a minister's week?" I felt reluctant to say anything about what was to happen, even to my closest friends. My records show that I had an audience of 250 that morning at the usual 11:00 o'clock service. I found it hard to be composed as I delivered my sermon, for I kept thinking about Miriam.

As soon as the service was over, I hastened to the nursing home. The baby had not yet arrived but came that afternoon. It was a girl, and since she was born on St. Patrick's day, we named her Patricia. We gave her no middle name as we agreed that should she get married the family name of "Drury" would be her middle name; but she never married.

On Monday, July 7, 1930, our second son was born. We named him Philip Edward. Our two youngest were nearly sixteen months apart in their ages. Within a couple weeks after his birth our little son developed difficulty in keeping down the milk given him. He did not gain weight as expected. I was placed in a difficult position, for I had been selected to be Dean of a Presbyterian Summer Conference which was to meet at Whitworth College just north of Spokane. The expected enrollment was set at 100. The committee in charge knew of no other qualified person to serve if I could not go. Miriam wanted me to remain at home, but our doctor, Dr. Einhouse, did not feel that this was necessary since Miriam had her sister with her. So I decided to go, but kept in daily contact by telephone. The baby's condition did not improve.

Upon my return home after the week long conference, our doctor advised taking our baby to a child specialist in Spokane. I was able to secure rooms for the family in one of Whitworth's dormitories. Early in September the five of us drove to the college. Muriel had other plans and did not go with us. Our baby was put into a hospital where the specialist diagnosed his trouble as being pyloric stenosis, which meant there was an obstruction at the bottom of the stomach.

This enlargement of the pyloric muscle had prevented the free flow of the food into the digestive system and this, in turn, had caused the frequent vomiting. Even though the baby was less than a month old, an operation was necessary.

The doctor performed surgery, opening the abdomen and cutting through part of the muscle to allow the food easy access to the intestine. The result was immediate; the baby kept down his milk and began to increase in weight. Miriam and I took turns driving into the hospital to see him; we were grateful he was able to survive.

Moscow was an ideal place to raise children. There were plenty of recreational activities and we had no fear about letting the children go where they pleased in the village. Moscow then had about 5,000 people; now it has close to 20,000.

WE BUILD THE FIRST UNIT OF OUR NEW CHURCH

Since we were so crowded for space for our various programs, the church already had begun thinking of building. A building committee was formed in May, 1929, and an architect was hired. We conducted a building fund campaign in April of 1932. My records indicate that we had $9,120 in our building fund in 1931. Since these were depression years, we felt that we could not build the entire church as desired, but compromised on building a large basement. By the end of 1934 we still had only $33,279 in the bank. However, this sum, plus a loan from the bank, enabled us to build the basement, which was ready for occupancy in 1934.

We now had a place for all of our youth activities and a dining room large enough to seat 200 for dinner. At the time we built the basement there was not a single school in Moscow with a gymnasium; so our basement was in demand by a number of groups, including some young men who played volley ball.

The basement contained a stage where our college students produced a number of plays. During my ministry in Moscow, I wrote three plays, based on biblical events, which were presented by the students.

Shortly after my arrival in Moscow, I was told of three elderly ladies who had emigrated from Scotland as little children, along with their parents and a cousin, and were now living on a farm a few miles out of Moscow. Since we had but recently come from Edinburgh, my wife and I called on them. They considered themselves to be Presbyterians, but were not church members and did not attend church. We learned their names were Annie, Allie, and Margaret Cameron. Allie and Margaret worked in the fields along with their cousin, Murdo Stewart. Miriam and I, with our children, called there many times and were always cordially received.

First Presbyterian Church, Moscow, Idaho
This 1930 photograph shows the old church.
Dr. Drury served as pastor here from 1928 to 1938.

At the time of our building fund campaign I called on them, hoping to get a contribution. They asked me how much I thought they should give; not knowing anything about their ability to contribute, I gave them the modest figure of $250.00. At the time I thought this would come from all four of them. Instead they took this to mean individually, and so, to my surprise, they gave $1,000.00. The Camerons were always very kind to us, and as long as we were in Moscow, they gave us a turkey for each Thanksgiving and a goose each Christmas. They will come again into this story in a following chapter.

IDAHO INSTITUTE OF CHRISTIAN EDUCATION

It so happened that in the early 1930's, in the midst of the depression, one of the fraternities located on Elm Street bordering the University campus was able to build a new house; this left their former one vacant.

Under the special leadership of Dr. Wayne Smith, a member of the University faculty and an active leader in the First Methodist Church of Moscow, together with the enthusiastic cooperation of Dean Eldridge, the idea was promoted of organizing a fraternity of Christian young men and buying the empty fraternity house. We were able to find enough students who were willing to become charter members of a local fraternity, which would be known by the Greek letters Alpha Chi which stood for the Greek words meaning Brothers of Christ or the Christian Brotherhood.

The Mormon church had erected a student center on the edge of the campus and were giving courses in religion for which the University was giving academic credit. Thus, a precedent had been set. Our immediate concern was to raise enough money to pay the salary of a director. We called a meeting of the men from the four interested churches — Baptist, Christian, Methodist and Presbyterian — and presented our cause. We were successful in raising about $3,000.00 in cash and pledges. On the basis of this we hired the Rev. Carl Wells, a recent graduate of the University of Southern California, to be the Director. He was a fine choice.

The first classes were held in the living room of the Alpha Chi house, but this proved to be unsatisfactory; so we converted a wide porch on the north side of the building into an extra room. It had its own entrance, and here the classes were held.

The financial situation of the Institute was in a precarious state. We soon discovered that when money was tight, our constituency preferred to keep up their denominational payments rather than the interdenominational work. Since we were able to raise only half of what was needed for the second year for Wells, he, out of financial necessity, left us to accept a position in a school in Washington, D.C. I was asked to teach a course in Church History, which I did for two terms in 1937-38. The attendance was small — only about five or six. I believe I am the only one of that founding committee still alive.

Nearly fifty years have passed since the Institute was founded. It is now well established and has received several bequests and annual contributions from several of the national church boards.

I GET MY COVETED PH.D. DEGREE

When we settled in Moscow I had my thesis about two-thirds written and plenty of source material at hand; but at first I was so busy with my church work that I had no time to work on my thesis. My wife kept prodding me and I owe much to her for my being able to finish it.

During the vacation month of August, 1929, I rented a cottage on the shore of Lake Coeur d'Alene where I was able to do some more writing. Miriam's mother joined us that summer and helped in the care of our baby Patricia.

Again, in August 1931, when we had two babies, we drove to San Anselmo where I was able to get the use of a cottage owned by the seminary. While I was at San Anselmo, I was able to complete the thesis. I then had three copies bound with the title stamped on the cover — CHRISTIAN MISSIONS AND FOREIGN RELATIONS IN CHINA, AN HISTORICAL REVIEW. I sent the first copy to my senior professor, Dr. Hugh Watt, at the University of Edinburgh; I sent a second copy to the Presbyterian Historical Society in Philadelphia; and gave the third copy to my Seminary in San Anselmo.

It had taken me nearly four years to finish the project. Dr. Watt replied on July 19th, saying that the two "internal examiners" appointed from within the faculty had turned in an "entirely favorable" report. But, and then came the bad news, the external examiner, an ex-missionary from Manchuria and a resident of Edinburgh, had turned in an unfavorable report. Usually the faculty refused to grant the Ph.D. degree when one of the three readers of the thesis turned in an unfavorable report; but, in this case, Dr. Watt was so convinced of the merits of the thesis that he persuaded the faculty to appoint another examiner.

Writing to me on November 2, 1932, Dr. Watt stated: "I shall fight my hardest that it be not rejected absolutely, but that a chance of revision be granted. What stuck in the throat of the Board was one sentence from the external examiner's report — 'That it showed commendable diligence, but no other commendable quality.' I did my best to point out the folly of this judgment, but it did remain to rankle in their minds."

Another external examiner or reader was appointed, a Dr. Simpson who happened to be the grandson of the Dr. Simpson who discovered chloroform. Within a few days after receiving the thesis, he submitted a favorable and even enthusiastic report. "The report," wrote Dr. Watt to me on December 9, 1932, went on to say that "he hoped the thesis would be published and published soon." Dr. Watt sent me a cablegram dated December 8th with but one word; but that was all sufficient: "Favorable."

The coveted degree, which has meant so much to me, was publicly conferred on me, in absentia, at a Graduation Ceremonial of the University of Edinburgh, held Friday, December 16, 1932. I would have liked to have been present for the occasion, but that was not possible. Anyway, the coveted degree was mine.

Dr. Simpson's recommendation that the thesis be published prompted me to send a copy to the Commercial Press of Shanghai, China. One of the editors there read the manuscript and also recommended publication, but this would have to be at my expense, and I would have to be responsible for sales. According to the estimated cost in U.S. money, 500 copies of a cloth bound book with 320 pages of text would have cost me $3.48 a copy or a total subsidy of $1,714.00. If 1,000 copies were printed, the subsidy would be $2,400.00. Kelly & Walsh, a leading bookstore in Shanghai, wrote on August 2, 1933, saying that if the thesis were published, they could sell at least 200 copies. However, those were the depression years in the United States and I did not have the money to pay for this cost of printing. So it happened, that the first book I wrote remains unpublished.

A Broken Dish and its Consequences

The above account has a sequel. In the summer of 1966, my wife and I spent three months in England, Scotland and Ireland. We returned to Edinburgh where I was delighted to learn that my beloved Professor of Church History, Dr. Hugh Watt, was still alive and was living in retirement with his wife. They kindly invited Miriam and me to dine with them. This was a thrilling experience for me to have fellowship with Dr. Watt again, after not seeing him for thirty-eight years.

The subject of how narrowly I had missed getting my doctor's degree came up for discussion. I asked Dr. Watt why the first external examiner had given such a negative report on my thesis.

Dr. Watt replied: "That external reader was Dr. Alexander McInnis (not his real name) who was a retired missionary from Manchuria. He explained that he rejected your thesis because you did not include Manchuria in your study."

The mention of the name of Dr. McInnis awakened memories of a most distressing incident which took place in his home when I was a student at the University, 1927-28. It occurred to me that here might be the reason for that unfavorable report. I explained to Dr. Watt.

"While my wife and I were living here in Edinburgh," I said, "Dr. and Mrs. McInnis, hearing that we came from Shanghai, kindly invited us to their home for tea. We explained that we had a two-and-one-half year old son and had no baby sitter. I offered to go alone and leave Miriam to take care of Bobby. 'No,' they insisted, 'bring him with you.' We had frequently taken Bobby with us to teas, and he always behaved himself; so we felt free to do so again." The story I then told is summarized as follows:

Upon our arrival at the McInnis home, we were ushered into a tastefully furnished dining room which contained many oriental objects. We noticed in particular the beautiful Chinese dishes which were on the table. The plates were richly embossed with Chinese designs. I voiced my admiration which evidently pleased Mrs. McInnis who explained that that dinner set was their pride and joy and was irreplaceable.

While seated in comfortable chairs before the fireplace, both my wife and I became so absorbed in the account Dr. McInnis was giving of life in Manchuria that we failed to notice what our little son was doing. Suddenly there was a crash of broken china and then we saw what had happened. Our son had taken one of the fireplace pokers and had swung it around and let it fall on one of the large dinner plates. It was broken beyond repair. Of course, I offered to buy another but was told that those dishes were irreplaceable. I remember the strained atmosphere which clouded the remainder of our visit.

After telling Dr. Watt about this experience, I asked: "Could it have been possible that Dr. McInnis was so disturbed by that broken Chinese plate that he reacted, either consciously or unconsciously, in a negative way to my thesis?" The fact that Dr. McInnis had written that while my thesis had "showed commendable diligence," there was no other "commendable quality." These words reflected a deep feeling of bitterness, and, as a result, I almost failed in getting my doctor's degree. I was glad that I was able to express in person my gratitude to Dr. Watt for his intercession in my behalf.

I Join the U.S. Navy Chaplain's Corps

Some time during the summer of 1933 I received a letter from my friend, Chaplain Tom Kirkpatrick, whom I first met in Shanghai, China, informing me that the Navy had started a Reserve Corps for chaplains; he urged me to enlist. The invitation appealed to me, and

I drove to Spokane on December 12, 1933, to meet with a Navy Recruiting Officer. At that time I became a member of this new unit with the rank of Lieutenant. Later I learned that I was the first Presbyterian in the United States to join the Chaplain's Corps Reserve. When Pearl Harbor day came there were fewer than 200 chaplains of all faiths on active duty, and only eight in the Reserve Corps qualified for service. As will be told later, I was called to duty at the time we declared war on Japan — December 7, 1941.

THE MUSICAL CONTRIBUTIONS OF MY WIFE

During the years that the Drury family occupied the manse of the First Presbyterian Church of Moscow, August 1928-July 1938, my wife made a most important contribution to the religious music of the Presbyterian Church, especially for children. She had a musical background, having been a pianist and organist for her church in Pacific Grove, California, during her high school days. When we were in Edinburgh, Scotland, in 1927-28 while I was studying for my doctor's degree, she took three hours of work a week at the University in Music. After we settled in Moscow, Miriam continued her musical studies at the University of Idaho from which institution she received her B.A. degree in music June 5, 1939.

Miriam became interested in writing songs for children when she was helping in the Sunday School of the church in Moscow. She found the songs which were printed in the weekly Sunday School leaflets for the children in the beginners and primary departments woefully lacking in quality. As she explained to me, a proper hymn or song must measure up in three particulars — good poetry, good music, and good doctrine. So many of the songs published by our church's Board of Christian Education were lacking in one or more of these categories. So my wife began writing her own songs.

By 1934 we had three children — Robert, age nine, Patricia, age five, and Philip, age four. Miriam would try out her compositions on the children. Hearing that Dr. Calvin W. Laufer, then in charge of the Editorial Department of the Board of Christian Education, was planning to compile and publish a series of graded song books for the children of the church's Sunday Schools, Miriam sent in about one hundred items consisting of words and music, or just music, or just words. The first of Dr. Laufer's series appeared in 1935 under the title *When a Little Child Wants to Sing*. This hymnal contained thirty-three items by Miriam — either words and music, or just words, or just music, and later proved to be in great demand. Some years ago I picked up one of the books in a church and found that it came from the thirtieth printing. Some of Miriam's songs have been taken from this book by other denominations, as the Methodists, Congregational, Baptist and Episcopalian.

Perhaps the most used song in the hymnal for children was the following:

> I saw a bird in the top of a tree,
> This is the song he was singing to me:
> "God loves us all in a wonderful way:
> Be happy, be happy, today."

Miriam kept on with her writing of poetry and music. Six of her compositions appeared in *Hymns for Primary Worship,* 1946, and three in *Hymns for Junior Worship,* 1940. In addition to the musical compositions, Miriam wrote children's stories which appeared in the Board's publications. I failed to keep a record of these, but they must have numbered at least twenty-five.

After we moved to San Anselmo, California, in the summer of 1938, Miriam wrote anthems for the Junior Choir. Anthem books, published by the Westminster Press, which contained one or more of her anthems, appeared in 1949, 1954 and 1961. The latter books contained anthems for the adult choirs. Two of her hymns, words only, appeared in the Presbyterian WORSHIP BOOK which was published in 1970.

PERSONAL FINANCES

We had a difficult time during the depression when the annual budget for current expenses dropped down below $5,000.00. The salaries of the University professors were cut; wheat sold for 25¢ a bushel. It was, therefore, inevitable that my salary should be cut. I was getting $3,000.00 a year, but in 1932 this was reduced to $2,400.00, or $200.00 a month. I had no help from the church to cover car expenses, and no secretary to help with correspondence. It was a constant struggle from one month to another. About 1937 the church restored 10% of the cut.

The two-door Chevy sedan I had bought in Detroit in 1928 was now too small for our family of six; so I traded it in on February 14, 1931, for a four-door second-hand Chevy. I was allowed $325.00 for my old car and was able to take title to the '29 car by paying $175.00 extra. My records show that I had driven that first car 7,075 miles at a cost of .017¢ a mile, and was able to make 15.42 miles per gallon.

Even though our finances were very limited, I managed to take advantage of our month's vacation each summer, usually in August. We made three trips during the ten years I was in Moscow to San Anselmo, 1931, 1934 and 1935. I was often able to do supply preaching during the vacation month and sometimes able to use the manse of the pastor whom I was assisting.

When I was married I was carrying $12,000.00 in life insurance; $2,000.00 from the Banker's Life in Des Moines, and $10,000.00 taken with the government when I was a soldier in World War I. During our residence in Shanghai I had to draw from the cash values of the policies in order to pay necessary bills. I also took an additional loan to pay expenses in Edinburgh. When we got to Moscow I was $1,000.00 in debt to members of my family on which I was paying 5% interest during the depression. These were difficult times, and I had to borrow more on my policies while in Moscow, as my salary of $200.00 a month did not cover expenses. The result was that I had to give up $9,000.00 of my insurance, as I was totally unable to repay the interest on what I had borrowed and keep up the annual premiums. This meant that my insurance was reduced to $2,000.00, which was my only estate if I should pass away first. At that time the church pension was still very small, and my precarious financial condition was a source of concern to me. When World War II came I was able to pick up $8,000.00 of government insurance which, in part, replaced what I had surrendered.

It was never my custom to accept a fee for a funeral which involved a church family; but sometimes people who were not members of our church would offer a fee for a funeral. My record book shows that I received on an average of $40.00 a year in funeral fees during the years 1929-32.

Occasionally I was called upon to lecture before school groups and would often get $10.00 as an honorarium for such appearances. Two years before I left Moscow to take up my new duties at San Anselmo, the church restored a portion of the cut. Those were difficult days which somehow we managed to get through. I was able to repay, with interest, all the money I had borrowed from relatives.

Pastoral Duties

As pastor of the First Presbyterian Church of Moscow, I had the usual routine of duties which would have come to any person serving as pastor of that church. These included conducting the Sunday services, sponsoring youth activities including the Sunday School, officiating at funerals and weddings, and endless calling on the sick and new people who had recently moved to town.

Our church program kept me busy every evening of the week. We always had our main mid-week service on Thursday with a covered dish dinner. Usually these evenings were given to Bible study, or to meetings with our Sunday School staff.

The declining interest in the Sunday evening service, and the increased activities with young people, made it advisable for me to give up those services, and this was a great help to me. Our young people's groups were then called Christian Endeavor. We had an active group in our High School C.E. and here I had the help of some devoted lay people of the church.

The College C.E. had a membership of over fifty. On Sunday afternoons we met at 5:00 o'clock for light refreshments; then, after a song service, the young people conducted the meeting. I soon learned that most of these young people were the students who had not joined a fraternity or sorority; so this became their social outlet. When weather permitted on Friday or Saturday evening, this college group usually went to the mountains for a picnic supper. It is hard now for me to believe that we charged only 25¢ for the entire evening. If we had thirty in the group, I would pay $1.00 to a neighbor to take us out in his truck; with the balance of the money I would buy ice cream, buns, weiners, potato salad, and coffee — all for 25¢ each!

I was much engaged with summer conferences for young people. The Presbyterian Board of Christian Education sent me to San Francisco to attend a conference of those who acted as deans for these summer conferences. With but few exceptions I attended at least one conference each summer for high school or college young people. On three occasions I acted as Dean of the conference, and at other times was one of the faculty members.

One of the members of my College C.E., when I first arrived, was a student by the name of Paul Rice. He comes again into our story several years later. Another student who figured largely in later years was Kenneth Platt, whom I baptized and received into the church. Kenneth and his wife, Jeannette, are now living in Moscow where both are active members of the church.

One of the happy memories of my Moscow ministry centered about our church picnics. Dean and Mrs. Eldridge had a cottage about five miles to the northeast of Moscow in a forest on Moscow Mountain, sometimes called Thatuna Hills. Often as many as 100 would attend these summer picnics; frequently at the Eldridge cottage.

The church had many consecrated and active members, and I must mention Dean and Mrs. Jay Eldridge, Mr. and Mrs. Harry Sampson, Mrs. Earl Clyde (daughter of the founder of the church), and many others who were of great help to me.

The church observed its fiftieth anniversary on December 18, 1930 and recently has celebrated its centennial.

COMMUNITY ACTIVITIES

During my ten year residence in Moscow I became active in several community organizations. Since I had joined the Masonic

Lodge in Early, Iowa in 1918, I now transferred my membership to the Lodge in Moscow. I served as Master in 1937. I also joined the Royal Arch Chapter and became High Priest during the first six months of 1938, or until I left for San Anselmo.

Since I was a veteran of World War I, I joined the American Legion Post in Moscow and served as Commander for one year. During this year the Post sponsored a fife and bugle corps. I joined those who used the drums. We took lessons from a drill sargeant attached to the student corps at the University. I found it took much practice to master even the simplest system of the various drum beats. I remember that on one Armistice Day I marched in the parade from the University to the City park with the other members of the Legion Post who were either drummers or played the fife. This was the limit of my musical activities.

For at least four years I served as chairman of the county's Red Cross chapter. During those days of depression there were many desperately poor in and around Moscow. I remember that the Government sent in, by rail, cars loaded with flour and cotton cloth for free distribution which the Red Cross handled.

I also joined the Kiwanis Club which met once a week in the Moscow Hotel for an evening dinner. The price was only 65¢, but often I was so short of funds that I waited until the dinner was served before attending. I kept up my Kiwanis activities after I left Moscow and now have a twenty-two year record of perfect attendance.

CHAPTER NINETEEN

As Author and Publisher

Many have asked me the questions: "How did it happen that you got started in writing so many books [now twenty-five], and scores of articles for historical and religious publications? What was your philosophy of history? Where did you find so much original and unpublished source material, and how were you able to get your books published when several sold for as much as $26.50 per volume?" To answer such questions was one of the main reasons I am writing this work. Perhaps some of my experiences in historical research and getting my books published will help others in similar projects.

After being in interdenominational work in China for over four years, I found that I was happy to be back within a denominational organization. No longer were questions raised as to which hymnbook or whose Sunday School literature we should use. Moreover, when back in the Presbyterian fold, I became a member of a pension plan; this was not available under an interdenominational organization.

When I arrived in Moscow, the Presbyterian church there belonged to the Presbytery of Walla Walla. After being cut off from meetings of Presbytery for several years, I found a real joy in having fellowship with brother ministers and elders again. The first meeting of the Presbytery, which I attended, was held in Walla Walla in the fall of 1928. It was at this meeting that for the first time I met a group of Nez Perce Presbyterians. I do not know exactly how many attended, but there were enough to make up a choir. They sang for us some of the gospel songs which Henry H. Spalding, the pioneer missionary who settled in this tribe in 1836, had composed or translated.

It was also at this Presbytery meeting that I learned about the coming of the first missionaries sent out by the American Board of Commissioners of the Board of Foreign Mission, hereafter to be referred to by the initials A.B.C.F.M. In this party were Dr. and Mrs. Marcus Whitman who settled in Waiilatpu seven miles west of present-day Walla Walla, and Henry and Eliza Spalding who moved into the Lapwai Valley about twelve miles up the Clearwater River from Lewiston. They were the first white American families to settle in what are now the states of Washington and Idaho. The fifth member of that 1856 party was a single man, William H. Gray. Gray returned to New York State in 1837 to find recruits for the Oregon Mission, and also to marry Miss Mary Dix. He persuaded the American Board to send out three newly married couples to Oregon in 1838. They were:

the Rev. and Mrs. Cushing Eells, the Rev. and Mrs. Elkanah Walker, and the Rev. and Mrs. Asa B. Smith, all of whom were Congregationalists. When the Gray party traveled west on its way to Oregon, it paused in Cincinnati where a young man, also a Presbyterian, Cornelius Rogers, joined the group. This brought the total number of missionaries in the American Board's Oregon Mission to thirteen. It was never any more.

This was the mission and these were the missionaries about whom I was to write and publish twelve volumes beginning with the life of Spalding in 1936 and ending with the story of Chief Lawyer of the Nez Perce Indians, one of Spalding's converts, in 1979. But such a project was far beyond my most fanciful dreams when I first heard that choir of Nez Perces at the Presbytery meeting in Walla Walla. I was then still working on my doctor's thesis. But the presence of the Nez Perce choir singing the gospel songs taught to their grandparents made a deep impression on me. But, so far as I can remember, I did not even drive out to Waiilatpu to see the great grave of those killed in the massacre of 1847.

I WRITE MY SPALDING BOOK

In the summer of 1934 I was invited to teach a Bible class at Talmaks, which was a summer conference grounds in the foothills of the Bitter Root mountains for the Presbyterian Nez Perces. At that time the Nez Perces had six Presbyterian churches, all of which had Nez Perces for their pastors. These native ministers had been trained by Sue and Kate McBeth, or by their niece, Mary Crawford. The McBeth sisters were both dead by the time I arrived on the field, but Mary Crawford was still alive.

I remember that at this summer conference of 1934 I looked forward to 1936 which would be the centennial of the coming of the first Presbyterian missionaries to the Nez Perce and Cayuse Indians. I felt this centennial should be remembered, not only by the Presbyterians, but also by the State of Idaho, and, indeed by the National Presbyterian Church and the entire nation.

On my way back home I visited the old Spalding Mission on the banks of the Clearwater River at the mouth of Lapwai Creek. I found this place to be in a dilapidated state; it was a junk yard. Weeds had grown around the tombstone of the Spaldings so that I had difficulty in finding it. I was shocked at the neglect of this historic place. When I returned home I told my wife that I planned to write a magazine article about Spalding in which I would call attention to the coming centennial.

My first need was to locate original source materials. Upon inquiry

I learned that Mrs. Henry Hart (Mary) Spalding, a daughter-in-law of Henry Harmon Spalding, was living at Almota on the Snake River, a few miles below Lewiston. Hoping she would have some source materials, I drove down into the Snake River canyon over a very dusty road on a hot day in August 1934 to see what I might find. To my delight, Mrs. Spalding had eight original letters written by either Henry or Eliza Spalding. The earliest was dated in September 1833 before the two were married; the second was dated in March 1834. The other six letters were written from Lapwai during the years 1837-44. Even a cursory glance through the eight letters impressed me with their importance. All were unpublished. Here was the basis, not for just a magazine article, but for a full-length book!

I offered to buy the letters and found Mrs. Spalding willing to sell. After some discussion we agreed on a price of fifty dollars for the lot. Today the letters would bring much more than that, but it should be remembered that in 1934 wheat was selling in the Inland Empire for 25¢ a bushel. I was reimbursed for my expenditure by the Presbyterian Historical Society in Philadelphia, where these revealing letters are now on deposit.

Meeting Mrs. Henry Hart Spalding made me realize I had entered upon the scene of Northwest history at the end of a generation that was rapidly passing. After making inquiry about other living descendants of the original mission band, I learned that the two daughters of Perrin Whitman, a nephew of Marcus, were living in Lewiston, Idaho. They were Mrs. Charles (Frances) Monteith and Mrs. Sophia Mallory. Their father had gone out to Oregon as a 13-year-old lad with his Uncle Marcus in 1843.

I called on the two elderly ladies one chilly evening in early September 1934. After telling them that I was planning to write a biography of Henry Spalding, I asked if they had any of their late father's letters or other documents pertaining to the Oregon Mission. "Oh, why did you not come a few weeks ago!" one replied. "We sat before this fireplace and burned the contents of a small trunk which contained our father's papers." My heart sank within me as I asked: "Did you not save anything " "Yes," one answered. She went into a adjoining room and brought back a packet about four inches thick, charred around the edges, and tied with a faded pink ribbon. The first document I examined was a letter from Gen. William T. Sherman, then in San Francisco, to John B. Monteith, Indian agent at Lapwai, giving directions regarding the Chief Joseph uprising. I was able to buy the bundle of papers, which I turned over at cost to the Spokane Public Library. From the very beginning of my collecting, I have followed the practice of placing the documents I was able to procure into some recognized repository, feeling that such would give a greater guarantee for their preservation than if I tried to build up a personal collection.

In search for material I wrote to Dr. Enoch Bell, secretary of the American Board with headquarters in Boston. In my naivete I asked him to send me copies of all the letters they had on file from their Oregon missionaries. It must be remembered that Oregon then included everything north of California and west of the Continental Divide, and extended up into what is now Canada. Dr. Bell replied saying that I did not know what I was asking, because there were over one million words in those letters.

Early in September 1934 I made a trip to Walla Walla to visit the site of Whitman's mission at Waiilatpu, and to see if Whitman College (named after the martyred missionary) had any manuscript sources. A copy of a letter I wrote on September 7 to Dr. Thomas C. Pears, then director of the Presbyterian Historical Society in Philadelphia, refreshes my memory.

I first called on T. C. Elliott, Walla Walla broker and well-known historian. He kindly offered to take me out to Waiilatpu and give me a guided tour of that historic site. At the time we visited it, the Whitman Monument Association had title to about eight acres that included a hill one hundred feet high crowned with a Whitman monument and the great grave where the remains of the victims of the massacre of November 1847 lie buried. The Whitman Mission National Historic Site now has title, not only to those eight acres, but also to an additional ninety acres that includes the sites of the millpond and the original mission buildings.

I still remember the thrill I experienced as Elliott conducted me around the grounds and, out of the richness of his detailed knowledge of the past, told me of the events that had occurred there. I was a novice standing at the very beginning of my career as a historian; he belonged to an older generation and had already established an eviable reputation as an authority in the field of Northwest history. For a few hours he was my mentor and I his student.

Elliott knew I was planning to call on Dr. Stephen B. L. Penrose, who had served for many years as president of Whitman College. Penrose was a staunch believer in the Whitman-saved-Oregon story; Elliott was not. He alerted me as to what I could expect from Penrose. Elliott explained that Spalding was the one who first advanced the theory that Whitman had made his dramatic ride east in the winter of 1842-43 to prevent the United States from trading off its claims to Old Oregon for a cod fishery off the Newfoundland coast. This impossible theory lies at the heart of the Whitman-saved-Oregon story.

After calling on Elliott I went to Whitman College and there met a professor of Geology, Dr. H. S. Brode, who, after learning what I wanted, took me to the attic of the library building where there was a trunk full of papers belonging to, the missionaries. I later learned that the Rev. Myron Eells, son of one of the pioneer missionaries, had written the life of Marcus Whitman which was published in 1909. After the publication of this book, the heirs of Myron Eells gave this collection of papers to Whitman College. These were the papers in the trunk Dr. Brode showed me. After making just a cursory examination of the contents, I was able to imagine how Captain Kidd felt when he opened a chest of gold doubloons. Here were the original diaries of Marcus and Narcissa Whitman, scores of their letters, letters from some of the officials of the important Hudson's Bay Co., and a wealth of other related material. I knew I would have to have the contents of that trunk before I could write my life of Spalding.

I asked permission to borrow the papers which Dr. Brode kindly granted; and I took home with me that day a suitcase full of the priceless documents. Today such liberties with such valuable source documents would not be permitted as the College is quite aware of their value and has catalogued and filed them away for use under strict supervision. I never could have written my Spalding books without those papers.

After taking the documents to my home, I sorted out those which related to Spalding and then sorted them by year, and month, and day and began writing. As the story of Spalding's life unfolded, I literally did not know the end from the beginning. I became so engrossed in my subject and had such a wealth of material at hand that, in spite of my church work, I was able to write an average of about 1,000 words a day, five days a week, for five months. The first draft of a manuscript of about 120,000 words was finished about the end of February, 1935.

It so happened that while I was living in Moscow, there was an evening train with a pullman car which left Sunday evening for Portland and returned Monday evening. I took many trips to the Oregon Historical Society to study copies of letters written by missionaries. I felt overwhelmed with the great wealth of material I had at my disposal.

Sometime early in the fall of 1934 the Atlantic Monthly announced a contest for the best biography of a western pioneer. I decided to enter and in the spring of 1935 submitted my Spalding manuscript. They gave it a quick reading and returned it to me. Later I learned that the prize went to Mari Sandoz who had written a splendid book about an early Nebraska pioneer called "Old Jules." Later when I

found so much more material about Spalding I was glad that I had
not won the prize. It would have been a mistake to have had that
first manuscript published, but at least the possibility of winning a
prize gave me motivation to finish the first copy by the early spring
of 1935.

By the spring of 1935 I realized I had to go back to New York State
and visit the birthplaces of Spalding and of Marcus and Narcissa
Whitman. How I managed to get the money for this trip I do not
now remember. I do know that I had ordered a new car which I
picked up at the factory in Detroit.

From the very beginning of my researching I always felt free to
write letters to anybody whom I thought could help me. Hearing that
Spalding had attended Western Reserve University, I wrote to the
librarian there and asked for information about Spalding. The letter
was turned over to Dr. F. C. Waite who, although a member of the
medical faculty, was a born historian. He immediately took an interest
in my project and sent me a wealth of information regarding Spalding's years spent at the college, 1831-33. Dr. Waite even found the
diary of a student who had attended Spalding's wedding.

When I told Dr. Waite that I was planning to go to New York
state and visit the birthplace of Spalding and the Whitmans, he kindly
offered to go with me. How fortunate I was to have him go with me
to these historic places. We visited Prattsburg and there I met an old
lady who was a historian of the town, Miss Charlotte Howe. She had
collected items regarding the Spaldings and Whitmans for many years.
Nobody there in Prattsburg happened to be interested in her collection; so she turned it all over to me. From these papers I learned much
of the early life of both Spalding and Narcissa Prentice [Whitman].

When I showed my manuscript to Miss Howe, wherein she read that
Spalding was a rejected suitor of Narcissa, she was greatly incensed.
I was just repeating a common rumor that I had heard. Spalding and
Narcissa attended the same school, the same church, and sang in the
same choir. The rumor I heard was that he had proposed marriage
and was rejected. Miss Howe, who knew more about the early life
of Spalding than anybody, was emphatic in denying the story; so I
left this out of my Spalding book. But later, when I was working on
the Whitman book, I found convincing evidence that the rumor was
true.

Spalding was actually born in a little village called Wheeler located about six miles south of Prattsburg. While in Prattsburg, I discovered that Spalding had been born out of wedlock and was raised
in a foster home at Wheeler. Dr. Waite and I visited the old Wheeler
cemetery where we found the gravestones of his foster parents.

On that same trip I visited the headquarters of the A.B.C.F.M. and met Dr. Enoch Bell, who took me into a room where the letters of the Oregon missionaries were stored. They were bound together in bundles and covered one wall of the room from floor to ceiling. I felt completely overwhelmed. I wanted to work from original documents, but this was impossible; so I had to be content with using the copies somebody had made for the Oregon Historical Society. All of this was before the days of microfilm and xerox, but it was a thrilling experience for me to read the original letters of the missionaries who went out to Oregon in 1836 and 1838.

I spent several months rewriting the manuscript, incorporating the new information I had found. I then sent it to an eastern publisher with the hope that he would accept it, but it was returned. Then one Sunday Providence smiled on me again. I noted a stranger in my morning congregation, and at the door after the service, he introduced himself as Mr. McCormick, a member of the editorial staff of the Caxton Printers at Caldwell, Idaho. I knew that this publishing house had majored in printing western histories; so I seized the opportunity to tell McCormick about my Spalding manuscript. I pointed out the fact that in less than a year Idaho, and the whole northwest, would be celebrating the centennial of the coming of the Spaldings and Whitmans. I emphasized the timeliness of publishing this book; McCormick was impressed and asked to take the manuscript to Caldwell.

Mr. J. H. Gipson, the managing director of the Caxton Company, saw the possibilities in publishing this book, and on September 21, 1935, I signed a contract for the publication of 1,000 volumes which would sell for $3.00 each. Actually 1500 volumes were published. In the contract I was responsible for the sale of 500 copies, for which I received no royalty. In other words, I was obligated to pay the publishers $1,500.00 which was more than one-half of my salary; but I so believe in my story that I did not hesitate to sign. After the first 500 were sold, I was to get a 5% royalty for the second 500, and after that 10%.

My publishers issued a four page folder which measured about six by nine inches describing the book. I sent these folders, with an order card, to about 500 of my relatives, friends, and a number of historians. These brought in 300 orders. A 10% discount was offered to all who paid in advance.

I was able to attend the Presbyterian General Assembly as a visitor in 1935, and here I was privileged to meet key members of the Board of National Missions and was successful in getting their cooperation in the publication of my Spalding book. The Board instructed one of its secretaries, Dr. Arthur L. Limouze, to raise $10,000.00 for the renovation of one of the Nez Perce Presbyterian churches at Lapwai, Idaho, which Spalding had founded. Dr. Limouze had never heard of Spalding; he wrote to me for information, and I sent him a copy of my manuscript. He was impressed and made arrangements with Caxton Printers to buy 300 copies at half-price. He then sent the 300 copies to as many Presbyterian ministers scattered throughout the nation with the request that they read the book and then take a collection for the restoration of the church. He got his $10,000.00 and I got the best publicity in the world.

It so happened that I had in my Moscow congregation a member of the faculty of the University of Idaho, Dr. Gordon Alcorn, whose wife, Rowena Lung Alcorn, was an artist. I gave a picture of Chief Timothy, one of Spalding's first converts, to Mrs. Alcorn and she painted a portrait of him which I used in my Spalding book and which Caxton used on the cover. Before the second edition appeared, I induced Mrs. Alcorn to paint the portrait of Henry Harmon Spalding which appeared on the cover of the second edition, and also was used in the body of the text. Both editions carried a black and white reproduction of a drawing by Mrs. Alcorn of the Spalding cabin at Lapwai.

Recognition has been given to Mrs. Alcorn by hanging a collection of twenty-two of her portraits of Nez Perce Indians in the Historical Museum of the Rocky Reach Hydroelectric Dam near Wenatchee, Washington. Two more of her paintings of important Nez Perce chiefs are at Whitman College. I take pride in realizing that my request to her to paint Chief Timothy's portrait for my Spalding book was the incident which started her on her illustrious career as a painter of the Nez Perces.

In order to conserve footnotes I compiled a chronological list of eighty-three Spalding letters which I had located, giving the date each letter was written, the place, reference to the writer — whether it was Henry Spalding or his wife — where the original is now kept, and reference to any publication of the letters. Thus, in the text of the book, when I wanted to refer to my source, all I had to do was give the number of a letter and my readers could then locate and read it.

Two thousand copies of my Spalding book were sold in the centennial year of 1936. The next thousand in the second edition sold more slowly, and it was not until January of 1957 that the last copy was sold. Although this book sold for $3.00 in those depression days, it has now become a collector's item, and I am told second-hand book dealers are now asking $50.00 and up. My total royalty received for the two editions came to $176.40 and was not enough to cover expenses. However, my real royalty was not in money, but rather in the reputation I had established as a careful and accurate historian.

When I finished this series in 1979 with the publication of my "Chief Lawyer" book, I started to rewrite my Spalding book. But, after writing some thirty thousand words, I laid it aside in order to write my autobiography. The unfinished manuscript of what I hoped would be a revised version of the Spalding book is now in the archives of the Idaho Historical Society in Boise, Idaho.

I Write My Whitman Book

Even before I had completed writing my Spalding book, I was gathering material for a book on Marcus Whitman. I discovered that Whitman had become the center of a historical controversy, and that a vast number of books, pamphlets, and magazine articles had been written about him. Spalding was the first one to advance the theory that the main purpose of Whitman's ride to Washington and Boston in 1842-43 was to prevent the United States from signing a treaty with Great Britain which would give most of the Oregon country to England. This theory was picked up by many until it was exposed as false by two eminent historians, Edward G. Bourne, and William I. Marshall. Writing about 1900-1907 these two authors proved that Whitman rode east on mission business; but it took a long time before the friends of the Whitmans could accept this revised theory.

It so happened that the librarian at the University of Washington at Seattle, Charles W. Smith, made a special study of the literature bearing upon the Whitman-saved-Oregon story. Smith compiled a bibliography of books, pamphlets and articles on this subject so exhaustive that the list ran to over ninety pages in an historical magazine. I had the good fortune to be able to visit Seattle sometime in 1936 when I was just beginning to collect material about Whitman. I wrote ahead to Mr. Smith and told him that I would like to see all the items in the library bearing on Whitman's story. When I called at the library I was amazed to find that he had filled two library trucks with items from that library bearing on the story. I was overwelmed. I did the only thing scholastically acceptable by starting anew from original sources. I did refer to some of the books listed, but for the most part, I turned to original sources and did not rehash what others had written.

Again I made a list of Whitman letters as I had done with the Spaldings. In my *Marcus Whitman, M.D.*, which appeared in 1937, I listed 223 letters written either by Marcus or Narcissa Whitman. Since the writing of that book I located eighty more Whitman letters, which I used in my two-volume work on Marcus and Narcissa Whit-

man, which appeared in 1973. I will have more to say about these
books at a later time.

In 1935 when I first visited Prattsburg and Rushville, the latter being
the birthplace of Marcus Whitman, I became acquainted with a young
school teacher by the name of Robert Moody who became one of my
best informants regarding the early life of Marcus Whitman. For the
most part the people at both Prattsburg and Rushville had forgotten
the full significance of the contributions that Spalding and Whitman
had made to the west. I remember going out to the cemetery at Rushville and finding the gravestones of Whitman's parents upside down
in the weeds. Moody took a special interest in restoring the stones and
cleaning up the graveyard. On the stone of Marcus' father, Beza
Whitman, I noted a quatrain which was very common on tombstones
in New England in that period. It read:

> Stop here my friend and think on me
> I once was in the world like thee
> This is a call aloud to thee
> Prepare for Death and follow me.

I later learned that in a nearby cemetery someone had written with
a piece of chalk underneath that same poem: "To follow thee, I'll not
consent, Until I know which way you went."

Moody also took me out to call on an old man named Carlton
Pratt. He was the son of Jonathan Pratt who was a classmate of Marcus
Whitman in medical school. Carlton was living in a decrepit condition; chickens were roosting in his house; he was sick, lying in bed.
Taking care of him was an ex-convict. Carlton had a few relics which
once belonged to his father, including a collection of old coins. Shortly
before we called, someone had purchased a desk that had belonged
to his father; and, at that time, the contents of a top drawer were
emptied out on the floor. I searched through the mass of papers and
located two of the oldest known letters written by Marcus Whitman.
Both had been written to Jonathan Pratt; one was dated September
11, 1827, and the other was dated February 5, 1828. We also found
a portion of Jonathan Pratt's diary. These discoveries opened up an
entirely new chapter in the life of Marcus Whitman. I was able to
get the letters and the diary. A few weeks later Moody wrote to me
saying that Carlton Pratt's home had burned and he had lost his life
in the fire. The ex-convict had disappeared and it was thought that
he took the coin collection with him.

On my way back to my home in Moscow I stopped off in New York
and called on a well known seller of second-hand books dealing with
the west, Edward Eberstadt. Eberstadt had an office in a high build-

ing overlooking the library in New York City. I was carrying with me in my brief case, the eight Spalding letters which I had secured from Mary Spalding in order to take then to the Presbyterian Historical Society in Philadelphia, where they are now.

When I entered Eberstadt's office I found him leaning back in his chair with his feet on the window sill enjoying a glass of liquid refreshment. He paid no attention to me until I mentioned the eight Spalding letters which I was carrying. Down came his feet from the window sill; he swung around and asked to see them. He wanted to buy them, but I told him I had already sold them to the Historical Society. Then he tried to bribe me. He said: "Reach out and touch that safe," which was standing in the corner of the office. I did, and then he taunted me by saying: "There are eighty Whitman letters in that safe." I then became the pleader; I wanted them for my new book on Whitman. "Let me see them," I urged; but he refused, saying: "The bloom would be off the peach." He refused to let me see them.

THE PRESBYTERIAN GENERAL ASSEMBLY

Even before my Spalding book appeared, I began lecturing on the Spalding-Whitman story. Between September 6th and the end of December in 1934 I had filled fourteen engagements — a total attendance of 832. This included three lectures before the Synod of Idaho at Twin Falls in October.

During 1935 the number of engagements grew to twenty-seven with a total attendance of 4,895. This included three lectures at the San Francisco Theological Seminary in October. I received no honorariums for these appearances, but usually had my expenses paid if I had to travel far. I appeared before service clubs, historical societies, high schools, teachers' conventions — I was telling a story that most of my hearers had never heard.

On February 19, 1936 I spoke to 550 people at the state meeting of the Washington Women's Clubs at Whitman College. This address was printed in pamphlet form.

Early in 1936 Dr. Arthur Limouze, of the Presbyterian Board of National Missions, wrote asking if I could speak at the General Assembly which was to meet at Syracuse during the first week of June. He offered to pay all of my expenses, and wanted me also to take part in the centennial observances being planned for Prattsburg, where both Spalding and Narcissa Prentice (Whitman) were born, and Rushville, where Whitman was born. Dr. Limouze assured me of some twenty dates to speak which would give publicity to the centennial and at the same time help me to sell my Spalding book.

The invitation offered an important opportunity and was most intriguing. I consulted my session and asked for a six week leave. I realized that I would have to have a car; this meant at least two week's travel time. The various centennial celebrations would take ten days. That would give me a few days for further research. I wanted to go to Harvard to see the Whitman letters, which Eberstadt had had in his safe, and which since had been deposited in the Widner Library at Harvard.

Miriam wished to go with me, and I wanted her to do so; but, what should we do with the children? I wrote to my relatives in Iowa, and my sisters, Blanche and Clara, agreed to take care of them. We decided to buy a new Chevrolet in Chicago; so on May 10th we took a train from Moscow to Carroll, Iowa, a few miles from Early, where my relatives would meet us and take the children. Understandably the children were somewhat apprehensive at being left with strangers, but we found that they made a good adjustment. They enjoyed their first experience on a Pullman train.

While at General Assembly I was under the direction of Dr. Limouze; my records show that I averaged two speeches a day before various church groups, schools, and historical societies. General Assembly opened on May 26th with a pre-assembly on Evangelism, and I was asked to give a short talk on the Whitman-Spalding story. About 1,000 were in attendance.

One of the mountain peak experiences in my life came on Monday when I was privileged to address the full Assembly to again tell the Whitman-Spalding story to about 2,000 people. I shared the program with Dr. Clarence MacCartney, an eloquent pastor of a Presbyterian church in Pittsburgh. With me at this Assembly was John Frank, a full blooded Nez Perce Indian and an elder in the First Presbyterian (Indian) church of Kamiah.

The day after General Assembly closed there were special commemorative services at Rushville and Prattsburg to honor the Whitmans and Spaldings. I had the opportunity to speak at each of these, as did John Frank who was certainly a living representative of the success of the missionaries.

The Rushville program, which began at 10:30 on June 4th, drew a crowd of about 500. The services were held out-of-doors in front of the Rushville Congregational Church which Marcus had attended in his youth. After lunch we went to Prattsburg where two services were held — one at 4:00 and the other at 7:45 p.m. I spoke at the earlier one. About 1,000 attended, including some of the commissioners to General Assembly who stayed over for these programs.

Beza Whitman, father of Marcus, died on April 7, 1810, leaving his widow with five small children. Mrs. Whitman turned to relatives for aid. Marcus, then eight years old, was sent to live with an uncle in Cummington, Massachusetts. I decided that while I was at Syracuse I should visit Cummington and also the nearby village of Plainfield where Marcus attended a fine church-sponsored academy. After making arrangements for Miriam to stay with friends, I left for western Massachusetts as soon as possible after the centennial observances. Marcus had lived in Cummington and Plainfield for ten years; here he came under strong religious influences from both his relatives and the school directed by the Rev. Moses Hallock. It was while he was here in school that he decided for the ministry, but discovered, when he returned to Rushville in 1820, that his mother was opposed to the idea.

My visit to the two villages in the Berkshire hills uncovered much information regarding the early life of Marcus Whitman. From there I drove to Cambridge to see the collection of some eighty Whitman letters which had been in the safe in Eberstadt's office when I had called there a year or so earlier. Eberstadt had sold the collection to a wealthy collector, W. R. Coe, who presented them to the Beinecke Rare Book and Manuscript Library of Yale University Library. That which had been denied to me by Eberstadt was now opened. Most of the letters in this collection were written by Dr. Whitman to Elkanah Walker, who was then a missionary of the American Board located at Tshimakain near present-day Spokane. These dealt largely with mission business and, therefore, were of little value to me. The library did have ten Whitman letters which had been stolen from the archives of the Oregon Historical Society after they had been published in the 1891 and 1893 issues of the *Transactions of the Oregon Pioneer Society*. These were important as the transcriptions which appeared in the T.O.P.A. were not accurate.

By June 15th I was back in Penn Yan where I picked up Miriam and we started for Iowa, arriving in Early by June 18. We had a happy reunion with our children, and I was surely grateful to my relatives who took care of three lively children so that both of us could go to the General Assembly. That trip meant much to me, for I was able to gain a national reputation as an authority on the Whitman-Spalding story; I found much new material for my Whitman book; and I was able to sell many of my Spalding books and even take orders for the Whitman one.

After spending only three days in Early, where we were entertained with one feast after another, we left for Moscow on the 22nd and were home by the 25th.

The success of the sales for my Spalding book prompted Mr. J. H. Gipson, head of the Caxton Printers, to offer me a contract for a biography of Marcus Whitman. According to the terms of the contract signed April 24, 1937, even before I had completed writing my Whitman story, I was to submit the finished manuscript by July 1, 1937. Knowing that the Whitman book would be larger than the Spalding one, Caxton offered it for sale for $5.00. The contract called for the publication of "1,000 or more" copies, but actually 1,885 were printed. The first 500 were autographed and numbered. Ten copies were bound in full morocco and sold for $10.00 each.

The terms of the contract were similar to those for the Spalding book. No royalty for the first 500 copies; then 5% for the second 500, after that 10%. Caxton Publishers sent out hundreds of flyers announcing the publication which was fixed as of December 1, 1936.

As with the Spalding book, the time was ripe for a new book on Whitman. My records show that during the first seven months after the book was released 785 copies were sold. My royalty on the 285 copies, above the 500 on which I received no royalty, was $74.37. The full edition of 1,885 was sold out by the end of 1951 and brought a total royalty to me of $480.22, not enough to pay for expenses involved in gathering materials. The book contained 473 pages and had an attractive red cover which bore a picture of the Whitman monument showing him standing by a wheel. For many years this statue was on the Witherspoon building in Philadelphia. It is now at the entrance of the Presbyterian Historical Society in Philadelphia.

The reviews given the book were excellent. On January 26, 1939, my publishers sent me the following note.

> The very scholarly *"Review of Religion"*, published by Columbia University of New York City, contains in its January issue a 6½-page review of Dr. Drury's MARCUS WHITMAN, written by Elliott Van N. Diller, of Mills College, in which Dr. Drury's work is given the very highest praise.
> ". . . Dr. Drury handles his material with the skill and enthusiasm of a dramatist . . . The massacre, in which Whitman, Narcissa and twelve others died, is graphically reconstructed by Dr Drury, and this forms one of the literary highpoints of the book . . . sincere, realistic, and consistent portrayal. . ."

To me, a good index is the key to any volume on history. Hence, I always compiled an index for each of my books. The index of my first Whitman book ran to seven pages.

Dr. F. C. Waite, the doctor-historian at Western Reserve University, provided information about Whitman's medical training; this had not ever been published before. Whitman attended the Fairfield Medical College in Herkimer County, New York. No medical school in the United States could have given Whitman any better training for his work as a frontier physician than that given by Fairfield. In that day the doctors had no fever thermometer, no anesthesia, no stethoscope. Dr. Waite located the records of the Fairfield Medical School in Albany and there learned that Whitman's thesis subject was "Caloric" which suggests that he was studying the possible relationship between bodily heat or fever and disease.

I began work on my northwest series just in time. In my Spalding book I acknowledged the help received from 23 people, all of whom have now passed away. In my Whitman book I gave credit to 28 people, all of whom are now dead except for my wife and Robert Moody. I am reminded of a verse in the book of Job which refers to one of the calamities which were visited upon him. All of his relatives were killed in a storm. A servant came with the bad news and said, "They are all dead and I alone have escaped to tell thee."

BEGINNING MY WALKER RESEARCH

The Walker family, with the Eells, settled on a trail which connected the Spokane River with Fort Colville. This fort was about seventy miles to the north of the Spokane River. The site was about thirty miles to the northwest of the present-day Spokane, and was called Tshimakain which meant the "place of springs." This was the third main station of the American Board's work in Old Oregon. These two families were from the reenforcement of 1838 and lived and labored here until May of 1848.

Four women of that 1838 reenforcement, together with two women who went out in 1836, were the first American white women to cross the Rocky Mountains through the south pass. This opened the door of the Rockies through which, in the following years, hundreds of thousands of emigrants flowed to both Oregon and California.

In 1894 the Rev. Myron Eells, a son of Cushing and Mary, published a life of his father in a book called *Father Eells, a Biography of Rev. Cushing Eells*. His story had been well told, but no one had brought out a biography of Elkanah Walker and his wife, Mary Richardson Walker. I felt the time had come for me to round out my trilogy and write about the Walkers. Mr. Gibson of Caxton Printers encouraged me to do so and offered me a contract on the same terms as with my previous two books.

Both Elkanah and Mary kept diaries while they lived at Tshimakain, and these now were in the Huntington Library at San Marino, California. I also had access to the letters written by Walker to the A.B.C.F.M., and to the many references to the Walkers in the writings of the Whitmans and Spaldings. To make the most of these materials I decided I needed to go to Maine and visit their early homes.

In doing this, I could probably also visit the General Assembly of 1938 which was to meet that year in Philadelphia, and also I wanted to meet church historians throughout the nation — especially those who were serving as professors of church history in theological seminaries.

For the third time in planning a trip to New England in search of original source materials for my books, I found it well to buy a new car. After having had three Chevrolets, including the one we got in 1928 when we returned to the States from Edinburgh, this time I decided to get a Plymouth. According to my records I traded my last Chevrolet for a new Plymouth with delivery to be taken at Detroit, Michigan. The car traded in had gone 25,340 miles in two years. By taking delivery at the factory, I saved $130.00. The cost to me at the factory was $906.00, plus $21.00 license and $74.65 insurance. I received credit from my Moscow dealer for my former car of $536.00, which meant that I had to pay an extra $307.00. I was able to pay only $100.00 cash; so took out a note for the balance. The new car was my first with a radio, and it was a joy.

The elders of my Moscow church granted me a five week leave; so on May 8, 1938, I took the train to Chicago. I started keeping a journal again, and in my entry for May 9th noted that throughout my Moscow ministry I had not missed a Sunday because of illness. Throughout my life, God has blessed me with vibrant health until I reached my early eighties.

I arrived in Chicago Wednesday morning and spent the day interviewing church history professors at the Chicago Theological Seminary and at the Presbyterian McCormick Seminary.

I took possession of my new Plymouth at Detroit and decided this was the best car I had owned up to this time. I remember it had a driving control device which kept me from going faster than 35 miles an hour; this was not removed until a week later.

On Friday, May 13th, I paid a call on Dr. F. C. Waite, who had given me so much help when I was writing about Dr. Whitman. Now Dr Waite told me of some of his teaching techniques. After the first lecture in any given class, he would begin the next one with a series of five questions — three from the previous day's lecture and two from assigned reading. From the scores of these daily tests, he was able to compile a daily grade, as well as have a roll of those present. I followed this plan throughout my seminary teaching, especially in required courses, and found it very satisfactory.

I then headed for Penn Yan, New York, where I was entertained by the Rev. and Mrs. Hendricks. Mrs. Hendricks took me to Rushville that afternoon to call on Robert Moody, who had been of great help to me while gathering material for my Whitman book. Mr. Moody took us to see an old lady of 104 years, a Mrs. Housel, who had personal memories of seeing Dr. Whitman when he went east in 1842-3. From Rushville, we drove to Prattsburg where I renewed acquaintance with several who had helped with material for my Spalding book.

On Monday, May 16th, while enroute from Penn Yan to Hartford, Connecticut, I drove through Cummington and Pittsfield, where Marcus Whitman had spent ten years of his youth. This was my second visit to these villages.

On May 18th I left my car in New Haven and took the train to New York, where I spent most of the day interviewing members of the National Board of the Presbyterian Church, then located at 156 Fifth Avenue. I had lunch with Dr Limouze, who was well pleased with the sale of the Spalding book. I spent the night with Mr. and Mrs. Gordon Thompson, former members of my church in Shanghai; this visit brought back many fond memories

Thursday, having returned to New Haven, I had the great pleasure of taking lunch with Charles Boynton and Mrs. Emory Luccock. When Miriam and I landed in Shanghai, we lived in the Boynton home for several months, and it was good to see him again. Mrs Luccock was the wife of my successor in Shanghai, the Rev. Emory Luccock. We had called on them on our way across country in 1937, at which time I had shared with Emory some of the criticisms I had received from a few members of the Shanghai church. After the Luccocks had returned to China and become acquainted with the work of the church, Emory wrote to me saying: "I hasten to add that you have greatly underestimated your work here. I find evidences of its sincerity and strength in many places, some of which I believe would be a surprise and a delight to you. Moreover, I have talked with a number of the people whom you felt in your conversation with them were most ready to have you terminate your relations with the church, and I find that a longer perspective has given them an entirely new appreciation of what you accomplished." This letter did much to ease the sting of some of that criticism which I had received, and I was most grateful to Emory for writing, and to Mrs Luccock now for her encouraging words.

I drove to Standish, Maine, which was near Baldwin where Mary Richardson was born. I found the old house, her birthplace, still standing, but empty. I also visited Yarmouth where Elkanah had spent his youth but was unable to locate his birthplace.

Even though I had not been able to locate any manuscript material, I felt that my trip to Maine was rewarding.

I started back to Moscow on Friday, May 27. On Sunday I was in Ames where I called on Dr Herbert J. Gilkay, a grandson of Elkanah and Mary Walker. Sunday afternoon I drove on to Early. This road took me by the old Drury farm where so many memories of my youth clustered. On arriving in Early I found my stepmother, Laura, had invited all of the relatives who lived nearby in for a Sunday evening dinner. The ties that bind the members of my family together have always been strong.

Tuesday morning I left for Moscow and on Friday, June 3rd, had a joyous reunion there with my family.

On Sunday afternoon, June 5th, I had the honor of giving the Baccalaureate sermon at Washington State College. I owed this invitation to Dr. E. O. Holland, then the President of the college. He had become so interested in my writings and research that he offered to pay my expenses wherever I wished to go in search of material, provided I turn over all material I found to the library at W.S.C. I had previously tried to get some help from Idaho, but no money was available. In the course of several years I turned over a number of boxes full of historical items to the college.

Dr. Holland favored me on several occasions. He was responsible in 1939 for making me an honorary member of Phi Beta Kappa when, at that time, only five in the entire state of Washington were so honored. He also recommended the inclusion of my biographical sketch for the 1938 edition of "Who's Who in America" and it has appeared in every issue since that time.

Hearing that the youngest son of the Walkers, Samuel, was still living in the old Walker homestead at Forest Grove, Oregon, I called on him one day later in the summer of 1938. Sam was the last living direct (i.e., of the first generation) descendant of any member of the Whitman band At first he was rather reluctant to cooperate with me. I later learned that he had had some unhappy experiences with antique collectors. Gradually I won his cooperation, especially when he learned that all items received from him were to be deposited in the library of Washington State University at Pullman.

When I called on him in the summer of 1938 he said to me: "My father and mother rode horseback over the Rockies 100 years ago this summer." He was the last living link with the past. Shortly before this visit, Sam had cleaned out some trunks and had assembled an apple box of items which he was now ready to turn over to me.

When I arrived at his home, he took me to his garage, or rather an open shed with a dirt floor. There, on the ground, was the collection of items, including a number of medical books, some of which might have come from Dr. Whitman's library, several of Mary Walker's diaries written before she left for Oregon, and after she and her family were forced out of their Spokane station and had moved to Forest Grove, several books from the mission library with notations in Spalding's handwriting, and a miscellaneous assortment of other items. Among the pile of materials Sam Walker had gathered was a French-English dictionary given to the Walkers in 1838 by Capt. John Sutter enroute to California by way of the Whitman mission station at Waiilatpu. A notation on one of the flyleaf pages in Mary Walker's handwriting told the story. That book is now on display at the Whitman Mission National Historical Site.

A few months after I secured this box full of items, fire destroyed the Walker home, and the old couple was barely able to escape with their lives. Here was another experience of mine that emphasized the importance of collecting such historical items and placing them in well-established depositories where they will be preserved and made available to qualified students for generations to come.

Both Mary and Elkanah applied to the American Board about the same time. Mary's application was rejected because she was an unmarried female. Likewise, Elkanah's application was rejected because he was not married. On March 30, 1837, one of the secretaries of the Board wrote to Elkanah saying: "You ought by all means to have a good, healthy, patient, well informed, devoutly pious wife. There is a Miss Mary Richardson of Baldwin, Maine, who has offered herself to the Board, but we cannot send her single. From her testimonials, I should think her a good girl. If you have nobody in view, you might inquire about her. May the Lord direct & bless you."

If Armstrong had only realized how very shy Elkanah Walker was, perhaps he would never have dropped such a suggestion to him. We have evidence that Walker was astounded at the idea. What did the Board expect him to do? Was he to rush down to Baldwin and propose marriage to a girl he had never met? He showed Armstrong's letter to his friend, William Thayer. Here again imagination must fill in the details. Thayer enthusiastically endorsed Armstrong's suggestion. Having met Mary on two occasions in 1836, Thayer was impressed. But Walker was hesitant and full of doubts. "How do I know but that she has someone else in view," he asked. "I'll write and find out," replied Thayer.

Fortunately for our story, Mary kept through the years the original letters she received from Thayer. Under date of March 23, which evidently was the very day that Walker received Armstrong's letter, Thayer wrote a four-page, foolscap size, letter to Mary. He was tactful. He began by inquiring about her interest in the foreign mission enterprise. He discussed items the two had talked about the previous September. Then came the crucial question: "Suppose Providence should bring to your hand a good-natured mission-spirited companion, not the strangest supposition in the world, after all. . ." The implication was clear — what would be her response?

Mary noted in her diary that she received Thayer's letter on March 26 and wrote: "T. wishes to learn what has become of me." Not knowing the urgency which lay behind Thayer's letter, she was slow in replying. Finally she wrote on April 11. Unfortunately, neither Thayer nor Walker saved the letters they had received from Mary so we do not know exactly what she said. Judging by later events, we can surmise that she gave a diplomatic and favorable answer to Thayer's hint regarding the designs of "Providence."

Even though he had learned that Mary was not engaged, still the bashful Elkanah was far from being convinced that he should make any move to win the heart and hand of this girl whom his classmate so highly praised. On the other hand, he remembered that he was scheduled to sail for Africa in four or five months. Time was short and whatever was to be done had to be done promptly. Thayer urged the necessity of immediate action, and it was he who planned the strategy to be followed.

As good fortune would have it, there was a small Congregational church at Sebago, about seven miles from East Baldwin, which had no pastor. Students from Bangor Theological Seminary had been supplying the pulpit. It was very simple to arrange a Sunday supply for Elkanah. Being in the vicinity of the Richardson home, he could then pay a casual call and meet Mary. Elkanah was far from being convinced that the plan would work but finally consented. So on April 15, the day after he had received Mary's letter of the 11th, Thayer wrote a letter of introduction for Elkanah to carry. "As good fortune would have it," he wrote, with tongue in cheek, "I have learnt today of an opportunity to send a line near you at least by the bearer, Mr. Walker, & perhaps he will pass through Baldwin, in which case I have invited him to call at your Father's on my account."

Still Elkanah was not convinced. Suppose he were able to gain a graceful entry into the Richardson home and suppose that Mary did make a favorable impression, how could he propose marriage on such short notice? Two days were spent in discussing the problems involved. Then on April 17, the resourceful Thayer wrote a third letter to Mary: "Here I am writing again at a date of only two days later than my last . . . but I should not wonder if this treads within six hours on its predecessor's heels. This, by the way, is a sort of 'corps de reserve' to be brought into action if the case requires. If you ever receive it, you will receive it as an introduction of the bearer — Mr. Walker — to your kind regards as a suitor for your heart and hand. Should he thus present himself to you, the act will not be so hasty on his part as might at first seem. He has not been wholly unacquainted with you for some length of time past — though personally unknown."

To follow the story, we must now turn to Mary's diary. On Saturday, April 22, 1837, Mary made a brief entry of the day's happenings in her diary. Then she met Elkanah and before writing more, she drew a line across the page. That was her continental divide which separated all that had happened to her before meeting him from everything that came after. She even repeated the date as she began another entry for that same day: "Apr. 22, 1837. Along some time about 3 o'clock perhaps, I was folding away some old newspapers and looked out and saw two gentlemen approaching." One she recognized as the local doctor. The other was " a tall and rather awkward gentleman."

Elkanah presented Thayer's letter of introduction. Mary's alert mind immediately suspected some collusion for she wrote in her diary: "Query: Is not the hand of Thayer with him in all this?" She noted that Elkanah was tall. She was short, standing about 5'3''. When I called on their youngest son, Samuel, in the summer of 1938 at his home in Forest Grove, Oregon, he told me that his mother could stand under his father's outstretched arm.

Elkanah spent Sunday night at the Richardson home. Monday was one of the most important days in Mary's life. She devoted about 1,000 words in her diary of the description of that day. Her first reaction regarding Elkanah was of regret that the Lord had not dealt better with her. Before breakfast was served, Mary found herself in the living room with Elkanah. In the conversation which followed Mary mentioned the fact that she had been rejected by the Board because she was an "unmarried female."

Elkanah explained to Mary that she had been recommended to him by both Armstrong and Thayer. He then gave Mary an unsealed letter which Thayer had written.

"Blushing, agitated, and confused," wrote Mary in her diary, "I took the letter, confessed my surprise and retiring to the furthest corner of the room, attempted to read." Just at that inopportune moment, Mary's mother called them to morning prayers. Breakfast followed the devotions. Mary then excused herself and, seeking the privacy of her bedroom, read and reread Thayer's letter. She was tantalizingly silent on just how or when she said: "Yes." But this we know, sometime that day, within forty-eight hours after she looked out of the living-room window and first saw the "tall and rather awkward" stranger coming up the path to the front door, Mary had accepted Elkanah's proposal of marriage. The major factor which induced the two to pledge their troth to each other on such short acquaintance was their mutual desire to be missionaries under the auspices of the American Board and the conviction that the "hand of Providence" had brought them together.

When I visited Baldwin, and Mary's now vacant original home, I stood in the living room and looked out the window at the road down which Walker had come. Although I have no further manuscript evidence of their betrothal; yet I could use my imagination and realize how Mary felt when she first saw her future husband.

While on my trip to Maine I met several people who remembered when Elkanah and Mary paid a return visit in 1871.

In the spring of 1837 both Elkanah and Mary were appointed by the American Board to go to South Africa as missionaries. However, because of the new need developing in Oregon, they were asked on December 12th if they would be willing to change their destination from South Africa to Oregon.

Finally on March 5, 1838 Elkanah and Mary were married at the ages of thirty-three and twenty-seven. After saying tearful goodbyes to their families, they were on their way to Oregon. It was necessary for them to obtain passports from the U.S. War Department to pass "through the Indian country to the Columbia River."

Written in Mary's diary, soon after departure, was this note: "Hope we shall like one another. But it seems to me I should not like to exchange husbands, & I think Mr. Walker would not like to exchange wives."

On Wednesday, August 29th the Walkers, with others in their party, arrived at Waiilatpu. They had experienced over four months of terrible hardship —grueling physical labor, illness, riding miles each day on horses (the women rode side-saddle), always the danger of being robbed or killed by wild Indians, having horses stolen, often traveling only eighteen or nineteen miles a day. There were many times when Elkanah regretted ever having started, but it was too late to turn back.

I have often visited the Tshimakain site where a few signs remain to mark the spot where these missionaries were buried, including a lilac tree which measures at least twenty-five feet high and is still growing. No doubt this tree was planted by the Walkers.

My Walker Book is Published

The success of my Spalding and Whitman books prompted the Caxton Company to offer me a contract for the publication of *Elkanah and Mary Walker: Pioneers Among the Spokanes,* in an edition of 1,456 volumes to be sold at $3.00 each. Twenty copies were printed in a deluxe edition and sold for $10.00 each. As with my former books, Caxton provided a cover for this book. The manuscript was not finished until after I left for San Anselmo. It came from the press on July 1, 1941.

The book contained 250 pages, which included a number of illustrations. This was the first book to appear which told the story of the Tshimakain mission. My records show that 522 copies were sold by January 1, 1942; then sales were rather sluggish for several years, and it wasn't until 1956 that the edition was exhausted. Since I did not have any royalties on the first 500 copies, and then only 5% on the nex 500, and after that 10%, my total royalties for the entire edition was only $156.00.

These three books, my trilogy, dealt with the three main stations of the American Board in Oregon — Lapwai, Waiilatpu and Tshimakain.

I always felt dissatisfied with the Walker book because I did not have access to the diaries in the Huntington Library in San Marino. But, after moving to Pasadena in 1963, the diaries were still there just waiting for me to transcribe. Since the writing of both Elkanah and Mary was hard to decipher, it took me months to make the transcription. On the basis of this new information, I wrote another book about the Walkers in 1976 entitled *Nine Years With the Spokane Indians, The Diary, 1838-1848, of Elkanah Walker,* published by The Arthur H. Clark Company.

CHAPTER TWENTY

San Francisco Theological Seminary

On January 1, 1937, Dr. Jesse H. Baird began his duties as President of the San Francisco Theological Seminary at San Anselmo, California. Dr. Baird had been a member of the Seminary's Board of Trustees and, at the time of his call to the Presidency, was pastor of the First Presbyterian Church of Oakland, California. His new task was herculean. The country was then slowly moving out of a great economic depression; the Seminary was in dire financial straits. The salaries of the few full-time professors had fallen to $2,500 per annum.

Dr. Baird was responsible not only to reverse the sagging financial situation, but also to recruit a new faculty. Five of the professors were past the retirement age of sixty-five or approaching it. There was but one "young man" on the faculty, and that was Gurdon Oxtoby, son of William H. Oxtoby who had been serving as President during the depression years.

Before leaving Shanghai for Edinburgh, I received a letter from Dr. E. A. Wicher, my New Testament professor at the Seminary when I was a student there, urging me to get my Ph.D. degree. I recall how he stimulated my imagination by writing that he hoped some day I would be a colleague of his on the faculty of the Seminary. The Seminary had no installed professor of Church History for about twenty years, but depended on the services of part-time men, usually from the Baptist Divinity School in Berkeley.

When Dr. Limouze sent out 300 copies of my Spalding book in 1936 to as many pastors with the request that they read the book and then take a collection for the Nez Perce work, a copy fell into the hands of Dr. Baird. This served to introduce me to him. I had the privilege of meeting him early in 1937, shortly after he became President of the Seminary. He was looking for someone who could qualify to be Professor of Church History, and asked me if I would be interested. It didn't take me more than a few seconds to enthusiastically respond: "I certainly would."

Dr. Baird was looking for an alumnus of San Anselmo who had earned a doctorate in Church History. I qualified; in fact, at that time I was the only alumnus who did qualify. He wanted someone who had pastoral experience. Since I had been in parish work for over fifteen years, I was qualified here. Because this person would take over the chair of Church History, he would also have to teach missions. Although, strictly speaking, I had not served as a foreign missionary,

my more than four years in Shanghai gave me a good understanding
of the subject; so, again I qualified. Also, being the author of two
books, while not required, was in my favor. Finally, Dr. Baird asked:
"The Seminary is on the verge of bankruptcy. Would you be willing
to give up your secure position as Pastor of the Moscow Church and
take a chance with us?" I had no hesitancy in replying: "I am willing."
So, it was then agreed that, if the Seminary's Board of Trustees approved, and if the financial outlook improved, I would be called.

Since the Trustees of the Seminary intended to use my name in its
publicity to raise funds, I found it necessary to tell the members of
my Session of the possibility of my leaving. Thus, for over a year, I
worked under the handicap of knowing that my service as Pastor
might end within a year or so.

In a letter to Dr. Baird, dated May 4, 1937, I wrote: 'Last Sunday
afternoon, I had some of our closest friends and best workers in our
home. I frankly told them the whole story and asked their advice as to
what was the best thing for me to do. They kindly expressed sorrow
at our going, but felt, that if the way was opened, I ought to accept.
The wife of one of the elders said: 'We would not feel so badly about
your going to the Seminary, whereas if you went to another church,
we would feel hurt.' "

About April 1, 1938, Dr. Baird informed me that the Finance Committee had succeeded in raising the necessary funds. The Board of
Trustees met on April 27 and confirmed the action of the Finance Committee, and the call to become the Professor of Church History at the
Seminary was extended to me. My salary was to be $3,000.00 a year,
which was then about $250.00 more than the Moscow Church was
paying; there would be participation in the church's pension plan,
and the use of a house on the campus.

Although the call from the Seminary in San Anselmo was the ful-
fillment of a cherished dream, yet when that dream became a reality,
my heart was filled with mixed emotions. We had spent ten happy
years in Moscow and the roots of friendships formed there were deep.
Yet, I looked forward eagerly to my new position.

By announcing my resignation months in advance, the Church had
opportunity to choose my successor, and they called the Rev. Leroy
Walter, D.D. Thus, there was no serious break in the leadership of
the Church as had been the case when I arrived in July of 1928.

On July 24, 1938, just a week before we were to leave for San Anselmo, I gave a report to the members of my Session. I recalled that
when I became Pastor in August of 1928, there were supposed to be
394 members; however, after examining the rolls, we found only 300
active members. During my ten year ministry, I welcomed 482 mem-

bers into the Church — 254 on confession of faith, 183 by certificate, and 45 were restored. During the same time we lost 444 members, leaving a net gain of only 38.

I reported that I had officiated at 158 weddings, 162 funerals, and had baptized 129 who joined the church on confession of faith and 59 infants. During that ten years I had delivered 568 sermons. The Church had received $69,688.00 for current expenses; $9,388.20 for benevolences; and $24,408.00 for the building fund.

My last Sunday in Moscow came on July 31st. My records show that 250 were present. I used the same sermon I gave on my last Sunday in Shanghai — "Remember Jesus Christ." Miriam and I were the honored guests at a reception held that evening in the new gymnasium, and were presented with a splendid sterling silver dining set complete for twelve settings.

Our Move to San Anselmo

We left for San Anselmo on Monday morning, August 1st, 1938. Christine went with us; so we had six in the car. I had purchased a trailer which was packed with a variety of items, including our cocker spaniel named Cocoa.

We arrived at our new home on campus at 118 Bolinas Ave. August 3rd. The whole family was delighted with its spaciousness — three bedrooms, a sleeping porch and two baths upstairs. Downstairs there was a large living room with a fireplace; a dining room; a maid's bedroom; a kitchen; and a study, which must have measured twelve feet square. It had a separate entrance, a fireplace, and shelf space for about 2,000 books. Never before had I been so blessed with such a fine study.

It was well that we arrived in San Anselmo more than a month before the Seminary opened, for we needed that time to get settled and have some repairs made to the house; also I needed time to prepare for the courses I was to teach. I had not taken any courses in education in college; nor did any of my colleagues on the faculty at San Anselmo give me any suggestions as to how to teach. Good textbooks were unavailable because of the depression. The library contained some good history books, but not enough to give each student a copy. I used Philip Schaff's *History of the Christsian Church* as my main reference, but was unable to buy copies for the class. I sent out word to former students of the Seminary who had used this text asking them to donate or sell their copies. This inability to get good textbooks was a real handicap.

I decided that I would have to write out my lectures. These I did not read, but used as a reference when speaking. I drew heavily on the notes I had taken when I studied under Dr. Remsen Bird in my two years at San Anselmo, 1919-1921, and also upon notes I had taken while a student in Edinburgh. I remember that there were days when I came to the end of my prepared notes just as the bell rang signaling the end of a class period.

School opened on September 13th with between seventy and eighty students enrolled, including five or six young women. I was asked to give the Convocation address. My formal inauguration as the California Professor of Church History occurred on November 28, 1938. I then spoke on the subject, "A Christian Philosophy of History." My former Professor of New Testament, who had recommended me for the Shanghai Church, gave me the charge. In a letter to my stepmother, dated October 20, 1938, I wrote: "The longer we stay here the more wonderful it seems. I have had many happy experiences in my life, but this seems to be one of the very best. Surely God has been good to me."

Shortly after my arrival at San Anselmo I was appointed editor of the *Chimes,* a quarterly magazine put out by the Seminary. Later I became Alumni Secretary, and for more than ten years, edited the *Alumni News.*

The Seminary closed its fiscal year in the spring of 1939 with a $9,000.00 deficit. Dr. Baird requested several of the faculty members to speak before the various Synods and in some of the larger churches in behalf of the Seminary. I was asked to represent the Seminary in the Synods of Washington and Oregon.

On Sunday, May 31st, I had the opportunity to stand again in the pulpit of the First Presbyterian Church of Moscow, where I had been pastor for several years. The sanctuary was filled to capacity; what a thrill to meet old friends again. I was a guest in the Eldridge home that night.

Among unusual experiences I had that spring was my first airplane ride. I was scheduled to speak at the morning service in a large church in Seattle, and then at 8:00 o'clock that evening to give the baccalaureate sermon at the State Teacher's College at Cheney, Washington. I took a plane from Seattle to Spokane, where a representative of the college met me with a car. I noted in my diary that I was somewhat nervous over the prospect of an airplane ride. This was the first of many that I took in following years.

Another unusual experience came when I spoke before an assembly at the Oregon University at Eugene. Although my records fail to give the exact date, it was, if I recall correctly, that same year. I had been asked to speak that evening on the Whitman-Spalding story. By that time I had given the story so many times that I no longer needed notes. The assembly room was filled, and a bad storm was raging outside. Just as I was introduced, a bolt of lightning struck a transformer and plunged the hall into complete darkness. Since I knew my subject so well, I gave my lecture. From time to time a flash of lightning showed me that my audience was still there; or when I told a humorous story, I could hear their laughter. The room remained in darkness throughout my hour's lecture. When I had finished, the Master of Ceremonies said: "Dr. Drury has spoken an hour and we are still in the dark."

During the latter part of July, 1939, my brother Billy, who was then living with his family at San Leandro, California, near Oakland, and I paid the way for Laura, our stepmother, to visit us. She was with us during the first week of July and then for a few days at the end of the month. The rest of the time she was with Billy.

Even though I had joined the Reserve Corps of the Navy in 1933 when I was still a pastor at Moscow, I had taken no further training until the end of December 1940, when I was given a two-week training period with Chaplain Harry M. Peterson, then District Chaplain of the 12th Naval District, in his office in San Francisco. It was then that I learned for the first time that I was near sighted and needed to wear glasses, and have needed them ever since. This was the only time I had any duty with the Navy before World War II broke out.

In the summer of 1941 the Drury family of five and our student helper, Christine Clayton, spent two weeks in Yosemite Park. I rented two tents, and we did our cooking out of doors. This was the last vacation Miriam and I were able to spend with our children, for within a year war broke out and our lives were drastically changed.

CHAPLAIN CLIFFORD DRURY, U.S.N.

CHAPTER TWENTY-ONE

Chaplain in World War II

I accepted an assignment to preach in December of 1941 for four Sundays in the First Presbyterian Church in San Jose, California. I have vivid memories of December 7 — Pearl Harbor Day. Following the 11:00 o'clock service, word reached the congregation that Pearl Harbor had been attacked and part of our Pacific fleet destroyed.

Later that day I learned that my dear friend, Chaplain Tom Kirkpatrick, who was serving aboard the *Arizona,* was among those killed. He was the first Navy Chaplain in World War II to lose his life. That tragic event, which took him out of the Navy, brought me into it.

My diary for Christmas day, 1941, begins with the following: "Yesterday I received my orders to report to the Navy for duty at the 12th Naval District Headquarters in San Francisco." At that time Chaplain Harry Peterson was the District Chaplain; and the Navy had one chaplain on Treasure Island and another at Mare Island. I was assigned to Chaplain Peterson's office to assist in taking care of Navy Relief. The Navy was bringing home from Honolulu all civilian dependents of Navy personnel. Those in charge of the project would sometimes take people from the streets and put them aboard ships, without giving them a chance to go to their homes for personal belongings. Ship loads of the refugees landed in San Francisco without money or proper clothing, and the Navy Relief had to step in and take care of them. We had to rent a hotel to house them temporarily.

Although I had never taken a course in Pastoral Counseling, I soon discovered that one of my major duties as Navy Chaplain was to counsel the naval personnel. Often it was money problems; fortunately I could draw upon the Navy Relief funds to help in emergencies. Also, there were marital problems. One woman called them "martial" problems.

One of the unique experiences I had as Chaplain in San Francisco was that of conducting telephone marriages, when the bride would be in my office and the groom in Honolulu in the office of the Jewish Chaplain, Herbert Straus. According to California law, common law marriages were recognized if the two parties signed a statement that they had been living together as husband and wife. I was careful to get the advise of a Navy lawyer before performing this service. Altogether I had eight such telephone marriages. In most cases the woman was pregnant and needed the financial allotment due her from her husband in the Navy. There was possibly some risk in performing these services by telephone. This prompted the regular chaplains not to take part; they were fearful of criticism which might affect a promotion. As Reserve Chaplain this worry did not affect me. So far as I know, only one of the eight marriages ended in divorce. One of the brides, who came from New Jersey to be married and arrived just after the ship had left port with her husband aboard. When the baby was born, a son, she gave the child Drury as its middle name.

Even though I reported for duty in the District Chaplain's office in San Francisco, I still had responsibilities at the Seminary. Chaplain Peterson felt that I should continue teaching my required courses. Arrangements were made at the Seminary for me to have the eight o'clock hour and occasionally a class at nine o'clock. I would then drive to the city and remain on duty until 5:00 p.m. In turn, I had duty on Saturdays, and, beginning early in 1942, I was assigned special duty at the Tiburon Net Depot in Marin County. This included conducting Sunday services in an unheated warehouse. During the remainder of the Seminary year, 1941-42, I met, evenings in my home, with six students who were writing theses under my direction. It was a heavy schedule, and I had little time to be with my family.

Fifteen or twenty of my students entered the Navy Chaplaincy, including David Burcham who remained on the Reserve roll and attained the rank of Captain. As long as I carried some teaching responsibilities, I and my family continued to live at 118 Bolinas Avenue.

Fearing the possibility of Japanese submarines entering the Golden Gate and torpedoing U.S. Naval vessels, the Navy stretched a huge net across the entrance inside of the Golden Gate bridge. Two tug boats, with crews taken from the Tiburon base, took care of the net When a vessel was authorized to enter, these boats would pull back the nets to provide entrance. From time to time the nets were brought back to Tiburon, stretched out on a cement slab, and cleaned. These were the men who attended my Church services; my records show an average attendance of eighty. After receiving orders to Tiburon, I spent two days a week there, Wednesdays and Sundays. The other days were spent in Chaplain Peterson's office.

The net which the Navy stretched across the Golden Gate proved to have been a wise precaution, for after the war a torpedo, which a Japanese sub had fired at the south pillar of the bridge, was found on the beach nearby. It had been deflected by a rock and beached.

From time to time I was asked to give the invocation at the launching of some Naval vessel, often a submarine or a liberty ship, at one of the Navy construction sites near Vallejo or at Sausalito.

Knowing that we could not continue to live in one of the Seminary houses when I was not teaching, we began looking for a house to buy during the early months of 1943. After some searching we found a two-bedroom house at 89 Marinita in San Rafael, which we purchased for $5,000.00. I borrowed from my Life Insurance and got some help from the Federal Housing Administration. I signed my first papers on June 4th; took possession on July 1st; and then, after making some repairs including the building of another bedroom, we moved in on August 10th. The cost of the repairs was $865.00. About half of the house was on two levels, with the bedrooms and a bath above a garage. At that time lumber was almost impossible to get; however, I was able to get some from a dump heap at Mare Island. We were within easy walking distance of San Rafael High School which our daughter, Pat, was to enter that fall.

Our eldest son, Robert, completed his course at Tamalpais High School in the spring of 1942, and on June 25th left for Berkeley to enroll in summer school at the University of California. Bob went through high school in three years, and I noted in my diary that he was the first one in the history of that school to do so. On June 7, 1943, just a day before he was eighteen, Robert joined the U.S. Army. He had just finished his first year at the University of California. He was not called to active duty until August of that year and was then sent to Fort McClellan, Alabama for his basic training. From there he was sent to the South Pacific. I recall that I, with my wife and our other two children, drove down to see him depart from the railroad depot in San Francisco; it was hard to see him go.

Bob was assigned to the 25th Division which was sent to Caledonia in the spring of 1944. His Division landed on Luzon with General Douglas MacArthur during the first part of January, 1945. No doubt he would have been a part of the U.S. force which would have invaded Japan had not the atomic bombs brought that conflict to an end. Bob was discharged on August 25, 1945, when I was on duty in Washington, D.C.

YARD CHAPLAIN, MARE ISLAND

In a letter from Robert D. Workman, Chief of Chaplains, dated April 2, 1943, I learned that I was to be transferred from the District Chaplain's office in San Francisco to be Yard Chaplain at Mare Island near Vallejo. I was to relieve Chaplain Charles Ellis. I began my duties as Yard Chaplain on May 15th. Shortly after I reported there for duty, four other chaplains were assigned to Mare Island, two Protestant and two Roman Catholic. This permitted me to assign one of the Protestant chaplains, Paul C. Allen, to the Naval Hospital on the island. I was given a room in the officer's barracks which made it possible for me to spend some nights on the island. As my home in

San Rafael was about thirty miles distant, I was able to commute home about half of the time.

One of the extra duties which came to me as Yard Chaplain was to serve the several ships which came to Mare Island for repairs. Several had been torpedoed but, even with great gaping holes in their sides, they were able to make it into port. Members of the crew were then usually urged to take leave and go home while their ship was being repaired. This often caught the crew personnel by surprise and without funds to pay travel expenses to their respective homes. Often the men from such ships turned to the Navy Relief for loans or grants. In a report to Chaplain Workman dated September 12, 1943, I stated that my office, which handled Navy Relief, had made $10,000.00 in loans in July and $6,000.00 in August. The Navy Relief work became so heavy that a special woman Ensign was assigned to handle the loans.

One of the attractions of duty at Mare Island was the pleasure of having a real church on the base — St. Peter's Chapel. This was erected in 1901 and was the first military chapel built in the United States to be used by both Protestants and Catholics. A Naval Appropriation Act of 1900 contained an item of $5,000.00 for the erection of the chapel. It contains a beautiful series of Tiffany glass windows. Many memorial plaques are fastened to its walls; as I recall, the chapel seated about 200 people.

On January 1, 1942, shortly after going on active duty, I was promoted to Lieutenant Commander. Knowing that it was the general policy of the Chaplain Corps to rotate its chaplains between shore and sea duty, I had reason to believe that I might get orders for sea duty at any time after I had been with the 12th Naval District for a year and a half. This was one reason I wanted to get my family settled in our own home. Miriam was licensed to drive and was a good driver; so I had no hesitancy to go on extended duty elsewhere and leave her to manage the household.

While on duty for a time at Tiburon, I had a room on the Delta King, one of two steamers which used to ply between San Francisco and Sacramento, along with its sister ship, the Delta Queen. The ship was being used as a barracks at Tiburon.

Ordered to Washington

On February 2, 1944, Captain Robert D. Workman, then Chief of Chaplains for the Navy, wrote to me asking for my opinion as to what should be included in a history of the Navy Chaplaincy, which was to be published. I did not know that Frank Knox, then Secretary of the Navy, had issued an order calling upon every ship, and every naval activity, to have an historian. Nor did I dream that Chaplain Workman was thinking of me to write that history.

I answered Workman's letter on February 9th writing 1½ single spaced pages listing the items which I felt should be included. Back came a letter from Workman, dated February 15th, in which he stated that I had more ideas on the subject than he and that he was issuing orders for me to be transferred to Washington to write the history. It so happened that I was the only chaplain on duty who had majored in history and who had already published books in this field. My wife and I talked about the possibility of my finding suitable living quarters in Washington and then she and the children would join me.

According to a letter to my family written from Washington on March 30, I was detached from duty at Mare Island on March 17th. Since I had not seen my relatives in Iowa for three years, I planned to spend a few days there while enroute to Washington. I arrived in Early on Thursday, March 23rd and the next three days were spent in visiting and eating. My relatives' idea of hospitality was to give a feast. On Friday, I borrowed my sister Clara's car and drove out to the farm, six miles south of Early, where I was born and where I spent the first sixteen years of my life.

A flood of memories swept through my mind as I revisited the scenes of my youth. I found that most of the maple trees, which once arched over the lane leading from the road to the house and farmyard, had been cut down. The orchard was gone as were most of the trees which once sheltered us on the west and north sides of our home. Some of the farm buildings were gone, but the two big barns and the silo were standing.

I was cordially received by Mr. and Mrs. Reuben Hokanson, then the renters of the farm. I was invited into the house. It seemed so small that I marvelled how we were able to sleep ten or twelve and still have a room downstairs called the "spare room." Several years later I was invited by the Hokansons to spend a night there. This was a moving experience, but things were different — no crowing of roosters, no mooing of cows, and no humming of the telephone lines. The Hokansons lived there longer than did the Drury family.

On Sunday I spoke in the Methodist Church at which time the members of the Presbyterian Church joined us. The church was packed. I told about the work of the Naval Chaplaincy. Fifty-five of my relatives were in the audience. Afterwards the Drury family held a dinner in the basement of the city hall.

I left that afternoon by train from Carroll, Iowa, for Boone where one of my college classmates, J. Stewart Brown, was pastor. The Rev.

E. Marousek, pastor of the Presbyterian Church of Jefferson, joined us and we three members of the 1918 class of Buena Vista joined in leading the evening service in Brown's church. I caught the midnight train that night for Chicago.

On Monday morning I arrived in Chicago and had time to call on the Rev. Emory Luccock, who was my successor in Community Church, Shanghai. We had much in common to talk about. Mrs. Luccock is now one of my neighbors at Monte Vista Grove Homes, where my wife and others are living in retirement. I reported for duty in Washington on Tuesday, March 28th. I found that the Chaplains Division was housed in what was once a large warehouse next to Arlington Cemetery.

When I reported for duty in Washington, I discovered that the Navy made no allowance for housing its officers beyond giving them a monthly rental allowance. I received $120.00 a month. Washington was over-crowded during those war years. I spent my first night in the city in a hotel and the next day succeeded in getting a small room in McLean Gardens, a housing project on Wisconsin Avenue, about an hour's ride by bus or street car from the Chief of Chaplain's office or from my office in the Navy Yard in Anacosta.

My brother-in-law, Hillis Lory, arrived in Washington on April 7th, and he also got a room in McLean Gardens. He had secured a position in the State Department which he held for many years. We were often together; each of us was looking for a house so that we could have our families join us.

I found the hour long ride on public transportation to my office to be most tiring. Often I had to stand all the way because of the over-crowding in the street car or bus. After some searching I found a basement room for rent at 2604 Branch Avenue in the Hillcrest District in Southeast Washington. My landlady was Mrs. Landman. My new location was only about one-third the distance to the Navy Yard as was McLean Gardens. The main disadvantage about the basement room was the lack of ventilation in hot humid weather. I had a good bed and my own bath room. I moved in on May 4th and lived here until September 1st when I was able to move into the house I had rented at 2125 34th St., S.E., about two blocks from where I had been living.

Living next door to Mrs. Landman were the Entwisles, Ted and Lorena, and their young son Stanley. The Entwisles had a summer home on the shore of Chesapeake Bay, a few miles south of Anapolis. They also had a modest sized yacht and delighted in going fishing in the Bay. We became acquainted when I was living at Mrs. Landman's, and I was often their guest on fishing excursions. Thus began a friendship which has continued through the years and whenever I have returned to Washington I have always tried to find time to call on them in their beautiful home in Edgewater, Maryland.

A few blocks down Branch Avenue from Mrs. Landman's home was a Baptist Church over which a Mr. Faucett served as pastor. On May 6th, just a few days after I had moved into my basement apartment, I called on the Faucetts. At this time Faucett told me that his neighbor, Mrs. Bertha Wineberger, who lived with her husband across the alley from the Faucett home, was planning to move and that their home would be available for rental. I hastened to call on Mrs. Wineberger that same day. Later I learned that Faucett had told the Winebergers that he had a friend who would like to rent their house. Evidently Faucett had forgotten about this when he sent me to see them, for the Winebergers thought that I was this friend. The house would be available on September 15 — actually I moved in on September 1st.

The Wineberger house, located at 2125 34th St., S.E., had been built only five years previously. It was a two-story brick building with three bedrooms and a sleeping porch and bath upstairs. Downstairs it had a living room with a fireplace, dining room, kitchen, half-bath, and a room under the sleeping porch which could be used as a bedroom or den, There was a full basement and a separate garage. The rent asked was $125.00 a month. I quickly told the Winebergers that I wanted the house and signed the lease on June 12th, paying a $50.00 deposit. The location was ideal and within walking distance of the school that Pat and Phil would be attending, and was only twenty minutes driving time to the Navy Yard. I felt that the Lord had smiled on me.

I let Miriam know. She had three months to sell the house, the car, and pack our household goods. The Navy would move 10,000 pounds for us. I advised her to store most of my books in the attic of the Seminary's office building, and Phil helped out in this. I made train reservations for the family to go east via New Orleans for Miriam wanted to see that city and the cost was the same as though they came straight across the country. The schedule called for their arrival in Washington on Thursday, September 7th. Miriam was able to get the household goods packed and shipped by August 8th. She and the children continued to live at 89 Marguerita with some items of furniture we were leaving and some borrowed pieces.

The Winebergers moved September 1st and I moved in that afternoon. I bought a double bed from Mrs. Wineberger and a table and six chairs from a neighbor. Mrs. Wineberger left a refrigerator in the house.

Being assured of a house and of having my family with me, my next problem was to buy a car. I visited the Priority Board on July 11, where I made application for a permit to buy a car. Previously I had visited some auto sales offices and located a new Commander Studebaker for $1,550.00. The prices of both new and used cars were then being regulated by the Government OPA. I figured that we could get about $1,000.00 for our car which was in San Rafael. I could not deprive Miriam of its use until she and the children were about ready to leave for Washington.

There were many who were eager to get a permit to buy a new car. When I learned that the Priority Board had rejected the application of a Colonel, I felt that I had little chance. But on July 16th in a letter to Miriam, I joyfully reported that I was granted a priority. I was told that the permit was granted because of my duties as District Chaplain in PRNC. In my letter to Miriam on July 18th, I stated that I had only two weeks to complete the purchase and that I would have to pay $500.00 down. The balance could be paid after we sold our house and car in California.

I took possession of the new Studebaker on July 27th and what a joy it was to have one's own transportation. Writing to Miriam that day I commented: "My next problem is to get gas and a parking space at the Navy Yard." I put in a request for sufficient gas stamps for 700 miles a month. Having a car, I was able to help my brother-in-law, Hollis Lory, look for a house. On July 31st, I noted that I took him to see three houses which were for sale. Finally, on August 4th, Hollis found a house which suited him and bought it. The Lory home was in N.E. Washington, about twelve miles from our home.

Miriam found a buyer for our home in San Rafael for $7,000.00. We paid $5,000.00 for it in 1941 but added more than $1,000.00 in improvements besides leaving a stove and refrigerator. Our net profit was about $250.00. She sold the car for $1,065.00. On July 21st she wrote: "It seems like getting out of jail to get the house sold." I told her that the Navy would send a van to get our household goods about August 8th. Then, according to our plans previously made, she and the children left San Francisco on September 1st, went through Glendale to visit her parents and other relatives, on through New Orleans, and arrived in Washington, D.C. September 7th.

I was at the Washington depot long before their train arrived. After being separated from each other for five months, we had a joyful reunion. I proudly showed them the new car and then drove them to our new home on 34th Street, S.E. I had hoped that the van with our household goods would have arrived before the family, but that was not so. Fortunately for us, within three hours after the family had arrived, a van came to our door with our household goods. It seemed to me that a kind Providence was surely looking after us. There we lived until July 1, 1946, when we started back to California.

Upon my arrival in Washington, I discovered that instead of working on the history as I had expected, I was to relieve Chaplain Stanton Salisbury who had been serving as District Chaplain of the Potomac River Command. Chaplain Salisbury had transferred to the Chief's office where he served as Acting Chief of Chaplains while Chaplain Workman and two other chaplains were making a tour of naval installations, especially in Northern Africa. In my new assignment I was responsible for all Naval funerals in Arlington Cemetery, and also for the delivery of all notices of death or missing-in-action reports to relatives who lived in the Washington area. In other parts of the country these notices went by telegram, but in Washington they were delivered in person. As I recall, the chaplains associated with me and I delivered over 400 of these messages.

There were twenty-two chaplains connected with the Potomac River Command who worked under my direction. Among the personnel in the District there were about 15,000 women in uniform; most of whom were in the Navy and were called Waves. Also in the District there were over a thousand Marine women and several hundred in the Coast Guard called Spars.

Miss Sylvia Paine of Bar Harbor, Maine, was assigned to me to be my yeoman secretary. She proved to be a faithful and valued assistant.

From November 1944 to November 1945, I served as President of the Washington chapter of the Army and Navy Chaplains' Association. Luncheon meetings were held each month from January to May inclusive and from September to November in the Continental Hotel with an average attendance of about seventy. At one of our meetings we had the privilege of having Mrs. Franklin D. Roosevelt as our speaker. I was privileged to sit next to her at the dinner table and to introduce her.

As District Chaplain, I made regular visits to all of the installations in this Command having a chaplain and counselled, advised, secured equipment for, and in other ways aided the chaplains on duty. Also among my duties was that of helping to indoctrinate new chaplains who were students at the Chaplain Training School at Williamsburg, Virginia. From time to time groups of ten or twelve chaplains would report to me, and I would assign them to various units within my district for first hand observation of a chaplain's duties.

I served as District Chaplain of PNRC from the 28th of March,

1944 to the 22nd of August, 1945, when I was transferred to the Chief
of Chaplain's office to work on the history of the Chaplains Corps.
World War II ended in August of 1945. At that time I could have
been relieved from active duty and could have returned to my teaching
at San Anselmo; but, upon the request of the Chief of Chaplains,
I decided to stay in Washington for another year and work on the
History of the Chaplains Corps.

CHAPTER TWENTY-TWO

A History of a History

During the first few months of my work as a District Chaplain I had little time to work on the History of the Chaplains' Corps.

Common sense and good scholarship demand that historians should build on the researches and writings of their predecessors in the field of their specialty. I came to this project fresh from civilian life. I was a Naval Reserve and not a Regular Navy chaplain. Until I was ordered to Washington to work on this project, I had taken no specific interest in the past history of the Chaplain Corps. So my first responsibility was to see what had been written on this subject.

I found that two regular Navy chaplains — Clinton A. Neyman and William W. Edel — had each done some research and writing in this field. Both generously shared with me their findings. At the time the Chaplains School was established at William and Mary College, Chaplain Edel was asked to write a short history of the Corps which could be used at the school. He wrote the seventeen, legal-sized page brochure, "Navy Chaplains, 1775-1917," which with a six-page syllabus on the same subject prepared by Chaplain Neyman was the principal source used at the school to teach the history of the Corps.

I also learned that two chaplains who preceded them in the Corps — David H. Tribou, who served from 1872-1910, and Roswell H. Hoes (rhymes with goose), 1882-1912 — had also worked on the history of the Corps. Both Neyman and Edel had used their materials.

Although the project as originally conceived was to write the history of Navy chaplains in World War II, I soon realized the importance of going back to the days of the Continental Navy. One could not appreciate the present status of the Corps without first tracing out its history. When I explained my convictions to Chaplain Workman, he gave me the green light for this larger work. We agreed that there would be two volumes of the narrative history, with September 8, 1939, as the dividing line. This was the date that President Franklin D. Roosevelt declared the existence of a state of national emergency. Chaplain Workman also approved my suggestion to compile a *Who's Who of the Naval Chaplaincy*. This was designed to be Volume III of the series but, as will be related later, was actually published first.

After having acquainted myself with the findings of chaplains Neyman and Edel, I then turned to the Library of Congress. Using the best list available of Navy chaplains, I checked each name with the author's index in that Library. This turned up a number of books written by chaplains. I also had the privilege of going through some of the original correspondence by John Paul Jones and therein found a few references to chaplains in the Continental Navy. But on the whole the resources of the Library of Congress were a disappointment in that they provided so little material.

I then turned to the Naval Records Collection in the National Archives to see what could be discovered in original manuscript sources. By patiently scanning the muster rolls in old log books going back to the very beginning of our Navy, I picked up the names of about fifty who were listed as "chaplains." These were unordained men and were usually selected out of the ship's company. Often they were pursers or ships' clerks who had the special duty, usually assigned in those days to the chaplain, of teaching the midshipmen. It is doubtful whether they performed any of the duties expected of an ordained minister. This search opened a new chapter in the history of the Chaplain Corps. Perhaps a word of explanation is needed at this point. Actually the term "Chaplain Corps" applies to the group of chaplains after 1917 when the first Director or Chief, John B. Frazier, was selected. I am using the term, however, to apply in a general way to the chaplains of the earlier years.

Our first Chief of Navy Chaplains, John B. Frazier, opened a folder for each chaplain in the Navy and this file was still in existence when I came to the period of World War I. Ever since the days of Chaplain Frazier, two files on Navy chaplains have been kept. One is the official file in the Bureau of Naval Personnel which contains the personnel data. The second is the file in the Chief's office which contains the personal correspondence of the individual chaplains to the Chief or to others in his office. These files were rich in historical materials.

When I began writing the history of the Chaplains Corps nothing was said about how it should be published. Believing that my volume on Who's Who in the Chaplain Corps would be sold by private subscriptions, I felt the necessity of making my sketches as brief as possible. My yeoman and I devised about 250 abbreviations, using many of those already in use by the Navy. I decided that each biographical sketch should have two paragraphs. The first would give vital statistics about the individual concerned, and the second would give his military record as a chaplain. The volume, when finished, carried the sketches of 3,353 chaplains covering the period from John Paul Jones to the end of 1946. In order to conserve space, most of the periods, as those usually found after abbreviations, were eliminated. The comma took the place of both a period and a comma. I estimated that about 60,000 periods were thus eliminated.

Long before the Who's Who was finished, I was at work writing the history of the Chaplain Corps covering the years from John Paul Jones to the declaration of a state of emergency by President Franklin Roosevelt in September 1939. Original source materials for this period were most difficult to locate. No file was kept on the activities of the chaplains of World War I by the Navy or by any historical society.

I had to rely upon the few books written by former chaplains, the most prolific of whom was Walter Colton, who was the first Protestant clergyman to settle in California. Colton was the chaplain for Commodore Stockton who raised the American flag over Monterey in 1846.

During most of the nineteenth century the Navy chaplains worked under great limitations. There was a time when they had no official standing in the Navy. They were usually given the poorest stateroom aboard the ship. There was no Chief of Chaplains. Assignments to duty were made by a woman clerk in the Navy Department.

I found great difficulty in obtaining illustrations for Volume I. Thanks to the historical interest of Chaplain Edel, Photographer's Mate 2c Clayton E. Braun, was assigned to painting chapels used by the Navy chaplains in the South Pacific during World War II. Braun also made about twenty portraits of early chaplains from photographs in Edel's possession. Twelve of these portraits were reproduced in Volume I.

Since nothing had been said about a method of publication, I assumed that when it was ready, an appeal would be sent out to all the chaplains to buy a copy of the history of the Chaplain's Corps. Later on my narrative history was used as a textbook by the Reserve Chaplains, but it was never written for that purpose. It was written for popular consumption.

In the spring of 1946, shortly before I was released from active duty, I went to New York City to interview several publishing firms to see if any would be interested in publishing the history. I met with no success. When in New York I got in touch with Chaplain Joshua Goldberg, the senior Jewish Chaplain of the Navy, who promised to find someone to subsidize the publication of the history. After returning to Washington, I received a letter from him saying that a friend of his, Henry Monskbey, who was then President of B'nai B'rith, had promised to subsidize the publication to the extent of $10,000. This assurance made me very happy; however, after I had returned to my home in San Anselmo, California, in the fall of 1946, I received a letter from Chaplain Goldberg saying that Mr. Monskbey had died. Nevertheless I continued to work on the history.

After I returned to my seminary teaching I was called back to Washington for periods of two weeks to two months during eleven consecutive summers from 1947 to 1957 inclusive.

An unexpected development came in 1948 when Congress passed Public Law 810 which carried provisions for the strengthening of the Reserves of all of the armed services. A new incentive was provided for Reservists to maintain an active relationship with their respective branches of the military by providing retirement pay for those who qualified. Navy chaplains, for instance, could qualify if they made fifty credits each year for a total of twenty years of satisfactory service. Credit was granted by law for past service. After 1948 the officers concerned had to spend some time each year on active or training duty, attend drills, or take corrspondence courses. Usually all three of these methods and other possibilities were needed to make the fifty points. This called for texts to be used for correspondence courses. Although the *History of the Chaplain Corps* was never written to be the text for such a purpose, the Chaplains Division promptly made the decision that the work would be suitable. Our publishing problem was solved by the Government taking over the full cost.

The first book of the history to be published was *United States Navy Chaplains, 1778-1945.* The United States Publishing Office published this book and it sold for $2.50. This was the first Who's Who of any branch of the Navy, and it proved to be an invaluable reference book for all chaplains on active duty, especially for the District Chaplains. The first volume of the narrative *History of the Chaplains Corps* appeared in 1949, an edition of 2,200 copies, paper bound, and 1,000 in hard cover, with another 1,000 paper bound printed in 1969. This also was published by the Government and covered the period from 1778-1949. Although this appeared after the volume giving the biographical sketches of the chaplains, it was listed as Volume I. Volume II of the narrative history appeared in 1950 and carried the story down to the end of World War II. This also appeared in an edition of 2,200 copies, paper bound, and 1,000 in hard cover.

I continued to work on a subsequent history of the Chaplains Corps, bringing it down to 1958. 1,500 copies of Volume II were reprinted in 1964 and 600 more in 1976 in paperback. Both Volume I and Volume II have been used as textbooks by Reserve Chaplains, and by new chaplains coming into the Corps.

After being transferred to the Chief of Chaplain's office, which was located in what had been a large warehouse about a mile west of the Pentagon and across the street from Arlington Cemetery, I had no regular Sunday duties. Often I spent part of those days working alone at my desk in the Chief's office. I was thus free to accept invitations to occupy the pulpits of several churches which needed a temporary supply. I was invited to preach at the Sixth Presbyterian Church of Washington, located on North 16th Street, on the last Sunday of 1945. The church happened to be without a pastor; the first invitation was followed by another, and so on for four months. I found this a delightful experience. About sixty lawyers were members of the congregation. After being there for about four months, the session of the church invited me to be its pastor. Although the offer was tempting, I declined as I wanted to return to my teaching position at San Anselmo. The Seminary had been holding the chair open for me.

While in Washington, I made the acquaintance of an artist of Russian birth — Gregory Stapko. At Stapko's suggestion, I sat for my portrait. He would come to the Chief's office late in the afternoon after all who worked there had gone home. I would then sit in the Chief's chair while Stapko painted me from life. This was not a full length portrait, but one only of the upper half of my body. I gave it to the Presbyterian Historical Society, now located at 425 Lombard Street in Philadelphia.

Many years later a former seminary classmate, Drury Haight, painted my portrait again; this was given to the library of Buena Vista College in Storm Lake, Iowa.

OUR ELDEST SON RELEASED FROM THE ARMY

As mentioned previously, our eldest son, Robert, had joined the United States Army, and was with the 25th Division. In the spring of 1945 Bob became ill and was sent back to the States. Since we were then living in Washington, he was sent to Norfolk, Virginia. To our great joy he spent most of June with us. I remember getting leave for a day or so in order to take him to one of the Civil War battlefields at Fredericksburg, Virginia; then to Kitty Hawk where the Wright brothers first flew their plane; and then to Roanoke Island to see the pageant, "The Lost Colony."

After spending about a month with us, in August he returned to the University of California for his second year of college.

I was promoted to the rank of Captain on March 20, 1945. I continued on duty working on the history project for about a year following the end of the war.

—2 Cor. 5 ~ 15—

Parrish Services —

—Oct—

CHAPTER TWENTY-THREE

We Return to San Anselmo

Since I was released from active duty on July 1, 1946, and since I had taken less than four weeks off duty during my nearly four years of active duty, I had about two months vacation available. On July 1st we sent our household goods by Mayflower Van to San Anselmo, and we left to drive up through New York and Boston on our way to Quebec. We stopped over the 4th of July to visit Mr. and Mrs. John C. White at Meredith, New Hampshire. I had become acquainted with the Whites when I was serving in the Sixth Church. They had a home on the shore of Lake Winnipesaukee. They also had tourist cabins on the lake which they put at our disposal.

We had several days seeing the sights of Quebec, and then boarded a steamer to go up the St. Lawrence River enroute to Buffalo.

On our way to Early, I was able to show Miriam and our two chilren, Patricia and Philip, the old Drury home on the farm where I spent the first sixteen years of my life. We arrived in Early about the 12th of July and were given a royal welcome. A family reunion was planned for Sunday, July 14th, and fifty-five relatives were present. I was still wearing my white uniform.

While at Early we decided to visit Yellowstone Park on our way to San Anselmo. We moved back into our former home at 118 Bolinas Avenue where we had lived for several years before I entered the Navy. It was good to be back home again.

We arrived back in San Anselmo on July 29, 1946, and to our great joy the van with our household goods arrived the same day. We were able to sleep in our regular beds that night.

I was soon back at teaching. I resumed my regular classes when Seminary opened in September. As I recall, I rarely had less than ten hours of lecturing a week, and occasionally up to fourteen.

These were college years for our older two children. Bob returned to the University of California and Pat enrolled in Occidental College in Eagle Rock, California, from which she was graduated in 1950 with a Phi Beta Kappa key. Phil began his high school work in Tamalpais High in southern Marin County, to which he commuted by the electric train. Our big house on Bolinas Avenue seemed lonesome with two of our children away.

One of the joys which came with our return to Marin County was the proximity to San Leandro, which lay just east of Oakland, where my brother Billy, his wife Elinor, and their daughter, Elizabeth, lived. We had frequent reunions. A sister of Elinor's, Alice, was married to one of my seminary classmates, Lloyd Carrick, who was serving as pastor of St. John's Presbyterian Church in San Francisco. It became our custom in those days to hold a family reunion on such occasions as Thanksgiving and Christmas in the dining room of Carrick's church. The usual attendance was between fifteen and twenty. I cherish the memories of such gatherings.

Shortly after I resumed my work at the Seminary, Dr. Baird asked me to write a pageant which could be presented at the 1947 commencement in recognition of the Seminary's 75th anniversary. Actually since the Seminary was founded in 1871, this occasion should have been recognized in the spring of 1946. I worked on the text of the pageant during the winter of 1946-7 and in the spring selected the cast. I called it "God Giveth the Increase." The pageant was presented at the 1947 Commencement in the Seminary's gymnasium which was filled to capacity with the audience. The closing episode referred to World War II. I invited all of the alumni who had served in the military, most of whom were chaplains, to come in their uniform. They remained behind the wings of the platform until the last scene. Then to martial music they marched across the platform one by one, being separated by about twenty feet. At least twenty took part, and the scene brought tears to the eyes of many.

A curtain had been hung at the back of the main platform which shielded the Seminary's choir under the direction of Prof. Milton Kelly. As the final finale the curtain was drawn and the choir sang Handel's Messiah.

MY TEPEE BOOK

The second book which I had published after my return to San Anselmo bore the title *A Tepee In His Front Yard*. The publisher was Metropolitan Press (now Binford and Mort) of Portland, Oregon; they printed 1,500 copies which appeared in the fall of 1949. This volume told the story of Spalding's return to the Nez Perces in 1871. He started a revival among the Nez Perces which resulted in more than 600 of them being baptized and the founding of six Presbyterian churches in that tribe. Spalding also visited the Spokanes where he baptized over 330. The Cowley family, descendants of Henry T. Cowley, a missionary with Spalding, subsidized the publication to the extent of $1,800.00. This volume of 206 pages was inspired by the discovery in the library of Whitman College of forty-two letters from Cowley to Spalding. Another collection of some fifty letters from Cowley to the Secretary of the Presbyterian Board of Foreign Missions, Dr. John C. Lowrie, was located in the files of the Presbyterian Historical Society in Philadelphia. Still other Cowley letters were located elsewhere.

Sometime during the summer or early fall of 1877 General W. T. Sherman, who was then based in San Francisco, visited Spokane. Sherman called on Cowley, who was then serving as a missionary to the Spokane Indians, and in blunt language told him that he was wasting his life in a futile aim. Years later, when Cowley was involved in a law suit over some real estate in what is now Spokane, he wrote to Sherman asking for a testimonial. In Sherman's reply, dated Jan. 30, 1888, he wrote: "As to Christianizing the Indians, of course you know it was a farce . . . You had one poor Indian in a tepee in front of your good house. . ." It was not so much an Indian tepee being in the white man's front yard as that of having a white man's house in the Indian's back yard. The Indian got there first and the very fact that Cowley was willing to live so near an Indian family was to his credit. So I called my book *A Tepee In His Front Yard.*

The Metropolitan Press, which published my Tepee book, gave it a jacket which pictured an Indian walking between a tepee and a white man's cabin. It also gave the following sub-title to the book, "H. T. Cowley and the Founding of Spokane." Each of my first three books, published by Caxton at Caldwell, Idaho, also had jackets. The Spalding book was given two jackets, one for each edition.

A Tribute from the Portland Oregonian

The September 18, 1949, issue of the Portland *Oregonian* carried the following editorial. This has been one of the finest tributes ever paid to me for my writings. The editorial follows:

A New Drury Biography

The Inland Empire, and the Pacific Northwest as a whole, are the richer because one Dr. Clifford M. Drury became pastor of the First Presbyterian Church at Moscow, Idaho in 1928, and continued there for ten years. Dr. Drury developed a great interest in the founding missionaries of the region, and prior to World War II he turned out a series of books, "Henry Harmon Spalding," "Marcus Whitman, M.D.," and "Mary and Elkanah Walker," which have made historical history.

We pay this tribute because, following distinguished service during the war and the writing of the official history of the navy's chaplain corps, Dr. Drury, now at the San Francisco Theological Seminary, has returned to his first love. Binford & Mort of Portland have just issued a new volume in his series on the Inland Empire missionaries — this one, "A Tepee in His Front Yard," telling the story of H. T. Cowley, one of the founders of Spokane.

The book has already been described in the news. What we wish to add here is that Dr. Drury is singularly objective, which is a rare quality among church historians. At the same time he is a fine, and not florid, stylist, which also is rare. In fact, we have that remarkable result — a definitive and fascinating set of books on a fascinating set of characters, and characters who suffered sadly from partisan biographies prior to Dr. Drury's arrival on the scene. He is an able writer and conscientious historian.

CONTINUED WORK ON CHAPLAINCY HISTORY

After returning to San Anselmo, I went back to Washington, D.C. for eleven summers during 1947-1957 in order to continue the history project. My summer service varied from two weeks to two months. I was given one point for each day on active duty which helped secure the fifty points needed each year to qualify for retirement pay, which I received when I was retired in 1957 at the age of sixty. At first I made the return trip to Washington by train and often read examination papers from my seminary classes while enroute. Later I went by air.

The first two summers in Washington I managed to get along without a car, but it was difficult. After World War II new cars were hard to get, for automobiles were not built for civilian consumption during the war. Orders for new cars piled up. In the summer of 1949, while in Washington on duty, John C. White, a member of the Sixth Presbyterian Church where I had supplied the pulpit for several months in 1946, bought a new Dodge sedan. He had placed his order several years earlier and so was able to get the car. He kindly turned this car over to me and waited another year to buy one for himself.

Five times during the following years, when called back to active duty, I turned my car over to the Buick dealer in San Rafael and then picked up a new car in Detroit. Since in those days auto dealers sold cars to patrons who picked up their car at the factory at a discount of about $160.00, or the equivalent of freight charges to California, and since I could collect travel costs from the Navy, I was able to get a new car during those years with a depreciation of about three cents a mile. This is no longer possible.

The volume of the *History of the Chaplain Corps* containing the biographical and service record sketches of the Chaplain Corps actually appeared before the two volumes of the narrative. Although it was not officially so numbered, it was actually Volume III of this series. The narrative was continued in volumes IV, V and VI.

A second "Who's Who" appeared in 1953 as Volume IV of the *History of the Chaplain Corps* in an edition of 1,000 copies. The title page bore the sub-title "United States Navy Chaplains, 1946-1952." This volume carried corrections and additions to 1,555 sketches which appeared in Volume III with the additions of 273 sketches of chaplains who had entered the Corps after January 1, 1946. This volume also contained sixteen pages of text which brought the history of the Corps up-to-date. The GPO sold this volume for $1.00.

A third volume of the "Who's Who" series appeared as Volume V of the *History of the Chaplain Corps* in 1957 and sold for $1.50. This volume contained the biographical and service-record sketches of 2,800 USN and USNR chaplains, including corrections and additions to 2,222 sketches which appeared in Volumes III and IV of the series. This volume included the sketches of 26 chaplains who had entered the service after January 1, 1953. Thus the three volumes together present the sketches of a grand total of 3,888 chaplains. Here in concise form is reference material of the greatest value.

One special feature of Volume V, which appeared in an edition of 3,000 copies, is that it "closed" the record on every chaplain who served during World War II and who did not remain on active duty. The possibilities were death, retirement, resignation, or release from the Reserve roll for a variety of reasons.

I received no royalty for my navy books for I was on duty when they were written, during which time I received the pay which accompanied my rank. The royalties received for books written before and after my navy books were published rarely were more than actual costs involved. The real royalty consisted of appreciation from discerning readers.

My first volume of the narrative *History of the Chaplain Corps* appeared in November, 1949. The first of a series of "fan" letters came from a Roman Catholic chaplain, Walter A. Mahler, who, on December 2, wrote: "I have just completed thumbing through the first volume of your *History of the Chaplain Corps*. This is indeed a magnificent piece of work, and I congratulate you most heartily on the finished product. I am consumed with admiration for the amount of detail and research that you have compiled within these pages. I predict a long and well-thumbed life for this volume and its subsequent companion. It will be quoted and requoted in all the years to come, and you can rest assured that you have made for yourself a lasting niche in the memories of all Chaplains, past and present."

After reading Volume II of my *History of the Chaplain Corps*, Chaplain Joshua Goldberg, the senior Jewish chaplain in the Navy, wrote: "It is my humble opinion that you have made a major contribution to the Chaplaincy — one that will not soon be forgotten."

In addition to these and other testimonials there were the reviews in the religious and secular press. Without exception these were highly favorable.

My last contribution to the written history of the Chaplain Corps came in the summer of 1958 when I was on active duty in the Chief's office for a month beginning July 1. At that time I began work on Volume VI of the *History of the Chaplain Corps,* which dealt with the work of the chaplains in the Korean War. I was able to write about one-third of the book before returning home and to outline what was to come. This work was completed by two of my successors — chaplains Paul S. Sanders and W. Ivan Hoy. After I left, several chaplains were assigned to the history project for varying periods of time. At present, Cmdr. H. Lawrence Martin, ChC, USN is the historian, and for several years has been giving full time to this activity.

Chaplain Martin visited me at my home in Pasadena on November 12, 1980 and remained for three days interviewing me on an "Oral History" project. After returning to his office in Washington the tapes were transcribed and corrected. Chaplain Martin added some pictures and some further information about my work in the Chaplain Corps and had it all bound into a book which contained 118 pages.

On the evening of November 30, 1982 a reception and dinner was held in my honor at the Officers Mess on Terminal Island, Long Beach, California. About sixty-five were in attendance, including Rear Admiral Neil Stevenson, ChC, USN, Deputy Chief of Chaplains, and also Chaplain H. Lawrence Martin. Also present was the Captain of the battleship New Jersey, which has recently been brought back into service. At this time the book prepared by Chaplain Martin was presented to me. In this book I added some information about how I happened to be able to write the *History of the Chaplain Corps.* The evening marked a highlight in my life. My wife was unable to attend because of ill health, but my grandson, Marcus Drury, age 24, and his mother, Shirley Drury, were present.

A Short Tour of Sea Duty

San Francisco Theological Seminary granted me sabbatic leave for the school year 1948-49. I returned to Washington on July 1, 1948 to continue work on my Chaplain Corps history. After finishing the writing of Volume II of the narrative, I found that I had some extra time on my hands. I felt the need of having some sea duty. With the exception of the Jewish chaplains, I was the only one in the Chaplain Corps who had attained the rank of Captain without having had some sea duty. I felt free to be gone for several months without inconveniencing my wife. I decided to investigate the possibility of getting a short term appointment as chaplain on some Navy vessel.

I approached Chaplain Stanton Salisbury, then Chief of Chaplains, with my idea and he approved. It was understood that there would be no pay involved, but that I would be able to travel around the Mediterranean and through Europe, and then return to the States by

Navy planes without cost. Salisbury made inquiries to see if there was a vacancy on some Navy vessel which usually had a chaplain, but there was none. He then learned that a large fleet oiler, the Allagash, which was 553 feet long and displaced 25,000 tons fully loaded, was to carry high test gasoline to the Sixth Fleet then at Gibraltar. He knew the Captain — John N. Kennaday — who expressed willingness to take me aboard.

I went aboard on Thursday, August 25th, 1949 and was assigned to a comfortable private cabin located about mid-ship. I met Captain Kennaday whom I described in my diary as "a fine Christian gentleman." He was an Episcopalian. The ship had a complement of 225. The Captain kindly invited me to take my meals at his table which was located in his private quarters.

When I left my home in San Anselmo I took with me my blue uniform, my gray uniform, and only one white uniform. Captain Kennaday always wore his white uniform for dinner. I was in a quandry as to what to do, as I could not wear one white uniform all the time. Captain Kennaday, however, made arrangements for one of the sailors to take my white uniform in the evening, wash it, and have it ready for me the next day.

We left Norfolk Friday, August 26th, for Corpus Christi where the ship was loaded. We then headed for Gibraltar. We ran into high seas, but I had no loss of appetite. I took my dinner every evening with the Captain.

An item in my diary for August 29th is as follows: "A sailor came to my cabin at 1400 which was the hour set for the funeral service of his father back in Minnesota. We had a short service of our own." My records show that I had about thirty out for each of my Sunday morning services. Captain Kennaday always took part by reading the scripture.

When we arrived at Gibraltar we joined the Sixth U.S. Navy fleet and suddenly I discovered that I was the ranking chaplain for the fleet.

I was able to see the sights of Gibraltar in a day or so, and since the ship was to be in port for at least another week, I decided to make a trip to Seville. But, before leaving Gibraltar, I secured from the Spanish Consul there a visa to enter Spain. At that time the U.S. had not recognized Spain.

I changed into my civilian clothes and was taken by one of the ship's boats across the bay to Algieries, which was in Spanish territory. There I was able to buy a ticket for a bus ride to Seville. I remember the evening when I arrived in Algieries having dinner in a restaurant, sitting near an open window. A crowd of boys, ages two to fourteen, soon gathered outside the window and begged for my bread, saying in Spanish, "La pan." They were hungry and I gave them all but one piece of bread.

I made the trip to Seville on a 1924 Reo bus. There were three classes of passengers — first and second class were privileged to ride inside; the third class rode outside on top of the bus. The bus had very poor brakes; I recall that we ran over several turkeys enroute. In Seville I was able to get a room in the King Alfonso XII Hotel for $2.00 a night. I visited the famous Archives of the Indies where some two million documents were stored, including letters from the Spanish explorers and priests in the new world. At the time I visited the Archives there was a woman there from Bancroft Library in Berkeley making microfilm of the records pertaining to California. She introduced me to the librarian who could not speak English. The librarian asked me if there was something particular I would like to see, and I replied that I would like to see the letters of Christopher Columbus. He brought out two bundles of letters; it gave me a thrill just to hold them in my hands.

After leaving Glbraltar the ship headed for Italy. I understood the ship might have to go to the Persian Gulf to get a cargo of gasoline, so I decided to leave the ship at Naples on October 6th. I remember that the Captain made it possible for me to avoid customs at Naples simply by putting me in a boat and rowing me ashore. At soon as I landed I was surrounded by a crowd of young men evidently all unemployed. One could speak a little English, and I hired him to take me to see the Navy Chaplain on duty there.

While in Naples I was able to visit Pompeii again, which my wife and I had seen in the summer of 1927 enroute to Edinburgh. The Navy Chaplain helped me make arrangements to go by train to Marseilles. I stopped off in Milan and at Pisa to see the Leaning Tower, which I climbed somewhat fearfully since it was leaning at what I thought was a rather dangerous angle.

From Milan I continued on to Marseilles where I had a few days free and decided to visit Avignon which was the seat of one of the Popes during the years 1309-78. This was during the time when the papacy was divided. At Marseilles I was able to get a ride on a Navy plane which was enroute to Morocco.

One day while at Gibraltar, I met an English man who was in his government's consular service. He asked me where I was from. I replied: "California." He then asked: "Where in California?" I replied "Marin County," to which he replied: "I served for a time as the English Consul in San Francisco and lived on Bolinas Avenue in San Anselmo.' I quickly replied: "We live at 118 Bolinas Avenue." We had lived almost across the street from each other. He gave me his card; he was the British Consul at Rabat, and urged me to visit him should I ever go to Morocco.

So, when I landed unexpectedly at Port Lyautey, Morocco, I remembered his invitation. Rabat was within easy driving distance of Port Lyautey. The Navy Chaplain at Lyautey got in touch with the English Consul who kindly invited us both to drive down for luncheon. When we entered his home, I was delighted to see pictures of Marin County hanging on his walls — the Golden Gate Bridge, Muir Woods, and Mt. Tamalpais. This is a small world!

After spending several days in Morocco I was able to get a ride on a Navy plane leaving for Washington. We stopped enroute at the Azores and at a base in Newfoundland, and then on to Washington, D.C., where I arrived near the end of October in 1949.

PRESBYTERIAN PANORAMA

In 1947 The Board of National Missions of the Presbyterian Church looked forward to its Sesquicentennial which would come in 1952, and they appointed a committee to make preparations for a proper observance of that anniversary. I was made a member of that committee. Dr. Herman N. Morse, then Secretary of the Board, indicated a need for a comprehensive history of the Board, and at the November 1948 meeting of this committee I was asked to write the history. They agreed to pay me $350.00 a month, plus all transportations costs.

None of my books was written under such pressure of time as this one, for I was still working on one of my Navy books and also had some teaching duties at the San Francisco Theological Seminary.

The lineage of the Board of National Missions goes back to 1802 when the General Assembly of the infant denomination appointed a Standing Committee of Missions. This Board Committee became the Board of Missions in 1916. Through the years that followed, the name was changed to the Board of Domestic Missions, then to the Board of Home Missions, and finally to the Board of National Missions. It was the oldest of the official agencies of the United Presbyterian Church. Today the name of the Board of National Missions has disappeared in the reorganization of the church. The geographical expansion of this denomination from the Atlantic to the Pacific and from Canada to Mexico is largely due to the activities of this Board under its various names.

After spending several months at home in San Anselmo, I returned East and spent all of the month of August 1950 in the Historical Department of the Presbyterian Church which was then located in one of the upper floors of Witherspoon Building. This depository now is housed in its own building at 425 Lombard Street, Philadelphia, with Wm. Miller as Director. At his request I am depositing many of the documents used in the writing of this autobiography in this Department of History.

Before my arrival in Philadelphia, I wrote to Charles Anderson, then Director of the Department, asking him to have one of his staff remove from the shelves all of the items pertaining to each of the Synods of the denomination and place them in chronological order on a long table in a reference room. I was then planning to write a brief history of each Synod, giving the name of the first Presbyterian minister to settle within the Synod and the name and date of the organizations of the first Presbytery and Synod in the area.

When I arrived, the books and papers containing the history of the various synods were neatly arranged in alphabetical order on a long table. I started with the story of Alabama and worked my way around the table to Wyoming, in each case giving the name of the first Presbyterian minister to settle in the area, the dates of the first Presbytery and Synod, and other pertinent items of interest. This appeared in a forty-eight page Appendix A to my *Presbyterian Panorama*. It became a useful guide to many Presbyterian bodies wishing to celebrate some significant anniversary.

In 1803 the Standing Committee of Missions appointed the Reverend Gideon Blackburn to be its first missionary to the Indians. He was sent to the Cherokees in what is now Tennessee. Either Blackburn or one of his successors left a spelling book in the schoolhouse when obliged to leave. An illiterate Cherokee Indian by the name of George Guess picked up the abandoned book. He called each page a "talking leaf." He reasoned that each letter represented a sound, but he was unable to distinguish between vowels and consonants. To him each letter represented what we call syllables. He assigned a syllable of his language to each, but since there were some seventy or more syllables in his language, as is also true of the English language, Guess had to devise additional signs to complete the syllabary. He taught his writing to a daughter and proved to the other members of the tribe that he had devised a written language for his people — a script which is still being used by his people.

George Guess's Indian name was Sequoia. In the early history a botanist — I believe he came from Austria — was naming the big trees of California. He also happened to be a student of languages and knew of the work of Sequoia in reducing his language to a written form; so he named the big redwoods after this Cherokee Indian — Sequoia Sempervirons for the smaller redwoods which grew along the coast; and Sequoia Gigantic for the mammoth redwoods which grew in the mountains near Yosemite Park.

I spent June and July at work on my Navy project, and then, after picking up a new car at Flint, Michigan, I met my daughter, Patricia, at Flint and drove her to Warren Wilson College in North Carolina where she spent the following scholastic year. I then returned to New York to continue research in the rooms of the National Mission Society.

My other duties kept me from giving full time to the writing of my Panorama book. By August 1951 I reported to Dr. Anderson of the Presbyterian Historical Society that I had written about 40,000 words that month and still had about 10,000 to go. I was informed that the deadline for my manuscript was September 13, 1951. Since the book was to be published by the Westminster Press and had to be ready for sale by April 15, 1952, I was working under pressure. But I secured the aid of a good stenographer and was able to meet the deadline. The Press brought out about 3,000 volumes with red binding and red jacket. It contained 458 pages and sold for $3.75.

The reviews were highly commendatory. Dr. Lefferts A. Loetscher of Princeton Theological Seminary wrote in the *Westminster Bookman* of September 1952: "This substantial volume is a mine of actual information about almost every conceivable phase of Presbyterian National Missions." Dr. W. C. Lamott, one of my fellow members on the faculty at San Anselmo, wrote in the June 1952 copy of the *Seminary Chimes:* "The selection of materials is superb, an indication of marvelous self-restraint on the part of the author, whose love for detail is well known."

According to a report from the Board, dated September 17, 1953, nearly 2,000 copies had been sold. Within a couple of years, the entire edition was exhausted.

I was the lecturer for five traveling seminars sponsored by the Presbyterian Board of Foreign Missions. These seminars took me into the states of California, Oregon, Washington, Utah, Idaho and Vancouver, B.C. We usually had enough to fill a thirty-five passenger bus. I remember that once we visited Talmaks, the camp ground of the Nez Perces churches. I had been telling the members of the seminar about the Nez Perce Indians. When we arrived at Talmaks, one of the Indian women, the widow of an Indian preacher — Rev. James Dickson — rushed to me, threw her arms around my neck and kissed me. Evidently memories of yesterdays had swept over her, for I had known her husband, and her son had been one of my students at San Anselmo. One of the members of the seminar, who saw what had happened to me, said: "Well, it is quite evident that you know your Indians."

In the summer of 1951 the Synod of Oregon celebrated its 100th anniversary. I wrote the script for the play which was presented one evening. The Synod met at Lewis and Clark College in Portland.

THE DRURY FAMILY, 1955
Left to right: Robert, Phillip, Gloria (Robert's wife),
Clifford (front), Patricia and Miriam.

GENEVA HALL AND STEWART MEMORIAL CHAPEL
San Francisco Theological Seminary, San Anselmo, California.

CHAPTER TWENTY-FOUR

Major Events of 1955-1963

My activities during the years 1955-1963 centered in three main areas — (1) the Seminary, (2) further writing for the Navy, and (3) writing and publishing my books.

The Seminary experienced phenomenal growth during the years that Dr. Jesse H. Baird served as president, 1937-1957. The student body increased from about seventy to over 300. A road was built around the hill which gave greater freedom of access to the top of the knoll, which was about sixty feet high. Two castle-like buildings had been erected there in 1890-91. One was Scott Hall which contained classrooms and a library, and the other was the three-story Montgomery Hall, which contained dormitory rooms for the men. A kitchen and dining room were in the basement. Now Geneva Hall and Stewart Memorial Chapel were built at the top of the knoll. Geneva Hall contained reading and class rooms and space for at least 100,000 books. These two buildings, which were joined together, were dedicated October 14-15, 1952.

Dr. Thomas Holden, a graduate of the Seminary and one of its trustees, was responsible for the design of the stained glass windows in the chancel. The rose window carried symbols that referred to the Reformation. The two windows in the chancel majored on the Old and New Testaments. I was asked to design the twenty-six windows in the nave. Each window had seven medallions — a large oval picture in the center with four small round medallions at each corner and a square or triangular medallion at the top and another at the bottom. The windows were made by the Wallis Wiley Studio in Pasadena.

Twenty-five of the windows were dedicated to Presbyterian pioneers in the six western states with smaller medallions referring to Hawaii and Alaska. Henry and Eliza Spalding were each remembered, as well as Marcus and Narcissa Whitman. The twenty-sixth window was dedicated to Sir Francis Drake and his chaplain Francis Fletcher. The first Protestant service in what is now the United States was conducted by Chaplain Fletcher on June 24, 1579 at some point near what is now called Drake's Bay, about thirty miles north of San Francisco. The top medallion of this window pictured the Russian church at Fort Ross and the Roman Catholic mission at Sonoma founded in 1824. When the mission was dedicated on April 4, 1824, the Russians took part in the service. This mission was the meeting place of the Eastern Orthodox Church and the Roman Catholic

Church. The world was then encircled with the gospel. The twenty-six windows contained 182 medallions, each with some historical interest. The windows were dedicated on May 26, 1955.

Other buildings erected on the seminary's campus during the presidency of Dr. Baird were three apartment halls for married students — Landon, Hunter and Oxtoby — an administration building, and Alexander Hall which contained a dining room and kitchen.

Beginning about 1952, and continuing for the following eleven years, I led caravans of students to Drake's Bay. We would stop at Olema enroute where the effects of the San Francisco earthquake of 1906 could clearly be seen. At that point the earth moved westward and northward for some seven or more feet. A road was divided. Whole trees were moved. All of the area west of the San Andreas fault, which includes the Pt. Reyes Peninsula has been called an island in time. The geological formation of this peninsula is the same as that of the Tehachapi mountains. It moves northward at about three inches a year.

In January 1954 the pastor of the First Presbyterian Church of Burlingame invited me to give a series of four lectures on our history. The subjects were "Why We Are Christians," "Why We Are Protestants," "Why We Are Presbyterians," and "Our Heritage On the Pacific Coast." The average attendance at these lectures was 300, and I received $100.00, plus travel expenses, for the series. I gave the series twenty-five times in as many churches before I was retired. After coming to Monte Vista Grove Homes at the end of 1963, I was again called upon to give these lectures, and did so another twenty-five times.

During the latter part of February, 1957, the Seminary offered me $150.00 a month if I would vacate the house where we had been living at 118 Bolinas Avenue. It was much too large for my wife and myself, and because of the expanding faculty, there was need for the house. After some investigation we bought a lot for $6,950.00 in Greenbrae which was near the highway that led to San Francisco. We signed a contract with a builder to erect a three bedroom house on this lot, which cost us about $18,000.00. I had to borrow all that I could from my government insurance, and take out a loan at the bank for the balance. Building was started on March 28, 1957; we moved on May 18th. My study had shelves for my 3,000 volume library. We sold the house, with some appliances, for $38,000.00 before we came to Pasadena. Recently I heard that it had resold for $150,000.00.

From the very beginning of my work at San Anselmo, I took a special interest in the library. Even though funds to buy new books were small — my allotment for church history got down to $25.00 a year — still I was able to collect many volumes from interested friends.

I took special delight in adding books to the rare book room. I found several copies in duplicate at the Huntington Library at San Marino which I visited when I was at Occidental College. Among the treasures was a copy of the first complete Bible printed by the Valdus Press in 1518. I bought some pages of an imperfect Gutenberg Bible for $400.00 from a man in Brazil who made more by selling individual pages than he ever would have by selling the imperfect copy. How I got the money I do not now know.

One of my unique experiences is worthy of special mention. In 1845 Andrew Rodgers joined a small group of Oregon-bound emigrants. He stopped off at the Whitman mission where he was welcomed and made the school teacher. Rodgers was a member of the Associate Presbyterian Church, one of the branches of the Scottish Covenanter movement, but after his arrival at Waiilatpu, he joined the Mission church. He was a deeply religious man and after his arrival at Waiilatpu decided to study for the ministry. The Mission appointed Elkanah Walker to supervise his studies, and on May 15, 1846, Whitman wrote to the Board in Boston and ordered eleven text books including six for his Hebrew and Greek studies. The books arrived at Waiilatpu in the fall of 1847.

Rodgers was one of the fourteen who lost their lives at the time of the Whitman massacre which began on November 2, 1847. At the time the forty-seven captives were rescued by the Hudson's Bay Company on January 2, 1848, most of the captives were able to take their personal belongings with them.

Someone took the books that had belonged to Andrew Rodgers. After the rescued captives arrived at Oregon City, the question arose as to what should be done with the books that had belonged to Rodgers. Someone suggested that they be given to the Rev. Wilson Blaine, a pioneer minister of the Associate Presbyterian Church who had arrived in Oregon a few years previously.

A few weeks after my family and I had moved to San Anselmo in the late summer of 1938, we visited my brother, Billy Drury, and his family in San Leandro. While there I learned that a grandson of Wilson Blaine lived in San Leandro. I called on him and was given an apple box full of books that had belonged to his grandfather. While unloading the books after I returned to San Anselmo, I came across an old Greek Lexicon. It so happened that Dr. Wicher was passing by at the time. I showed him the Greek Lexicon and asked if it was worth anything since it had been printed before 1846. Dr. Wicher gave the book a cursory glance and then said: "It might be worth ten cents," and gave it back to me. I then opened the book and found written on the fly leaf, in his handwriting, the name "Andrew Rodgers." Here was one of the few remaining genuine relics

of the Whitman massacre. This book is now in the museum at the
Whitman Mission National Historic Site.

SAN ANSELMO ACTIVITIES

I was happy in my teaching responsibilities and had from ten
to fifteen class hours a week with over 1,500 students during my
teaching years. After my retirement in 1963 I taught Presbyterian
Polity and History at Fuller Theological Seminary in Pasadena for
five terms.

For more than ten years at San Anselmo I was in charge of the
Wednesday Assembly at which time we heard representatives of the
various Boards and Synods and other distinguished speakers. Hearing
that Alexander Kerensky, who headed the only democratic government in Russia, was at Leland Stanford University, I wrote to him
and asked if he would speak at our Wednesday Assembly. He kindly
consented to do so, and thus I had the opportunity of getting him at
Palo Alto and taking him back. I remember asking him how he managed to escape from Russia when all of the other members of his
cabinet were either killed or captured. He explained how the peasants
shielded him; he went through Finland and then travelled to the
United States.

Dr. Baird had the custom of giving each faculty member the names
of twenty or twenty-five students for whom he was to be the advisor.
Miriam and I invited those whose names were given to us to a social
hour in our home on Wednesday evening, October 23rd. While serving ice cream, I started around one end of the table just as a student
shifted his chair. One leg of the chair came down on the outside of
my right foot. I spun around in an effort to save the dishes of ice
cream and went down on my back. One of the dishes was broken, but
the other was not. But more seriously, the tibia in my right leg was
broken.

I was taken that evening to the Marin General Hospital where the
leg was set and put into a cast which reached from the bottom of
my foot to nar the hip. The doctor said the cast weighed only five
pounds, but it seemed like fifty to me. I was told that I would have
to wear it for three months. I was using crutches the second day and
was home after six days. I was able to drive my car using my left
foot. The leg healed well.

ANOTHER TRIP TO EUROPE

In 1956 I enjoyed a sabbatic leave from my teaching at San Anselmo. I returned to Washington and continued work on Volume V
of the Chaplains Corps history. I was then recording the events
which had taken place in the Corps and bringing the Who's Who up

to date. I asked for, and received, orders to travel to Europe by Navy transportation. I received no pay for this journey and it was limited to four weeks.

I had two reasons for going. First, I wanted to write a report of Navy chaplains at work in Bremerhaven, Naples, and London. Secondly, I knew that in 1959 Presbyterian/Reformed churches around the world would be remembering the 400th anniversary of Presbyterian polity, for in that year the first Synod met in Paris. I dreamed of editing a book which would contain chapters by reputable historians from each country which had a Presbyterian or Reformed church. In English speaking countries the word Presbyterian is used, whereas on the continent the word Reformed is used. Among the Protestants, there are more Presbytrians/Reformed than any other denomination. The Lutherans would come next, but they are largely limited to Germany and the Scandinavian countries. I wanted to contact Church History professors in various countries to get their cooperation.

Having secured Navy air transportation on a space available basis that left Washington on February 20, 1956, we touched down in Newfoundland, then on to Paris. From Paris I flew to Frankfurt where I arrived on the 22nd. I visited a replica of Guttenberg's shop and learned that he did not invent moveable type, but rather type metal . . . when lead is heated, it expands; when antimony is heated, it contracts. By putting these two metals together, Guttenberg found a metal which could be poured in a mold and keep its shape.

From Frankfurt I flew to Bremerhaven where I was housed in the quarters of the former German naval commander, Admiral Donetz. While there the Navy chaplains suggested that I go to Berlin. I had never dreamed of going there, but readily gave consent. A nightly train ran from Bremerhaven to Berlin. My chaplain friends soon got official permission for me to go through Eastern Germany; also they made arrangements with some American officials in Berlin to take care of me. I stayed in a military barracks for $1.00 a day. In Berlin I was given use of a car with a driver who took me wherever I wanted to go. I sought an interview with Bishop Otto Dibelius, who was in charge of all Protestant work in both East and West Germany. I also was taken to see the impressive Russian monument to their dead in East Berlin. The wall dividing the city had not been built. I visited a refugee camp where people fleeing from East Germany by the subway were temporarily housed. I remember asking a German young woman why she had come; she replied that she wanted to avoid being drafted into the army.

I spent about two busy days in Berlin and then went back to

Bremerhaven. From there I flew to Naples to study the work being done there by Navy chaplains. While in Naples, I was able to visit the ruins of Pompeii again. Then I went to London via Geneva and Paris. While in London I got in touch with a former student, Conway Lanford, an Army Chaplain. He took me in his car to the village of Hawstead, the Drury's ancestral home. The first Drury in England came with William the Conqueror in 1060. He was from a village in Normandy called Rouvray — hence the name DeRouvray or Drury. It lies in Suffolk County near Bury St. Edmunds.

My report on the work of the Navy Chaplains in Bremerhaven, Naples and London was never printed.

400 YEARS OF WORLD PRESBYTERIANISM

During this trip to Europe I had interviews with faculty members of eight different seminaries, including the Waldensians in Rome and the Reformed in Geneva, Paris and London. In England I visited both Oxford and Cambridge. Dr. Marcel Pradervand, Secrtary of the World Alliance of Presbyterians/Reformed church, was of great help to me in supplying names and addresses of church historians in the various countries around the world.

I also visited Scotland and North Ireland. I returned to the States on an Air Force plane which left from Prestwick, Scotland and arrived back in Washington on March 17th. The total cost to me for the entire trip was about $900.00.

As I recall, I received some twenty-two different chapters from as many different countries. I wrote the account of Presbyterians in the United States. Altogether these chapters contained about 400,000 words. I sought to get help from some Presbyterian agency without success. Dr. Robert E. Speer, for many years General Secretary of the Presbyterian Board of Foreign Missions, read the manuscripts and strongly recommended their publication. The publication of the work demanded a subsidy which I was unable to provide. Finally, I decided to have the material microfilmed. I wrote to the Librarian asking if I could copyright a microfilm. He replied, saying it never had been done, but he saw no reason why I could not do so. I did it. I made about thirty copies and advertised them for $10.00 each in several church historical publications. Copies went into the principal libraries of the country. I made no money on this venture. Several of the chapters were published in the Journal of the Presbyterian Historical Society.

A TRIP TO HAWAII

I learned that it was possible to get a free trip, with the exception of the cost of meals, to Honolulu for myself and my wife on one of the Navy cargo ships which plied between San Francisco and Honolulu. I put in my application for a cabin on October 14, 1959, on the U.S.N. Gaffey scheduled to sail on Wednesday, December 2nd. I was told that all seven of the cabins set aside for non-active military personnel were already taken, but if there was a cancellation I would be notified. We made preparations to go, believing there would be a cancellation, by making arrangements with a student to drive us to the wharf where the ship would be berthed and to look after our house while we were gone.

On the day the ship was to sail, we were notified at 10:10 a.m. that one cabin was available, but that we would have to be at Fort Mason at 1:30 that day. We hastily called the student and finished packing our bags. It was little less than an hour's ride from our home in Greenbrae to Ft. Mason, which was near the southern end of the Golden Gate bridge. After eating a hastily prepared lunch, we left about 12:00 o'clock for the ship. At 3:00 p.m. the ship sailed under the Golden Gate bridge, and we were on our way to Honolulu.

Even though the sea was rough, we did not get sea-sick. Indeed we had encircled the globe by water without getting sea-sick. Both of us were delighted with the ocean voyage.

The ship docked in Honolulu at 7:30 p.m. Decmber 7, 1959. I spent some time in the library of the Hawaiian Mission Children's Society where I found a number of letters written by the members of the American Board's mission to Oregon. The Hawaiian Mission was founded by this Board in 1820. This was the same Board which sent the Whitmans and Spaldings to Oregon in 1836. The Hawaiian Mission supplied the Oregon missionaries with sugar, molasses, and finally the printing press which Spalding used at Lapwai. The press is now in the Oregon Historical Society in Portland, Oregon.

On Monday we flew to Hilo on the big island of Hawaii for a three-day outing. We took a bus for the thirty mile ride to the Kilauea military camp established to provide "rest and recreation" to the military. It was at an elevation of 4,000 feet and within a couple of miles of Volcano House near the mouth of Kilauea volcano. We were given a comfortable cabin, paid for our own meals; it was a delightful experience.

The first night after our arrival, we were awakened by the management saying that the Kilauea volcano was erupting, and they were providing a bus to go to see it. We hastily dressed and soon were standing with others on the edge of the big depression about a mile from the volcano which was shooting molten lava some 800 feet into the air. Although we were a mile away, we could feel the heat. We could see it, feel it, smell it, and hear it — an awesome sight.

Standing near us was a mother with her young son, perhaps four or five years old. We heard him ask: "Mother, where are the fire engines?"

The volcano continued active for about two weeks. Sometimes it would die down completely, and then again it would shoot up to 1,700 feet. The temperature of the lava was about 2,100F, which means that it then flowed like water.

We saw the mongooses which were imported from India to prey on the rats; but the rats climbed trees to safety and continued to multiply. The mongooses stayed on the ground and also multiplied.

After three thrilling days on the big island of Hawaii, we flew back to Honolulu. Not being able to return to the mainland by ship, we secured passage on one of the Navy planes which was due to leave on Thursday morning, December 24th. We left Honolulu at 7:30 a.m. and had a ten hour ride to Travis Air Base near Vallejo, California. We had made no arrangements to get home, but an officer at the base detailed a car to take us the forty or so miles to our house. We arrived there about 9:30 on Christmas eve, delighted to be home again. We found our youngest son, Phil, there. We were away just twenty days, from December 4 to the 24th.

California Imprints, 1846-1876

When I began teaching Church History at San Francisco Theological Seminary in the fall of 1938, I found myself at a loss to provide church history text books. The excellent six-volume work on the History of the Christian Church by Philip Schaff was long out of print. Through advertising in Seminary publications, I secured some copies from former students. I had more difficulty in getting suitable texts for American Church History. I used W. W. Sweet's book, "The History of the American Church," but that only gave one or two paragraphs on the history west of the Rocky Mountains; so I decided to write a History of Christianity on the Pacific Coast.

I began by making 3x5 cards listing author and subject and location. I wanted information about writings by ministers, or others, on social, educational and religious subjects. I also wanted a list of early newspapers and their locations. I started with the date of 1846 with a proclamation of Captain John Montgomery prohibiting the holding of slaves in California. The only known copy is one that I found in the National Archives, Washington, D.C. I ended my study with 1876 when the first volume of F. Leypold's volume *United States Catalog* appeared. I felt that such a bibliography as I planned to write would be necessary to anyone who sought to write a history of Christianity in California.

I worked on this project for several years. I secured the services of a fine young woman typist who typed up the cards. The main bibliography contained 958 items printed in California. There followed three appendices. The first contained 59 items relating to items printed outside of California during the years under review, which bore upon the religious, educational, and social history of the state. Appendix II contained a list of 43 religious periodicals or newspapers printed within the state. Appendix III contained a list of 36 manuscripts, books, and pamphlets printed after 1876. This brought the total to 1,096. 'I checked with 77 libraries or depositories.

The Arthur H. Clark Company of Glendale brought out 514 copies by the offset method in 1970 which sold for $10.00 a copy. The title page stated that the book was "Privately printed for the author." Moreover I indexed the Occident (the only complete file of which is in the San Francisco Theological Library) for the years 1869 to 1900, and the Pacific for the years 1851-1869. Microfilms of these indices were made which are in several libraries, including Huntington in San Marino, California. I never wrote a history of Christianity in California, but I feel that I laid the foundation for someone else to do so.

The book barely paid for itself, including what I paid the typist. This was a labor of love.

THE DIARY OF TITIAN RAMSEY PEALE

While working on my narrative history of the Chaplain Corps, I heard about a Navy chaplain who served under Lieutenant Charles Wilkes when he was sent out to explore the South Pacific and the west coast of what is now the United States. The expedition visited the Hawaiian Islands in 1840, where this chaplain committed some indiscretions which led to his dismissal. When the squadron arrived in San Francisco in 1841, the chaplain was discharged and sent back to the States. I was eager to find out the cause for the chaplain's dismissal, and so went to the Library of Congress to examine the Wilkes papers. I did not find what I wanted, but to my surprise, I did find a diary of Titian Ramsey Peale, the son of Charles Willson Peale, a well known portrait painter of the Revolutionary War period who founded a museum in Philadelphia. So far as I could discover, this portion of the diary which Titian was keeping had never been published..

While at San Francisco, Lt. Wilkes ordered one of the smaller ships of his squadron, the *Peacock,* to sail north on an exploring tour to the mouth of the Columbia River. Titian Peale was ordered to go on this vessel. The *Peacock* was wrecked on a bar at the mouth of the Columbia and became a total loss. The ship's company of nearly thirty men escaped, including Peale. The stranded crew made its way to Fort Vancouver where the officials of the Hudson's Bay Company provided supplies and horses for the inevitable overland trek to San Francisco.

The diary begins with an entry for September 22 when the party left for San Francisco, and continues to November 1 when they reached their destination. Knowing that Glen Dawson, proprietor of the Dawson Book Shop in Los Angeles was bringing out a series of small books on Early California Travels, I wrote to him in January 1955 suggesting that he take the Peale diary as one of the series. Dawson was interested. I supplied a transcript of the diary and I secured copies of several of Peale's paintings from Bancroft Library, Berkeley. The late Carl S. Dentzel, once Director of the Southwest Museum, Los Angeles, wrote about one-half of the twenty-five page introduction. The small book was published as No. 36 of Dawson's Early California Travel Series in a limited edition of 300 copies which sold for $10.00 each. I received no royalty, but was given five copies. The book was reviewed in the February, 1958, issue of the *Pacific Historical Review*. The reviewer stated: "The diary is rich in nature notes as well as in descriptions of experiences of the travelers."

This book was selected as one of the 50 "books of the year" by the American Institute of Graphic Arts, more because of its beautiful typography rather than its content.

DIARIES OF SPALDING AND SMITH, 1958

The first book of mine issued by the Arthur H. Clark Co. of Glendale dealing with the Oregon Mission of the American Board was *The Diaries and Letters of Henry H. Spalding and Asa B. Smith Relating to the Nez Perce Mission, 1838-1842,* which appeared in an edition of 1,200 copies in 1958. It contained 368 pages and sold for $12.50. The Spalding diary, the original of which is in Whitman College, ran to over 33,000 words; the Smith diary, now on deposit in Houghton Library, Harvard University, contains over 15,000 words. These diaries, together with related materials, cover four critical years, 1838-1842 in the history of the Whitman-Spalding mission.

Asa B. Smith had a choloric disposition. He joined the 1838 re-enforcement to the Oregon mission on the spur of the moment and deeply regretted his decision when only a few days out of Independence, Missouri; but it was then too late to turn back. Before the party of four couples and a single man arrived at Waiilatpu, the clash of personalities was so great that none of the other three couples wanted to be in the same station with him. Finally, Spalding consented to have the Smiths live with him at Lapwai.

In these diaries one sees Smith as the critic and Spalding as the criticized. There were differences of opinion as to how the mission work was to be pursued. Finally, in the summer of 1839, the Smiths moved some sixty miles up the Clearwater River and started a fourth station at Kamiah. This was contrary to the advice of all of his fellow workers. There the Smiths lived for about two years, enduring all manner of hardships. Their lives were threatened. Sarah Smith was in ill health. When they did leave in the spring of 1841, she was unable to ride a horse and had to be taken down the river in a canoe.

The two diaries, never before published, supplemented each other. Spalding reduced the language to writing; Smith compiled a dictionary and the grammar. In its review of this book which appeared in the *Chicago Westerners Brand Book*, the statement was made: "Probably no other single volume is quite so indispensable to an understanding of this episode in the history of the Northwest."

The book remained in stock for nearly eighteen years. I received no royalty on the first 500. After that I received 10%. My total royalties amounted to $834.96.

SAN FRANCISCO YMCA, 1853-1953
ONE HUNDRED YEARS BY THE GOLDEN GATE

Beginning in January, 1951, the Young Men's Christian Association, through its General Secretary, Roy Sorenson, invited me to write the one hundred year old history of this organization. I was to be paid $350.00 a month while working on this project, the same as when I wrote *Presbyterian Panorama*. Actually I spent some ten years before I turned over my manuscript of about 90,000 words. I spent about four months upon the project and received a little over $1,400.00 for my work. This was one of the hardest books I ever wrote, for I found it far more difficult to write about some organization than I did about people, living or dead.

San Francisco had a population of about 50,000 at the end of 1853. Most of them were men. About 34,000 had landed in 1853. Drawn by the lure of gold, they came from all over the world. The authors of *The Annals of San Francisco*, published in 1855, wrote: "San Francisco was, at the time we have discussed, and still is in a state of moral ferment . . . The scum and froth of its strange mixture of peoples, of its many scoundrels, rowdies and great men, loose women, sharpeers, and few honest folk, are still nearly all that is visible. The current of its daily life is muddied by the wild effervescence of these unruly spirits."

The Christian Advocate, a Methodist paper published in the city, reported that in 1853 a month before the YMCA was founded, that there were 537 places within the city where liquor was sold. With the rooming houses and hotels packed with young men, the gambling houses, bars, and brothels had a lucrative source of customers. Where was the lonesome young man to spend his leisure hours if not in the gaudily decorated dance hall or the richly festooned saloon? The city did not have a free library until June 1879. Motion pictures were then unknown. The whole amusement life of the city was monopolized by men whose primary motive was money and not morality.

In July 1855 San Francisco boasted of having eleven Protestant churches, several Roman Catholic churches, a Jewish synagogue, and one Unitarian church. The sum total of all the religious forces within San Francisco raised but a feeble dam against the moral turpitude which had engulfed the city. Among the few who were concerned for the spiritual welfare of the young men in particular was a young lawyer from Dayton, Ohio, William K. Osborn, who had joined the First Presbyterian Church in November 1850. After a residence of about three years in the city, Osborn felt that something should be done to help the young men. He found a few young men who shared his concerns and together they decided that it would be a good thing to form a YMCA. So it happened that on July 18, 1853, the San Francisco YMCA was founded with sixty-four charter members. This was the first YMCA to be organized west of New Orleans and the thirteenth in all of the United States.

Fortunately for me I had access to the original records which came through the earthquake and fire of 1906. The record books were in a safe and although the covers were badly scorched, the text was still readable. These, together with other source materials, provided the information necessary for this book. For eleven years, 1853-1864, the YMCA carried on its activities in rented quarters. A building was secured in 1864 at 522 California St. The Y made two more moves before the earthquake and fire of 1906. After the fire the Y erected its present handsome building at the corner of Golden Gate and Leavenworth.

In my history I traced out the significant events which occurred before the administration of Roy Sorenson in 1946. I turned in the finished manuscript on January 2, 1962, and the book of 256 pages, with cover, appeared in January 1963, in an edition of 1,000 copies, 500 copies in cloth and 500 in paper. The cloth bound copies sold for $8.00 per copy. The book was published by the Arthur H. Clark Company of Glendale which sold 226 copies, with a royalty of 75¢ for each volume turned over to me. The YMCA assumed the balance of the cost of printing. The reviews of the book were very favorable.

WILLIAM ANDERSON SCOTT — "NO ORDINARY MAN"

Shortly after I joined the faculty of San Francisco Theological Seminary, in the fall of 1933, I became aware that no serious study had been made of its founder — William Anderson Scott. As the years passed, the stronger became the conviction that I must write his biography, for he was the founder of the Seminary at San Anselmo. The coming of the Seminary's centennial in 1971 only increased my desire.

My first problem was to find source materials. My first discovery was three chests in the basement of Scott Hall, named for Dr. Scott. It appears that after Dr. Scott's death in January of 1885, the bulk of his manuscripts were given to his son-in-law, A. W. Foster, who lived in San Rafael. They filled three chests and were put into the basement of the Foster home. At some unknown time, fire broke out in the home and the basement was filled with water. No attempt was made to dry out the papers, and after many years the three chests were deposited in the basement of Scott Hall on the campus of San Francisco Theological Seminary. There they remained for more years. When I opened the chests, I saw the mass of dried out papers which gave off a pungent odor. Dr. Scott wrote out his sermons and class room lectures. Often he tore open envelopes which brought him his letters, and used the opened envelopes as scrap paper on which he wrote notes to be inserted into his lecture notes. I was able to peel off the stamps, some going back to the first ever issued by our post office department, and sell them. The money thus secured was used to pay for some paintings by Gregory Stapko which now hang in the library of Geneva Hall, San Anselmo. Most of the papers had disintegrated so badly that they were of no use, but I did find some items of value, such as the diary he kept when he was chaplain in the Black Hawk war, beginning in March 1832 when he was only nineteen years old. Most of the contents of the three chests had to be discarded.

A granddaughter of Dr. Scott was living in Marin County and had a collection of some 800 letters, which included copies of some letters written by Dr. Scott, as well as some he had received. I was hoping that she would give this collection to the Seminary, but instead she gave it to Bancroft Library in the University of California. I made many trips to Berkeley to read all of these letters and to make notes.

Since I was to have a sabbatic leave from the Seminary in the spring of 1962, my wife and I planned to spend it visiting the churches connected with Dr. Scott's ministry. I applied for scholarship aid of $600.00 from the American Philosophical Society of Philadelphia. My request was granted. I needed local color, so I planned to visit all of the parishes of Scott before he came to San Francisco in 1842. These included Opelusas, Louisiana where he was ordained a minister of the Cumberland Presbyterian Church on March 13, 1835; then to Winchester and Nashville, Tennessee where he spent four years; then to Tuscaloosa, Alabama for the next two years; and from there to New Orleans for the next twelve years, 1842-1854. From New Orleans he went to San Francisco. While in San Francisco, Scott founded Calvary Church, launched a religious magazine and started a college. Then, because of his sympathies for the Confederacy, he was forced to leave. After an exile of about eight years, 1861-1869, he returned to San Francisco where he founded St. John's Church and, in 1871, the San Francisco Theological Seminary.

Miriam and I left on Tuesday, February 27. We drove that day to Pasadena and visited Monte Vista Grove Homes where we completed our arragements to retire there at the end of 1963. MVGH is unique as it ministers exclusively to Presbyterian ministers, their wives or widows, and single woman church workers. It is located on a fifteen-acre campus and can accommodate about 175 residents. It has a forty-bed health center and a common dining room. The next day we started for El Paso, Texas. We visited Carlsbad caverns on Sunday, March 4th — an awesome experience.

We reached Opelusas on Wednesday, March 7th, but I found nothing there that applied to W. A. Scott. We arrived in New Orleans the afternoon of the same day. I called on Dr. Hunter, pastor of the First Presbyterian Church where Scott was pastor from 1842-1854. Dr. Hunter was very helpful to us, and I was able to get considerable material about Dr. Scott's ministry in that city. After spending more than a week in New Orleans, we left for Tuscaloosa where Dr. Bryant, pastor of the church Scott once served, was most helpful. I was invited to preach on Sunday, March 18th. Dr. Bryant was concerned about integration. When I preached, some men of the congregation were stationed at each entrance to keep Negroes out.

From Tuscaloosa, we headed for Miami, but took a sight-seeing trip to Key West, and then arrived at Miami on Saturday, March 24th. There I parked the car, and on Monday, the 26th, Miriam and I flew to Jamaica to visit Paul Rice and his wife. Paul was in my Moscow church. He was in the U.S. service as an entomologist on Jamaica. We flew on a Dutch airline which came down in Havana, Cuba, but the passengers were not allowed to leave the plane. We spent a delightful week in Jamaica. I was invited to speak in a Congregational church on Sunday, April 1st. About 7% of the congregation of 350 were white; the others were black. They had no guards at the doors to keep the whites out. Because of our friendship with the Rices, we saw much more of Jamaica than the average tourist sees.

Then back to the mainland where we resumed our journey to the north. Near St. Augustine I took a side trip to see the monument to Ribault who led a party of French Huguenots to the mouth of St. John's River in 1562. No minister was in the party, and the little colony was wiped out by the Catholics, who were in St. Augustine, sometime after 1565. Thus ended the first contact of Protestant Christianity within America.

From St. Augustine we drove to Montreat, North Carolina, where the Southern Presbyterian Church maintains its historical depository. Here I had opportunity to study Presbyterian records, including the original minutes of the First Presbyterian Church of New Orleans during Dr. Scott's ministry. From Montreal we drove into eastern Tennessee visiting Nashville and the home of General Andrew Jackson. For a time Scott, as a young man, was pastor of the Heritage Church on General Jackson's estate. After a disastrous fire, thought to be incendiary, the church was rebuilt, and I was asked to give the dedicatory address on May 1, 1969. Loaded with new materials, I felt ready to begin writing.

On our way home from Tennessee we stopped in Early, Iowa to visit relatives, then on to Kansas City to see our son Bob and his family, and then on to Ghost Ranch in New Mexico. By the second week of May we were back home. I was able to write about 25,000 words on the Scott story before school opened. We celebrated our 40th wedding anniversary on November 17th, and more and more we were thinking of retiring to MVGH at the end of 1963.

The Arthur H. Clark Company of Glendale accepted the manuscript and brought out an edition of 2,500 copies in 1967. The book had an attractive jacket, and was to sell for $6.50. The size of the edition was large because I thought that the Seminary would help in its sale, since it appeared so near the centennial of the Seminary. In this I was disappointed. The low price was made possible by a subsidy of $3,000.00 given by Mrs. Martha Abbot, a granddaughter of Dr. Scott. In spite of most favorable reviews, sales, after the first 1,500 copies were sold, lagged. On April 13, 1970, I reported to Mrs. Abbot that the Clark Company still had 1,187 copies on hand. Many copies were given free to colleges and individuals. I bought 100 copies which I gave to the Seminary for promotional purposes. Even though the sales were disappointing, I consider this to be one of my best books.

CHAPTER TWENTY-FIVE

Retirement

On Thanksgiving Day, 1962, Mr. McDill, Director of Monte Vista Grove Homes in Pasadena, called me and stated that the party who was to occupy the other half of our duplex wanted to build at once, and if we wanted the other half, we would have to act at once. I passed my sixty-fifth birthday on November 7, 1962; so was eligible for retirement. However, I found great joy in my teaching and was happy in my relationships at the Seminary; yet we both wanted the site we had picked out on the campus of MVGH on El Nido street. It was hard to say: "Go ahead, we will pay our share of the cost of building the duplex." We were given about 1,200 square feet. The Grove let us plan the interior. The building was started in the spring of 1963. The building was to cost about $22,000.00. It would have a large living room, two bedrooms, one bath, tile roof, and an enclosed porch about ten by twelve feet.

The building was completed in September, and we moved that month. Our home in Greenbrae was put up for sale, and we sold it the next spring. Miriam stayed alone in Pasadena while I returned to complete my fall teaching and to live in the empty house at 25 Via Hermosa, Greenbrae. I made several trips to Pasadena, each time packing the car with as many of my books as possible. I would go down Friday and return on Sunday or Monday. The life was lonely for each, but Miriam preferred it to having the house always opened for would-be buyers.

I was past my 66th birthday when I was retired. We came to Monte Vista Grove Homes in the late fall of 1963. In August 1978 I suffered a moderate heart attack and went into the hospital, called my former daughter-in-law and my grandson, Marcus, to call on me, which they did. Since then we have developed a warm relationship. In the summer of 1982 I found that I had diabetes. We decided to move into two units which were empty and connected so that I could be near the dining room and health center. It was one of the wisest things we ever did. It was hard to give up our home at 403 El Nido, but it had to be done. I turned my car over to Marcus, and we gave him our big Persian rug and other furniture. Marcus calls on me at least once a week and is able to run errands for me. My diabetes is ever with me.

After bing retired I was able to establish a warm relationship with Dr. John Bonner, pastor of the Christ Presbyterian Church in Lakewood, California. This church holds a midwinter conference at its

retreat house at Crestline in the mountains north of San Bernardino.
I was able to be the featured speaker for at least ten times.

I often appeared before service clubs and spoke at least five times
before the Los Angeles Corral of Westerners, and six times before the
Crown City Kiwanis Club. In 1982 I received a pin signifying I had
attended Kiwanis Club regularly for twenty-one years. After retirement I had ten more books published by the Arthur H. Clark Co.
and twenty-four articles were published in magazines.

Our son, Phil, died on March 29, 1969. In September 1978 I baptized Marcus Drury and his mother Shirley in the San Marino Community Church.

Some time in the summer of 1980 I heard that the Community
Church in Shanghai which was built during my pastorate, and dedicated on March 8, 1925, had been turned back to the Christian Chinese. I wrote to the pastor, Shen-Yi-fan, and learned from him that
he and his assistants were holding two services every Sunday in the
church with about 1,000 attending each time. I was greatly pleased
to hear this. When I was pastor the most we could get into the church
at any one time was 600, but now the church is packed and people
stand. I hear there are more Christians in China now than before the
Revolution.

After retirement I began getting my church pension, social security,
and Navy retirement pay, which together about equalled the salary
($10,000.00) the Seminary was giving me at the time of retirement.
Our house was not sold until the spring of 1964. It had to stand
empty for several months. I had gotten rid of many of my books;
I once had a library of 3,000 volumes. I took about 600 with me to
Pasadena.

Our Trips to Mexico, Alaska and England

We made an auto trip into Mexico during the Christmas holidays
in 1955, going down on the western route and returning through the
central part of the country. We did not use our car much in Mexico
City for the traffic was terrible. We did drive to Cuernavaca. We
took an airplane to Oaxaca where we saw some interesting ruins.

In the summer of 1965 we went to Alaska. One of my students
was pastor of the First Presbyterian Church of Anchorage. He was
to be away for five weeks and asked me to fill the pulpit while he
was gone. He offered me the use of an old car and an apartment.
We left from Vancouver, B.C. about the middle of June and sailed up
the Inland passage to Skagway, where we took a plane to Sitka where
we spent several days at the Sheldon Jackson College, then on to
Anchorage. I received a warm welcome my first Sunday in the pulpit

of the Church, on July 20, 1965. Invitations came to speak before both the Kiwanis and Rotary Clubs of Anchorage. This was the year after the bad earthquake of 1964, and since I was retired from the Navy, I was given a free plane ride to Kodiak Island Navy Base. The earthquake had caused the island to dip about five feet so that the ocean water flooded the airfield at times. We returned late in August.

In 1966 we took a three months trip to England, Scotland, and Ireland. I applied for, and received, a $1,000.00 grant from the American Philosophical Society, which made the trip possible. I was then working on my Whitman books and needed to examine the archives of the Hudson's Bay Company in London. These archives have now been moved to Winnipeg, Manitoba, Canada. I spent several weeks going through the HBC records, but found little which related to the Whitman-Spalding mission; but at least I had the satisfaction of knowing that I had made the search.

After spending about six weeks in London, we traveled by train to Grimsby in Lincolnshire, from which place my grandfather came when he was about sixteen years old in 1854. He settled with relatives near Bryant, Clinton County, Iowa.

In Lincolnshire I examined some eighty wills on file in their archives. I was interested in linking up the Drury family of Hawstead (near Bury St. Edmunds) with the Drury family of Grimsby. I was not successful.

Then on to Edinburgh, Scotland, where my wife and I had spent eight months in 1927-28. My senior professor, Dr. Hugh Watt, was still living and he told me the story of how I had so narrowly missed getting my Ph.D. degree.

Before leaving for England and Scotland, one of our Moscow friends, Mrs. Earl (Lola) Clyde, asked us to look up members of the Cameron family and tell them about an American inheritance which should be theirs. While we lived in Moscow we became acquainted with three women — Maggie, Allie, and Anne Cameron — who were farming several hundred acres of fine wheat land, with the help of a nephew. Both Allie and Anne had died and Maggie went to live with a cousin, a single woman who managed to get all of the property (several hundreds of thousands worth) put into her name. Lola Clyde wanted me to see their cousins in Scotland and file a protest. The woman who was caring for Maggie had hired a lawyer to go to Scotland and get the relatives to sign a paper giving her the land. This he did. Lola wanted me to call on the relatives and explain to them how they had been cheated.

I wrote ahead and told them we were coming. When we landed in London, I received a telephone call from one of the cousins.

She was interested and wanted to see me. When taking a bus trip around the northern end of Scotland, we stopped at a little village called Aviemore, where we met several of the cousins. I showed them newspaper clippings and other documents. They told me that a lawyer had given them money to sign some papers. I replied by saying that in the United States we paid the lawyers; they did not pay us. They asked me what they should do. I suggested the name of a Moscow, Idaho lawyer and suggested that they cable him to take the case. This they did and, as a result, they received the large inheritance.

From Glasgow we went to Belfast and then made a tour around Ireland. When we arrived at Cork, Miriam became too ill to continue; so we dropped out of the tour. I visited Limmerick Castle, near Cork, and kissed the Blarney Stone. I recall that while descending the stairway built within the walls, I met a short heavy-set woman who asked me how far it was to the top. I told her that she had a long way to go. She then asked me if I had kissed the Blarney Stone. I told her that I had; suddenly she leaned over and kissed me. When one kisses the Blarney Stone, he is supposed to gain eloquence. When the woman kissed me, I felt that she got the magic charm and I reverted to being an historian again, more interested in accuracy than in eloquence. I asked her where she lived, and she replied, "Santa Monica, California," which is not far from Pasadena. From Cork we flew back to London and soon returned to the States after having had three of the most interesting months of our lives.

Marcus and Narcissa Whitman

In 1973 the Arthur H. Clark Company brought out two volumes on Marcus and Narcissa Whitman and the Opening of Old Oregon. The revision of my Whitman book of 1937 was made necessary by the fact that I now had access to the eighty letters which Edward Eberstadt had and to which mention has already been made. These letters landed in the Yale University Library and were thus made available to me. I had found so much new material regarding the Whitmans that a revision was necessary. I had access to two drawings believed to be of Marcus and Narcissa Whitman, which were drawn by Paul Kane and were in the Royal Ontario Museum in Toronto, Canada. A friend of mine, Drury Haight (no relation) painted portraits from these sketches. They were reproduced in color in the new work on the Whitmans. 1,250 sets were published, and sold for $38.50 per set. The reviews were excellent and the edition soon sold out.

I planned to rewrite my Spalding book and was able to write

about 30,000 words before I had to give up. I sent this manuscript to the Idaho Historical Society in Boise, Idaho. I consider my two volumes on the Whitmans, which appeared in 1973, to be my best work.

I assisted in the promotion of the sales of all of my books, especially of the two volumes on the Whitmans. Expecting that the books would be ready by a certain date, I arranged a speaking tour to begin June 28, 1973 and continue until July 6. For years it had been my custom to keep the names and addresses of those who had purchased my earlier books on three by five cards. Of course, the Arthur H. Clark Company had its list of purchasers. We put these lists together, and the Clark Company sent a letter to all, announcing when and where I would be speaking. Due to a paper shortage, the books were not ready when expected. The first volume of the set was given a temporary binding so that I could have something to show.

My lecture series began on Thursday evening, June 28, in the new wing of the State Historical Society at Tacoma. Bruce LeRoy was the Director. 164 people were present, including a few who came from Seattle. I then flew to Spokane where my friend, Cecil Hagen, had reserved the dining room of a fine cafe. Dinner was served to ninety-six after which I spoke.

I was in Moscow on Sunday, July 1st. I gave my Whitman lecture in the church that evening to seventy people. From Moscow I went to Lewiston where another friend, Marcus Ware, made arrangements for a dinner to be served to 180. On the 4th of July I was with the Presbyterian Nez Perces at Talmaks, where I spoke to about 100. On the 5th of July I was at the Whitman Mission National Historic Site. Their auditorium held only about 125; I filled it twice. People waited while I gave my first lecture. On the 6th I was in Portland and addressed the City Club, where there were about 150 present. That evening I spoke before some thirty or more in the First Presbyterian Church. Then back to my home in Pasadena. By the end of 1973, over 700 sets of my *Marcus and Narcissa Whitman* had been sold. The speaking tour had been worthwhile. This book was completely sold out by July of 1979. I received a royalty of about $3,105.93.

RUDOLPH JAMES WIG

I first met "R.J.," as he was affectionately known, in the fall of 1946. He was then serving as one of the Trustees of San Francisco Theological Seminary. After I had retired at the end of 1963, I found that his wife had died and that he was living in one of the cottages on the grounds of the Huntington-Sheraton hotel. I called on him, and he kindly invited me to dinner in one of the hotel's dining rooms. I found that he was lonely. Soon after calling on him, he asked me to write his biography. I hesitated. I had been writing about people who were deceased. Never before had I written about one still alive. Finally, after some urging, he induced me to visit his cottage and see what he had. I found that he had a wealth of source materials — annual reports of various organizations in which he had been interested, correspondence, and other relevant material. His papers filled his bedroom, and every closet was full. The wealth of information was overwhelming.

His three married daughters promised to cooperate and brought me their mother's diary. I was invited to his home at Balboa, his second home on the seashore, about fifty-five miles from Pasadena. Here, too, were stacks of papers.

I started writing in the fall of 1966, and as I finished a chapter I would read it to "R.J." while one of his daughters was present. Never once did he try to dictate what should or should not be included. I spent many hours with him in his home, especially during the summer of 1967.

"R.J." acquired a modest fortune in two specialized fields. The first was in working with diatomaceous earth which is used as a filter in the production of a variety of items, such as sugar, fruit juices, cheese products, etc. The diatomaceous earth was in a deposit at Lompoc, California. Wig was connected with the Seaweed Firm which majored in mining the deposits at Lompoc for eight years, 1920-1928. Financially speaking, these were the most important years of his life.

Wig's second venture was in harvesting seaweed from which certain products were secured by the American Can Company for sealing its tin cans, and in many other products, especially in the manufacture of ice cream.

Wig's major interest, however, was with the church and education. He made notable contributions to the cluster of colleges centered at Claremont, California, and to the Presbyterian Church in both local and national activities. He was one of the most active laymen in the Presbyterian Church, nationally known for his administrative abilities.

My biography of Wig appeared in 1968 from the press of the Arthur H. Clark Company and sold for $6.50. The edition contained 1,000 volumes. The family subsidized the work. Most of the books were given to friends of the family and to educational institutions. Wig did not live to see the finished volumes, but did see the manuscript in proof form.

First White Women Over the Rockies

One day while calling on my publishers, I suggested that I felt it was time for me to write about the women of the Oregon Mission. I had written about Spalding, Whitman and the other men of the mission, but practically nothing about the women. I knew where the diaries of five of the women were, and felt that an editing of these would make one, perhaps two, books. Mrs. Marcus (Narcissa) Whitman and Mrs. Henry H. (Eliza) Spalding came over the mountains with their husbands in 1836. The other four women came in 1838; these were Mrs. Elkanah (Mary) Walker, Mrs. Cushing (Myra) Eells, Mrs. Wm. H. (Mary) Gray, and Mrs. Asa B. (Sarah) Smith. I knew where I could get copies of the diaries of the first five, but I did not know whether Mrs. Smith kept one or not. My publishers encouraged me; so I began work on the diaries at hand.

Narcissa kept field notes as she made her trip over the mountains. These were owned by Mrs. Ginera Whitman Lutz of Bellingham, Washington; she refused to let me see the notes. Following the death of Mrs. Lutz, the notes were turned over to the library of Whitman College. While at Fort Vancouver, following the trip over the mountains, Narcissa wrote two diaries from these notes — one for her mother and another for her husband's mother. The diary written for her mother, and also Eliza Spalding's diary, are at Whitman College. Narcissa's diary for her husband's mother is in Bancroft Library, University of California at Berkeley.

The 1838 reenforcement sent out by the American Board to Oregon consisted of four couples. The women were Mrs. Elkanah (Mary) Walker, whose diary was in Huntington Library, San Marino, California; Mrs. Cushing (Myra) Eells, a copy of her diary is in the Oregon Historical Society for the original was lost in a fire; Mrs. Gray's diary was in private hands and was written after she reached Oregon, May to August, 1840. I did not know if Mrs. Smith kept a diary or not.

I took the five diaries, with some letters, and turned the manuscript over to my publishers. They brought out two volumes in 1963 which sold for $21.00. The edition contained 1,500 sets. Within eleven years all were sold and I received $1,526.83 in royalties.

An unexpected result of the publication of these two volumes came when Bruce LeRoy, Director of the Washington State Historical Society in Tacoma, wrote a review of the two volume set for the *American Heritage*. In his review he said that Sarah Smith "left no known diary." This magazine fell into the hands of Richard Smith of Chevy Chase, near Washington, D.C., who happened to be the great-nephew of Asa Smith. He wrote to me and said that Sarah's diary was in the Denver public library. I wrote at once to the librarian asking for a xerox copy of the diary. The librarian replied that they did have the diary, but that they intended to publish it. I wrote back begging them to reconsider. I said that I knew more about these missionaries than anyone else and asked them to look at my books. The librarian did as I requested, and then wrote that they were sending me the xerox of the diary. This became the heart of volume III of my *First White Women Over the Rockies*, which was published in an edition of 1,500 copies in 1966 and which sold for $11.00. By the end of 1974 the stock was down to forty volumes.

The Diary of Elkanah Walker, 1838-1848

In 1976 the Arthur H. Clark Company brought out the eleventh of my books on the history of the American Board's Mission in Old Oregon under the title *Nine Years With the Spokane Indians, the Diary of Elkanah Walker, 1838-1848*. This volume contained 547 pages and sold for $26.50. I never dreamed when I began this series with my life of Henry Harmon Spalding that the series would ever grow to this size.

After my retirement at the end of 1963, I had time to explore the wealth of northwest history in the archives of Huntington Library, which was only two miles from my retirement home at Monte Vista Grove. There I found the original diaries of both Mary and Elkanah Walker. Neither had been published in its entirety. Huntington Library had acquired these diaries some fifty years before I turned to them. They were waiting for me to come along. It took me several months to transcribe them, for in both cases the handwriting was difficult to transcribe. Mary's diary appeared in volume II of my *First White Women Over the Rockies*. Now I turned to her husband's diary. Mary wrote especially of what went on inside the home; Elkanah wrote about what occurred outside the home. Here was the story of how he reduced a language to writing, and of the difficulties he encountered when trying to convert the Indians. The Walkers lived among the Spokane Indians for nine years without winning a single convert. Then after some twenty-five years, Spalding visited the Spokanes and baptized 357 men, women and children. It took a long time for the Christian seeds sowed by the Walkers and Eells to germinate.

The Clark Company printed 1,250 copies. It took several years for the edition to be sold. Most of the royalties received went to pay the subsidy I had to advance to get the book published.

Walker printed a Spokane primer on the mission press at Lapwai in 1842. Only two perfect copies of his primer are known to be extant. Clark reprinted about fifty of the pamphlets which were sold for $2.00 each. The book contained reproductions of paintings made by John Mix Stanley of Elkanah and his daughter, Abigail.

So far as I know, there has been no mission of any Protestant Church so fully documented and written up as the Oregon mission of the American Board. I am glad that I was able to write these eleven volumes. I know that they will live long after I am gone.

CHIEF LAWYER OF THE NEZ PERCES, 1796-1876

Chief Lawyer was one of the forgotten Indians of the Nez Perces. Historians have majored on Joseph who led the rebellion of 1877. Lawyer refused to join in the rebellion and kept about two-thirds of the tribe on the reservation. He has been called a traitor to his tribe and a "Red Judas," but he chose the wiser course.

He took a leading part in the councils of 1855 and 1863. He became a Christian in his old age and was baptized by Spalding.

In 1979 the Arthur H. Clark Company brought out my Lawyer book of 304 pages which sold for $22.75. The edition contained 1,000 copies. The edition was sold out by the summer of 1982. This was a labor of love, for to me he was the greatest of the Nez Perce chiefs.

LAST NAVAL DUTY

In June, 1950, I received a telephone call from Washington asking if I could serve as the Protestant Chaplain aboard the St. Paul, a cruiser, which was to take some 1,200 midshipmen on a cruise. I was free; so put on my uniform again and went. As we were entering Pearl Harbor on June 25th, word came over the loud speaker that fighting had broken out in Korea. The St. Paul returned to San Diego where the midshipmen disembarked. I got off also and another Protestant chaplain took my place. The ship already had a Catholic chaplain.

Then in April of 1965 one of my former students, Bob Warren, a Navy chaplain on Midway Island, made arrangements for me to visit him during Holy Week and give a series of addresses. I put on my Navy uniform again and drove to Travis Air Base near Vallejo and took a plane for Honolulu. There I spent several days with Navy chaplains and then took a smaller Navy plane to Midway. This proved to be a most interesting experience. The gooney birds were everywhere and very tame. I spoke four times and then returned. That was my last official Navy duty.

FAMILY EVENTS

On August 24, 1978 I suffered a moderate heart attack and was in the hospital. I made a quick recovery and returned home on September

7. On March 16, 1980 Miriam fell in her bedroom and broke the pelvic bone of her left hip. She had to undergo an operation in the Huntington Hospital, and on March 8th was transferred to a convalescent home. I was able to bring her home on May 7. Her doctor bill, hospital, and convalescent home bills came to a little over $9,000.00, which was all covered by insurance.

Our youngest son, Philip, died of cancer on March 29, 1969. He was an engineer with the Lockheed Company. I brought him to the Health Center at the Grove, where he passed away. He left a ten-year-old son, Marcus, who now lives with his mother, Shirley, about four miles from MVGH. Marcus now has his own home, and when we moved to smaller quarters in July 1982, and I could no longer drive, I gave him my Buick Skylark, as well as many items of furniture.

My brother, Billy, who was very close to me, died on November 23, 1980. I miss him so much.

In Conclusion

This is the end of my *Road From Yesterday*. The book will appear in a limited edition in July or August of 1984, and will sell for $25.00. I have written for the benefit of my family, my friends, and those who are interested in knowing how I was able to publish twenty-five books on history.

Throughout my writing I have done all my own typing until I got to this last chapter. Then three fingers of my left hand became paralyzed and this brought my typing to an end. I have had to rely on the help of a good typist to finish the book.

I feel that it is fitting that I should bring my readers up to date regarding the members of my family. Of the twelve children of Will Drury only five are now living. Clara (Mrs. Elmer Evans) is now in a Methodist Retirement Home in Fort Dodge, Iowa. I am here at Monte Vista Grove Homes with my wife, Miriam. We celebrated our sixty-first wedding anniversary on November 17th, 1983. We are very glad that we are here, only one-half block from the dining room and one block from the Health Center. Sarah (Mrs. Hillis Lory) is in a medical facility in Sun City, Arizona. The two children of my father's third wife, Laura, are Dean, who lives with his wife Joyce at Madras, Oregon, and Joyce (Mrs. Clarence Hind) at Early, Iowa.

My wife and I have been blessed with having three children. Robert M. Drury served for seventeen years as librarian of a Baptist Seminary in Kansas City, Kansas. He and his wife Gloria have twin daughters who have recently been graduated from the Kansas State University at Emporia, Kansas in Physical Education. Our daughter Patricia, who never married, is on the faculty of Delta College near Bay City,

MARCUS D. DRURY
Grandson of Clifford
Drury.

CLIFFORD AND MIRIAM DRURY
At a party held in their honor on November 17, 1982,
their sixtieth wedding anniversary.

Michigan. Philip, as noted earlier, died in 1969, leaving his wife, Shirley, and a son, Marcus.

I have been very fortunate in having good health thorugh most of my life. In the summer of 1982 I discovered that I had diabetes and must now take an injection of insulin every morning. In September of 1983 I found that I had shingles, which is a very painful affliction. My driving days are over. Because of my paralyzed fingers my writing is finished. My wife Miriam is in better health now than I am. We are very glad that we are in this retirement home.

Looking back on my eighty-six years of life I feel that a divine providence has guided me. My history of the Navy Chaplain Corps could never be written again as so many of my sources have been destroyed. I know that my books on the history of the missionaries in the Pacific Northwest will live. I feel that I saved the story of Marcus Whitman and Henry Spalding from oblivion. Already these books are collector's items.

Most of the source material used in the writing of this book has been sent to the Presbyterian Historical Society, 425 Lombard St., Philadelphia. Part of my historical collection has been deposited in the following libraries: Eastern Washington State Historical Society, Spokane, WA; Washington State University at Pullman, WA; Idaho Historical Society, Boise, ID; Whitman College, Walla Walla, WA; and a full set of my writings has been sold to a college in Santa Barbara, CA. I am very glad that I wrote on these subjects and thus saved a great story for the future.

Appendix

I. A selected chronological list of magazine articles by C. M. Drury
  1. "Oregon Indians in the Red River School," Pac. Hist. Rev., Vol. VII, March, 1936.
  2. "The Columbia Maternal Association," Oreg. Hist. Qtly., June, 1938. Reprinted in pamphlet form for WA State meeting of Women's Clubs, 500 copies.
  3. "Gray's Journal of 1836," Pac. N.W. Qtly., July, 1938.
  4. "Presbyterianism on the Pacific Coast," *The Presbyterian*, April, 1939.
  5. "History of the First Presbyterian Church of San Jose," Pamphlet issued by the Church, 1939.
  6. "The Nez Perce Delegation of 1831," Oreg. Hist. Qtly., Sept. 1939.
  7. "Ninetieth Anniversary of the First Presbyterian Church of Stockton, California," pamphlet printed by the church, March, 1940.
  8. "Botanist in Oregon in 1843-44 for Kew Gardens, London," Oreg. Hist. Qtly., June, 1940. Containing a review of K. A. Geyer life.
  9. "The Beginnings of the Presby. Church on the Pacific Coast," Pac. Hist. Rev., June, 1940.
  10. "Presby. Journalism on the Pacific Coast," Pac. Hist. Rev., Dec. 1940.
  11. "John White Geary and his brother, Edward," Calif. Hist. Qtly., March, 1941.
  12. "Spalding-Lowrie Correspondence," Jl. Dept. Hist. Presbyterian Church, March, June, Sept., 1942.
  13. "Sixty-five Years, History of First Presby. Church, Berkeley, Cal.," Pamphlet published by the church, April, 1943.
  14. "Early American Contacts With the Japanese," Pac. Hist. Qtly., Oct., 1945. Being Chap. II of *The Northwest Mosaic,* edited by J. R. Halseth and B. R. Gkasrud.
  15. "Famous Chaplain Teachers of Midshipmen," *U.S. Naval Proceedings,* May, 1944.
  16. "A Chronology of Protestant Beginnings in Cal.," Calif. Hist. Soc. Qtly., June, 1947.
  17. "George Frederick Whitworth," Jl. Hist. Presby. Church, March, 1948.

18. "Protestant Missionaries in Oregon," Oreg. Hist. Qtly., Sept., 1949.
19. "Centennial of the Synod of Cal.," Pages 144-152 of Minutes of Synod of Cal., 1951. 250 copies in pamphlet form.
20. "Chronological List of Churches in Cal.," Synod of Ca., 1954.
21. "Chronological List of Churches in Oregon," Minutes Synod of Oregon, 1955.
22. "Biography of George Burrows," Jl. Dept. Hist. Presby. Church, Sept., 1955.
23. "Walter Colton, Chaplain and Alcalde," Calif. Hist. Soc. Qtly., June, 1956.
24. "Presby. Beginnings in New England and the Middle Colonies," Jl. Dept. Hist. Presby. Church, March, 1956.
25. "Irish Background of Makemie," Jl. Hist. Presbyterian Church, June, 1957.
26. "History of San Jose Presbytery," Jl. Hist. Presby. Church, Sept. 1958.
27. "The Beginnings of the Synod of Oregon," Jl. Hist. Presby. Church, Dec., 1959.
28. "I, the Lawyer," Westerners, New York Posse Brand Books, April, 1960. 250 reprints.
29. "First White Women Over the Rockies," Jl. Hist. Presby. Church, March, 1951.
30. "Hanged Twice in Effigy — W. A. Scott in San Francisco," Jl. Hist. Presby. Church, June and Dec., 1963.
31. "Sketch of Mrs. Eliza Spalding," *Biographical Dictionary of notable American Women,* 1963.
32. "John Knox," Biographical article in *New American Encyclopedia,* Vol. 16, 1964.
33. "The Oregonian and the Indians' Advocate," Pac. Hist. Rev., Oct., 1965.
34. "The Origins of Presbyterian Policy," So. Calif. Presbyterian, Jan., 1966.
35. "The Right to Disagree: A Presbyterian Heritage," So. Calif. Presbyterian, Oct., 1966.
36. "Gold Rush Churches of California," L.A. Westerners Brand Book, 1966.
37. "Adventures in Americana," Pamphlet, Denver Posse of Westerners, July, 1966.
38. "A History of a History," July-August, 1966 issue of *The Chaplain.*
39. "No Ordinary Man," So. Calif. Presbyterian, Oct., 1967.
40. "Negative Reports on Oregon," L.A. Brand Book, No. 13.

41. "Charles Compo," In Vol. VIII by Hafen, *Mountain Man of the Fur Trade of the Far West.*
42. "Anson Burlingame, China's First U.S. Ambassador," Pac. Hist., Summer, 1971.
43. "Eliza Spalding," in *Notable American Women,* 3 vols., Harvard University Press, 1971.
44. "Reminiscences of an Historian," Pacific Corral, the *Northwesterner,* Nov. 1972.
45. "Christian Beginnings in California and Indian Mission Beginnings in Old Oregon," *Stockton Corral Far Westerner,* Oct., 1972.
46. "Another Myth Answered," Pac. Rev., Spring, 1973.
47. "Joe Meek Comments on Whitman Massacre," Oreg. Hist. Qtly., March, 1974.
48. "Reminiscences of an Historian," West. Hist. Qtly., April, 1974.
49. "Growing Up on an Iowa Farm," Annals of Iowa, Winter, 1974.
50. "Is This Marcus Whitman," *American West,* Nov., 1974.
51. "Tshimakain,Indian Camp Ground," Pac. N.W. Qtly., Jan. 1976.
52. "Wilderness Diaries," Diaries of Elkanah and Mary Walker, *American West,* Nov./Dec., 1976.
53. "Chief Lawyer," *Idaho Yesterdays,* Feb., 1979.
54. "More About the Whitmans," Pamphlet with four recently discovered Whitman letters issued by WA. State Historical Society, Tacoma, March, 1979.

II. Books written or edited by C. M. Drury, exclusive of books published for the Navy.

Henry Harmon Spalding, Pioneer of Old Oregon (1936)

Marcus Whitman, M.D., Pioneer and Martyr. (1937)

Elkanah and Mary Walker, Pioneers Among the Spokanes (1940)

A Tepee in His Front Yard: A Biography of Henry T. Cowley (1949)

Presbyterian Panorama (1952)

Diary of Titian Ramsay Peale, Oregon to California, 1841 (1957)

The Diaries and Letters of Henry H. Spalding and Asa Bowen Smith, Relating to the Nez Perce Mission, 1838-1842 (1958)

Four Hundred Years of Presbyterianism, edited and copyrighted, microfilm (1961)

The San Francisco Y.M.C.A.: One Hundred Years by the Golden Gate (1963)

First White Women over the Rockies: Diaries, Letters and Biographies of the Six Women of the Oregon Mission, 1836 and 1838 (vols. I and II, 1963; vol. III, 1966)

William Anderson Scott, "No Ordinary Man" (1967)

Rudolph James Wig: Engineer, Presbyterian Layman, Pomona College Trustee (1968)

A Bibliography ofCalifornia Religious Imprints, 1846-1876 (1968)

Marcus and Narcissa Whitman and the Opening of Old Oregon (2 vols.) (1973)

Nine Years with the Spokane Indians: The Diary, 1838-1848, of Elkanah Walker (1976)

Chief Lawyer of the Nez Perce Indians (1979)

III.   Honorary Degrees and Citations received by C. M. Drury

D.D. — Buena Vista College, Storm Lake, Iowa, May 30, 1941

Litt.D. — Whitworth College, Spokane, Wash., Sept. 26, 1955

D.H.L. — Whitman College, Walla Walla, Wash., June 7, 1964

Litt.D. — Azusa Pacific College, Azusa, Cal., May 4, 1974

Letter of Commendation, with medal, Secretary of the U.S. Navy, Dec. 12, 1957

Distinguished Service Award, Presbyterian Historical Soc., Phila., Penn., Oct. 14, 1960

Capt. Robert Gray medal, Washington State Historical Soc., Tacoma, Wash., May 4, 1963

Distinguished Alumnus Award, Buena Vista College, Storm Lake, Iowa, 1968

"Hide Decor," Los Angeles Corral of Westerners, in recognition of books (first time awarded), Sept. 4, 1976

Distinguished Alumnus Award, San Francisco Theological Seminary, San Anselmo, Cal. (first time awarded), June, 1981